LIVE & WORK IN
SAUDI
& THE GULF

Louise Whetter

Published by Vacation Work, 9 Park End Street, Oxford
www.vacationwork.co.uk

LIVE AND WORK IN SAUDI ARABIA AND THE GULF

First Edition 2000

by Louise Whetter

Copyright © Vacation Work 2000

ISBN 1-85458-239-9 (softback)

Publicity: Roger Musker

Cover design by
Miller Craig & Cocking Design Partnership

Typeset by Worldview Publishing Services (01865-201562)

Printed by William Clowes Ltd., Beccles, Suffolk, England.

Contents

SECTION I – LIVING IN SAUDI ARABIA & THE GULF

OMAN

QATAR

SECTION II – WORKING IN SAUDI ARABIA & THE GULF

EMPLOYMENT

STARTING A BUSINESS

MAPS

APPENDICES

Foreword

What better way of beginning the twenty-first century than to make a fresh start overseas? The Arabian Gulf may not be foremost in everyone's mind as a prospective destination but this first edition of *Live & Work in Saudi & the Gulf* reveals how there is more to the Gulf states than vast expanses of desert and meandering camels, women hidden under black wraps and rich Arabs flaunting their wealth. The Arabian peninsula still holds that certain mystique about its people and culture that makes it one of the most challenging and exciting places in which to live and work.

This book is the latest addition to the popular series of publications that provide a guide to the opportunities for work, starting a business and living conditions in different countries around the globe. These books are specifically designed to act as an information base for the many and diverse regulations and practicalities involved in moving abroad. Complications are inherent in purchasing a new home and beginning a new job simultaneously in a country that has very different laws and procedures to those with which you are familiar. Nevertheless, by using *Live & Work in Saudi & the Gulf* as a reference manual you will be able to make the awesome transition briefed with the knowledge of what to expect rather than leaping head-first into the unknown and finding yourself caught up in a nightmare situation. The book is divided into two halves, *Living in the Gulf* and *Working in the Gulf* respectively, which cover all aspects of such a move from how to find a job, work practices in the Gulf, business opportunities, how to set up a business, to Arab etiquette, language and culture. There is no chapter on how to retire in the Gulf as quite simply you can't – your residence visa in each country is only valid for as long as you have employment or are dependent on someone employed there.

Thousands of UK nationals currently live and work in the Arabian peninsula with the most favoured states being the larger and richer of the six: Saudi Arabia, the United Arab Emirates (UAE) and Kuwait. The Gulf states – Bahrain, Kuwait, Oman, Qatar, Saudi Arabia and the UAE – comprise a conflicting mixture of the ancient and modern, traditional and the novel. The countries are both the most up-to-date in terms of modern structures and conveniences, and the latest technology, yet simultaneously, the most steeped in ancient customs and tradition. Wages are high, the standard of living extremely good and if you get beyond the religious formalties that enshroud these nations you will find very welcoming and generous hosts.

Business and work-related opportunities abound in the Gulf countries where the economies of the states – though mostly dependent upon oil prices – are incredibly healthy. Over the last 30 years or so since the discovery of oil in the Arabian peninsula the six countries have transformed from being relatively backward communities whose vulnerable economies were reliant upon the pearling, fishing and trading of local merchandise, to highly prosperous countries some of which are rated among the wealthiest nations in the world and leading players in the global business markets.

There are enormous differences between the culture and lifestyles lead in the Arab and Western worlds that can pose a formidable challenge to anyone moving out to the Gulf, especially females. However, that is what can make the experience particularly rewarding as you discover more about the intricacies of the Arab religion, Islam, that dominates every aspect of Muslims' lives, and manage to overcome and grow to respect what may at first appear to you inherent prejudices within the Arab culture but are in fact not seen as such by Arab nationals – for instance the many restrictions placed on women from dress codes to various other facets of daily life and how these do or do not affect their lives for the better or worse. There are of course plenty of other fascinating traditions to experience in the Arab world which have a more positive appeal, such as the emphasis placed upon hospitality and the enjoyment of ancient sports such as camel racing, falconry, dhow racing and horse racing. Living in a society so disparate from that which you are used to can only be an enriching experience as your perception of the world and how different people operate is broadened. This book aims to tell you how, where and why to seek the Gulf experience.

Louise Whetter
Oxford, May 2000

Acknowledgements

The author and publishers would like to thank the many people who provided information and help in compiling this book. Special thanks go to all those who agreed to supply case histories of their own experiences of living and working in the Gulf. Further, for all their generous assistance throughout the writing of this book I feel express thanks are due to my colleagues, contacts and contributors, amongst whom are: Noelie Groult, all the staff and members of Corona Worldwide – specifically Pat Yaxley, everyone at the Middle East Association – in particular Jennifer Webb, Overseas Jobs Express for kind permission to reprint the table of driving regulations in Saudi Arabia, Rohan Badenhorst of the Binzagr Villa Compound, Saudi Arabia, for his contribution to the Saudi 'Setting Up Home' chapter, and above all those family and friends – especially Oi Yee Wong for the literary encouragement, and Alfred Chubb for his sense of humour – who offered the moral and logistical support necessary in completing a project of this kind. Finally, enormous thanks are due to my brothers, Patrick and Jeremy, for their invaluable assistance in compiling the expatriate tax and other sections of this book.

I would like to dedicate this book to my parents and sister, Charlotte.

NOTE: While every effort has been made to ensure that the information contained in this book was correct at the time of going to press, some details are bound to change within the lifetime of this edition, and readers are strongly advised to check facts and credentials themselves. If you have any updated or new information that you feel would be of interest to readers of the next edition, please write to the author at Vacation Work, 9 Park End Street, Oxford OX1 1HJ. Contributors will be sent a free copy of the next edition, or a Vacation Work title of their choice.

SECTION I

Living in the Gulf

General Introduction

Bahrain

Kuwait

Oman

Qatar

Saudi Arabia

United Arab Emirates

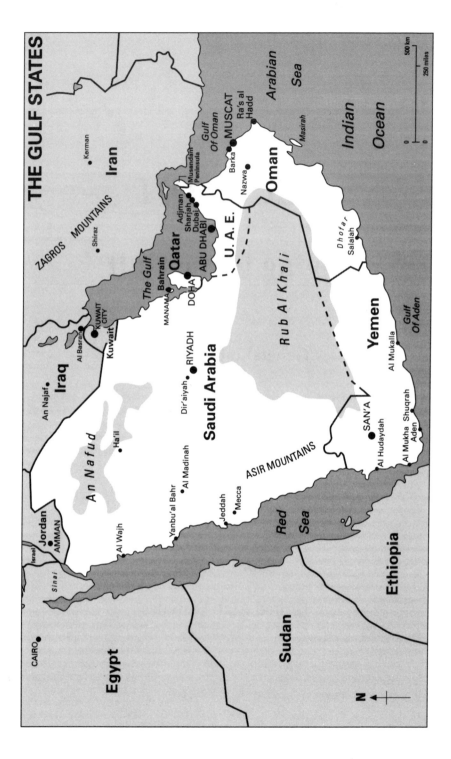

Living in the Gulf

General Introduction

The purpose of this chapter is to give a broad overview of what the Gulf region is like and what the six Arab Gulf states have in common, for example what cultural aspects they share. The subsequent chapters detailing individual country profiles show that despite those similarities which they have within their infrastructures each state has its very own individual identity.

Destination the Gulf States

The Arabian Peninsula comprises the following countries: the State of Bahrain, the State of Kuwait, the Sultanate of Oman, the State of Qatar, the Kingdom of Saudi Arabia and the United Arab Emirates (UAE). Apart from being geographical neighbours these countries are principally linked through their strong faith in Islam. However, despite sharing the same essential Islamic beliefs and all being wealthy Arab countries whose economies have been built on trade and later the discovery of oil, the individual countries are quite different from one another in many ways, from the lie of their land to the practice of their faith (within Islam there are two distinct branches of believers who are in turn divided into sects), and treatment of and attitude towards women (see below).

There are countless opportunities for skilled Western expatriates seeking employment in the Gulf but why choose to live and work in the Arabian Peninsula? For the majority of expatriates the choice is very much influenced by the size of the pay packet and improved standard of living over that which they might be able to afford in their home country, especially as there are no personal taxes to pay on their quite substantial earnings. Contracts with major companies can also include many added bonuses such as accommodation or a housing allowance and the payment of school fees, which are pretty hefty throughout the Gulf region.

Millions of foreign nationals are resident throughout the Gulf either from other Arab countries – Egypt, Syria, Lebanon, Jordan and the Sudan, or from countries such as India, Pakistan, the Philippines, Sri Lanka, Bangladesh, Iran, Europe, and the USA. Those from Western countries are recruited to professional and skilled positions in management, oil, gas, and power, education, and health care. Those of other nationalities tend to be employed as housemaids or drivers or workers at a similar level. There is still unfortunately a certain degree of prejudice throughout the Gulf in the choice of employees recruited, not only your gender and race but even whether you look what is considered 'pleasing to the eye' can bias an employer's decision to employ you or not. The extent to which this is evident varies from state to state. Moreover, all the Gulf countries are currently trying to gradually replace their foreign work force with their own nationals. Nevertheless, this has not yet particularly affected the demand for highly qualified Western workers whose skills are still very much sought after and respected. However, you cannot get too comfortable with your life in the Gulf as you can only remain resident there as long as you are employed or dependent upon someone with an employment contract – retirement there is not a viable option for expatriates.

For many it is not only the lure of money that attracts them to the Gulf but the excitement of discovering a new life in a country with a culture totally unlike that with which they are familiar. Only by experiencing what it is actually like to live in one of the Gulf states will you really be able to know which stereotypes and personal preconceptions are real and which are false. Some find it hard to visualise the Gulf as anything but a somewhat backward area with vast stretches of desert with camels and Bedouin roaming about. Perhaps this picture was not far from the truth some fifty plus years ago but since the discovery of oil in the region in the 1930s all the countries have developed greatly with ultra-modern capital cities boasting skyscraper skylines comparable to Manhattan's. But despite the outward appearance of 'high-tec' modernity each state still retains – to a lesser or greater extent – its sense of the traditional both in the restoration or remains of ancient structures, such as the many old forts and wind towers, and the maintenance of the Bedouin souks, and above all in their adherence to the Islamic faith which governs the overall lifestyle within each country and the actions of all Muslims (see *Islam* below).

The Arab people are widely thought to be very hard to get to know and expatriates throughout the Gulf often joke that in Saudi Arabia the Saudis attempt to avoid western cultural 'pollution' by keeping foreign nationals enclosed in compounds whereas in the UAE it is the UAE nationals who keep themselves enclosed in residential areas while they let the expatriates move around freely. This would suggest that there is a certain hostility felt by the Gulf nationals towards expatriates in their countries but the truth is that if you are lucky enough to have close contact through work or indeed make friends socially with any of the Gulf nationals you will find that they are a very warm, welcoming and generous people. Once you have gained the trust of a Gulf national you are assured of their continued friendship and loyalty. The ease with which you can meet Gulf nationals differs in each country with Saudi Arabia perhaps being one of the most difficult places to make friends with Saudi nationals and Bahrain and Kuwait the most likely places where you could mix with the respective countries' citizens.

Perhaps some of the most evident differences between your home country and one of the Gulf states are the rules governing dress and alcohol. Throughout the Arabian Peninsula both men and women are expected to dress conservatively with arms and legs (at the very least) covered in public. Respect for this ruling is particularly important in Saudi Arabia where the *mutawwa'iin* (religious police – see section in Saudi Arabia *Daily Living* chapter) patrol the streets to ensure that foreigners abide by the dress code and other religious laws. The purchase and consumption of alcohol is strictly prohibited in both Saudi Arabia and Kuwait but in the other Gulf countries there are certain outlets selling alcohol to holders of liquor licences and alcoholic drinks can be bought at licensed hotels and restaurants. However, despite Saudi Arabia and Kuwait being officially 'dry' states, within the compounds (closed off residential areas for expatriates) and private homes expatriates find that they can quite easily brew and consume alcohol provided that they are discreet. Local authorities will on the whole turn a blind eye to the illicit activities which may be going on within the compounds unless rules are flagrantly being broken. Additionally, the police will occasionally crack down on censured behaviour by carrying out random searches on homes looking for damning evidence of misdemeanours of an alcoholic or extra-marital kind, etc. On no account should you ever offer alcohol to a Muslim.

You will find that your social life in the Arabian Peninsula will tend to be centred around the expatriate community and despite the many restrictions in force throughout the Gulf – in Saudi Arabia there are no cinemas, bars, clubs, etc. – you will find plenty of activities available to occupy your leisure time. In all the Gulf countries you can pursue practically any sport that you may wish to from water sports – scuba diving, snorkelling, wind surfing, canoeing, fishing, etc. to a wide range of land sports – desert driving, racket sports, golf, caving, hockey, horse riding, etc. Additionally all the states have a myriad of expatriate associations and clubs covering all different interests and there is of course the natural landscape to explore, archaeological excavations and numerous museums to visit, as well as amazing five star hotels and fantastic restaurants to spend your time and money in.

The Gulf is notorious for its harsh laws and severe punishments imposed on offenders, and it is true there are certain rules and regulations which must be abided by that may seem somewhat inordinate or not very 'politically correct' by western standards, such as the many restrictions placed on women and the penalties that can be incurred for adultery or theft or even minor driving violations like going through a red light. Punishments can include arrest, heavy fines, public flogging, imprisonment, amputation of the hand (for theft) and in extreme cases public stoning to death or beheading (for adulterers, murderers, drug smugglers, those found renouncing their Islamic faith or practising witchcraft). In Saudi Arabia the figures recorded for the year 1999 up to the month of October revealed that the number of people judicially killed reached a total of 95 – 49 being foreigners, including 12 Pakistanis, 10 Nigerians (three were women), nine Afghans, six Indians, in addition to citizens from Thailand, Indonesia, the Philippines, Syria, Jordan, Ethiopia, Chad and Yemen.

Foreigners resident in the Gulf found in violation of the local laws are subject to the same penalties that Gulf nationals are. However, Western offenders although not guaranteed total immunity from the infliction of severe penalties, do have the advantage of the global media to draw attention to any sentence they may receive that appears inhumane by Western standards. This was exhibited in the 1998 case of the two British nurses, Lucille McLauchlin and Deborah Parry, accused of killing a colleague. The focus placed on their plight through the international media saved them from serving the death penalty provided that they pay blood money to the deceased's relative. The laws are not in force to instil fear in people but to protect them and ultimately the positive result of having such a system is reflected in the low crime rate found throughout the Gulf.

Each Gulf state imposes the law to different degrees and one thing you can be assured of is a strong sense of personal safety in all the individual countries as long as you respect the local customs. Women should generally try not to travel anywhere unaccompanied although the extent to which they should adhere to this varies from state to state. Each country in the Arabian Peninsula has so much to offer anyone deciding to relocate there not only in material terms but in less tangible ways, subjective and hard to quantify, such as personal development through gaining an understanding of, and learning to live with, the all pervasive Islamic culture.

For all those seeking new challenges, opportunities and experiences, the Gulf is a perfect destination to fulfil all these needs and much, much more. In fact many expatriates initially placed in the Gulf on just one or two year contracts find that they relish the experience so much that they arrange to stay for longer periods in the same country or move to different countries within the Arabian Peninsula. Patience and the ability to adapt to an Arab lifestyle are the keys to making the most of your stay in the Gulf. Relocating to the Gulf offers you the chance to earn lots of money, and at the same time make hundreds of new friends and participate in the infinite number of activities on offer as well as learn about an unfamiliar culture, and above all to enjoy yourself.

Preparing to Go

When considering a move abroad, especially to one of the Gulf states where the Arab culture and lifestyle is so different to that in the West, it is essential to gain some knowledge of what to expect in order to avoid too much culture shock. One of the best ways to prepare yourself for a move to the Gulf is to talk to as many people who have undergone the experience themselves and can answer any queries that you may have and advise you on what to bring, things to remember, dos and don'ts, etc. If you do not already have any contacts in the Arabian Peninsula then you can soon establish contacts by either joining an expatriate association such as Corona Worldwide (c/o The Commonwealth Institute, Kensington High Street, London W8 6NQ; tel/fax 020-7610 4407; e-mail hq@coronaww.prestel.co.uk Website www.commercepark.co.uk/coronaww) or make friends with individuals currently resident in your destination country on-line through one of the many expatriate clubs on the internet (see below).

Corona Worldwide is a voluntary organisation that now welcomes male members as well as females and has branches internationally including in Saudi Arabia. The society offers practical information, advice and support to help you settle in Bahrain, Kuwait, Oman, Qatar, Saudi Arabia and the UAE. Members are introduced to someone with first hand knowledge of your destination country, who can listen to and dispel any anxieties that you may have and tell you how to prepare and what to expect from the move. Amongst the publications they produce are: *Culture Shock! What it's like to live in a country not your own*, a guide to preparing your departure, what to take and leave, what to expect on arrival, coping with strange situations, homesickness, settling in, enjoying the new environment; *Living in a Muslim Country*, a guide to understanding the behaviour and restrictions determined by religious belief or established traditions. Corona Worldwide also provides comprehensive support and assistance to those returning to the UK after a period overseas. Many relocation companies now offer a similar service (see *Relocation Companies* below) although they do not provide the personal contacts that Corona Worldwide can offer.

For businessmen and women intending to relocate to the Arabian Peninsula, *The Centre for International Briefing* (Farnham Castle, Farnham, Surrey GU9 0AG; tel 01252-720416/9; fax 01252-719277; e-mail marketing@cibfarnham.com Website www.cibfarnham.com) is the market leader in international effectiveness training. The Centre runs hundreds of different programmes every year which aim to assist people going overseas to work more effectively in their new environment. Strands include business briefings, country briefings, intercultural team building programmes, cross-cultural awareness workshops, management of expatriate personnel, award-winning intensive language tuition programmes, and repatriation briefings. Programmes include an up-to-date overview of the country or region, the political and economic situation today, as well as a study of the people and their business practices and social culture. Other organisations offering similar services are listed below under *Useful Addresses*.

Embassies (see separate country entries under *Regional Guide* for addresses) can also be worth contacting for information on the countries they represent, or you could contact the *Middle East Association* (33 Bury Street, London SW1Y 6AX; tel 020-7839 2137; fax 020-7839 6121; e-mail mail@the-mea.co.uk Website www.the-mea.co.uk), which provides its members (primarily small, medium, and large sized companies or Middle Eastern businessmen) with a range of services to inform them of the business markets throughout the Middle East, including the Gulf states. Additionally, the *Foreign and Commonwealth Office* (Consular Department, Room CL 605, Clive House, Petty France, London SW1H 9HD; tel 020-7270 4137/42; Website www.fco.gov.uk) can send copies of Consular Department publications with details of those services which consuls abroad can and cannot provide. Their website contains full, current information on recent travel advice, diplomatic missions, and foreign policy issues; the American equivalent can be found on the Bureau of Consular Affairs' website at www.travel.state.gov.

Useful Addresses

Centre for Professional Employment Counselling (CEPEC): Lilly House, 13 Hanover Square, London W1R 9HD; tel 020-7629 2266; fax 020-7629 7066. Provides careers counselling and a resettlement service for corporate-sponsored professional expatriates returning to the UK. Their counselling service covers career, personal and financial matters.

Expatriate Management Ltd: St Clements House, 2 St Clements Lane, London EC4N 7AP; tel/fax 020-7280 7732. Handles the administration of expatriate employees for companies, but also organises orientation and training courses. Prospective expatriates should enquire about a briefing.

Global Integration Limited: Wyvols Court, Swallowfield, Reading RG7 1WY; tel 0118-988 0148; fax 0118-988 0335; Website www.global-integration.com; e-mail us@global-integration.com. Provides individually tailored cross-cultural training programmes for senior managers and executives.

Going Places: 84 Coombe Road, New Malden, Surrey KT3 4QS; tel 020-8949 8811; fax 020-8949 6237. Provides half-day, one-day, and two-day training courses for individuals, couples and company delegates, varying from country to country and meeting specific requirements. The scheduled company-specific briefings can bring you useful contacts with other professionals who will be moving to the same country.

On-line Resources

The following is a list of websites linking expatriates located around the world, providing useful information about destination countries as well as allowing members to contact one another to compare notes on their situations or offer advice to others about what to expect from the relocation, what to bring, what to beware of, dos and don'ts, etc.

Across Frontiers: www.acrossfrontiers.com
American Citizens Abroad: www.aca.ch
Escape Artist: www.escapeartist.com
Expat Exchange: www.expatexchange.net
Expats: www.expats.co.uk
Living Abroad: www.livingabroad.com
Outpost Expat: www.outpostexpat.nl
Transition Dynamics: www.transition-dynamics.com

Useful Publications

Equitable Guide to Working Abroad: Bloomsbury, 2 Soho Square, London W1V 6HB. Written by William Essex, this book has useful chapters on financial planning for UK citizens, as well as on dealing with family-related issues, such as international schooling.

Resident Abroad: Financial Times Publications, Maple House, 149 Tottenham Court Road, London W1P 9LL; tel 020-7896 2525; fax 020-7896 2276. Expatriate magazine with general interest articles and a focus on tax and financial planning issues.

Together on Assignment: ECA International, tel 020-7351 5000. Self-help tool to guide expatriate families through the difficulties they are likely to face particularly when over 90 per cent of international postings involve male employees, and in many cases women who accompany their partners leave behind fulfilling careers of their own, resulting in frustration and boredom in their new environment. The three-part package includes a 'Partner's Guide' containing case studies, a checklist and information on children and work issues, and an activity planner. Cost £125 plus VAT.

A NEW LIFE ABROAD!

How often have you pictured yourself living abroad? Enjoying a brand new lifestyle somewhere new and different?

It's an ambition you share with lots of people, of all ages and backgrounds.

But most fall at the first hurdle, unsure where to start and daunted by the prospect of cutting through all the red tape and bureaucracy that is involved. What a pity they didn't know about First Point International.

Whether you'd like to work, run your own business or even spend your retirement abroad, First Point will secure that crucial visa and provide all the advice and practical assistance you're likely to need.

YOUR NEXT STEP

To find out how you could soon be on your way to a new life abroad, call or send for our Information Pack today.

+44 (0)20 7724 9669

(24 Hours.) Please quote ref. LSG

www.firstpointinter.com
info@firstpointinter.com

Transitions Abroad: 18 Hulst Road, PO Box 1300, Amherst, Massachusetts 01004, USA; tel +1 413 247-3300; fax +1 413 256-0373. Bimonthly magazine with excellent articles on living and working in foreign countries and letters from readers abroad. It also contains contact addresses for organisations which can arrange work abroad and promotes 'active involvement as a guest in the host community rather than as a tourist.' They also publish the *Alternative Travel Directory* with country-by-country listings including study programmes and volunteer opportunities, and can send back issues and planning guides on a single subject or country.

Useful Addresses

The following bookshops both have sections specialising in the Middle East.

Probsthain & Company: 41 Great Russell Street, London WC1; tel 020-7636 1096.

The Travel Bookshop: 13 Blenheim Crescent, London W11; tel 020-7229 5260.

Removals

There are numerous firms that specialise in removals abroad and it is strongly advisable to contact one of these when embarking on a move out to the Gulf. A list of such companies is available from the *British Association of Removers* (*BAR*, 3 Churchill Court, 58 Stations Road, North Harrow, Middlesex HA2 7SA) in return for a stamped self addressed envelope. Make sure that you ask for a list of international removers as these are a sub-group of the association's members. The BAR also publishes a free leaflet of handy hints for those contemplating removals overseas on application at the same address. As removal companies are not regulated by law, contacting a firm affiliated to the *Association of International Removers*, or to the BAR, is the best guarantee of protection. Affiliated companies are inspected for their business practices and for their financial security, and they are also covered by shipping guarantees and bonds in case they go out of business while your goods are being shipped over to the Gulf. Most companies will offer a certain number of weeks' free storage, and will undertake to move absolutely anything door to door, including motorbikes, cars and pets. Costs vary widely depending on the destination: shipping to a port is generally reasonable but as soon as goods need to be transported any distance inland, the price escalates.

More details can be obtained by contacting one of the firms listed below.

Useful Addresses

Throughout the Gulf:

Bishop's Move: Overseas House, Stewart's Road, London SW8 4UG; tel 020-7498 0300; fax 020-7622 1794; e-mail overseas@bishops-move.co.uk Website www.bishops-move.co.uk

Davies Turner Worldwide Movers: 49 Watesway, Mitcham, Surrey; tel 020-7622 4393.

Vanpac International: 1340 Arnold Drive, Suite 231, Martinez, CA 94553, USA; tel +1 925 313-0989; fax +1 925 313-0971; e-mail info@vanpac.com Website www.vanpac.com

Bahrain:

Al-Dana Freight Forwarders: PO Box 10340, Manama, Diplomatic Area, Bahrain; tel +973 702-670; fax +973 701-073; e-mail aldanafw@batelco.com.bh

FourWinds Bahrain: PO Box 11131, Manama, Bahrain; tel +973 536-665; fax +973 530-212.

Gulf Agency Co (Bahrain) WLL: PO Box 412, Manama, Bahrain; tel +973 530-022; fax +973 530-063.

Saudi Arabia:
Continental Express Systems: PO Box 91572, Riyadh 11643, Saudi Arabia; tel +966 1 476-3980; fax +966 1 473-1092.
Four Winds Saudi Arabia: PO Box 4223, Jeddah, Saudi Arabia; tel +966 2 691-8883; fax +966 2 691-7190.
International Cargo Services: PO Box 696, Al Khobar 31952, Saudi Arabia; tel +966 3 898-3266; fax +966 3 899-1347.
Namma Cargo Services: PO Box 1498, Al-Khobar 31952, Saudi Arabia C.R. 9359; tel +966 3 895-2222; fax +966 3 894-6888; e-mail 104742.3320@ compuserve.com

United Arab Emirates:
Abu Dhabi Shipping Agency: PO Box 46103, Abu Dhabi, United Arab Emirates; tel +971 2 789-783; fax +971 2 789-783.
Ahmed Saleh Packing & Forwarding: PO Box 2606, Dubai, UAE; tel +971 4 854-000; fax +971 4 854-884.

Settling in Services
In Touch Consultants (Relocation & Settlement Services): PO Box 9550, World Trade Centre, Dubai, United Arab Emirates; tel +971 4 381-358; fax +971 4 389-168; e-mail rowlands@emirates.net.ae Website www.angelfire.com/me/rowlandsdubai/index.html
RESCO: Dubai, UAE; tel +971 4 329-285; fax +971 4 329-372; e-mail resco@emirates.net.ae Website www.newsofa.com

Renter/Home Insurance
American Interntaional Underwriters: 505 Carr Road R23-7A, Wilmington, DE 19809, USA; tel 800 343-5761 (freephone in the US), +1 302 761-3107 (outside the US); fax +1 302 761-3302; e-mail aiuna@ix.netcom.com

Pets

Moving pets to the Gulf region can be a lengthy process involving reams of paperwork and much stress however this can be taken care of for you by the *British Veterinary Centre* (BVC) based in the United Arab Emirates. They can offer assistance and advice with the import of your pet at all stages of the process. Full details of the services that they offer and answers to any queries about what is involved in the move can be obtained from BVC (tel +971 2 650085; fax +971 2 650014; e-mail britvet@emirates.net.ae Website www.britvet.com). Additionally information can be acquired from the *Ministry of Agriculture* and other specialists in vet travel are listed below.

Due to the large number of abandoned pets in Saudi Arabia it is extremely difficult to arrange to bring any animal into the country with you. In fact the importation of cats is strictly prohibited and although it may be possible to import a dog. Alternatively, you could adopt one of the many stray cats and dogs while you are in Saudi Arabia. To move pets to Oman involves giving advance notification and obtaining an official import permit from the Omani agriculture department. Several health checks and treatments must be done within a short time prior to travel. Oman is also very strict about the port of entry used.

Useful Addresses

Bishop's Move Pet Line: Overseas House, 102-104 Stewart's Road, London SW8 4UG; tel 020-7498 0300.
Ministry of Agriculture, Animal Export: Hook Rise South, Tolworth, Surbiton,

Surrey KT6 7NF; tel 020-8330 4411. Information and application forms for Ministry of Agriculture export certificate; also lists of Official Veterinarians.

Ladyhaye Livestock Shipping: Hare Lane, Blindley Heath, Lingfield, Surrey RH7 6JB; tel 01342-832161.

Worldwide Animal Travel: 43 London Road, Brentwood, Essex CM14 4NN; tel 01277-231611; fax 01277-262726.

Relocation Companies

Relocation companies not only provide all the services that removal companies offer but additionally handle all aspects of your move from your home country to wherever you are moving, such as helping you find accommodation and schools in your destination country, giving you orientation and induction to the new environment, etc. A comprehensive list of relocation firms can be obtained by contacting the *Association of Relocation Agents* (PO Box 189, Diss IP22 1PE; tel 08700-73 74 75; fax 01359-251508; e-mail info@relocationagents.com Website www.relocationagents.com).

First Point International (York House, 17 Great Cumberland Place, London W1H 7LA; tel 020-7724 9009; fax 020-7915 5265; Website www.firstpointinter. com) is a relocation specialist with experience of assisting individuals with the legal, lifestyle and career aspects of moving abroad.

Other companies that offer comprehensive relocation packages to both companies and individuals and specialise in international removals include *Crown Worldwide* (tel 020-8709 1200; fax 020-8709 1249; e-mail schigami.gblob@ crownworldwide.com Website www.crownworldwide.com) and *Transeuro Worldwide Movers* (Group Head Office, Drury Way, London NW10 0JN; tel 020-8784 0100; fax 020-8451 0061; Website www.transeuro.com). *Crown Worldwide* not only has a UK office but additionally has offices situated in the United Arab Emirates (PO Box 44669, **Abu Dhabi**, UAE; tel +971 2 343-491; fax +971 2 317-840; e-mail general.aeauh@ crownworldwide.com; PO Box 51773, **Dubai**, UAE; tel +971 4 444-982; fax +971 4 493-984; e-mail general.aeaxb@crownworldwide .com) and in Bahrain (PO Box 828, Manama, Bahrain; tel +973 227-598/224-858; fax +973 224-803; e-mail general.bhbah@crownworldwide.com).

Bishops Move (Overseas House, Stewart's Road, London SW8 4UG; tel 020-7498 0300; fax 020-7622 1794; e-mail overseas@bishops-move.co.uk Website www.bishops-move.co.uk) specialise in removals but also offers corporate relocation services.

Insurance

When relocating abroad, it is strongly advisable to take out a range of insurance policies to cover you and your family for all eventualities.

Norwich Union is one of the UK's largest insurance groups, with over 7 million customers serviced by some 16,000 staff worldwide. Norwich Union has been providing insurance services in the Arabian Peninsula since 1950 when the Yusuf Bin Ahmed Kanoo Group of Companies were appointed as Norwich's local agents in Bahrain. Later further offices were opened in Dubai, Abu Dhabi, Sharjah, and Jebel Ali in the UAE, and in Riyadh, Jeddah, and Al Khobar, in Saudi Arabia, and in Muscat, in the Sultanate of Oman, to meet the growing insurance needs of governments, multinational companies, and individuals, throughout the Gulf region. A comprehensive range of insurance packages are offered to meet the requirements of all clients. For more details contact Norwich Union on one of the following numbers:

NORWICH UNION

Looking to Live and Work in Saudi or the Gulf ?

When starting a new job in a foreign country the last thing on your mind is insurance.
Insurance needs to be planned to ensure you, your family and property are adequately protected during your stay abroad.

Norwich Union has been in Saudi and the Gulf for 50 years and has a wealth of experience in providing those people working abroad with the right insurance coverage to suit their needs.

We offer a comprehensive range of insurance products which includes:

Motor
Home Contents
Group Medical
Personal Accident
Travel
Commercial

So when starting a new life in the Middle East think Norwich Union for your insurance needs. We can be contacted on the following Telephone/Fax numbers.

NORWICH UNION MIDDLE EAST OFFICES

JEDDAH (K.S.A.)
Tel. 9662-664 6655
Fax 9662-660 9505

AL KHOBAR (K.S.A.)
Tel. 9663-8822813
Fax 9663-8820063

RIYADH (K.S.A.)
Tel. 9661-477 6706 / 478 0293
Fax 9661-478 0418 / 478 6869

BAHRAIN
Tel. 973-213515
Fax 973-213308

DUBAI (UAE)
Tel. 9714-324 3434
Fax 9714-324 8687

ABU DHABI (UAE)
Tel. 9712-774444
Fax 9712-766282

JEBEL ALI (UAE)
Tel. 97184-819696
Fax 97184-816095

SHARJAH (UAE)
Tel. 9716-561 3186
Fax 9716-562 0953

OMAN
Tel. 968-704382 / 708078
Fax 968-799385

CELEBRATING 50 YEARS IN THE GULF
NORWICH UNION

Bahrain: tel +973 213515; fax +973 213308.
Oman: tel +968 704382/708078; fax +968 799385.
Saudi Arabia: tel +966 2 664-6655; fax +966 2 660 9505 (Jeddah).
    tel +966 3 882-2813; fax +966 3 8820063 (Al Khobar).
    tel +966 1 477-6706/478-0293; fax +966 1 478-0418/478-6869 (Riyadh).
United Arab Emirates: tel +971 2 774444; fax +971 2 766282 (Abu Dhabi).
    tel +971 4 324 3434; fax +971 4 324 8687 (Dubai).
    tel +971 6 561 3186; fax +971 6 562 0953 (Sharjah).
    tel +971 8 481 9696; fax +971 8 481 6095 (Jebel Ali).

John Wason (Insurance Brokers) Ltd (72 South Street, Reading, Berkshire RG1 4RA; tel 0118-956 8800; fax 0118-956 8094; e-mail info@johnwason.co.uk Website www.johnwason.co.uk) also specialises in all areas of overseas insurance from 'Contents' to 'All Risks', 'Personal Money' and 'Medical and Repatriation Expenses.' As well as offering a 'Comprehensive' insurance package that includes cover for contents, all risks and money, medical and repatriation expenses, personal accident and sickness, their 'Essential' insurance policy is specifically designed to provide full cover for those living in company houses or apartments overseas or for those who rent whilst living or working abroad. Contact John Wason direct at the above address, or visit their website for further information.

Details of other insurance brokers specialising in expatriate insurance policies are available from the *Association of British Insurers*, 51 Gresham Street, London EC2V 7HQ; tel 020-7600 3333; fax 020-7696 8999; Website www.abi.org.uk.

ISLAM

To understand the lifestyle and culture of the Arabs in the Gulf it is essential to gain some knowledge of their religion, Islam, which permeates every aspect of their daily lives. When translated from the Arabic, Islam literally means 'active submission to the will of God.' A Muslim (or Moslem) is one who submits. Absolute faith and complete submission to the will of God are intrinsic components of a Muslim's creed.

Muslims believe that God ordains every single event that occurs on earth. Hence when you arrange to meet with a Muslim at a specific time his response is commonly *In Sha Allah* (if God wills), a sentiment that is held very strongly by the speaker who will make it to the meeting if it was meant to be but if he does not, it is not what God willed.

The Islamic faith not only promulgates a profound and fundamental spiritual dogma but additionally outlines a detailed code of conduct as found in its Holy Book, the Koran (Qu'ran), and other holy writings. Every action in a Muslim's life is labelled with a degree of consequence from compulsory, advised, disapproved, prohibited to neutral.

The existence of Islam in the Gulf is all-pervasive. Public worship is unreservedly performed taking priority over nearly everything else that is going on, religious texts are notably present in all homes, offices and cars, and public speeches (regardless of subject matter) continually contain references to God and His Prophet Mohammed. 'In the name of God, the Compassionate, the Merciful,' heads most letters and in countries where there is a stricter adherence to Islamic doctrine the consumption or possession of alcohol is forbidden and specific dress codes imposed.

The Islamic Creed

Muslims believe in one God, *Allah*, and that His last prophet was Mohammed, born in Makkah (Mecca) in AD 571. Prayers take place five times daily at dawn (*fajr*), midday (*dhuhr*), mid-afternoon (*asir*), sunset (*maghreb*), and evening (*isha*). Exact times are published in local newspapers every day. During these prayers all Muslims face towards the direction of the sacred *Ka-abah*, a black cube-shaped stone in Makkah's Holy Mosque. The sacred book of Islam, by which all Muslims abide, is the Holy Qu'ran in which the Five Pillars of Islam are prescribed:

FAITH (*shahada*). The First Pillar is the avowal of faith: There is no god but Allah and Mohammed is the prophet of Allah.

PRAYER (*salah*). The Second Pillar stipulates the rituals of prayer to be performed five times a day with individuals facing the Holy Ka-abah in Makkah.

ALMS GIVING (*zakat*). The Third Pillar requires all Muslims to pay a fixed proportion of their possessions for the welfare of the whole community and particularly for its most impoverished members.

FASTING (*sawm*). The Fourth Pillar concerns the ninth month of the Islamic calender, Ramadhan, during which all Muslims must abstain from all food, drink and sexual activity from dawn to sunset.

PILGRIMAGE TO MAKKAH (*hajj*). The Fifth Pillar bids all Muslims to make a journey to Makkah at least once in their lifetime. The *hajj* is the specific pilgrimage made annually by thousands of Muslims united in the act during the closing month of the Islamic year, *Dhul Hijah*. Visits made by individuals at other times of the year are known as *umrah*.

Makkah, the birthplace of Islam and the Prophet Mohammed, and Madinah, where the Prophet's Mosque and his burial place are situated, are considered by Muslims as their two holiest cities. Entry into these Saudi cities is strictly forbidden to non-Muslims.

Muslim Sects

Arab custom dictates that a leader's successor should be elected by consensus of the community (*ijma*). Consequently, the Prophet Mohammed had not himself specified who was to replace him as Khalifat Tasul Allah (caliph or successor to the messenger of God) after his death in AD 632.

Two rivals for the position emerged: Abu Bakr, father of the Prophet's preferred living wife Aisha, and Ali ibn abi Talib, cousin of the Prophet and the husband of the Prophet's daughter Fatima. Abu Bakr was chosen by popular consensus and was succeeded in 634 by Umar ibn Khattab who was followed in 646 by Uthman ibn Affam (Mohammed's son-in-law). In 656 Uthman was murdered and Ali became caliph but then he too was killed by a splinter group, the Kharijites, in 661. His death marked the end of an age of Muslim unity. The followers of Ali, the Shiat Ali (from which the term Shiite is derived) refused to acknowledge the new successor which caused a break with the Sunnis responsible for today's divisions within the faith. The Shiites considered only the house of Ali as having legitimate claim to Mohammed's succession and because the choice of Imam (prayer leader) was so important the election of caliph continues – even today – to be antagonistic.

THE SUNNIS

The Sunnis are the orthodox Muslim group. 'Summa' translated from Arabic means 'customary procedure.' The vast majority of Muslims belong to this sect. With the exception of Iraq, Bahrain, Lebanon and the Yemen Arab Republic, Sunnis prevail in all Arab countries. They consider that the Shiites place a certain divinity on Imams which is sacrilegious. Sub-groups of the Sunnis are:

The Wahhabis. The teachings of the Wahhabis are the most austere of the Muslim sects. The Wuwahhidun (Unitarians – title given to followers of this sect) promulgate spiritual and moral reform, encompassing a return to the purity of Islam as exercised by the Prophet and the caliphs who succeeded him. They refuse to accept the special relationships of the Shiite Imam to Allah and consider all believers to have equal access to God. The name derives from Mohammed ibn Abd al Wahab (born 1703) who took the teachings of the Qu'ran literally and the sect grew closely associated with the political power of the Al Saud family the founders of today's Kingdom of Saudi Arabia. Saudis do *not* like to be referred to as Wahhabis, they prefer to be called Muwahidoon (the United Ones).

The Ibadis. This sect derives from the moderate branch of the Kharjites (wiped out within a few centuries of their establishment due to their belligerent actions and beliefs). They treat true believers with amity (*wilaya*) and all others with enmity (*bara's*). Unlike the Kharjites, Ibadis do not agree with the slaughtering of other Muslims solely on the basis of religious beliefs. Within their worship a puritannical style code is upheld.

THE SHI'A
The Shi'a derive their name from 'Shi'at Ali' or 'Party of Ali.' They hold the opinion that the Imamate (leadership of Islam) rightfully belongs within the family of Ali, the Prophet's son-in-law who challenged the Orthodox Caliphate and was killed in AD 661. The majority of Shiites are convinced that the line of Imams descended from Ali came to an end in the ninth century when the twelfth Imam seemed to have disappeared but that he is still in some way present and will return to lead Islam again. The Shi'a prevail in Iran and are the majority sect in Iraq, the Yemen Arab Republic, Bahrain and Lebanon. They also have a notable presence in Kuwait and the Eastern Province of Saudi Arabia. Among the Shi'a sub-groups are:

The Ithna-Asharis (the 'twelvers'). This sub-group of the Shiites prevail in Iran and constitute just over half the populations of Iraq and Bahrain with substantial numbers present in other Gulf States and Lebanon.

The Zeidis. The Zeidis are the leading group in the Yemen Arab Republic and their name derives from Ali's great grandson Zeid.

The Ismailis or Suba'iya (the seveners). The Aga Khan is the spiritual leader of this group that limits its number of Shi'a Imams to only seven. Within this sect are further sub-groups including the Nazaris who are interspersed worldwide.

The Muslim Calender
The Islamic calender dates from the Hegira and in Western terms Muslim years are suffixed AH (Anno Hegirae – in the year of the Hegira).The year is founded on lunar cycles consequently it is 11 or 12 days shorter than the Gregorian year. The traditional Muslim regards the day beginning at sunset (6pm) rather than at dawn.
The Islamic months are *Muharram* (30 days), *Safar* (29 days), *Rabi'al-Awal* (30 days), *Rabi'al-Thani* (29 days), *Jumad al-Awal* (30 days), *Jumad al-Thani* (29 days), *Rajab* (30 days), *Sha'ban* (29 days), *Ramadan* (30 days), *Shawal* (29 days), *Dhul-Qa'dah* (30 days), and *Dhul-Hijah* (29 days – 30 in a leap year).

Holy Days and Festivals

	1999/2000 (1420AH)	2000/01 (1421 AH)	2001/02 (1422 AH)	2002/03 (1423 AH)	2003/04 (1424 AH)
Ramadan starts	8 Dec	27 Nov	16 Nov	5 Nov	25 Oct
Eid-al-Fitr starts	7 Jan	27 Dec	16 Dec	5 Dec	24 Nov
Eid-al-Adha starts	17 Mar	6 Mar	23 Feb	12 Feb	1 Feb
Moslem New Year	17 Apr	6 Apr	26 Mar	15 Mar	4 Mar
Prophet's Birthday	25 Jun	14 Jun	3 Jun	23 May	12 May

Exact timing of these dates is dependent on the sighting of the moon hence those recorded here may be one or two days out of the precise date but it is noticeable that each date falls about eleven days earlier every year.

Ramadan

During the full lunar month of Ramadan all Muslims have to abstain from all food, drink, tobacco and other pleasurable activities between the hours of sunrise and sunset. This is particularly demanding if it is summer when even water is not permitted during the daylight hours. The degree of abstinence varies according to how strict the individual Muslim regards himself to be. When living in Arab countries during Ramadan out of respect for their custom, it is advisable not to eat, drink or smoke in the presence of a Muslim throughout the daytime. Indeed in some countries it is a punishable offence to do so. Additionally a Western woman should ensure that she is dressed conservatively covering bare arms and legs.

The end of Ramadan is celebrated with a feast.

Eid-al-Fitr (festival of breaking the fast)

The end of Ramadan on 1 Shawal (the tenth month) is marked by Eid-al-Fitr and runs over the following two days. It is a time of celebration and happiness when friends and relations get together and children receive presents of money or clothing. Additionally, everyone has to pay a specific amount of food or money to a charity, *the Sadaqah al-Fitr*, which provides or purchases a meal for someone in need. The festival also involves an extra congregational prayer.

Eid-al-Adha (festival of sacrifice)

This festival takes place on 10th Dhul-Hijjah and the subsequent three days. It marks the occasion when Abraham was prepared to sacrifice his son Ismael as a symbol of his complete devotion to God. This proof of Abraham's total dedication to God was rewarded by a sheep being killed in place of his son and since that time the practice of sacrificing a domestic animal has been continued to signify a Muslim's willingness to sacrifice everything as prescribed in the Islamic faith. The meat of the slaughtered animal is split into three equal portions – one for the family, one for friends and neighbours, and one for the needy. This represents the special charity of Eid-al-Adha. It was also at the time of this festival that the final divine revelations were made to the Prophet Mohammed. Hence like the Eid-al-Fitr there is great celebration and joy amongst the communities with an extra congregational prayer occurring.

During the time of both Eids it is usual to congratulate an Arab, or if you know him well send cards to arrive a day or two prior to the festival. Additionally, at these times it is customary for important individuals to hold audience in their palaces or homes, which means that you should enter the house, greet them, take coffee and depart after a sufficient pause.

Holy Days

Lailat-al-Qadr (Night of Power or Determination).
This takes place on one of the odd-numbered nights during the last ten days of Ramadan (commonly the night before 27th) and marks the night on which the first divine revelations of the Qu'ran were received by the Prophet Mohammed. Lailat-al-Qadr involves a night-long devotion, recitations of the Qu'ran and charitable acts.

Lailat-al-Mirai (Night Journey to Heaven).
This takes place on 27 Rajab and marks the vision of the Prophet Mohammed in which he was received by God and observed the glory of Heaven.

Mawlid-al-Nabi (Prophet's Birthday).
This takes place on 12 Rabi'al Awal but its commemoration is traditional rather than Islamic as Islam does not focus on any single mortal. Gatherings are held, orations given and prayers offered.

Ras-is-Sana (Head of the Year).
This takes place on 1 Muharram and commemorates the time of the Prophet Mohammed's move from Makkah to Madinah regarded as the inception of Islam.

Ashura.
This takes place on 10 Muharram and is marked by the Shiite as the time when the Prophet's grandson Husayn was killed at the Battle of Kerbela in 680. Shiites refused to acknowledge Yazid (the second Ummayed caliph) and their attempts to overthrow him were unsuccessful.

Muslim Diet Rules

In the Qu'ran are prescribed foods which Muslims are allowed to eat (*halal*) and those which they are not (*haram*). Muslims are forbidden to eat: animals that have perished naturally or have been slaughtered for reasons other than food; blood; pork and its derivatives – e.g. lard and gelatine; animals sacrificed to a pagan deity or in a way not ordained in the Qu'ran; alcoholic and all fermented liquids which includes foods containing alcoholic extracts (e.g. Christmas cake).

Alcohol Prohibition

Prophet Mohammed did not initially promulgate a ban on alcohol but after excessive consumption among believers began to affect their worship he expressed marked disapprobation of the habit. Alcohol was only officially prohibited when the ritual five prayers a day became common practice. The enforcement of the ruling varies from one Gulf State to another.

In Saudi Arabia and Kuwait the sale and consumption of alcohol is strictly forbidden. Customs officials are ever watchful and offenders are severely dealt with. Bahrain is known as the place where alcohol is more readily available than elsewhere in the Gulf but due to its ties with Saudi Arabia continually strengthening more constraints may be introduced and there has already been a campaign launched against drunkenness. Currently you can import into the country one bottle of spirits duty free and alcohol can easily be purchased from bars, licensed hotels and restaurants and certain shops. In Oman alcohol cannot be imported but some hotels and restaurants do sell it. Expatriates resident in Oman have the option of obtaining a liquor licence from their embassy which allows them to purchase alcohol from special shops. Severe penalties are imposed on those caught drunk in public. In Qatar, alcohol can only be bought by resident non-Muslim expatriates with a special liquor licence. You are not allowed to import alcohol into Qatar and consumption of it is restricted to within private homes. Harsh penalties face anyone caught contravening these rules. In the United Arab Emirates (with the exception of Sharjah) alcohol is sold in most licensed restaurants and hotels and a liquor licence is required in order to purchase alcohol from special shops to drink at home.

Shari'a (Shariah) Law

The laws in all the Gulf countries are largely based (though not entirely, see separate country entries for details) on the Islamic Holy book, the Qur'an; this system is commonly known as 'Shari'a.' Shari'a outlines two categories of crime: those that are carefully defined, and those that are implicit in the requirements and prohibitions of the shari'a. For the former category, there are specified penalties; for the latter, punishment can be prescribed by a *qadi* (judge) of a shari'a court. Among the carefully defined crimes with prescribed penalties (*hadd*) are: personal injury, adultery, fornication, theft, and homicide.

The extent to which penalties are applied to those caught in violation of shari'a laws varies from state to state, with Saudi Arabia noted for upholding the strictest rules and the most severe punishments for offenders. Beheadings and the amputation of a thief's right hand regularly take place in front of the main Mosque on Fridays after mid-day prayers. Crimes which carry a death sentence include murder, apostasy (renunciation of the Muslim faith), and sexual immorality such as adultery or homosexual acts. Murder is deemed as a crime against another individual rather than a crime against society and as such shari'a entitles the victim's family to demand punishment, grant clemency, or demand blood money (*diya*) – a fixed price in recompense for the crime (in Saudi Arabia the current rate for a Muslim man's life is 100,000 Saudi Riyals and a Christian's about half of this amount). Throughout the Gulf unmarried single men and women are not permitted to live together and in Saudi Arabia single women in public outside the compounds should, as a general rule, be accompanied at all times by a close male relative.

Special attention should be paid to the following aspects of Shari'a law upheld throughout the Arabian Peninsula:

Non-payment of debt. Shari'a law stipulates that non-payment of debt is a crime that can result in imprisonment. However, imprisonment does not discharge debt.

Alcohol. Throughout Saudi Arabia and Kuwait, alcohol is strictly prohibited. Evidence of drinking such as drunken brawling, careless drink-driving accidents, noisy parties, or roaming around in the middle of the night/early morning can result in the offenders serving prison sentences from a few weeks to some months. Those caught smuggling, manufacturing or distributing alcohol can expect to receive several years. Sentences also often include the punishment of flogging and smugglers will have to pay a large Customs fine. Although the other Gulf states permit the consumption of alcohol in licensed hotels and restaurants, and the purchase of alcohol by non-Muslims in possession of a liquor licence, they still have strict rules governing drink-related offences and the amounts of alcohol that can be bought by an individual. Severe penalties will be imposed on anyone found in contravention of the stipulated regulations.

Drugs. Drug trafficking is severely punished throughout the Gulf with the death penalty commonly imposed upon offenders in Saudi Arabia. Possession of even the tiniest quantity can result in a two year prison sentence in addition to lashes and a fine. In October 1998 a London headmistress and a British male teacher were each sentenced to four and a half years in an Abu Dhabi prison for possessing alcohol and three grammes of cannabis (enough for just two joints). The drug was found in a camera case that had been given to them by a friend. The couple were also told to pay a fine of £140 and are to be deported upon completion of serving their sentences. Despite appeals for clemency by family members of the accused no audience has yet been granted with any government officials.

If you intend to bring any medicinal drugs with you to the Gulf then you should always carry your doctor's prescription. Extra care needs to be taken when bringing any everyday pharmaceutical products into one of the Gulf states as they may be prohibited and you will be detained until the matter has been resolved. In Saudi Arabia sleeping pills and any drug containing codeine are banned and even poppyseeds and nutmeg are considered hallucinogens and therefore outlawed in the country.

Other prohibitions. In addition to the restrictions placed on drugs and alcohol in the Arabian Peninsula, the following items are also prohibited: pork and its derivatives, religious books and material (in Saudi Arabia only), obscene literature or videos showing scantily dressed women or intimate male-female contact. Any books or videos you bring into the Gulf will be seized on your arrival and will either be kept or returned heavily censored. Even fashion magazines such as 'Cosmopolitan' are deemed scandalous.

Imprisonment

Gulf prisons are not aimed to rehabilitate but rather to punish inmates. They are usually very overcrowded and hot. It is not uncommon to watch fellow prisoners flogged. Any exercise which you may be allowed is an infrequent privilege. Regular visits are permitted but generally under trying conditions.

Embassy/Consular Aid

Your embassy or Consul in the Gulf country in which you are resident will do everything in their power to assist you if you are caught breaking any of the local laws. However, this help is normally restricted to offering advice and trying to make sure that the standard correct Gulf legal processes are adhered to. You are not protected against receiving customary punishment e.g. long prison sentences and public flogging, for offences that you have committed. Muslims and non-Muslims alike are subject to the full penalties ascribed to violations of the Shari'a law.

If you are arrested you will be taken to a police station to be questioned and asked to make a statement while an investigation occurs. During this investigation you will not be allowed the aid of any outside contact (with employers, friends, consul, or lawyer). If the police do decide to bring charges against you, you will be detained in custody and then transferred from the police station to a prison until you appear before a judge to verify that your signed statement is correct and was not made under actual physical duress.

Your Consul/embassy representative will have unlimited access to you while you are in police custody but once you have been imprisoned only restricted access will be permitted. After your initial appearance before a judge you will be returned to police custody until your trial which will be conducted in accordance with Qur'anic law. No jury is present and you have no rights to a lawyer or embassy representative, although consular attendance may be granted in some cases. The court will provide an interpreter. If you are convicted of a crime you will be sentenced by the judge then asked to sign an acceptance of the sentence (unless you intend to appeal against the conviction to a higher court).

The whole process can take three months or more depending upon the complexity of the case as those involving foreigners are handled with extra special care. A higher court, the Provincial Governor, the Ministry of the Interior and in serious cases the Council of Ministers have to confirm (or increase) the judge's sentence. Appeals can take up to twelve months to be heard. Some expatriates found guilty of an offence are just deported after a few days or weeks in police remand but this is a very rare occurrence.

Social Practices in the Gulf

Arabs are a very polite, hospitable and generous race and when living in Arabia it is very important to take note of some of the following customs in order to gain a greater understanding of their culture and to avoid inadvertently offending their sensibilities.

Shaking hands. Must always be done on greeting and departing. A handshake lasting longer than it would in the West symbolises friendship. If the handshake on departure is held for longer than on arrival it means that you have made a good impression.

Coffee. When coffee or tea is offered it should always be accepted. Generally sweet milkless tea is served first followed by sweet Arabic coffee in small traditional handleless cups. To take two cups of coffee is deemed the well-mannered number to consume, to take just one cup is seen as an insult and any more looks greedy, although different countries have different rules on this and it is advisable to follow your host's example. To prevent your cup from being continually refilled by the pourer gently shake it before handing it over.

Soles of feet. It is considered a calculated insult to expose the sole of your foot to an Arab due to it being thought of as unclean in the Arab world. Therefore, be careful when sitting with one leg crossed over the other and equally try not to sit too stiffly with both feet firmly fixed to the ground looking awkward.

The Right Hand Rule. Never accept food or anything else with your left hand. The right hand should be used not only for accepting everything and eating but for all major gestures. It is extremely offensive to beckon anyone with the forefinger of the right hand. Indeed if you need to beckon someone at all it is best to point all the fingers of the right hand downwards and pull the hand towards the body.

Expressing Admiration. Best to avoid showing too much interest in any of your host's belongings as it may be seen that you are asking for something as a gift which your host will probably insist that you keep.

Personal Appearance. It is important to always look well presented when visiting an Arab. Many Gulf Arabs find men publicly wearing shorts or sleeveless vests without a shirt offensive. Men should be covered from their navels to their knees at the very least; women should be covered from head to toe with only their face and hands exposed. The degree to which this dress code is enforced varies in different countries but out of respect for Arab nationals women should publicly dress quite conservatively saving skimpy clothes for the beach resorts, hotels and private swimming pools, etc.

Language. English is widely spoken throughout the Gulf but it is considered very good manners to learn some of the most common Arabic greetings and everyday phrases.

Photography. When taking photographs in the Gulf you should always double check whether it is permissible or not especially if you are taking pictures of Arab nationals. Taking photographs of military installations, police stations or Muslim women is strictly prohibited.

Dogs. The Arab people believe dogs to be unclean and that ownership of a dog holds off good fortune although dogs can be kept for hunting, herding and guarding.

Public prayers. When a Muslim is praying in public it is considered very rude to stare or walk in front of the individual praying.

Taboo subjects. When talking with an Arab never ask him directly about his wife only ever ask after 'the family.' Discussing politics is another area to avoid especially the Palestinian and Israeli question. The term 'Persian Gulf' should no longer be used, instead the area should be called the 'Arabian Gulf' or more simply 'the Gulf.' You should also be very careful about how you approach, and what you say concerning, the Islamic religion. Last year a British teacher was dismissed from their job in Kuwait and their teaching licence revoked, for composing an imaginary letter from Mohammed to the Archangel Gabriel requesting him for a position as a prophet.

Dining out

Meals at an Arab's house are generally very short and involve sitting cross-legged on the floor. It is polite practice to leave straight after coffee has been served. Men and women eat separately but some non-Muslim women are occasionally invited to join the men. Before eating a traditional Muslim will speak the words *Bismillah ar-Rahman* (In the name of God, the Merciful, the Compassionate). He is likely to concentrate more on his guests than on his food as self-discipline is a key attribute and hunger is preferable to gluttony, physical appetites should be tempered.

Arab Names

When addressing an Arab either face to face or in a letter it is very important to ensure that the right names are used. Some names can sound similar but are written differently and careful attention should be paid to the accurate spelling of the names. For example, Mahmood is not the same as Muhammad, Maajid differs from Majeed, and Saalim from Saleem. Most Arab names will have various English spellings due to the transliteration involved from one alphabet to the other but keep to the version used by the Arab himself as written on his card or letter heading. Mohd is the abbreviated form of Mohammed and when an apostrophe is used it signifies a glottal stop which is not found in the English language, e.g. Sa'ad.

Arabs in the Gulf tend to have their name set out in one of two ways. Either their personal name is followed by their father's name and then grandfather's name – e.g. Abdul Aziz bin Jassim bin Sulman, or their personal name is followed by their father's name and then their family or tribal clan – e.g. Abdul Aziz bin Jassim al Khalifa. 'Bin' or 'ibn' means son of and in both these examples the man would be addressed as Abdul Aziz. The latter name structure is more customary and is the one employed by ruling and other distinguished families. Women do not adopt their husband's name on marriage.

Arabs have many names for God such as Aziz and Rahman. These titles are popular throughout the Arab world preceded by 'Abdul' meaning 'slave of.' You should never address anyone as simply 'Abdul' but add the subsequent name 'Abdul Aziz' or 'Abdul Rahman' etc.

Arab Dress

Throughout the Gulf Arabs may be seen wearing traditional national dress. A man's attire includes a loosely fitting, ankle-length garment generally made of cotton referred to in Kuwait, Oman and the UAE as a *dishdasha* or *kandoura*, and in the other Gulf states as a *thobe*. On their heads they wear the *gahfia* or *tagia*, a small white crocheted skull cap usually covered by the *gutra*, a long cotton cloth. A double black woollen braid, the *igal*, worn around the crown of the head keeps the gutra in place.

Women tend to wear a long-sleeved, full-length dress, also called a *kandoura*, which is commonly lavishly embroidered with traditional designs. Under the kandoura are worn trousers, *sirwal*, and over the top of the outfit, when women go outside their homes, is worn a black cover, *abaya*. Hair is always covered by an abaya or a black scarf *shaela* and in some countries Muslim women cover their faces with veils and masks too so only their eyes and hands are left exposed.

Women in the Gulf

To many Westerners, who are accustomed in their home countries to women being treated as equals to men in all areas of daily life, women throughout the Arabian Peninsula appear to lead very repressed lives in which they seem to be treated with little or no respect by the men of these countries, and the restrictions they appear to be constrained by, dictated by the Islamic faith. There is certainly a degree of truth in this viewpoint, women in the Gulf do not have the same freedom to live as they wish as women in Western states and women *are* treated very differently to men, and yet the situation for and attitude towards women varies greatly within the individual Gulf states and Islam actually places great importance on the role of Muslim women and their rights within society.

The woman's position in the Islamic Gulf countries is by no means a simple black-and-white state of affairs. In some countries, more so than others, women are definitely treated like second-class citizens although their presence in the work place (see below) is steadily increasing (with the exception of Saudi Arabia), in the face of widespread traditional strong feelings that the woman's place is in the home. In the United Arab Emirates, the President, Shaikh Zayed bin Sultan Al Nahyan, acknowledges the validity of women in the work force as well as in the home, and his wife, Shaikha Fatima, leads the Women's Federation, promoting the training, education and advancement of the status of women.

Dress

Throughout the Gulf women are generally expected to dress in a particular style that covers them from head to toe (see *Arab Dress* above). Many foreigners may consider this somewhat restrictive but a dress code is also expected of men, and beneath the usually plain black, long, loose coverings (*abbayas*) women tend to wear very extravagant designer outfits. Moreover, the argument for such modest dress in public places is that it is serving to protect the dignity of a woman, so that she is valued as a person and for her mind, not for her looks. It is not obligatory for women to cover their faces, in addition to the rest of their bodies (with the exclusion of hands and feet), except in certain areas of Saudi Arabia. Furthermore, when performing the *Hajj* (see above) all women should leave their faces exposed.

Education

Islam states that it is every Muslim's duty to seek education, male or female, in order to acquire knowledge that can be used for the good of the community. Indeed, the early Muslim world actively encouraged women to study and many women – including Aisha, one of the wives of the Prophet Mohammed – became notable religious scholars, writers, poets, doctors and teachers. In all the Gulf states the numbers of women receiving schooling has dramatically increased over the last thirty years or so (see *Schools and Education* in individual country chapters). All Islamic schools are segregated and in universities male lecturers deliver papers to female students via a television screen. Recent figures reveal that women now constitute 58 per cent of university students in Saudi Arabia and in Qatar, female graduates and post-graduates outnumber men by three to two. In Kuwait, 2,000 women graduated from Kuwait University in 1996 compared to 600 men and in the UAE, since the late 1980s, women graduates have outnumbered men by a ratio of two to one at the United Arab Emirates University.

Marriage

Muslim women retain their own names and thus, arguably, their own identity when they marry, rather than adopting their husband's name. Although some now follow the Western convention of using their husband's family name, for example when travelling.

Islam views marriage as a partnership between wife and husband in which mutual care and respect are vital facets of the union. Traditionally men are seen as ultimately responsible for providing for their families while women play an important role in supporting their husbands and maintaining a strong family unit. It is the fear that working women will neglect their familial duties, which will then lead to the break up of the family unit, that accounts for most individuals' opposition to women obtaining paid employment.

Despite the majority of Muslim marriages being 'arranged', Islam dictates that a woman has to give her consent to any union. Moreover, a woman has the right to request a clause in her marriage contract which forbids her husband from wedding another wife for the duration of their marriage. Once a marriage contract has been signed, the terms are binding. If a marriage fails Islam does permit a woman to seek divorce as well as a man although the extent to which this ruling is enacted in reality is very much dependent on each Arab country's own customs and dictates regarding divorce cases.

The Islamic law allowing men to take more than one wife was apparently initiated to offer a woman protection. The reasoning for this being that during the period of tribal wars many men died leaving widows with children without a provider and young girls unable to find husbands. Consequently, by allowing men to marry more than one woman everyone could, in theory, be cared for. The condition for having more than one wife is that all wives are treated equally, both materially and spiritually. Although the ruling still exists today, polygamy is very rare nowadays.

Suffrage

In 1999 women gained voting rights in Qatar and in Kuwait, the emir issued a decree in May to permit women to hold public office and vote in the next parliamentary elections in 2003. However, the draft law granting women full political rights was rejected by the all-male parliament in November – 32 voted against the draft, 30 in favour, 2 abstained. Nevertheless, the voting figures show that it is only a matter of time before women may gain their just voting rights in the state. Women's suffrage does not yet exist in any of the other Gulf countries.

Property and Inheritance Rights

A woman has the right to own property and there are no restrictions on her ownership and management of money or real estate or on performing any legal transactions concerning her properties. She can freely: purchase, sell, mortgage, borrow or lend, donate, act as a trustee, sign contracts and legal documents, and establish a business or company.

When an estate is divided men tend to inherit a larger share than women but this is due to the fact that Islam places a greater weight on men providing for their families whilst any money that a woman inherits is for her use only, she is not expected to put it towards the support of her family. Women are commonly entitled to half the male share of an inheritance.

Driving Restrictions

Saudi Arabia is the only country in the Gulf where women are *not* allowed to drive although there are rumours that this ruling may change at some unspecified time in the future.

Women in the Work Place

A lot of Arab men retain the traditional views that a woman's place is in the home. However, this is by no means felt by all Gulf Arabs and in certain states women have actively been encouraged to enter the work force, e.g. in Kuwait and Bahrain (see also *Women at Work* in the 'Employment' section). In the last five years the number of women in work in Bahrain has risen by over 40 per cent, increasing by over 3,500 to almost 14,000. Throughout the Gulf, the proportion of working women ranges from 23 per cent in Kuwait (a third of the indigenous work force) to 12 per cent in Bahrain, 9 per cent in Oman and the UAE, to a mere 7 per cent in Qatar and Saudi Arabia.

Women have tended to work in more 'feminine' professions such as health care, education, air travel and banking although now many also run their own businesses and there has been a marked interest among the Gulf females to enter more male-dominated fields of work such as law, the media, engineering, retail and even in the multinational consumer sector. In 1996, an emiri decree in Bahrain appointed two women to very senior civil service posts – Ms Samia Al-Moayed became Director of the Department of Management and Organisation at Bahrain's Civil Service Bureau and Ms Sabah Al-Moayed became the General Manager at the head office of Bahrain's leading bank, Al-Ahli National Bank.

Only last year the DTI (Department of Trade and Industry, Kingsgate House, 66-74 Victoria Street, London SW1E 6SW) and COMET (Committee for Middle East Trade, 33 Bury Street, London SW1Y 6AX; tel 020-7839 1170; fax 020-7839 3717; e-mail enquiries@comet.org.uk) organised a successful conference on 'Women in Business in the Arab World.' About 70 British businesswomen and 35 of their counterparts from throughout the Arab world (managers, owners, sales and marketing directors and executives from a wide range of business fields) were present at the event in which awareness for the growing role of businesswomen in the Gulf and other Arab regions was highlighted and future business transactions encouraged in those areas. Amongst the speakers at the conference was Assilah Al Harty, Chief Executive of the Al Harty Complex in Oman and Managing Director of the Al Harty Group. Her recent appointment to the Board of Oman Chamber of Commerce reflects the gradual shift towards educated young women in the Gulf attaining executive roles in the business world and managing their own companies. Further, one of the results of the event was to inspire Kuwaiti delegates to contemplate establishing a women's business group in Kuwait.

More and more opportunities are opening up for Arab women (as well as men) to work in the Arabian Peninsula especially as all the Gulf countries in the region are looking to replace their expatriate work force with their own nationals in the private and public sectors. However, the prejudices are weighed heavily against women and even those men who are not opposed to females working, give their approval with the condition that the sexes are segregated at work. Women generally earn a third of what their male counterparts earn for the same job, and women are on the whole excluded from decision-making and management roles.

For a Muslim woman to attain a career in the Gulf is very much dependent on the support of her family and friends. Traditionally a woman is under the guardianship of a close male relative, be it her father, brother, uncle, or husband, without the consent of her guardian/provider she will not find it easy to accomplish any of her career aims. Then, even after she may obtain the consent of her father, she may receive outrage from other male relatives and so women face a constant struggle to dispel the inherently biased opinion formed against their presence in the male-dominated business world. At the 'Women in Business in the Arab World' conference, Jordan's Princess Basma bint Talal, concluded that, the 'Many constraints faced by women are social or cultural and not the result of a discriminatory religion – as is often maintained by those who do not understand Islam in its original form, or those who wish to distort its message.' The Arab world is not likely to experience a female revolution on the scale of an Emmeline Pankhurst revolt, but in their own slow but sure way women are beginnning to assert themselves and be recognised for their worth in the work place outside the home.

Desert Activities

Desert Driving

Generally known as 'wadi bashing', driving around the desert in a 4WD (four wheel drive) vehicle is a particularly popular activity amongst expatriates in the Arabian Peninsula. On the whole these desert safaris are a one day event but some people like to camp out as well especially in Oman, Saudi Arabia and the United Arab Emirates. Desert driving can be the perfect getaway from the urban confines of city life offering expatriates the chance to explore the more varied and beautiful landscape that can be found throughout the Gulf outside the main cities.

Many tour operators in the individual states arrange specific 'wadi bashing' trips. One company in particular, *Off Road Emirates* (PO Box 47360, Abu Dhabi, United Arab Emirates; tel +971 2 333232; fax +971 2 336642), operates in the UAE, Oman and Yemen, and offers more specialised journeys for groups of four to twelve people. The company assists with every aspect of your desert safari from planning your route to supplying all the necessary equipment and providing on the spot expertise. In Oman, *Zubair Tours* (PO Box 833, Ruwi 112, Sultanate of Oman; tel +968 708081; fax +968 787564; e-mail toursinb@alzubair.com Website www.alzubair.com) also offers a range of wadi bashing, dune driving, and overnight desert camping tours.

For all those embarking on a desert drive it is well worth reading Dariush Zandi's *Off Road in the Emirates* and Kem Melville's *Staying Alive in the Desert*.

Traditional Arab Spectator Sports

Throughout the Arabian Peninsula you will find plenty of opportunities to experience watching some traditional Arab sports such as camel racing, dhow racing (wooden boats powered by a single sail that catches the wind), and perhaps even falconry (if you are lucky enough to receive an invite by an Arab national). In some areas you may also have the chance to witness some bloodless bullfighting such as in the East Coast of the UAE. In this activity two bulls are pitted against one another, locking horns and wrestling until one turns tail and flees. Horse racing is very popular throughout the Gulf as well. Most of these sports generally take place in the cooler winter months as it is far too hot during the summer season.

The Arabic Language

English is widely spoken throughout the Gulf so learning Arabic is not a necessity. However, if you make the effort to learn some basic Arabic words and phrases it is considered very polite, and greatly appreciated by the Arab nationals.

Finding courses to learn Arabic when resident in the Gulf is not easy as the few schools that do cater for expatriates learning Arabic have low attendance records and only offer language learning courses intermittently. Local Islamic groups may advertise Arabic lessons in regional English language papers but care needs to be taken to discover whether they are teaching Koranic Arabic or the Arabic commonly used everyday. In Saudi Arabia it is well known that many of the courses offered are accompanied with a strong dose of Islamic proselytism.

Details of any language courses that are available can be found in the local press or by contacting the foreign embassies or cultural centres based in the Gulf who often offer language courses of their own in their own native speech, e.g. French, German, etc. The *British Council* has branches in all of the six Gulf states and frequently offers lessons in Arabic, visit their website www.britishcouncil.org and look under *Schools and Education* in the individual country chapters for contact addresses.

Useful Words & Phrases

Peace be with you (greeting)	*AsSalam alaikom*
And with you be peace (response)	*Wa alaikom asSalam*
Hello (informal)	*Marhaba*
Good morning	*Sabah al kheir*
Good morning (response)	*Sabah al noor*
Good evening	*Masa al kheir*
Good evening (response)	*Masa al noor*
Welcome	*Ahlan wa sahlam*
Welcome (response)	*Wa bikum*
How are you? (to a man)	*Keif haalak*
(to a woman)	*Keif haalik*
(to a group)	*Keif haalkum*
Well/good	*Zein*
By God's grace	*Al-hamdu lillah*
God willing	*Insh'allah*
Thank you	*Shukran*
Not at all	*Afwan*
Please (formal) (to a man)	*Min fadlak*
(to a woman)	*Min fadlik*
(to a group)	*Min fadlikum*
Please (do)	*Tafaddal*
Goodbye	*Ma-as-salamah*
Yes	*Na'am*
No	*La*
Sorry	*Muta'assef*
Excuse me	*Ismahlee*

BAHRAIN

Currency

The unit of currency is the Bahraini Dinar (BD) which is divided into 1,000 fils.

1 Bahraini Dinar (BD) £1.5977; £1 BD 0.6259
1 Bahraini Dinar (BD) US$2.6526; US$1 BD 0.3770

Introduction

Destination Bahrain

The official name of Bahrain is the State of Bahrain although it is generally referred to simply as Bahrain or 'the Island'. The local long form of the name is *Dawlat al Bahrayn*, and the short form *Al Bahrayn*. Bahrain is the only island-state in the Arab world and it was here that the discovery of oil in the Gulf first took place in the early 1930s. Consequently, the Island was among the first of the Gulf states to exploit the wealth that came from oil revenues and begin the development of its health care and education among other necessities that have contributed to the country's present ultra-modern condition. It is the most 'western' of all the Gulf states in appearance but the nation still retains its Arab culture and fundamental Islamic principles, and expects foreigners to respect its beliefs (see *Islam*, Gulf States' 'General Introduction' chapter).

Due to the limited size of Bahrain's oil reserves, the country was compelled to look at diversifying its economy far earlier than the other Gulf states and now boasts a healthy economy and one considered to be the most diversified in the Arabian Peninsula. There is currently a focus on the tourism and financial services sectors and other private sector industries which make Bahrain a prime destination for job-seekers in the Gulf as employment opportunities are plentiful.

Pros and Cons of Moving to Bahrain

Despite being one of the most open and liberal of the Gulf states, Bahrain is still, compared to the West, very conservative in its outlook. Women are regarded with respect perhaps more so than anywhere else in the Arabian Peninsula and yet it is still advisable for western women to keep shoulders, arms, and legs covered in public out of respect for the nation's customs. Men should also avoid wearing overly tight clothes and exposing their chests in public.

As in the other Gulf states the salaries and employment packages tend to be far more generous than those you would receive in your home country and with no personal taxes to pay you will have even more money to save or spend as you wish. Furthermore, the comparative cost of living in Bahrain is estimated to be far lower than that in European and North American countries.

Bahrain is a very lively country with an extensive range of land and water sports available as well as numerous hotels, bars, and licensed restaurants where you can purchase alcohol. Unlimited amounts of alcohol can also be bought from certain outlets throughout the island. However, the down side to this liberality is that it attracts large numbers of visitors from Saudi Arabia who, unable to indulge in their own country, come to Bahrain to get drunk, leer at the women, and generally behave badly. The establishment of a causeway linking Bahrain to Saudi Arabia has made the crossing into the country even easier for weekend visitors.

Nevertheless, Bahrain is on the whole a relatively safe country in which to live with a low crime rate. Political tensions have been present in the country since 1994 (see *Government* below) and in 1996 several bombings took place which led to increased security measures being implemented but foreigners were not the targets for these attacks and there has not been any further trouble since then. Residents these days need to worry more about the cars on the road as the standard of driving in the country is so appalling.

From a Western perspective, the main pros and cons of living in the State of Bahrain can be summarised as follows:

Pros: Higher salaries than in your home country.
No personal taxes to pay.
Offshore banking facilities.
Bahrainis considered the most welcoming of Gulf nationals.
Sociable expatriate community.
High standard of health care and educational institutions.
Low crime rate.
English widely spoken.
Public practice of non-Islamic faiths permitted.
Less restrictions and expectations placed on women than in other Gulf states.
Alcohol widely available.
Extensive range of leisure activities.
Beautiful scenery.

Cons: Volatile internal politics.
Influx of hostile weekend visitors.
High rate of road traffic accidents.
Sweltering summers.

Political and Economic Structure

Bahrain was once attached to the Arabian peninsula but has been an island since about 6,000 BC. Its historical name is Dilmun meaning 'land of life' or 'sacred land' and it has also been referred to as the legendary Garden of Eden and described as 'paradise' in the Epic of Gilgamesh. The island attracted settlers in 3,000 BC due to its natural resources of fresh water and fertile soil at a time when surrounding areas lacked both. Records of its existence as an important seaport between Mesopotamia and the Indus Valley have been found in Sumerian, Babylonian and Assyrian inscriptions.

From the second millennium BC, Bahrain became a vital centre for trade in metals, textiles, pottery and agricultural products with pearling acting as the backbone of the country's economy for thousands of years until the relatively recent collapse of the natural pearl market in the 1930s. However, the discovery of oil in 1932 provided the country with a very profitable replacement industry that has made Bahrain the wealthy country it is today.

Due to its strategic location, much sought after natural resources and strong economy, Bahrain has had a long history of ownership conflicts. From 1521 to 1622 it came under Portuguese rule but was continually being attacked by various tribes and national groups until the eighteenth century when the al-Khalifa family assumed control. Between 1861 and 1971 the country became a British Protectorate. On the British departure in 1971, Bahrain became an independent state under the rule of Shaikh Isa bin Ali al-Khalifa.

The Economy

Oil has been the primary support of the Bahrain economy since its discovery in 1932 but due to its limited resources, Bahrain has spent the last twenty years pushing for a more diverse economy so that today it has one of the most diverse economies in the Gulf region with oil now counting for only 10 per cent of Bahrain's GDP (Gross Domestic Product). Areas such as the financial service sector and tourism are undergoing considerable growth and the iron-ore processing, natural gas production and aluminium smelting also play substantial roles in keeping the economy buoyant.

But with the anticipated lower revenues from its oil-related export and a projected GDP increase of just 1.8 per cent, Bahrain is relying upon more private sector involvement and greater participation of foreign investors. In order to encourage foreign investment, rules and regulations related to free trade have been re-examined by the Bahrain government to the extent that in 1995 the Heritage Foundation of Washington DC pronounced it as the third in the world in overall economic freedom concerning trade.

Bahrain officials continue to strive to make Bahrain the Singapore or Hong Kong of the Middle East as regards its finance industry. A position strengthened by the opening, the first of its kind in the Middle East, of the Baring Asset Management Office. This office brought with it 181 financial institutions and 236 investment funds that are now operational in Bahrain. Added to this came the establishment of the CitiBank Islamic Investment Center, a one hundred per cent owned subsidiary of Citicorp Banking Corporation, capitalised at US$20 million.

In response to the country's employment concerns, Bahrain is promoting a 'Bahrainisation' programme which involves a series of training schemes for the younger generation with the aim being to eventually replace the substantial foreign labour present at all levels of the economy with Bahraini nationals.

Economic Outlook

With the focus on privatisation and creation of more employment opportunities, Bahrain offers foreign companies a healthy economy of which to become a part. However, despite the measures to maintain the country's reputation as a regional stable financial centre, a close eye should be kept on the slightly more precarious political government of Bahrain.

Government

Bahrain is ruled by a traditional Arab monarchy headed by an emir chosen from the al-Khalifa clan through an appointed cabinet (Council of Ministers) led by a prime minister. The current emir is Shaikh Isa bin Sulman al-Khalifa; his brother, Shaikh Khalifa bin Sulman al-Khalifa is the prime minister. Political parties are strictly prohibited and no elections occur at any level of government. A forty-member consultative council, the *Majlis as-Shura*, appointed by the emir may advise the ruler and Council of Ministers but ultimately has no official authority.

A division has grown between the country's rulers and their subjects that threatens Bahrain's stability. The rift has stemmed from both religious and economic factors. The government is Sunni, the Conservative Islam of the Arabian Peninsula, most Bahrainis are Shiite, the more fundamental Islam of Iran. Sunnis

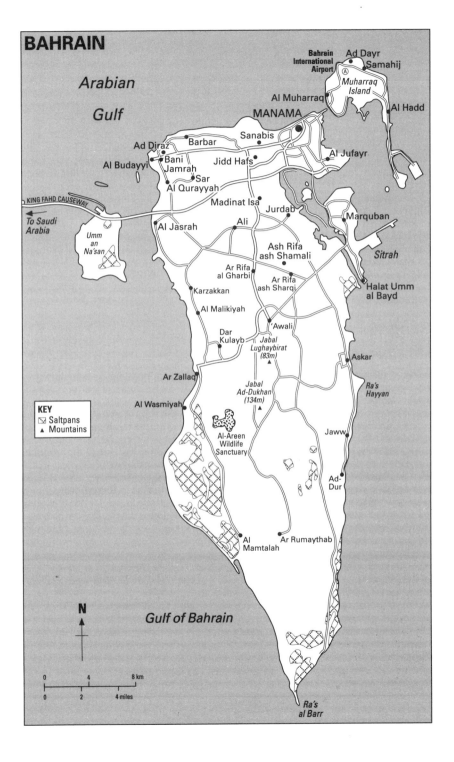

comprise a minority of the population but handle the majority of the country's wealth. Shiites, regardless of their greater numbers are given little say in the running of their country. The lack of reforms by the Sunni monarchy to advance the country towards democracy and political accountability has driven militant Shiites to random outbursts of violence such as a series of bomb attacks that started in 1996. Cars, buildings, hotels and banks were targetted. The level of violence was curbed by the government's promotion of a Bahrainisation programme and the increase in price of new visas and work permits for foreign workers but the situation remains volatile. In December 1999, the current emir pledged to re-introduce municipal polls in order to give ordinary citizens – both male and female – a say in their government. However, exactly when this is to take place has yet to be decided.

Details of the latest political position in the country and high-risk areas can be obtained by contacting one of the following telephone numbers of specialised travel advisories:

The British Foreign and Commonwealth Office: 020-7238 4503; Website www.fco.gov.uk/travel/countryadvice.asp?BA

US Department of State Overseas Citizens Services: +1 202 647-5225.

The Canadian Travel Advisory Line: 800 267-6788 (in Canada); +1 613 944-6788 (outside Canada).

Geographical Information

Area and Main Physical Features

Bahrain, the smallest of the Gulf States, is a country comprising 33 islands with a total land area of over 700 square kilometres. Its name comes from two Arabic words *thnain Bahr* meaning 'two seas' which refers to the unusual source of sweet water springs running below the sea mingling with the salty water.

The archipelago is situated on the western shores of the Arabian Gulf, 22 kms (14 miles) off the eastern coast of Saudi Arabia, to which it has been linked by the King Fahad Causeway since 1986. Qatari coast lies 28 kms (17 miles) due south of Bahrain. Bahrain island, where the capital Manama is located, is the largest of the islands constituting 85 per cent of the total land area of the country, with Sitra, lying south-east of the capital, being the second largest and joined to Bahrain island by a causeway. Also to the south-east of the main island lies a group of 16 small islands, the largest of which is similarly shaped to Bahrain hence its name Hawar meaning young camel in Arabic. Most of the surrounding islands are uninhabited except by the annual visits of hoards of migrating birds.

Bahrain's land is low lying peaking at a height of just 134 m above sea level at Jabel Dukhan. The majority of the land is barren limestone rock covered with a thin rocky soil or *sabkha* (salt flats) and low sand dunes so only the hardiest of desert vegetation can exist in these areas. However, there is a narrow strip of fertile land in the northern and north-eastern region of the island which does allow the cultivation of small farms and date plantations. This area was once the location of a great number of natural springs which irrigated the land as they still do today although to a lesser extent, and is now the region where the Bahraini population is mainly concentrated.

Population

The population of Bahrain is currently estimated at 616,342 which includes 224,640 foreign nationals. Population growth is 2.09 per cent per annum. 63 per cent of the population are Bahraini nationals, 13 per cent are Asian, 10 per cent are from other Arab countries, 8 per cent are Iranian and the remaining 6 per cent are expatriates from other countries. 75 per cent are Shi'a Muslim, 25 per cent are Sunni Muslim.

The official language of Bahrain is Arabic, although English, Farsi and Urdu are widely spoken. 85.2 per cent of the population (aged 15 and over) are functionally literate.

Climate

Bahrain experiences a typical desert climate, swelteringly hot in the summer months (from June to September), pleasantly cool and sunny in the winter (October to May). Some relief from the heat and humidity in the summer is brought in by cool, northerly winds, *shamal*. The little rainfall that does occur will be in the winter months.

Weather Chart
Average temperature (Celcius), rainfall (mm), sunshine in hours per day, humidity percentage.

	Jan	Feb	Mar	Apr	May	Jun	Jul	Aug	Sep	Oct	Nov	Dec
Bahrain												
Max	20	21	24	29	33	36	37	38	36	32	28	22
Min	14	15	17	21	26	28	29	29	27	24	21	16
Rainfall	5	20	10	5	0	0	0	0	0	0	20	20
Rainy Days	1	2	1	1	0	0	0	0	0	0	1	2
Sunshine	7	8	8	9	10	11	11	11	11	10	9	7
Humidity	78	77	75	71	67	67	68	70	70	73	75	81

Regional Guide

Bahrain's strategic location in the centre of the Gulf region has made it one of the favoured local tourist resorts and an important business centre. With the opening of the King Fahad Causeway in 1986, linking the main island with Saudi Arabia, in addition to its excellent port and airport services and its increasing popularity as a stop-over point for major international flights, the country has become a hub of communications not only within the Gulf States but worldwide. It offers both its business and tourist visitors a comprehensive range of opportunities spanning both sectors and is well-known for its welcoming and comparatively liberal attitude towards its guests and foreign nationals.

English is widely spoken throughout the country and the standard of living is generally very high.

Information Facilities

Bahrain's tourist industry is booming and in addition to a tourist information desk at its airport there are a wide range of sources from which to find out more about the country as listed below under *Useful Addresses* and *Useful Websites*. Tour operators (a list of which can be found in the *Getting There* section) also provide you with all the information you need on Bahrain as well as being able to arrange all sorts of tours for you to explore the country.

Useful Addresses

Tourism Directorate (Ministry of Cabinet Affairs and Information): PO Box 253, Manama, Bahrain; tel +973 211-026; fax +973 211-717.

Bahrain Tourism Company (BTC): PO Box 5831, Manama, Bahrain; tel +973 530-530; fax +973 530-867.

Embassy of the State of Bahrain: 98 Gloucester Road, London SW7 4AU; tel 020-7370 5132/3; fax 020-7370 7773; e-mail information@bahrainembassy.org.uk Website www.bahrainembassy.org.uk

British Embassy: PO Box 114, Manama, Bahrain; tel +973 534-404/719; fax +973 536-307; e-mail britemb@batelco.com.bh

Embassy of the State of Bahrain: 3502 International Drive, NW, Washington, DC 20008, USA; tel +1 202 342-0741/2; fax +1 202 362-2192.

Embassy of the United States of America: PO Box 26431, Manama, Bahrain; tel +973 273-300; fax +973 272-594; e-mail usismana@batelco.com.bh Website www.usembassy.com.bh

Useful Websites

Arab Net: www.arab.net
State of Bahrain Index: www.cnnhotels.com/hotels/mideast/bahrain/bahrain.htm
Hotels and Travel in Bahrain: www.hotelstravel.com/bahrain.html
World Travel Guide: www.wtg-online.com
Excite Travel: www.excite.com/travel
Bahrain Tourism: www.bahraintourism.com

BAHRAIN ISLAND

Bahrain is the largest and most densely populated of the country's islands. Manama is the capital of Bahrain spread out over the north-eastern corner of the island. The city is dominated by modern architecture but there are traces of the traditional in the form of the souk situated in the heart of the old town. Additionally, you can find out more about Bahrain's history by visiting the city's National Museum or Heritage Centre. The capital is home to the country's leading hotels, most active nightlife, foremost tourist attractions and excellent shopping. *Bab al Bahrain* (Gateway to Bahrain) erected by the British in 1945 lies in the centre of Manama where all the government buildings are located and is distinguished by a large arch.

Surrounding the capital there are plenty of opportunities for visiting cultural sites. A few kilometres to the west of Manama lies *Qalaat al Bahrain*, a compound of four archaeological excavations dating back to 2,800 BC when the island was inhabited by the Tumulis (Dilmun) race. You will also find here a 400 year old Portuguese fort, the remnants of an eleventh century Arab fort, Assyrian ruins and an ancient bit of city wall. Just beyond this area is the Barbar Temple, dedicated to Enki (the god of springs) and dated over 3,000 years old. Travelling further on from Qalaat al Bahrain will take you to the villages of Sar and A'ali where there are pottery workshops and important grave mounds. Tumuli grave mounds dating from 2,800 - 1,800 BC can be found throughout the northern region of Bahrain.

In the central and southern desert regions of the country are located the emir of Bahrain's Palace, *Ar Riffa*, the nation's highest peak, Jabal ad Dukhan (or *Jebel Dukhan*), palaces of Sakhia demonstrating nineteenth century Arabian architecture, and the Al Areen Wildlife Park which accommodates some five hundred endangered Gulf species. Situated south-east of Jabal ad Dukhan is the Tree of Life, nourished by a spring and the begetter of the legend that Bahrain is the original Garden of Eden.

MUHARRAQ ISLAND (Al Muharraq, Muharriq)

Muharraq is Bahrain's second most eminent island and the location of the nation's chief airport. The city is linked to Manama by a 2 km (1 mile) causeway. There is nowhere to stay on the island but plenty of sights to see including the old town, the National Museum and Civic Centre, Shaikh Isa's House, *Bait Shaikh Isa*, and the Abu Mahir and Qalaat Arad forts. The National Museum houses several amazing exhibits such as objects excavated from the Tumuli mounds, and is rated among one of the best museums in the Arab world.

Trips to some of Bahrain's smaller islands can be arranged by travelling on dhows. Popular choices include *Jirada*, to the east of the main island known for its idyllic beach of golden-white sand, and *Al Baina* situated between Al Khobar and Bahrain. Journeys to either island take about two hours. Those wishing to try their hand at fishing can charter fully equipped dhows.

Getting to Bahrain

Air

The most convenient mode of transport by which to travel to Bahrain is by air. Bahrain is served by numerous international carriers including American Airlines, British Airways, Gulf Air, KLM, and Kuwait Airways. The flight time from London to Bahrain is about 6 hours and from Los Angeles 21 hours, from New York 14 hours. Bahrain's international airport is 6.5 km (4 miles) north-east of Manama and serviced by buses and taxis that run across the causeway to the main island.

Sea

There are three major ports offering a quick and convenient entry into Bahrain at Mina Salman, Mina Manama and Mina Muharraq. On the north-east of the island are the deep-water oil tankers.

Road

You can drive from Dhahran (in the Eastern Province of Saudi Arabia) to Bahrain across the King Fahad Causeway. The journey takes about one and a half hours and the relevant visas must be held by all travellers to and from the countries. Those travelling out of Bahrain must pay a toll fee of BD2.

Useful Telephone Numbers

Airlines
American Airlines: 0345-789789; Website www.aa.com
British Airways: 0345-222111; Website www.british-airways.com
Gulf Air: 020-7408 1717; Website www.gulfairco.com
KLM: 0990-7509000; Website www.klm.com
Kuwait Airways: 020-7412 0006.

Tour Operators
Al Bader Travel & Tourism: +973 213-333.
Al Danah Travel & Tours: +973 533-099.
Al Darwish Travel & Tours: +973 714-500.
Al Khunaizi Travel & Tourism: +973 213-618.
Alpha Travel & Tours: +973 532-777.
Arab World Tours: +973 963-737.
Sunshine Tours: +973 223-601.

Insurance

When visiting Bahrain it is strongly advisable to take out comprehensive insurance. Among the many insurers offering reasonable and flexible premiums are the following:

Atlas Travel Insurance Ltd: 37 King's Exchange, Tileyard Road, London N7 9AH;
    tel 020-7609 5000; fax 020-7609 5011; e-mail quote@travel—insurance.co.uk
Columbus Direct Travel Insurance: 17 Devonshire Square, London EC2M 4SQ; tel
    020-7375 0011; fax 020-7375 0022; Website www.columbusdirect.co.uk
Our Way Travel Insurance: Foxbury House, Foxbury Road, Bromley, Kent BR1
    4DG; tel 020-8313 3900; fax 020-8313 3652; e-mail ourwayins@aol.com
    Website www.members.aol.com/ourwayins/ourway
Travel Insurance Agency: tel 020-8446 5414/5; e-mail tia.london@virgin.net
Worldwide Travel Insurance: tel 01892-83 33 38.

Residence and Entry Regulations

The Current Position

With the exception of other GCC nationals and those in transit, all individuals entering Bahrain must be in possession of a visa. Israeli passport holders are not allowed entry into Bahrain and holders of Israeli visas or Israeli stamps in their passports can only pass through Bahrain airport provided that they leave on the same through aircraft. Those whose profession is marked 'Journalist' in their passports must validate their journey to Bahrain with the Ministry of Information (PO Box 253, Bahrain; tel +973 781888; fax +973 210401). All visas must be acquired before arrival in Bahrain except tourist and 72 hour/7 day visas.

Tourist Visas

Citizens of the European Community, USA, Canada, Australia, New Zealand, Japan or Hong Kong can obtain tourist visas at the Bahrain International Airport or at the King Fahad Causeway. The visas are vaild for up to two weeks and the cost is BD 5. Applicants for tourist visas must have legitimate passports and return tickets in addition to no criminal record or involvement in activities that could pose a threat to public order or national security. Those with tourist visas are not permitted to seek employment during their stay in Bahrain.

72 hour/7 day Visas

These visas are obtainable on arrival in Bahrain at the Bahrain International Airport or at the King Fahad Causeway. Their primary purpose is to serve business visitors, trade delegations, attending exhibitions and seminars. In order to have their application processed, the applicant must have a confirmed return or onward journey ticket in addition to a valid passport. 72 hour visas are automatically granted to foreign nationals who have lived for at least six months in another GCC State. The cost of a 72 hour visa is BD 10 and for a 7 day visa BD 15.

Visit Visas

Visit visas are intended for foreign nationals wishing to visit relatives or friends in Bahrain. A sponsor in Bahrain must make the application for a visit visa at the

General Directorate of Immigration and Passports (GDIP). Generally the visit visa is valid for a period of one month but can be extended to a maximum of three months stay. Those on a visit visa during their time in Bahrain are not permitted to engage in any business activities whilst there. The cost of a visit visa is BD 22.

Business Visas

Business visas are designed for those intending to do business in the country and are available from your local Bahraini Consulate (or Consular Section at the Embassy). The period of time for which the visa is valid varies according to individual application and the attainment of a 'No Objection Certificate' (NOC) from a Bahraini sponsor. When applying for a business visa you need to submit: a completed application form, passport, passport-sized photograph, stamped self-addressed envelope and cheque for £3 to cover the return of your passport if applying by post, a fee of £20, and a letter from your employer. The visas usually take a couple of days to process.

Family Visas

These visas are for the spouse and children of their partner/parent working in Bahrain. Holders of family visas are not allowed to take up employment in Bahrain but can stay in the country as long as their partner is working there. The cost of a family visa is BD 22.

Employment Visas

Employment visas are a prerequisite to legally working in Bahrain and are also needed in order to become a resident of the country. To obtain an employment visa you need to pay a fee of BD 15 and submit a work permit from the Ministry of Labour & Social Affairs and an NOC from the Directorate of Immigration & Passports.

Registering with your Embassy/Consulate

On arrival in Bahrain, expatriates should ensure that they register with the regional Embassy or Consulate of their home country. This registration enables the home country's authorities to keep emigrants up to date with any information they need to be informed of as foreign nationals resident overseas and also enables them to trace individuals in the event of an emergency. The Consulates can also assist with information concerning an emigrant's status overseas and advise on any diplomatic or passport problems. They may also be able to help in an emergency e.g. in the unfortunate event of the death of a relative abroad. However, the Consulates do not function as a source of general help and advice, nor act as an employment bureau and they make this quite evident in response to any such enquiries.

Useful Addresses

The regulations regarding Bahraini visas are subject to change. The details given above are the latest facts but before travelling it is worth double-checking the costs/requirements by contacting one of the following:

Directorate of Immigration & Passports: Bahrain International Airport, PO Box 331, Manama; +973 528883; fax +973 531593.

Ministry of Foreign Affairs: PO Box 547, Bahrain; tel +973 262277; fax +973 210575.

Ministry of the Interior: Department of Nationality & Immigration Administration, PO Box 398, Abu Dhabi; tel +971 2 462244; fax +971 2 415780/449720.

Ministry of Labour and Social Affairs: PO Box 32333, Manama, Bahrain; tel +973 223-366; fax +973 215-508.

Embassy of the State of Bahrain: 98 Gloucester Road, London SW7 4AU; tel 020-7370 5132/3; fax 020-370 7773; e-mail information@bahrainembassy.org.uk Website www.bahrainembassy.org.uk

British Embassy: PO Box 114, Manama, Bahrain; tel +973 534-404/719; fax +973 536-307; e-mail britemb@batelco.com.bh

Embassy of the State of Bahrain: 3502 International Drive, NW, Washington, DC 20008, USA; tel +1 202 342-0741/2; fax +1 202 362-2192.

Embassy of the United States of America: PO Box 26431, Manama, Bahrain; tel +973 273-300; fax +973 272-594; e-mail usismana@batelco.com.bh Website www.usembassy.com.bh

Setting Up Home

Bahraini land or property can only be owned by Bahraini or other GCC citizens hence foreign nationals have no other option but to rent housing. For many expatriates their accommodation or a housing allowance may be included in their employment contracts. For those who must seek housing independently it is highly recommended to rent from one of the many real estate agents in operation (a comprehensive list can be found in your local yellow pages directory www.bahrainyellowpages.com). Estate agents will handle all the relevant paperwork involved and deal with the landlord on your behalf. Expatriates can choose to live in either apartments or villas which come furnished or unfurnished.

More details can be obtained by contacting individual estate agents.

Useful Addresses

Serviced Apartments

Universal Travel Apartment Service: PO Box 113, Manama 304, Bahrain; tel +973 210-050; fax +973 214-828.

Al Bander: +973 701-201.

Al Maner Apartments: +973 293-557.

Bait Al Hoora: +973 713-971.

Mansouri Mansions: +973 292-927.

Mishal Complex: +971 533-336.

Sheza Tower: +973 721-010.

Utilities

Electricity & Water

To get your home connected to the power mains you need to apply to your local electricity office with your passport, residence visa and rental agreement. The Ministry of Electricity and Water will then turn on your power. Check your lease agreement to discover whether electricity and water charges are included in the contract.

The electricity supply in Manama is 230V AC, and in Awali 110V AC. British type three-pin electrical sockets are widely used, and adaptors are widely available where necessary. Water can be drunk from the tap in certain areas although it is generally advisable to drink bottled water if only for its greater palatability.

Gas

There are no mains gas systems in Bahrain but canisters can be bought and delivered to your door for fuelling gas cookers. Contact your local gas company for more details (addresses can be found in your regional yellow pages directory www.bahrainyellowpages.com).

Telephones

Bahrain's highly advanced telecommunications and information services are run by Batelco (Bahrain Telecommunications Company). Batelco has ensured that Bahrain stays at the forefront of telecommunications in the region and in 1969 the country became the first in the Middle East to enter the era of satellite communications when it launched its first earth station. In 1992, Bahrain became one of the few states worldwide to accomplish 100 per cent digitalisation of its national and international switches. Services provided by Batelco include: Global System for Mobile (GSM), Integrated Services Digital Network (ISDN), Maritime communication, International Direct Dialling (IDD), internet, faxmail, paging, and an extensive range of voice, data and value-added services. New products and services are constantly being introduced to meet the rising demand and to keep up with the latest global developments.

Every household in Bahrain now has at least one telephone installed, and it is estimated that two out of ten people have a mobile phone and that pagers are employed by fifteen out of every one hundred individuals.

To get your land-line connected contact Batelco for details. New line installation takes on average 5 working days from application date. Residential and business lines cost BD 20 to install and quarterly rental is BD 3.5 for residential lines and BD 6.5 for business lines. Bills are issued monthly and include the following information: charges for local and international calls and operator assisted calls (where applicable), telephone line and equipment rental, services such as maintenance or connection, and any credit due. If you have any billing queries call +973 881111. Bills can be paid by post, through banks, by telephone, in person at Batelco service centres (by cash, cheque or credit card), or by Direct Debit. All bills must be paid within 21 days from the date stated on the bill.

Further details on products and services offered by Batelco can be obtained by writing directly to the company or by visiting their website (see below for addresses).

Useful Addresses

Bahrain Telecommunications Company: PO Box 14, Manama; tel +973 884337; fax +973 611898; Website www.batelco.com.bh
Ministry of Housing, Municipalities & Environment: PO Box 5802, Manama, Bahrain; tel +973 533-000; fax +973 534-115.
Ministry of Electricity & Water: PO Box 2, Manama, Bahrain; tel +973 533-133; fax +973 533-035.

Daily Life

Bahrain is generally considered to be one of the easiest states in the Gulf to adapt to, however living on the island is still very different to what you may be familiar with in your home country. The purpose of this chapter is to provide all the necessary practical information to successfully cope with a range of aspects of life in Bahrain so that armed with this knowledge your move to this country may be made that little less daunting.

Schools and Education

In addition to the state schools offering an Arabic curriculum mainly attended by Bahraini nationals and Arab expatriates, Bahrain is host to several private international schools that either specialise in providing an American, or British or other European, Indian, Pakistani, etc. style education, or that can accommodate the teaching of a selection of the different education systems for children from kindergarten ages (3/4 years old) up to the ages of 17/18. Those offering an American curriculum attract not only western expatriates but Arab expatriates and Bahraini nationals as well; those with a British curriculum are mostly attended by Europeans but sometimes Arab and expatriates of other nationalities also attend. As the majority of schools in Saudi Arabia only enrol children up to the ages of 14, many expatriate children over this age resident in the Kingdom go on to attend boarding schools in Bahrain such as St Christopher's School (Isa Town) and Bahrain International School (Juffair).

The standard of teaching in the private schools is generally very high and the British schools are regularly inspected by the UK Department of Education and Science as well as OFSTED (Office for Standards in Education). To find out more about individual schools it is best to contact them directly and to ask friends and colleagues for more information on the schools and their reputation. A list of schools is detailed below with the ages of students given in brackets. All these schools are co-educational and students are required to wear a uniform. Fees range from BD 1,115 to BD 2,030 (£1,823 to £3,328) per year at the Al Hekma International School or at Bahrain School (Juffair): BD 4,547 to BD 5,026 (£7,454 to £8,239). Additional registration fees may also be payable. It is worth checking the conditions of your employment contract as major employers may include school fees in your employment agreement.

Due to the demand for places in these schools it is strongly advisable to apply for entry as early as possible.

Useful Addresses

English Medium Schools

British School of Bahrain (3-16): Aldiya, PO Box 315775, Bahrain; tel +973 710-878; fax +973 710-875; e-mail bsnah@batelco.com.bh

The Infant School (2-11): Shaikh Salman Highway, PO Box 26625, Bahrain; tel +973 252-346; fax +973 263-362.

Habara School (2-11): PO Box 26516, Bahrain; tel +973 712-868; fax +973 256-779.

St Christopher's Awali School (3-7): Awali, PO Box 25225, Bahrain; tel +973 753-632; fax +973 753-663; e-mail stcinfan@batelco.com.bh

Dilmun School (3-11): Adilya, PO Box 26425, Bahrain; tel +973 713-483; fax +973 213-484.

St Christopher's School (8-17): Isa Town, PO Box 32052, Bahrain; tel +973 685-621; fax +973 780-927; e-mail st.christ@batelco.com.bh or juniors@batelco.com.bh

Sacred Heart School (4-16): Isa Town, PO Box 388, Bahrain; tel +973 684-367; fax +973 680-252.

International Schools

Al Hekma International School (9 months to 17 years): PO Box 26489, Adilya, Bahrain; tel +973 620-820; fax +973 624-800; e-mail ahmis@batelco.com.bh Website www.alhekma.com

Al Noor International School (3-17): PO Box 85, Bahrain; tel +973 736-773; fax +973 735-650; e-mail roonlasc@batelco.com.bh

Bahrain Bayan School (3-17): PO Box 32411, Isa Town, Bahrain; tel +973 682-227; fax +973 780-019; e-mail bayan@batelco.com.bh

Bahrain School (3-17): PO Box 934, Juffair, Bahrain; tel +973 727-828; fax +725-714; e-mail Sandra.Daniels@odedodea.edu

Ibn Khuldoon International School (3-17): PO Box 20511, Isa Town, Bahrain; tel +973 780-661; fax +973 689-028; e-mail iknset@batelco.com.bh

Naseem International School (3-17): PO Box 28503, Isa Town, Bahrain; tel +973 689-684; fax +973 687-166; e-mail naseem@batelco.com.bh

Further information on schools and education in Bahrain can be obtained from:

The British Council: PO Box 452, Manama 356, Bahrain; tel +973 261555; fax +973 276001; Website www.britishcouncil.org

The Media, Post and Telecommunications

The Media

All printed matter, films and videos displaying scantily-dressed women, sexual contact between men and women, religious propaganda or politically-sensitive matter will be seized by the Ministry of Information (PO Box 253, Bahrain; tel +973 272111; fax +973 262169/270463). Any books or personal videos discovered in luggage coming into the country will be reviewed by the Information Ministry to be returned (or not) to the owner in due course.

Television

Programmes in English are broadcast on Bahrain's channel 55 and on channel 57 you will find the BBC World Service Television on air 24 hours a day. English stations broadcasting from Abu Dhabi, Qatar, Saudi Arabia, Dubai, Oman and Kuwait can also be picked up with a good antenna. CNN and other satellite services are available upon subscription.

Radio

To find out the frequencies for the BBC World Service in Bahrain contact: tel 020-7557 1165; e-mail worldservice.letters@bbc.co.uk Website www.bbc.co.uk/ worldservice. A monthly international programmes guide, *BBC On Air*, which includes information on World Service Radio, BBC World and BBC Prime television services can be obtained by contacting the BBC at tel 020-7557 2211; fax 020-7240 4899.

Radio Bahrain broadcasts in English 24 hours a day on FM stereo 96.5 Mhz and 101 Mhz. Regular news summaries are read throughout the day.

Books and Newspapers

Bahrain's English language newspaper is the *Gulf Daily News* issued every day except Fridays with comprehensive listings of 'What's On' information. Foreign newspapers and magazines can be bought from the major hotels and certain other outlets such as supermarkets.

Bookshops and hotel bookstalls throughout Bahrain sell a limited range of English language books at inflated prices so if you are an avid reader it is advisable to bring plenty of books with you for your stay.

Post

The postal service in Bahrain is relatively efficient with airmail letters and parcels to Europe and North America taking about three to four days delivery time. Mail to Australia takes a few days longer. Surface mail takes up to nine weeks. Courier services are available. Sending post within Bahrain costs 80 fils per 20g letter weighs. Postage to other Gulf States is 80 fils per 10g, to other Arab countries the cost is 100 fils per 10g, to Europe and the Indian subcontinent 200 fils per 10g, and to anywhere else in the world 250 fils per 10g. Aerogrammes are charged at a fixed rate of 150 fils no matter where there destination. Poste restante facilities by which to receive mail in Bahrain are available at post offices.

Courier Services
DHL: PO Box 5741, Manama; tel +973 723636; fax +973 826400.
FedEx: tel +973 530440; fax +973 532022.
UPS: PO Box 113, Manama; tel +973 9660083; fax +973 224467.

Telephones

The international dialling code for Bahrain is +973. There are no area codes within the country. Both coin payphones and card or credit card phones are widespread.

Useful numbers

Local directory enquiries	181
International directory enquiries	191
Speaking Clock	140
Weather update	268700
News	268912
Sports	268222
Healthline	268914
Touristline	268444

Cars and Motoring

It is obligatory for all those in the front seat of cars, whether driving or not, to wear seat belts. Those caught contravening this rule will be fined BD 10. Driving is on the right hand side of the road and speed limits are strictly enforced. Drink driving offenders will incur hefty penalties. Despite the high quality of the modern road network in Bahrain, the general standard of driving in the country is very poor. Comprehensive insurance cover is a must as accidents frequently occur in the state. It is imperative in the event of an accident not to leave your vehicle or attempt to move it until the police have arrived on the scene and have assessed the situation. They will decide who is responsible for the accident and hand over reports to the concerned parties who can then present these to their insurance companies in order to have the necessary repairs carried out.

Purchasing a Vehicle

Purchasing a car in Bahrain is comparatively easy and far cheaper than you would find in Europe or North America. Numerous dealers selling both new cars and second hand cars are located throughout the country (addresses of car dealers can be found in your local yellow pages directory www.bahrainyellowpages.com). Advertisements for the sale of second hand cars can also be found in the Classified section of local papers or on supermarket notice boards.

Car dealers showroom opening hours are typically from 8am to 1pm and 4pm to 7pm, Saturday to Wednesday. Adjoining service centres are usually open from 7.30am to 7pm, Saturday to Wednesday, and 7.30am to 1pm on Thursdays, although hours may vary.

Useful Telephone Numbers

New Car Dealers
Ahmed Zayani and Sons: +973 232085.
Almoayyed Motors: +973 292555.
Euro Motors: +973 750750.
National Motor Company: + *+973 403444.*
Zayani Motors: +973 703703.

Second-hand Car Dealers
Al Baraka Cars Centre: +973 212442.
Al Dana Buying and Selling: +973 333573.
Al Fadhalah Car Showroom: +973 228892.
Al Fajer Car Showroom: +973 728337.
Al Jassim Cars Exhibition: +973 691580.

Car Hire

A number of major international car rental companies have branches in Bahrain alongside numerous local ones. Unlike the other Gulf states, an international driving licence is compulsory in order to rent a car in Bahrain, except for GCC nationals, and must be stamped by the Directorate of Traffic and Licensing. Car rental costs from about BD 13 per day or BD 70 to BD 80 per week including unlimited km. Further information can be obtained by contacting one of the companies listed below.

Car Rental Companies
Al Bader Car Hiring: tel +973 276087; fax +973 291791.
Avis Car Hiring: tel +973 531144; fax +973531441.
Budget Rent-A-Car: tel +973 534100; fax +973535402.
Europ Car Interrent: tel +973 321249; fax +973 321999.
Express Rent-A-Car: tel +973 234111; fax +973 532526.
Hertz Rent-A-Car: tel +973 321358; fax +973 321359.

Transport

Air

Air travel within Bahrain is relatively painless and convenient with over 300 flights a week leaving Bahrain International Airport (tel +973 325555; fax +973 324096) for other destinations within Bahrain.

Taxis

Taxis in Bahrain have orange side-wings and black-on-yellow number plates. Fares are regulated but always agree on a price before travelling anywhere as cost will depend on where you are going and from where and at what time. A telephone booking system is offered by *Speedy Motors* (tel +973 682999) but taxis can also be hailed on the street or hired from ranks outside hotels and major tourist sights. The telephone number for Airport Taxis is +973 320982. The minimum fare between the hours of 2200 and 0600 is BD1,200. Taxis hired outside hotels may charge more. Some taxis, recognisable by a yellow circle with the licence number painted in black on the driver's door and by their white and orange number plates, can carry up to five passengers and the fare shared.

Buses

The bus service in Bahrain is cheap – the standard fare to all destinations is 50 fils – however it is also somewhat unreliable. Nevertheless, most of the country's towns and villages are served by bus transport.

Sea

Travel between the main island of Bahrain and its smaller islands is by dhow or motorboat. Local travel agents can provide details.

Banking and Finance

Bahrain has established itself as an international financial centre home to 180 financial institutions: 19 commercial banks, 2 specialised banks, 48 offshore banking units, 28 investment banks, 41 representative offices, 10 investment advisory and other financial services, 27 money changers, 6 foreign exchange and money brokers. A full range of services covering both conventional and Islamic banking principles are offered. The Bahrain Monetary Agency (BMA) oversees the licensing, supervision and regulation of all the banks and financial institutions and is responsible for the thriving development of the industry. The island is strategically located midway between east and west time zones which allows financiers to do business with for example both Tokyo and New York in the same working day. Furthermore, the financial sector is aided by the country's tax free environment – total absence of corporate and personal taxes, highly advanced telecommunications, and macroeconomic stability.

The Bahraini Dinar is a convertible currency with no restrictions on its import or export. Banks and moneychangers will change currency and are located throughout Bahrain. There are numerous cash card machines in the country and hotels, restaurants and larger shops all accept major credit cards. Banks offer an extensive range of services comparable to those that you would find in your home country. Opening hours are generally 7.30am to 12pm and 3.30pm to 5.30pm, Saturday to Wednesday, and 7.30am to 11am on Thursdays. Some offshore banking units are closed on Sundays. During Ramadan opening hours are from 10am to 1.30pm.

Offshore Banking

If you are working for a large company in the Gulf you are likely to be earning quite substantial amounts of money some of which you will undoubtedly be looking to invest. One of the primary financial advantages of being an expatriate is that you can invest this money offshore in tax havens such as the Isle of Man, the Channel Islands, Gibraltar, and Bahrain thus accruing tax-free interest on your savings. Many such facilities are as flexible as UK high street banking and range from current accounts to long-term, high interest earning deposits.

In the increasingly complex world of multiple financial products, *Brewin Dolphin* concentrates on providing clients with an innovative and comprehensive service, based on communication, flexibility, continuity, and integrity. This approach has resulted in the group becoming one of the leading private client investment managers in the UK, managing funds in excess of £15 billion (US$24 billion) for onshore and offshore clients. They have been involved in the Gulf region for many years, making regular visits, and advising clients on direct investment in the world's principal stock and bond markets.

Among the companies listed below handling expatriates banking concerns is the *Lloyds TSB Overseas Club* which is particularly helpful in providing a full range of financial services for the expatriate in the Gulf, a representative office is located in Dubai specifically set up as a local point of contact for their clients resident there. *Ambrose Associates* primarily handle UK expatriate tax issues such as the tax implications of your departure and any continuing obligations under UK tax law, but additionally assist with determining matters of Residence and Domicile, advise on tax effective remuneration packages, cover property matters – rental, second home, overseas investment, and aid with national insurance planning.

The Lamensdorf Group (Regency House, 1-4 Warwick Street, London W1R 5WB; fax 020-7287 0511; e-mail admin@lamensdorf.co.uk Website www.lamensdorf.co.uk), a firm independent of any bank, building society, insurance company or investment manager, also specialises in offering comprehensive unbiased advice in a range of financial matters including: offshore planning, lump sum investments, private client banking, trust planning/asset protection, etc.

More information on the financial services available can be sought by contacting the individual companies themselves.

Useful Addresses

Ambrose Associates: Rydal House, 29 Rydal Drive, Bexleyheath, Kent DA7 5EF; tel 020-8301 2986; fax 020-8301 4609; e-mail ambrose.associates@virgin.net

Brewin Dolphin Securities: 5 Giltspur Street, London EC1A 9BD; tel 020-7248 4400; fax 020-7236 2034.

Lloyds TSB Overseas Club: PO Box 12, Douglas, **Isle of Man** IM99 1SS; tel 01624-638104; fax 01624-638181; Website www.lloydstsb-offshore.com; PO Box 3766, **Dubai**, United Arab Emirates; tel +971 4 3422550; fax +971 4 3422705.

Nationwide International Ltd: PO Box 217, 45-51 Athol Street, Douglas, Isle of Man IM99 1RN; tel 01624-696000; fax 01624-696001; Website www.nationwide-int.com

Woolwich: PO Box 341, La Tonnelle House, Les Banques, St Peter Port, Guernsey GY1 3UW; tel 01481-715735; fax 01481-715722.

Offshore Banking Units in Bahrain:

Allied Banking Corporation: PO Box 20493; tel +973 225420; fax +973 226641.

Arab Asian Bank E.C.: PO Box 5619; tel +973 532129; fax +973 530976.

Bahrain International Bank: PO Box 5016; tel +973 534545; fax +973 535141.

British Bank of the Middle East: PO Box 57; tel +973 224555; fax +973 226822.

Chase Manhattan Bank: PO Box 368; tel +973 535388; fax +973 535135.

Gulf International Bank BSC: PO Box 1017; tel +973 534000; fax +973 522633.

Hong Kong & Shanghai Banking Corporation (HSBC): PO Box 5497; tel +973 336992; fax +973 325563.

Standard Chartered Bank PLC: PO Box 29; tel +973 223636; fax +973 225001.

Tax and the Expatriate

There is no income tax or social security for expatriates to pay in Bahrain nor do any other taxes exist for foreign nationals resident in the country. As a non-resident of your home country (i.e. for UK nationals spending fewer than 183 days in aggregate in Britain) you will not be subject to your home country's tax on earnings either. For more details on what you may or may not be entitled to or subjected to regarding tax regulations (on earnings, relocation expenses, investments, etc.) as an expatriate you should consult a specialist tax advisor. Useful contacts can be found in magazines such as *The Expatriate* and the large accounting/financial advisory companies like PriceWaterhouseCoopers (Plumtree Court, London EC4A 4HT; tel 020-7583 5000; fax 020-7822 4652) publish handy booklets giving detailed information on the tax implications for foreign nationals working in other countries.

Health Care in Bahrain

Public health care in Bahrain is generally considered of a very high standard and the areas covered include: in-patient and out-patient dental care, general medical care, maternity care, orthopaedic care, paediatric care, and psychiatric care. Emergency treatment is free of charge at the public hospital in Salmaniya and almost all other primary and secondary treatment within the state services is provided at no cost to citizens and foreign residents. Nevertheless, it is strongly recommended to take out medical insurance to cover unforeseen circumstances so that private treatment can be obtained if required, although all large companies are obliged to cover their workers against accidents. More detailed information on the health services available in Bahrain can be obtained by contacting the *Ministry of Health*, PO Box

12, Manama, Bahrain; tel +973 289810; fax +973 289864 or by visiting its website www.batelco.com.bh/mhealth/cgi-bin/MoH/hcentres.htm.

Bahrain's five main hospitals are:

American Mission Hospital: PO Box 1, Manama; tel +973 253447; fax +973 234194.

Awali Hospital: Awali; tel +973 753366; fax +973 753598.

Bahrain Defence Force Military Hospital: PO Box 245, Manama; tel +973 663366; fax +973 650808.

International Hospital of Bahrain: PO Box 1084, Manama; tel +973 591666; fax +973 590495.

Salmaniya Medical Centre: PO Box 12, Manama; tel +973 255555; fax +973 289083.

Useful Telephone Numbers

Health Centres
Muharraq: +973 675955/676723.
Isa Town: +973 683736/689476.
Hammad Town: +973 410364/412414.
East Riffa: +973 773737.
West Riffa: +973 661230.
Zallaq Clinic: +973 632263.
Jaw & Askkar Clinic: +973 840261.

Private Medical Insurance

Private medical care in Bahrain is rated at a very high standard but it is also by no means cheap. Taking out health insurance cover for you and your family is essential.

BUPA International has designed its own Lifeline scheme that offers maximum choice and flexibility. There are three levels of cover: Gold, Classic and Essential, all of which provide full refund for hospital accommodation and specialists' fees so you never need to be concerned about unexpected bills for in-patient treatment such as an operation. Cover for emergency ambulance charges and sports injuries is also standard. The Gold and Classic schemes offer out-patient treatment which may be a very wise precaution in Bahrain. The most comprehensive cover is available with the Gold scheme which includes the cost of primary care treatment and home nursing. BUPA International has a 24 hour multi-lingual service centre dedicated to their expatriate members with an experienced team on hand to deal with any queries. Claims are paid promptly in any currency that you require, and you are covered anywhere in the world. For more information call +44 (0) 1273-208181.

Expat Financial (www.expatfinancial.com) caters for expatriates of any nationality around the world in the area of insurance and financial plans. They provide a wide range of international life, health and disability insurance and investment packages for the expatriate living abroad. It is well worth visiting their website to discover the full extent of services on offer including help with finding employment abroad.

To find out more about other international health insurance schemes available to the expatriate either contact one of the companies listed below or get in touch with Medibroker International a firm that specialises in offering medical insurance advice to expatriates moving abroad or returning home. Medibroker is an organisation run by expatriates for expatriates, completely independent of any insurer or product house and the advice that they give to their clients is totally free of charge. Their remuneration is gained through placing business and introducing clients. Medibroker acts as both broker and advisor to their expatriate clientele.

They do not handle any of the money transactions as all payments/contracts are made directly with the insurers that are recommended to you. Their service has recently been expanded to include advice and assistance with offshore investing, pensions, off shore banking and taxation affairs. For further details contact Medibroker International at: Ellerslie House, Hugletts Lane, Heathfield, East Sussex TN21 9BX; tel 01435-867484; fax 01435-867776; e-mail medibroker@aol.com Website www.medibroker.com.

Useful Addresses

BUPA International: Russell Mews, Brighton, BN1 2NR, UK; tel 01273-208181; fax 01273-866583; e-mail advice@bupa-intl.com Website www.bupa-intl.com

Cigna International Plan: Tower House, 38 Trinity Square, London EC3N 4DJ.

Expacare Insurance Services: Dukes Court, Duke Street, Woking, Surrey GU21 5XB; tel 01483-717801; fax 01483-776620.

Medicare (SBJ International): 100 Whitechapel Road, London E1 1JG.

New York International Group: 1328 Broadway, Suite 1024, New York, New York 10001, USA; tel +1 212 268-8520; fax +1 212 268-8524; e-mail nyig@aol.com Website www.nyig.com

PPP Healthcare: PPP House, Vale Road, Tunbridge Wells, Kent TN1 1BJ; tel 01892-512345; fax 01892-503329; e-mail sarah.marfleet@pppgroup.co.uk

Primary International Healthcare Ltd: Springfield House, Springfield Road, Horsham, West Sussex RH12 2RG; tel 01403-225110; fax 01403-225114; e-mail primaryih@aol.com Website www.pih-expathealthdirect.com

USAssist Inc: 6903 Rockledge Drive, Suite 800, Bethesda, MD 20817, USA; tel +1 800 895-8472; fax +1 301 214-8205.

WPA Health International: Rivergate House, Blackbrook Park, Taunton, Somerset TA1 2PE.

Bahraini Law

Bahrain's legal system is based on a number of sources, including customary tribal law (*urf*), three different schools of Islamic shari'a law (see *Shari'a Law* in Gulf States' 'General Introduction' chapter), and civil law as exemplified in codes, statutes, and regulations. Shari'a law includes the Maliki school of Islamic law (from Abd Allah Malik ibn Anas, an eight century Muslim jurist from Madinah) and the Shafii school of Islamic law (from Mohammed ibn Idris ash Shafii, a late eight century Muslim jurist from Makkah). Sunni Muslims (see *Islam* in Gulf States' 'General Introduction' chapter) recognise both these schools whereas Shi'a Muslims recognise the third school of Twelver Islam as introduced by the eight century Jaafari (from Jaafar ibn Mohammed, also known as Jaafar as Sadiq, the sixth imam). English common law greatly influences the country's civil law as it was drawn up by British legal advisors during the 1920s and continued to develop until Bahrain's independence in 1971.

The Bahraini judiciary is an independent and separate branch of government as stipulated in the 1973 constitution. However, the Minister of Justice and Islamic Affairs, the highest judicial authority, is selected by, and answerable to, the Prime Minister, who is currently the emir's brother, Shaikh Khalifa bin Sulman al-Khalifa. The emir himself holds ultimate authority over the whole judicial system and it is he who retains the power of pardon in all cases.

Both civil and shari'a courts are in existence in Bahrain. The latter courts, situated in all communities, foremost handle cases of a personal nature (e.g. marriage, divorce, inheritance). The only shari'a Court of Appeal is located in the capital, Manama. Appeals that surpass the jurisdiction of the shari'a Court of Appeal

Moving overseas?

Take along a trusted name from home

There's a sense of adventure about moving overseas. But when it comes to something as important as your health, you won't want to take any risks. That's why one million members in over 180 countries put their trust in the award-winning name of BUPA International.

You'll have the reassurance of our 24-hour multi-lingual helpline, 365 days a year. Plus the comfort of treatment wherever possible in one of our well equipped international hospitals.

For further information about our range of schemes, just contact us, quoting LWS, by:

Phone: +44 (0) 1273 208 181
Fax: +44 (0) 1273 866 583
e-mail: advice@bupa-intl.com

Web: www.bupa-intl.com

1999
WINNER OF
THE QUEEN'S AWARD
FOR EXPORT
ACHIEVEMENT

BUPA International
A world of experience in health care.

are dealt with by the Supreme Court of Appeal which constitutes part of the civil system. The civil court system comprises summary courts and a supreme court, the former of which are found throughout the country and deal with *urf*, civil, and criminal cases. The supreme courts hear appeals from the summary courts and beyond this appeals are taken, as in the instance of shari'a appeals, to the Supreme Court of Appeal that is the top appellate court in the state.

For further details on the legal system in Bahrain contact the *Ministry of Justice & Islamic Affairs* (PO Box 450, Manama; tel +973 531333; fax +973 531284).

Social Life

Bahrain is known for being one of the more lively of the Gulf states in terms of nightlife. Plenty of restaurants, nightclubs and hotels offer a variety of entertainment for residents and in the main towns cinemas show English language films. Additionally, there are the numerous expatriate clubs covering a wide range of interests (details can be obtained from your local embassy/consulate – addresses in *Residence and Entry* chapter). Both land and water sports are also very popular throughout Bahrain. The opportunities are endless and include activities such as scuba diving, snorkelling, game fishing, water-skiing, yachting, para-sailing and golf, horse-riding, rugby, cricket, football, etc. Most expatriates are also members of health and fitness clubs, and there are the usual choice of traditional Arab spectator sports (see relevant section in Gulf States' 'General Introduction' chapter).

Food and Drink

Bahrain is host to an extensive range of restaurants serving cuisine from all over the globe. In fact, places where you can experience Arabic food are far outnumbered by those serving European, Chinese, Japanese, Lebanese, Mexican and American. Arabic food tends to be very spicy and pungent with lamb being the principal meat but chicken, turkey and duck also widely served. Salads and dips are also customary. Most people drink water or *arak*, a grape spirit flavoured with aniseed. The consumption of alcohol is not actively encouraged but can be bought by non-Muslims in hotels, licensed restaurants and nightclubs except during Ramadan. Strong Arabic coffee and tea are other popular drinks.

Shopping

You can buy almost anything that you need in Bahrain. The country's international airport offers a wide range of duty free goods not only to passengers departing but those arriving or in transit. Both traditional souks and modern multi-storey air-conditioned shopping malls allow the shopper a choice of purchasing the old and new. The souks are ideal for buying carpets (Persian, Pakistani, Kashmiri and Chinese), cloths, gold and jewellery, spices and local produce at bargain prices. Bahraini pearls are particularly worth looking at. Bartering is a must but bear in mind that the Bahrainis are famed throughout the Gulf for their bargaining skills. Designer labels and all the latest items can be bought in the modern shopping malls and prices will generally be comparatively less than those in the West. Local produce can be bought at low prices but imported goods are much more expensive. The opening hours of shops and supermarkets are typically 8.30am to 12.30pm and 3.30pm to 7.30pm Saturday to Thursday with some open on Friday mornings as well, although times vary.

KUWAIT

Currency

The unit of currency is the Kuwaiti Dinar (KD) which is divided into 10 dirhams which is 1,000 fils.
1 Kuwaiti Dinar (KD) £2.0200; £1 KD 0.4950
1 Kuwaiti Dinar (KD) US$ 3.2706; US$1 KD 0.3058

Introduction

Destination Kuwait

The official name of Kuwait is the State of Kuwait with many simply referring to it as Kuwait. The local long form is *Dawlat al Kuwayt*, shortened to *Al Kuwayt*. The Iraqi invasion and consequent Gulf War at the beginning of the 1990s (see below) catapulted Kuwait into the forefront of the global public eye. Since that time traces of the devastation that the Iraqis left behind them have almost all disappeared as Kuwait has worked hard to restore the nation to its former state. Despite the modern architecture and appearance of the country being nearly an exact replica of how it was before the invasion, the atmosphere of the state has altered greatly with the Kuwaiti citizens being far more open and welcoming to foreigners than they once were – indeed Kuwait is considered one of the few places in the Gulf where expatriates will find it relatively easy to make friends and socialise with local nationals.

Like its fellow Gulf states, Kuwait is a country that combines the ancient and traditional with the modern and new, both architecturally and culturally. Kuwait's present wealth is largely founded on its extensive oil reserves which helped enormously in the country's healthy recovery from the war with Iraq. Although there are ongoing plans to replace the expatriate work force with Kuwaiti citizens, there is still a great need for the expertise of foreigners and an abundance of employment opportunities exist in the country for non-nationals.

Pros and Cons of Moving to Kuwait

The financial benefits of going to live and work in Kuwait are much the same as will be found anywhere in the Arabian Peninsula – high salaries, no personal taxation, accommodation or a housing allowance, school fees, etc. included in your employment contract. But what most notably distinguishes Kuwait from its fellow Gulf countries is its relaxed, welcoming atmosphere and hospitable citizens. Although the Arabs throughout the Gulf region are known for their generous hospitality, it is only in Kuwait that expatriates are likely to gain the opportunity to experience this first-hand.

Kuwait is an Islamic country and as such you should recognise and respect that Islam is all pervasive. Foreigners should dress conservatively at all times in public and be mindful of the other customary rules and regulations dictated to by the local shari'a law (see *Social Practices in the Gulf* and *Shari'a Law*, Gulf States' 'General Introduction'). Penalties for certain offences may seem extreme by western standards and yet may have a lot to do with the very low crime rate in the state.

The standard of living in Kuwait is very high although the cost of living is not cheap by Gulf prices. However, you will easily be able to purchase just about anything that you may want (except alcohol and pork). Local produce is priced averagely, but imported goods are very expensive. Public transport – buses or taxis – is widely available although owning a car is practically a necessity in order to avoid being cut off. Nevertheless, great care needs to be taken on the roads because despite the high quality network of roads, the general standard of driving in the country is very bad and accidents are frequent occurrences.

Socially the expatriate community in Kuwait is very lively with numerous parties being held within private homes where alcohol may be served discreetly. You may not be allowed to purchase or import alcohol into the country but many people brew their own in their private homes. However, you should exercise particular caution if you are considering violating the local laws in this way as anyone caught flagrantly breaking the law will be severely dealt with, and at the very least, receive heavy fines.

The opportunities to pursue any number of sporting or non-sporting activities and interests abound in the country and there are plenty of clubs which you can join representing a limitless range of hobbies. The quality and range of different restaurants in Kuwait are also very impressive, as well as the luxury hotels.

From a Western perspective, the main pros and cons of living in Kuwait can be summarised as follows:

Pros: High wages.
No personal taxes to pay.
Very sociable expatriate community.
Friendly, generous, and welcoming Kuwaiti nationals.
Relatively low crime rate.
English widely spoken.
Tolerance of non-Muslim faiths and cultures.

Cons: Alcohol prohibited.
Cost of living not cheap.
Hazardous driving conditions.
Not all the landmines left over from the Gulf War have been cleared.

Political and Economic Structure

Kuwait was founded at the beginning of the early eighteenth century, when several clans from the Al Ariza tribe migrated there from the Najd region in central Arabia. An oligarchic merchant state was established by the settlers, whose economic wealth was built on trade, fishing and pearling. Within this state, the Al-Sabah family rose to power and were officially declared rulers in 1756. They are still Kuwait's governors today.

Throughout the eighteenth and nineteenth centuries, Kuwait developed into a strong trading port, holding its own despite its powerful Saudi, Ottoman and Rashidi neighbours. However, towards the end of the nineteenth century, Kuwait became fearful of Ottoman invasion and entered a pact with the British. In return for their protection, the British received the assurance from Kuwait that it would not enter into any dealings with any other foreign power without their consent. In addition to protecting the state from invasion, Britain also provided it with advisors to assist its new-born bureaucracy and in 1922 and 1923 it established Kuwait's borders. In 1932, Iraq attested its border with Kuwait in its application to the League of Nations for membership as an independent state. However, as modern

history has shown the Iraq-Kuwait relations became extremely volatile during the twentieth century.

In June 1961, Kuwait attained independence from Britain. This move triggered off Iraqi antagonism as Iraq would not accept that Kuwait was now an independent state. Iraq claimed that Kuwait had once been part of Iraq and in response to their military threats British troops were deployed in the country. The British were soon replaced by an Arab League Force which managed to quell the immediate conflict. Kuwait became a member of the United Nations in 1963. Subsequent to this Iraq consented to abandon its threats and acknowledge Kuwait's independence and borders in a treaty signed by both governments. However, border clashes still occurred in 1973.

By the 1960s, Kuwait had developed into one of the richest states in the world on a per capita basis due to its oil production and revenues. Oil was initially discovered in the country in 1938 but the effects of World War II had delayed the capitalisation of the industry until the mid-1940s from which time it made a rapid and healthy development. However, the security of a stable and prosperous economy and settled relations with its Iraqi neighbour was severely challenged in the 1980s due to the Iran-Iraq War, terrorist attacks in Kuwait City, and economic problems caused by a worldwide oil surplus and the 1982 collapse of Kuwait's unofficial stockmarket, the Suq Al-Manakh. In August 1990 Iraq invaded Kuwait and so began the Gulf War that brought so much media-attention to this area of the world.

The Gulf War. Iraq justified its occupation of Kuwait by claiming that Kuwait was damaging its economy by refusing to lessen its oil production, and once again asserted that historically Kuwait had been part of Iraq. Due to the invasion, many Kuwaitis were driven from their homes to neighbouring countries and Kuwait set up a government in exile in Saudi Arabia. An international coalition of thirty states, lead by the United States, joined forces against the Iraqis ejecting them by force from Kuwait at the end of Operation Desert Storm in February 1991. Nevertheless, the Iraqis did anything but accept their defeat gracefully. As they were forced out of Kuwait, they looted homes and businesses, and set ablaze 742 of the country's 1,080 oil wells, which greatly harmed not only the country's oil industry but the environment as oil flowed into the desert and sea. Additionally, thousands of Kuwaiti prisoners were abducted.

Kuwaiti independence and a UN-demarcated border were officially accepted by Iraq in November 1994. However, only partial compensation for the property and environmental damage inflicted has so far been paid by the Iraqis and UN resolutions requiring Iraq to repatriate all prisoners of war have been ignored. Iraq still holds 605 prisoners of war captive (of whom 570 are Kuwaiti citizens).

The Economy

Kuwait is one of the world's chief oil producing states with its economy heavily dependent on oil revenues. Recovery in the oil sector from the Gulf conflict was relatively healthy with a loss of only 3 per cent of its total reserves and the acquirement of eleven wells from Iraq. However, Kuwait suffered from the sharp downturn of oil prices in 1998 and early 1999, experiencing zero economic growth during 1998. In addressing this state of affairs, the government aimed to increase revenues and reduce government subsidies, which provide services to Kuwaiti citizens at nominal or no cost. One of the ways this has taken shape is through the privatisation process of health care, electricity, and telecommunications assets.

In the oil sector, the Kuwaiti constitution prohibits foreign ownership of Kuwait's mineral resources, but the Kuwaiti government is advancing towards permitting foreign investment in upstream oil development under provisions allowing for per-barrel fees to the foreign firms rather than traditional production sharing agreements (PSAs) in order to increase its country's revenues. New Foreign Investment Law also stipulates that foreign companies may now be allowed 100 per cent ownership of local businesses (previously limited to 49 per cent), in addition to further incentives such as tax breaks and custom duty exemption. More detailed information on the new reforms are available from the British Trade International's Kuwait Desk (tel 020-7215 4811/8084; fax 020-7215 4831).

Attempts to diversify the region's economy are greatly hampered by the small size of the domestic market and the deficiency of natural resources besides hydrocarbons. In 1989, agriculture and fishing attained its peak of non-oil GDP (Gross Domestic Product) at 1.1 per cent but the aftermath of the Iraqi invasion significantly reduced the influence of these sectors. Now the agriculture sector mainly comprises vegetables, fruit, trees and timber production, with only a small livestock industry in existence. The focus for development in non-oil industries has thus fallen on finance and banking, and industry and manufacturing sectors.

Outlook

Kuwait continues to attract a substantial number of international investors in government projects and tenders. The country's oil and defence sectors look favourable, and government programmes to develop power, public works, and housing industries will aid economic expansion. Other sectors such as telecommunications, electric power, tourism, health care, and airlines are government-run, but on the verge of privatising. With privatisation, opportunities for new joint ventures will arise.

Government

In 1962, a new constitution was sanctioned by the hereditary monarchy of Kuwait and a National Assembly was established. The emir, currently Shaikh Jaber Al-Ahmed Al-Sabah who has been in office since 1977, presides over the government and appoints the Prime Minister and the Council of Ministers (the Cabinet). Legislation can be decreed by the emir through his Cabinet but all his actions must be endorsed by the National Assembly.

The Judiciary. The Kuwaiti legal system is based on the Egyptian model but is also a combination of Islamic law, English common law, and the Ottoman civil code. Family and personal affairs such as inheritance and divorce are overseen by separate family courts practising under religious laws, each religious faith (e.g. Sunni, Shia, Christian) having its own set of laws and courts.

Legislature. The National Assembly (*Majlis al-Umma*), consisting of 50 members elected by a select electorate, makes Kuwait unique in that it is the only country in the Arabian Peninsula with an elected parliament. Members are in office for four year terms and the whole body stands for election simultaneously. The emir has the authority to adjourn the Assembly for a spell not in excess of one month and can also dissolve the Assembly and within two months call for new elections. The Assembly has the power to question Ministers' performance and to overturn any emiri decrees that may be made during parliamentary interregnum. It can also veto and impose government laws so that parliamentary approval must be attained for any bill to become law in Kuwait.

The Electorate. Only men who resided in Kuwait before 1920, their male descendants and the descendants of naturalised citizens can currently vote in Kuwait. There are plans to enfranchise women to allow them to vote in the year 2003 but the matter is still under discussion. The minimum age for voters is 21. Members of the military and police are not permitted to vote in the interests of keeping the armed forces politically neutral. The present electorate constitutes only 15 per cent of Kuwaiti nationals.

Political Groups. There are no official political parties in Kuwait, however, several 'caucuses' have formed in their place. The more prominent of these being:

Independents: those lacking specific classification and commonly associated loosely with the ruling family or with other political groupings.

Islamic Constitutional Movement (ICM) and *Islamic Popular Grouping*: two Sunni fundamentalist groups.

Islamic National Alliance: the main faction for Shi'a Muslims.

Kuwait Democratic Forum (KDF): vague alignment of secular groups with Nasserist, pan-Arabist foundations whose power has been declining for a number of years.

National Democratic Group: consisting of mainly secular progressives with liberal tendencies.

Tribal Confederations: arrange, have held primaries, and acquiesce to vote for certain candidates who are generally closely associated with either the government or the Islamists. Their chief objective is the protection of tribal interests.

Geographical Information

Area and Main Physical Features

Kuwait is situated at the head of the Arabian Gulf and covers an area of approximately 17,818 square kilometres. To its west and north lies Iraq, to its east the Arabian Gulf, and to its south Saudi Arabia. Its topography is mainly flat with only occasional low hills and shallow depressions. One of its chief topographic features, the Zor Ridge, borders the north-western coastline of Kuwait Bay and rises to a peak of 475 feet/145 metres above sea level.

Despite having a coastline that stretches for 325 kilometres (195 miles), Kuwait has no inland rivers or lakes. Camel herds of the Bedouin rely on the vital desert basins throughout the northern, western, and central sections of the country, that fill with water after winter rains. Sebihiya, south of Kuwait city, is the location of the only true oasis still remaining in Kuwait.

Only 8.6 per cent of the country's terrain can be cultivated at present, however, rises in agricultural investments will promote irrigated and reclaimed land. Currently, local farming produces much of the region's tomatoes, cucumbers, green vegetables, and strawberries. Scrub constitutes the majority of the countryside's vegetation, although over 400 species of flora have been reported. After winter showers the desert blossoms with flowers.

Population

Before the Iraqi occupation the population of Kuwait was over 2 million, of whom only about 28 per cent were Kuwaiti citizens, this number dropped dramatically after the invasion but figures now show an upturn. The population is currently estimated at over 2.2 million which includes over one million non-nationals. Population growth is set at about 2.7 per cent per annum. 45 per cent of the population are Kuwaiti, 35 per cent are of other Arab descent, 9 per cent are South Asian, 4 per cent are Iranian and those of other nationalities make up 7 per cent. The majority of the country is Muslim (Sunni 45 percent, Shi'a 40 per cent), and those practising other faiths (Christian, Hindu, Parsi, etc.) constitute 15 per cent of the population.

The official language of the region is Arabic but English is widely spoken. 78.6 per cent of the population (15 and over) are functionally literate.

Climate

Kuwait experiences a characteristic desert climate: extremes of temperature, little and unpredictable rainfall, lots of sunshine and habitual dust storms, *tauz*. During the hottest seasons, July and August, the weather can be unbearably hot with temperatures rising to a maximum of 40-50 degrees centigrade, while from November to April the climate is mild and pleasant. December and January are the cooler months with night temperatures being comparatively low.

Rainfall occurs between November and April, generally only in light infrequent showers but occasional thunderstorms can bring up to five centimetres of rain at a time. Winds from the north-west are cool in the winter and spring months but hot in the summer. During July and October, hot and damp winds blow in from the south-east. At this time humidity can reach a particularly uncomfortable 90 per cent. In the late spring and summer, there are frequent strong dust storms that can last several days and it is advisable to keep all house and car windows firmly shut. There is a very strong risk of sun burn and sun stroke in the summer months. Sun protection is imperative as well as the intake of additional fluids and salt to replace losses through excessive perspiration.

Weather Chart

Average temperature (Celsius), rainfall (mm), sunshine in hours per day, humidity percentage

	Jan	Feb	Mar	Apr	May	Jun	Jul	Aug	Sep	Oct	Nov	Dec
Kuwait City												
Max	16	18	22	28	34	37	39	40	38	33	25	18
Min	9	11	15	20	25	28	30	30	27	23	17	12
Rainfall	22	22	26	3	1	0	0	0	0	2	10	26
Rainy Days	2.0	2.0	2.0	0.9	0.3	0.0	0.0	0.0	0.0	0.5	1.0	3.0
Sunshine	8	9	9	8	10	10	10	11	10	10	8	7
Humidity	69	65	67	61	61	56	43	48	52	62	63	71

Regional Guide

Kuwait was divided into three towns by Emiri decree in 1961: Kuwait City (the capital), Hawalli Town and Ahmadi Town. In 1971 Jahra was established followed by Farwaniya in 1988. The commercial centre of the country which houses the government offices and the major banks is Kuwait City. Due to the hazard of left over mines from the Iraqi invasion, any plans to explore the country should be made carefully and with an individual/company who can inform you which parts are safe to visit and how to get to them.

Information Facilities

Kuwait does not have a tourist industry as advanced as some of the other Gulf States such as the UAE, but as it has been recovering from the Gulf War so it has begun to rebuild itself not only to accommodate its residents but to attract the foreign visitor and investor. Local tourist offices do not exist as such but the addresses below can act as a good start to finding out more about the country. Useful websites include: www.kuwait.org – provides information on Kuwait's constitution as well as a detailed map of Kuwait; www.kuwait1.net – Red Pages (equivalent of the British Yellow Pages) directory of businesses in Kuwait.

Useful Addresses

Department of Tourism: Ministry of Information, PO Box 193, 13002 Safat, Kuwait; tel +965 243-6644; fax +965 242-9758.

Kuwait Information Centre: Hyde Park House, 60-60a Knightsbridge, London SW1X 7JU; tel 020-7235 1787; fax 020-7235 6912; e-mail kuwait@dircon.co.uk Website www.kuwait-information-centre.org.uk

Kuwait Information Centre: 2600 Virginia Avenue, Suite 404, Washington, DC 20037, USA; tel +1 202 338-0211; fax +1 202 965-3463.

Kuwait Tourism Services Company: PO Box 21774, Safat, 13078 Kuwait; tel +965 245-1734/6/8; fax +965 245-1731; e-mail ktsc@qualitynet.net

Touristic Enterprises Company of Kuwait: PO Box 23310, Safat 13094, Kuwait City, Kuwait; tel +965 565-2775/1; fax +965 565-7864.

KUWAIT CITY

Kuwait City has a population of about 189,000 and is situated on the coast of the Arabian Gulf. It has more or less completely recovered now from the 1990 Iraqi invasion although its museums which once housed the best collections of Islamic Art were badly looted and are still missing much of their original contents. As well as its museums Kuwait offers its visitors the following sights: the Al Seef Palace, home of the emir and the first building to be reconstructed after the Iraqi occupation; the Grand Mosque, which can cater for over 5,000 worshippers at one time; the ruins of the old city walls and gates; and the Kuwait Tower, which is a collection of futuristic steel towers offering a magnificent view of the city and harbour. Beyond this, Kuwait has little else to entertain its visitor except the strange sight of perfect green golf courses amidst the vast arid expanses of desert.

HAWALLI

Hawalli is the largest city in Kuwait although the smallest governate in terms of area and is in reality little more than a suburb of Kuwait City. Located 8 km (5 miles) south-east of Kuwait City, Hawalli is mainly a residential and commercial region well-known for its fresh water. The country's first fresh water well was discovered here.

AHMADI

Ahmadi has a population of approximately 25,400 and is located 35 km (20 miles) inland south of Kuwait City. Tourist attractions include public gardens and a small zoo. Visitors here are strongly advised to stick to the roads as mines still pose a serious risk here. Mina al-Ahmadi is the chief port of the country; other ports in this governate include Shuaiba, Abdullah and Al-Zour. The town, named after the former emir, Shaikh Ahmed Al-Jaber Al-Sabah, is renowned for its oil fields and wells.

JAHRA

With a population of 111,000, Jahra is situated 30 km (20 miles) west of Kuwait City near the Al Mutla ridge. The ruins of an Iraqi column line the roadside. Jahra is the site of the famous red palace in which a notable Gulf War battle took place. Umm Al-Esh Satellites Station, Rawdatain Oil Fields, Umm Al-Esh, Al-Marakish and Rawdatin fresh water fields are also located here. The town governs two islands, Warba and Bubiyan.

FARWANIYA

Located inland south of Kuwait City with Jahra to its west, Farwaniya is primarily a residential region with very little to offer the tourist.

DOHA VILLAGE

Located 15 km (10 miles) west of Kuwait City, this small town is the site of Entertainment City, the biggest amusement park in the Middle East. On the outskirts of the park is a settlement where you can view local craftsmen build dhows.

ISLANDS

Kuwait governs several islands of which the most prominent are: Bubiyan, Failaka, Kubbar and Qaruh.

Bubiyan is the largest of the country's islands and lies 35 km (20 miles) north-east of Kuwait City, near both the Iraqi and Iranian borders. Conflict over ownership of the currently uninhabited island was a contributing factor to the Gulf War. Bubiyan is connected to the Kuwaiti mainland by a bridge.

Failaka (Faylakah) is the only major island inhabited and is situated 30 km (20 miles) east of Kuwait City. Visitors reach the island by dhow. Failaka is known for its beachfront properties and sites of interest such as the local museum and archaeological digs.

Getting to Kuwait

Air

The easiest way to get to Kuwait is by air. *Kuwait Airways (KU)*, Kuwait's national airline, runs non-stop flights to Kuwait from London. Other major airlines serving Kuwait include *British Airways*, *KLM* and *Lufthansa Airlines*. The flight from Kuwait to London is about 6 hours, to New York 13 hours, Los Angeles 19 hours and Sydney 17 hours. 24 hour flight information can be obtained from the country's international airport, *Kuwait (KWI)* (tel +956 433-4499). KWI is located 16 km (10 miles) south of Kuwait City.

Road

For the more adventurous ones who wish to brave driving to Kuwait there are two favoured routes from the Mediterranean: Beirut-Damascus-Amman-Kuwait, and Tripoli-Homs-Baghdad-Basra-Kuwait. The former route follows the Trans-Arabian Pipeline (TAP line) through Saudi Arabia; the latter runs across the Syrian desert. Due to the current political and military positions in both Lebanon and southern Iraq it is strongly advisable to check with the embassy before choosing a car route.

Useful Telephone Numbers

Airlines
Kuwait Airways: 020-7412 0006 (Admin.); 020-7412 0007 (Reservations).
British Airways: 0345-222111.
KLM: 0990-7509000.
Lufthansa Airlines: 020-8750 3500.

Useful Websites

City.net: www.excite.com/travel/countries/kuwait
Hotels and Travel: www.hotelstravel.com/kuwait.html
Hotel Book: www.hotelbook.com/static/MiddleEast/kuwait.html
Kuwait Airways: www.kuwaitair.de/cities/kwi/hotels/index.asp
CDC Travel Information: www.cdc.gov/travel/mideast.htm; provides latest health information requirements for those travelling to Kuwait and the Middle East.

Insurance

All visitors to Kuwait are strongly advised to take out comprehensive travel insurance. A list of addresses for some of the major insurers offering reasonable and flexible premiums can be found in the *Getting to Bahrain* chapter under 'Insurance.'

Residence and Entry Regulations

The Current Position

All individuals require a visa to enter Kuwait with the exception of other GCC nationals, expatriate residents of the GCC, and transit passengers who do not leave the airport. In general visas are relatively easy to acquire provided that the applicant is not Israeli and has no Israeli stamps in their passport.

Visit Visas

Visit visas are valid for periods of three and six months and are required by all those entering Kuwait for short term stays. The permits must be obtained in advance from a Kuwaiti Consulate abroad, or from the Ministry of the Interior in Kuwait through the visitor's sponsor or host. In order to procure a visit visa British citizens resident in the UK should submit the following documents to the Embassy of Kuwait (2 Albert Gate, Knightsbridge, London SW1X 7JU; tel 020-7590 3400): two completed application forms (available from the embassy), their passport, three passport size photographs, a covering letter from their UK employer and a fax invitation from their sponsor in Kuwait. A single entry visa valid for three months costs £30, for six months £48. If applying by post, a registered self-addressed envelope must be enclosed with the application documents. Once the visa application has been approved it should only take 24 hours for the permit (comprising a white slip of paper for entry and a pink slip for departure) to be issued.

Multiple Entry Visas

Multiple entry visas can be obtained by certain British nationals, e.g. businessmen. The holder of a multiple entry visa is entitled to make any number of visits to the country within a period of 6 months, 1, 2, or 5 years, for up to a one month stay per visit. Application is similar to that for visit visas, contact the Embassy of Kuwait in your country for the latest regulations. The cost of multiple entry visas is: £66 for 6 months, £75 for 1 year, £96 for 2 years, and £180 for a 5 year period.

Residence Visas

The No Objection Certificate

The first step towards obtaining a residence visa for Kuwait is to acquire a No Objection Certificate (NOC) issued by the Ministry of Social Affairs and Labour and arranged by your sponsor. The Ministry of the Interior will only approve your application for residency on the strength of your NOC which can be organised in advance of your arrival or subsequent to it. If your NOC is processed by your sponsor in advance then you can enter Kuwait directly for employment. In such cases a residence permit can generally be arranged within two months of your arrival. If your NOC has not been processed prior to entry into Kuwait then you must enter on a visit visa, and subsequently apply for an NOC. After your application has been approved then you must leave Kuwait, either to return to your home country or to a neighbouring country e.g. Bahrain or the UAE, providing you have the consent of the Kuwaiti authorities. You can then re-enter

Kuwait on the NOC and expect your residence permit to be processed within two months of re-entry.

The Residence Permit

To obtain the residence permit for his employee/family member, a sponsor generally takes charge of all the paperwork involved in the procedure but needs to have the employee's passport, a copy of the NOC, a medical certificate of fitness (which involves a blood test for HIV and an X-ray) and a local police clearance certificate (which involves fingerprinting). The medical examination costs KD 10 and the permit itself costs KD 10 annually. For those working in the government sector who wish to sponsor their spouse and up to three children, they must be earning a minimum wage of KD 450 a month. Each permit again costs an annual fee of KD 10 but for each additional child over the three allowed there is a fee of KD 100 for the initial year, with subsequent years being charged at the normal KD 10 rate. For those working in the private sector, a minimum monthly wage of KD 650 is required in order to sponsor family members and the charges for permits for the initial year are KD 100 per person, and KD 200 for any additional children over the first three, subsequent years only KD 10 is charged per person.

Registration

British nationals seeking residency in Kuwait or on a long visit, are strongly advised to register with the British Embassy Consular Section as soon as possible after arrival. Registration should be renewed yearly, and any change of address or employment should be reported to the Consulate in addition to final departure from the country.

Civil ID

After a residence visa has been secured, it is obligatory to register for a Civil ID card which must be carried on your person at all times. A completed application form available from the Public Authority for Civil Information, should be submitted to this department along with photographs and passport photocopies.

Useful Addresses

Ministry of the Interior: PO Box 12500, Shamiya 71655, Kuwait; tel +965 243-3804/6; fax +965 243-6570.

Ministry of Social Affairs & Labour: PO Box 563, Safat, Kuwait; tel +965 248-0000; fax +965 241-9877.

Public Authority for Civil Information: tel +965 266-9111; fax +965 243-2440.

Embassy of the State of Kuwait: 2 Albert Gate, London SW1X 7JU; tel 020-7590 3400; fax 020-7259 5042.

British Embassy (Consular Section): PO Box 2, Safat 13001, Kuwait City, Kuwait; tel +965 240-3334/5/6; fax +965 242-5778; e-mail britemb@ncc.moc.kw

Embassy of the State of Kuwait: 2940 Tilden Street, NW, Washington, DC 20008, USA; tel +1 202 966-0702; fax +1 202 966-0517.

Embassy of the United States of America: PO Box 77, Safat 13001, Kuwait City, Kuwait; tel +965 539-5307/8; fax +965 538-0282; Website www.usia.gov/posts/kuwait

Setting Up Home

Renting Property

Those moving to Kuwait have no other option than to rent housing as Kuwaiti land or property can only be owned by Kuwaiti or other GCC nationals. For many expatriates their accommodation may be included in their employment contracts. For those who must seek housing independently it is highly recommended to rent from one of the many real estate agents in operation (see useful numbers below) who will deal with all the relevant paperwork on your behalf rather than directly face the landlord yourself.

One of the leading companies for furnished apartment services in Kuwait is *AAA Housing* (PO Box 823, Safat, Kuwait 13009; tel +965 2465888/2452700; fax +965 2433625; e-mail house@aaahousingq8.com Website www.aaahousingq8.com), which provides expatriates with high standard furnished accommodation in a number of locations: Kuwait City, Salmiya, Salwa, Fahaheel, Mangaf, Farwaniya. *AAA Housing* assist with all aspects of leasing a new furnished apartment, and its range of complexes are designed to cater for all needs and budgets. Among the services and facilities available on *AAA Housing* complexes are: free 24 hour maintenance, housekeeping cleaning services, round the clock security, satellite TV, children's play area, swimming pool, and other recreational facilities such as basketball and tennis courts, etc. Contact *AAA Housing* direct or visit their website for more detailed information.

Further advice on finding housing in Kuwait may also be available from the Ministry of State for Housing (tel +965 246-6300; fax +965 242-1412) or from *Al-Khaleejia Apartment Service*, Al Kazemi Buildings, Khaalied bin Walid Street, Al Sharq, Kuwait; tel +965 245-6545; fax +965 246-0738.

Useful Telephone Numbers

Al Duaij Real Estate Office: +965 240-2662.
Al Hashimiya Real Estate Co.: +965 243-6088.
Al Imad Real Estate: +965 240-9600.
Al Ritaj Real Estate Co.: +965 261-1615.
Aldwaysan Real Estate: 240-5177.
Arab Center for Commerce & Real Estate: +965 265-1422.

Boushahri Real Estate Co.: +965 574-4017.
Frost Real Estate: +965 564-3149.
Guide Real Estate Center: +965 574-0256.
Kuwait Real Estate Co.: +965 244-8330.

Utilities

Electricity

To get your home connected to the mains you need to apply to your local electricity office with your passport, residence visa, rent contract and a refundable deposit of KD 100. The Ministry of Electricity and Water will then turn on your power. Check your lease agreement to find out whether electricity charges are included in the contract.

Electric power is supplied at 220 or 240 volts, and both European and British standard prong configurations are in common use. Where necessary transformers are available in hotels and shops.

Water

Due to the lack of resources of natural water in Kuwait, the government has established several vast sea water distillation plants, one of which was the largest in the world with an output of about 200 million gallons of drinking water per day. The plants suffered with the Iraqi invasion but are now back to operating capacity. It is advisable to filter all domestic tap water and boil it before drinking – although, widely available bottled water is probably a much tastier and safer bet. A filtration system attached to your water pipes is recommended for the use of kitchen appliances such as dishwashers and washing machines to avoid staining.

Gas

There are no mains gas systems in Kuwait but canisters can be bought and delivered to your door for fuelling gas cookers. Contact your local gas company for more details (addresses can be found by consulting the Red Pages www.kuwait1.net – Kuwait's equivalent of Britain's yellow pages directory).

Telephones

To install a telephone line you must apply to the Ministry of Communications with the following documents: passport and residency visa photocopies, photocopies of your accommodation lease contract and an electricity bill, a certificate to verify that there are no outstanding costs on past phone bills, and a refundable deposit of KD 500 or security bank guarantee if you want to have an international line.

Telephone bills are issued at your local telephone exchange. Local calls are free and can generally be made from shops on request or, for a minimal fee, from your local telephone exchange. International calls can be made at the telephone exchange or by using phone cards.

Useful Addresses

Ministry of Communications: PO Box 318, Safat, 11111 Kuwait; tel +965 481-9033; fax +965 484-7058.
Ministry of Electricity, Water & Public Works: PO Box 12, Safat, 13001 Kuwait; tel +965 489-6000; fax +965 489-7484.

Daily Life

The purpose of this chapter is to provide all the necessary practical information to successfully cope with a range of aspects of life in Kuwait so that armed with this knowledge your move to this country may be made that little less daunting.

Schools and Education

Kuwaiti nationals receive free education in government schools where tuition is in Arabic. Certain groups of foreign nationals may put their children in these schools but demand far exceeds the availability of places. There are numerous international schools covering a range of different country's education systems although the most popular are the American and British style schools. Children of all nationalities may attend these schools but the majority of students are western. The Ministry of Education has ultimate authority over the private schools, setting their fee rates, inspecting them, and arbitrating in cases of complaint. All international private schools are co-educational and cater for children at all levels from kindergarten to A-levels/High School/College. Those working for large companies should check their contracts to see if payment of school fees is included. More detailed information on schooling in Kuwait can be found on the country's website (www.embassyofkuwait.com/Information—Section/Education/index.html).

There are nine schools in the suburbs of Kuwait City teaching a British curriculum. All these schools are run by British teachers and early application to them is strongly advised. Fees range from KD 700 (for Kindergarten years) to KD 2,140 (for A-level students) per annum. Contact addresses are listed below with the age groups (in years) catered for in brackets.

English Schools

The English School (Salmiya) (4-11): PO Box 379, Safat 13004; tel +965 563 7206; fax +965 563 7147.

The New English School (Jabriya) (4-18): PO Box 6156, Hawalli 32036; tel +965 531 8060/1; fax +965 531 9924; Website www.neskt.com

The Kuwait English School (Salwa) (3^1/2-18): PO Box 8640, Salmiya 22057; tel +965 565 5216/563 2130; fax +965 562 9356.

The English School (Fahaheel) (4-18): PO Box 7209, Fahaheel 64003; tel +965 371 1070/7263; fax +965 371 5458; e-mail esf@ncc.moc.kw Website www.skee.com

The Gulf English School (4-18): PO Box 6320, Hawalli 32038; tel +965 565 9361; fax +965 565 0758; e-mail gesadmin@ges.edu.kw Website www.mdrass.moc.kw/ges/contacts.html

The British School of Kuwait (3-18): PO Box 26922, Safat 13030; tel +965 562 1701/2701; fax + 965 562 4903; Website www.bsk.edu.kw

The English Academy (3^1/2-11): PO Box 1081, Surra 45701; tel +965 534 0427/8; fax +965 534 0421.

The Kuwait National English School (2^1/2-13): PO Box 44273, Hawalli 32057; tel +965 265 6904; fax +965 265 2459.

The English School for Girls (3-18): PO Box 12592, Shamiya 71653; tel +965 561 9134; fax +965 563 9435.

American Schools

The American International School of Kuwait: PO Box 17464, Khaldiya 72455, Kuwait; tel +965 564-5083; fax +965 564-5089; e-mail admin@ais.edu.kw

American School of Kuwait: PO Box 6735, Hawalli, 32042 Kuwait; tel +965 266-

4341; fax +965 265-0438; e-mail ask@ask.edu.kw Website www.ask.edu.kw
The Universal American School: PO Box 17035, Khaldiya, 72451, Kuwait; tel +965 562-0297; fax +965 562-5343; e-mail uaskuwait@hotmail.com

Further information on international schools and education in Kuwait can also be obtained from *The British Council*, PO Box 345, 13004 Safat, Kuwait; tel +965 2515512; fax +965 2520069; e-mail bckuwait@kuwait.net Website www.britishcouncil.org.

For those who would like their children to become proficient in both Arabic and English there is the *Al-Bayan Bilingual School* (PO Box 24472, 13105 Safat, Kuwait; tel +965 531-5125; +965 533-2836; e-mail bbsadm@ncc.moc.kw Website www2.kems.net/users/bbs) which takes children from the ages of 3 to 18. Both an American and a Kuwaiti syllabus are taught and pupils are prepared for university study.

Special Needs Children. There is a very useful website (www.safat.com), Kuwait Information Page for People with Special Needs, that lists schools, clubs, associations, research centres and institutes which are concerned about people with special needs in Kuwait. It is well worth visiting this site to find out just how much there is on offer to those physically and/or mentally disadvantaged in Kuwait.

The Media, Post and Telecommunications

The Media

All printed matter, films and videos showing scantily-dressed women, sexual contact between men and women, religious propaganda or politically-sensitive material will be seized by the Ministry of Information (PO Box 193, Safat 13002, Kuwait; tel +965 241-5301). Any books or personal videos discovered in luggage coming into the country will be reviewed by the Ministry of Information to be returned (or not) at a later date.

Television

Kuwait TV operates three colour television channels, one of which broadcasts imported Western programmes in English. Most expatriate apartment blocks now have satellite TV installed which means access to a wide choice of programmes covering a range of subjects.

Radio

The BBC World Service can be accessed on short wave radio in Kuwait for more details contact tel 020-7557 1165; e-mail worldservice.letters@bbc.co.uk Website www.bbc.co.uk/worldservice. A monthly international programmes guide, *BBC On Air*, which includes information on World Service Radio, BBC World and BBC prime television services can be obtained by contacting the BBC at tel 020-7557 2211; fax 020-7240 4899.

On medium wave you can listen to Kuwait Radio broadcast daily in Arabic or on FM stereo there is an all music station broadcasting from 1am to midnight daily. FM is also the frequency on which to find the US Armed Forces Radio station broadcasting.

Newspapers and Magazines

Newspapers and magazines are widely available in Kuwait from hotel shops, supermarkets and bookshops.

The two major English language dailies found in Kuwait are: *The Arab Times* (PO Box 2270, Safat 13023; tel +965 422-5187; fax +965 422-4649) and the *Kuwait Times* (PO Box 1301, Safat 13014; tel +965 483-5616; fax +965 483-5621).

Books and Bookshops

A range of English or European language books covering a spectrum of subjects are available from bookshops throughout Kuwait amongst which are the following:

Al Baker Book Shop: +965 261-6559.
Al Noori Bookshop: +965 571-3391.
Coronet Book Shop: +965 241-7533.

Post

Most residents and businesses in Kuwait have post box numbers to which their mail is sent as door to door delivery is very rare. Post offices can be found in most districts and will arrange a postal address for you on application. Airmail letters to and from Europe and North America can take from one week to one month. For international mail weighing less than 20 grams the charge is 150 fils; for mail weighing 20-50 grams the charge is 280 fils. Major courier services such as DHL, FedEx, TNT and UPS are available.

Telephones

Coin-operated payphones can be found throughout Kuwait taking 50 and 100 fils coins; card payphones are also in use. There are no area codes for calls within Kuwait. The code for dialling Kuwait from the UK is +965.

Useful Numbers

Emergencies	777
Billing Enquiries	123
Directory Enquiries	101
General Enquiries	484 4484
Telephone Enquiries	117

Cars and Motoring

Driving in Kuwait

Within Kuwait City there is a high standard road network and good motorway connections to other towns. But driving in Kuwait, as in all the Gulf States, is itself an extremely risky business. It is all too common to encounter other drivers speeding, swerving, lane drifting, pulling out suddenly, driving too close to vehicles in front, and ignoring traffic light signals. As a result the police are clamping-down on even the smallest of traffic offences and putting offenders in jail overnight or for more lengthy periods.

Driving in Kuwait is on the right and speed limits are 45 kmph in urban areas and 80 to 120 kmph on the major highways. Visitors can drive for up to a month on an International Licence based on their valid Western licence. Third party insurance taken out with a local company is a prerequisite. Buying new cars in Kuwait is as expensive as in the US or in Europe but petrol is cheap at 40-50 fils per litre. However, insurance is very expensive.

Word of Warning. Landmines are still to be found in Kuwait. Keep to the tarmac roads when travelling outside Kuwait city.

Car Rental

Self-drive hire cars are available in Kuwait but are costly (at least KD 8 per day or KD 38 per day for car with driver). Full insurance cover, guaranteeing compensation in the event of injury or death to an accident victim, should be included in your rental package but this should be double-checked. Car rental companies will give full advice on procedures.

Useful Telephone Numbers

Al Mulla Rental & Leasing of Vehicles and Equipment Company WLL: +965 2431 434.
Avis: +965 2453 827/8.
Budget: +965 4810 844.
Europcar: +965 4842 988.
Hertz: +965 4848 034.
Rent-al-Mulla/InterRent: +965 3980 533.
Thrifty: +965 2460 339.

Buying a Car

Owning a car in Kuwait is a popular choice as it is one of the most convenient modes of transport within the country. Residents in Kuwait can choose to buy either a new car or a second-hand car.
New cars generally cost as much as in the US or Europe but insurance fees are substantially more. For example, a year's fully comprehensive insurance can cost from KD 80 to KD 250 dependent on age and model of car. A standard scheduled service and tune-up at a dealer's garage can cost from KD 40 to KD 50. However, there are some positives to purchasing a new car, fuel is relatively cheap compared to most other countries and buying a new car, not only includes comprehensive insurance with the initial downpayment, but ensures a warranty period of at least three years and should mean that the car is more reliable than some second-hand cars. Most major car dealers can be found in Kuwait such as: Toyota, Subaru, Honda, Nissan, Fiat and Mitsubishi. Foreign residents usually require a Kuwaiti guarantor in order to purchase a car, unless they pay in cash.
Second-hand Cars can be a very economical alternative to buying brand new cars as very occasionally bargains on used cars in good condition can be found for as little as KD 500. However, usually you should be looking to spend from KD 600-1,000 in order to purchase a car in reasonable working order. You can seek deals on second-hand cars either from friends or colleagues, by looking in the Classified section of the local newspapers, from dealer showrooms who will often give a limited warranty of one or two months and arrange financing, or from the used car souk (Souk al Haraj) in Kuwait city. It is advisable to take out comprehensive insurance for your car (cost from KD 40-120) and for convenience, to stay with the owner's insurance company. Always double check your insurance company's definition of 'fully comprehensive.'

When you buy a second-hand car it is obligatory to register the transfer of ownership with the Traffic Department. Assistance is usually offered by the owner.

The process means first going with the seller to the insurance company to change the insurance – the seller must take with him his insurance papers, driver's licence and registration book, the buyer must bring his passport with residency visa and driver's licence. Then the seller, with the same documents that he has taken to the insurance company, must go to the Traffic Department in the area where he lives. It is possible to complete the transfer in one day.

Vehicle Registration and Inspection

All cars must be registered annually and those more than three years old should undergo yearly inspections. Failure to re-register a vehicle or have a car tested on time will result in a fine. For re-registration you need to apply to the Traffic Department with your residency visa, ownership details, and vehicle test results. Car inspection takes place at the Vehicle Testing Station in the governate in which you are located. The test simply involves checking that the body of the car is in good, clean condition with all lights working, that the engine does not smoke when the accelerator is pressed, and that the brakes (and brake lights) are working.

When driving, you should carry your car's registration book and driving licence with you at all times. It is advisable to make photocopies of these documents to ease the replacement process if loss of the originals occurs.

Breakdowns and Accidents

Kuwait has two automobile services: the Kuwait Automobile Club and the Gulf Automobile Association, both of which are affiliated with international associations. For a yearly road service charge of KD 10, they will provide free towing and mechanical consultation and will assist with the annual registration of your car. For a nominal charge, they will also provide help in exporting a car or in obtaining an international driver's licence.

In case of an accident all parties involved must remain at the scene until the police have conducted their own investigation. Applications for repair costs should be made to the individual's insurance company as soon as possible.

Driving Licences

An international driver's licence is valid with a residency or visit visa for a period of up to one month. After which time a Kuwaiti driver's licence must be acquired. To obtain a Kuwaiti licence requires persistence, patience, and perseverance in order to wade through all the red tape involved. First of all the following documents need to be collated: a salary letter, a housing letter, your passport and two photocopies of your residency visa, passport size photographs, a valid foreign driver's licence or international licence and two photocopies, and an Arabic translation of your driving licence by an approved translator at a cost of KD 5. The translation has to be verified by your embassy, then approved by the Foreign Ministry at a charge of KD 2. An application form for the Kuwaiti licence should then be procured from the Traffic Department and completed in Arabic – again you will most likely need the assistance of a translator. In addition to all this, you will need to provide a statement of your blood type, which may involve taking a blood test before continuing if you do not know your blood type. An eye test may also be required. Finally, once all this has been presented to your Traffic Department you should receive your Kuwaiti licence.

The whole process at a push could take as little as five days, including obtaining the translation, but more realistically it could take up to three weeks. Once you have acquired your licence it is strongly advisable to photocopy it straightaway. Having made your way through the long drawn-out procedure of actually getting a licence it should be of great comfort to know that it is now valid for the length of your residency permit and you should not have to undergo the same palaver again for the rest of your stay.

Useful Addresses

Gulf Insurance Company KSC: PO Box 1040, Safat, 13011 Kuwait; tel +965 242-3384; fax +965 242-2320.
Kuwait Insurance Company: tel +965 242-0135/9; fax +965 246-1855.

Transport

The most convenient way of travelling around urban areas in Kuwait is by taking the regional taxis. Local buses are not generally used by Western expatriates due to the ease of taxi-ing everywhere. Whether travelling in buses, taxis, wanaits (pick-ups) or waiting at bus stops, women may receive unwanted attention. It is strongly recommended to look absorbed in the business of watching for the bus, looking out of the window, or reading a book, in order to avoid direct eye contact. The 24 hour call taxis (service taxis), are probably the best bet for single women using public transport.

Buses

Buses in Kuwait are blue and white and a bargain at 100 or 150 fils for a standard fare. The network within greater Kuwait City is extensive although not necessarily the most reliable especially on Sundays when rush hour traffic may cause delays. In order to make up for lost time some drivers may take short-cuts, missing out certain stops, so it is advisable to check before boarding whether the bus is actually going to your destination – this may also cause problems as not all drivers speak English.

If only the driver is collecting fares, then you enter the bus at the front, if there is a fare collector on board then men enter the bus at the back and women and very young children enter at the front. Unaccompanied females normally sit in the front seats with men vacating these seats when women board. A female accompanied by a man can sit anywhere. If pressing the red button on the vertical posts or press bands fails to alert the bus driver to stop then try banging noisily on the metal above the exit door. Most bus stops have shelters and are marked by a round sign with a dark blue background and white lettering.

Express buses on particular routes have air conditioning, make fewer stops, and charge at least 150 fils for a standard fare. These buses have three-digit numbers.

Taxis

Call taxis. These are plentiful in number throughout Kuwait with the majority of their dispatchers and drivers accustomed to serving expatriates and speaking English. Rates are government regulated and can be checked against written charts at the company's main office. Fixed rates are from point to point with most companies charging similar competitive rates. As the fare is fixed, the more passengers, the more economical the journey as the total cost can be shared. Regular daily pick-ups at home or work can be arranged either via the company or the driver. Call-taxis are usually big, clean, American cars with the name of the company printed on the doors.

As call-taxis work on a pre-arranged fee basis, there is no need to tip the driver. Call-taxis cannot be flagged down casually on the street but must be ordered initially through a dispatcher. See the following list of call-taxi company telephone numbers:

Al Ebrahim Taxi: +965 240 0013.
Al-Samiya Taxi: +965 5722 931.
Burqan Taxi Establishment: +965 2415 500/9.
Gulf Shields Taxi: +965 2450 777.
Kuds Taxi: +965 2410 988.
Mustafa Karam Call Taxi: +965 3980 044.

Orange taxis. These type of taxis do stop on the street for passengers. They are driven by Kuwaiti owners and are not radio-dispatched. If you know what the rate should be and are good at bargaining then the orange taxis are generally cheaper than call-taxis. Fixed rates only apply to journeys from the airport. Set routes are taken by these taxis and often the journey is shared with other people picked up along the way. The more people in your party the more you pay. Drivers of these taxis are not used to expatriate passengers and frequently speak little or no English.

Wanaits (Pickups)

Usually driven by their owners, wanaits are little pick-up trucks of various colours and of two particular types: those marked *naql khass* in Arabic on the back (private vehicles), and those marked *naql-aam* in Arabic (public vehicles). Only the latter variety are used for public transport so when trying to flag down a wanait do not be surprised if several pass you by without stopping as they are most probably of the former kind. This type of transport can only be used if you are transporting some form of goods. Wanaits are not permitted to compete with taxis by picking up passengers without loads. Bargaining – especially if you test your Arabic – is the key to getting record low fares to your destination, that is better stated in terms of landmarks than street names.

Sea

Trips to offshore islands can be made by chartering dhows and other small craft.

Banking and Finance

The banking sector in Kuwait is regulated by the Central Bank of Kuwait. There are seven commercial banks, four specialised credit institutions, seventeen investment companies and numerous merchants, moneylenders and money changers operating in the country. A wide range of traditional banking services comparable to those found in western banks are provided in the commercial banks. Credit cards are an accepted form of payment at most establishments and numerous cash-points are located throughout the state. Typical banking hours are from 8am to 12pm, Sunday to Thursday with some banks open in the afternoons; during Ramadan the hours are generally from 9.30am to 1.30pm.

Useful Addresses

Central Bank of Kuwait: PO Box 526, Safat 13006; tel +965 244 9200; fax +965 246 4887.
National Bank of Kuwait: PO Box 95, Safat 13001; tel +965 242 2011; fax +965 243 1888.
Gulf Bank: PO Box 3200, Safat 13032; tel +965 244 9501/3; fax +965 245 0634.

Commercial Bank of Kuwait: PO Box 2861, Safat 13029; tel +965 241 1001; fax +965 245 0150.

Bank of Kuwait & the Middle East: PO Box 71, Safat 13001; tel +965 245 9771; fax +965 246 1430.

Al Ahli Bank: PO Box 1387, Safat 13014; tel +965 240 1916; fax +965 241 7282.

Burgan Bank: PO Box 5389, Safat 13054; tel +965 243 9000; fax +965 246 1148.

Offshore Banking

If you are working for a large company in the Gulf you are likely to be earning quite substantial amounts of money some of which you will undoubtedly be looking to invest. One of the primary financial advantages of being an expatriate is that you can invest this money offshore in tax havens such as the Isle of Man, the Channel Islands, Gibraltar and Bahrain, thus accruing tax-free interest on your savings. Many such facilities are as flexible as UK high street banking and range from current accounts to long-term, high interest earning deposits. For more details and addresses of offshore banking units see *Offshore Banking* section in 'Bahrain Daily Living' chapter.

Tax and the Expatriate

There is no income tax or social security for expatriates to pay in Kuwait nor do any other taxes exist for foreign nationals resident in the country. As a non-resident of your home country (i.e. for UK nationals spending fewer than 183 days in aggregate in Britain) you will not be subject to your home country's tax on earnings either. For more details on what you may or may not be entitled to or subjected to regarding tax regulations (on earnings, relocation expenses, investments, etc.) as an expatriate you should consult a specialist tax advisor. Useful contacts can be found in magazines such as *The Expatriate* and the large accounting/financial advisory companies like PriceWaterhouseCoopers (Plumtree Court, London EC4A 4HT; tel 020-7583 5000; fax 020-7822 4652) publish handy booklets giving detailed information on the tax implications for foreign nationals working in other countries.

Health Care in Kuwait

Before the Iraqi invasion, Kuwait once boasted one of the best medical services in the Gulf. Since the invasion it has managed to re-build its high standard of health care comparable to that in the West. It has a state medical service with local clinics (and larger polyclinics) and a number of good general hospitals and more specialist hospitals. Out-patients do not have to pay for treatment but in-patients do, and there is a charge for private rooms. However, emergency treatment is free. It is advisable to register with a clinic on arrival in Kuwait to avoid any later inconvenience when health care is sought. Proof of legal residency in Kuwait will be required (passport or civil ID).

If you would rather seek private health service, there are hundreds of doctors and dentists in private practice, private hospitals and nursing homes but fees are monitored by the State and very expensive. Health insurance is a must if you want to seek private treatment.

Useful Addresses

Ministry of Public Health: PO Box 5, Safat, 13001 Kuwait; tel 246 2900; fax 243 2288.

Useful Telephone Numbers

Private Hospitals/Clinics
Al Salem Hospital: 253 3177; 253 3178; 253 3179.
Hadi Private Clinic: 531-2555.
International Clinic: 574 5111.
Kuwait Clinic: 573 5111.
Mowasat Private Clinic: 571 1533/42.

Government Hospitals
Mubarak Al Kabir Hospital: 531 1437/2700.
Sabah Hospital: 481 2000/5000.
Al-Adan Hospital: 394 0600.
Amiri Hospital: 245 0005.
Farwaniya Hospital: 488 8000.

Government Clinics
Salmiya Clinic: 572 3741.
Salmiya Polyclinic: 572 3500.
Farwania Polyclinic: 472 6033.
Faiha Polyclinic: 254 5188.
Shamiya Clinic: 484 2090.

Dentists
Al Maidan Dental Clinic: 245 0017.
Dental Department: 253 3177/8/9.
International Clinic: 564 5111.
Kuwait Medical Centre: 575 9044/45.

Private Medical Insurance

Private medical care in Kuwait is of a very high standard but it is also by no means cheap. Taking out the proper health insurance cover for you and your family is essential when moving out to the Gulf.

BUPA International (Russell Mews, Brighton, BN1 2NR; tel 01273-208181; fax 01273-866583; e-mail advice@bupa-intl.com Website www.bupa-intl.com) has designed its own Lifeline scheme that offers maximum choice and flexibility. There are three levels of cover: Gold, Classic and Essential, all of which provide full refund for hospital accommodation and specialists' fees so you never need to be concerned about unexpected bills for in-patient treatment such as an operation. Cover for emergency ambulance charges and sports injuries is also standard. The Gold and Classic schemes offer out-patient treatment which may be a very wise precaution in Kuwait. The most comprehensive cover is available with the Gold scheme which includes the cost of primary care treatment and home nursing. BUPA International has a 24 hour multi-lingual service centre dedicated to their expatriate members with an experienced team on hand to deal with any queries. Claims are paid promptly in any currency that you require, and you are covered anywhere in the world. For more information call +44 (0) 1273-208181.

For more details on other international health insurance schemes available to the expatriate and contact addresses see *Private Medical Insurance* in 'Bahrain Daily Living Chapter.'

Kuwaiti Law

The legal system in Kuwait is largely based on civil law with Islamic law (see *Shari'a Law* in Gulf States' 'General Introduction') carrying great significance in personal cases. For more details see *Government* above.

Social Life

Kuwait does not have the reputation for a pulsating nightlife as say Bahrain or the UAE may have, and yet there are plenty of things in which the expatriate in the country can participate, such as numerous clubs representing a wide range of interests – sporting or otherwise. Moreover, there is a great deal of socialising that takes place within the expatriate community, private parties, dining out, etc. and Kuwait is one of the few states in the Gulf where foreign residents can and do socialise with Gulf nationals.

For details on the tourist areas to visit in the State of Kuwait see *Regional Guide* above.

Religion

Although Kuwait is predominantly an Islamic country, the practice of other faiths is allowed and some Christian churches do exist in the state such as St Paul's Church (Anglican), Ahmadi, tel +965 398 5929, and the Church of the Holy Family (Roman Catholic), PO Box 226, Safat 13003; tel +965 243 4637 ext. 113.

Institutions & Societies

The following is a list of just a handful of the many clubs which you can join when you are in Kuwait. More detailed and continually updated information can be obtained from your local embassy/consulate.

American Women's League of Kuwait: PO Box 77, 13001 Safat, Kuwait; tel/fax +965 263 8052; e-mail awlkuwait@excite.com Website www.fawco.org/clubs/kuwait.html
The British Ladies Society: tel +965 538 4526.
The Caledonian Society: tel/fax +965 5710081.
Hash Runners: tel/fax +965 563 8973.
Kuwait Academicals Football Club (The Accies): tel +965 908 8043.
Kuwait Little Theatre: tel +965 398 2680.
Kuwait Nomads Rugby Club: tel +965 372 8201.
Kuwait Players: tel +965 564 3409.
Premier Darts League: tel/fax +965 265 8535.
Scouts: tel/fax +965 551 6815.

Shopping

Kuwait is certainly no match for Dubai in terms of shopping but you will have no problem in finding available everything that you need.

Food & Domestic Goods

Raw foods can be bought from *bakalas* (groceries) or at local co-operative supermarkets. The 'co-ops' also cater for all your basic necessities. The largest most popular stores are in Salmiya, Rawda and Shamiya. Prices are usually more reasonable in the co-ops than in private supermarkets and attached to them are often fruit and vegetable shops and bakeries. Large quantities of goods can be bought from the wholesale sections. Both bakalas and co-ops open early in the morning and close late at night with some co-ops open 24 hours.

Medical clinics, post offices, banks, hardware shops, opticians, pharmacies, bakeries, etc. can be found in most district centres as well as at least one fast-food outlet. Some shopping areas even have playgrounds for children. A wide selection of American and European food can be found in private supermarkets although it is more expensive than the same goods bought in the home countries. Fresh fish and seafood can be bought at local fish markets at very reasonable prices. It makes a lot of sense to your daily budget to buy local foods at cheap prices than those far more expensive imported goods.

Traditional Shopping

A great selection of American and European clothes and shoes, etc. can be found in Kuwait but at a cost, although designer labels tend to be cheaper in Kuwait than in the West due to the absence of import tax on clothing. However, it is far more interesting to shop in the local traditional souks (covered bazaars). Everything from household and electrical goods to spices, clothing, antiques, weavings, carpets and jewellery, etc. can be found in these bazaars. The main Old Souk in the heart of Kuwait City, starts alongside Safat Square and runs down towards the sea. The key to shopping in these areas is to haggle, haggle and haggle some more.

One of the most favoured purchases in Kuwait souks is Kuwaiti gold frequently of 22 or 24 carats. All gold is stamped with a hallmark revealing its gold content. The weight usually decides an item's price but additional charges may be added for workmanship. Old gold jewellery can be melted down and re-designed. The majority of dealers negotiate and discounts are often given.

Souks can also be good places to buy good value fabrics to have made into clothes by one of the many tailors that can be found in the region. In addition to selling the more interesting, traditional goods such as Bedouin coffee pots, Persian carpets, Kuwaiti doors, etc. the souks also sell the mundane necessities such as tools, appliances, beach towels, sandals, etc. They are a definite must for both visitor and resident.

OMAN

Currency

The unit of currency is the Omani Riyal (OR) which is divided into 1,000 baizas (baisas).
1 Omani Riyal (OR) £1.6044; £1 OR 0.6233
1 Omani Riyal (OR) US$2.5977; US$1 OR 0.3850

Introduction

Destination Oman

The official name of Oman is the Sultanate of Oman with the majority referring to it simply as Oman or the Sultanate. The local long form of the name is *Saltanat Uman* and the short form *Uman*. Oman is distinct from the other Gulf states not only because of its location on the eastern corner of the Arabian Peninsula which makes it technically not a Gulf country at all, but also because of its reputation as one of the most beautiful countries in the region with a relatively unspoilt coastline stretching 200 km and breath-taking areas of verdant mountains, turquoise sea and vast expanses of golden desert.

It was not until the current Sultan, Qaboos bin Said, seized power in a bloodless coup in 1970 that Oman began to undergo dramatic changes that have altered it from being one of the most backward and insular of the states to being a far more open and well-developed nation welcoming foreign visitors and residents. Not that long ago even other Gulf Arabs required visas to enter the Sultanate and in 1970 the country had only one hospital, two schools and 10 km of paved road. Now Oman has plenty of hospitals offering a very high standard of health care, hundreds of schools – state and private – catering for both boys and girls, and a network of highways linking the major cities and towns totalling some 32,800 km. In 1995 figures estimated a total of 40,000 tourists to the country a number which continues to rise annually as tourism is now actively promoted.

Oman intriguingly combines the ancient with the modern, most noticeably demonstrated in its capital city, Muscat, where old structures or ruins stand side by side with ultra-modern new buildings, museums with business centres, twentieth century five star hotels next to the remains of seventeenth century forts. Traditional souks are intermingled with brand new shopping malls selling the latest designer labels. In so many ways the country is extremely up-to-date in its outlook and yet its society still very much retains its distinctive Arab culture both in the traditional dress of the citizens – men wear white angle-length robes (*dishdasha*), women black silk robes – and the nation's strong commitment to Islam, respect for strangers and family solidarity.

Pros and Cons of Moving to Oman

Oman is not as wealthy as some of the other Gulf states and so the salaries and employment contracts tend to be less generous than those found in the rest of the Arabian Peninsula. Nevertheless wages are still higher than the equivalent you might expect in your home country and with no personal taxes to pay and accommodation or a housing allowance included in your employment package you will still find that working in Oman can be a lucrative move. The cost of public transport and daily items such as groceries may be slightly greater than in other Gulf states but buying a new car is still much cheaper than it would be in Europe or North America.

The night life and shopping in the Sultanate are certainly not what attracts individuals to this country as both fall far short of what can be found in the neighbouring UAE. However, Oman excels in its favourable climate and stunning natural landscape that continually draws thousands of visitors to the country for desert driving and camping and general exploration of the mountains, unspoilt coastal regions and green valleys. Although Oman has modernised over the last 30 years or so, it has developed at a steady pace retaining its traditional and historical aura amidst a not too overbearing presence of the new.

Omanis are on the whole a very relaxed and hospitable nation and despite upholding strong Islamic principles and laws (see Gulf States' 'General Introduction' chapter) they place few restrictions upon the expatriate lifestyle within their country. Individuals of faiths other than Islam are free to openly practice their beliefs. Women can shop, drive and work relatively freely compared to limitations placed on them in other states such as Saudi Arabia. They are not required to wear an *abaya* but should dress conservatively in public places, i.e. cover chest, upper arms and knees. Alcohol can be bought by resident expatriates in possession of a liquor licence at certain outlets and all the major international hotels have bars where foreigners can drink. Strict penalties are imposed on offenders in the country, no matter of what nationality they may be, but this may be a very positive condition as the rate of crime in the country is much lower than in European or North American nations.

If you intend to stay in Oman for a long time a car is practically essential as the public transport system, although cheap, is very unreliable. As in the other Gulf states, the driving standard on the roads tends to be poor and accidents are not uncommon but Oman is definitely not quite as bad as the other countries.

From a Western perspective, the main pros and cons of living in the Sultanate of Oman can be summarised as follows:

Pros: Higher wages than in your home country.
No personal taxes to pay.
Welcoming Omani nationals.
Very sociable expatriate community.
Low crime rate.
English widely spoken.
Extensive range of water and land sports.
One of the most favourable climates in the Gulf.
Some of the most breath-taking scenery that can be found in the Gulf.

Cons: Salaries and employment packages not as good as in other Gulf countries.
Cost of daily living slightly higher than in the rest of the Arabian Peninsula.
Limited night life.
Unreliable public transport system.
Education and hospital fees expensive.

Political and Economic Structure

Oman is one of the oldest states on the Arabian peninsula and was once an important Sultanate whose power was in evidence as far away as Zanzibar and Pakistan. Its

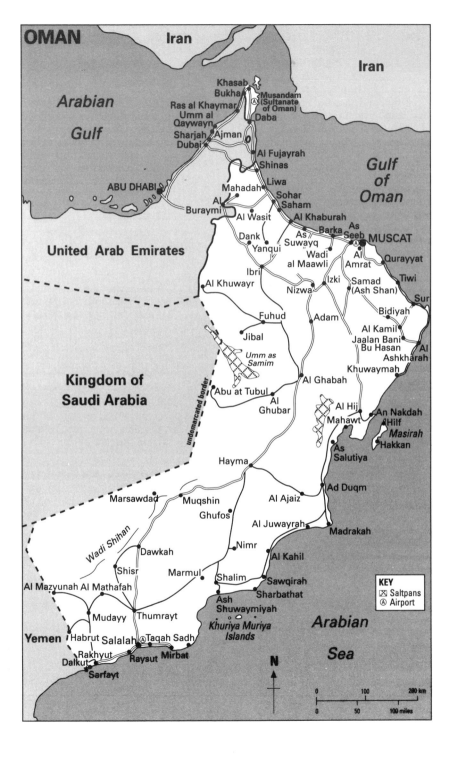

population and culture reflects a combination of African, Indian and Arabian influences with a hint of British practices and customs inherited from their rule in the mid-nineteenth to mid-twentieth centuries. For a more detailed history of the area see the *Reading List*.

Although Oman does not have the profuse oil wealth of its neighbour, the United Arab Emirates, the standard of living in Oman is still much higher than in several of the other Arab countries. Since the present Sultan came to power in 1970, the economy has become one of the best managed in the region and modernisation programmes have ensured that even the most remote mountain villages are serviced by roads, electricity, water, health clinics and schools. Prior to the discovery of oil in the country, Oman's underdeveloped economy was supported by subsistence agriculture and fishing.

The Economy

Oman's economy is heavily dependent on its oil exports which account for over 90 per cent of the country's GDP (Gross Domestic Product) and nearly all of its export income. Due to its desert land Oman's agriculture is limited to the coastal plain and a few irrigated regions inland. Limes, dates, and alfalfa (a plant which is used commercially as a source of chlorophyll) are the chief products; some livestock is also reared. Mineral deposits of copper, chromite, marble, gypsum and limestone are also being exploited with manganese ore and coal reserves yet to be extracted and processed.

Oil revenues have greatly contributed to the advanced development of other industries in Oman such as construction, agriculture and tourism, as well as aiding the make up of the country's infrastructure. Oman's principal trading partners include the UAE, Iran, the UK, Japan and Germany.

Government plans to strengthen the country's economy include: promoting 'Omanisation' – the replacement of expatriate workers with Omani nationals, diversification of the economy, increase and active encouragement of domestic and foreign private investment, implementation of privatisation programmes in the services sector, and onward progress with natural gas based projects.

Government

The Sultanate of Oman is an absolute monarchy headed by Sultan Qaboos bin Said, who is not only ruler of the country but Prime Minister, Foreign Minister and Minister of Defense also. Sultan Qaboos took office in 1970 replacing his father Sultan Said bin Taimar. In 1981, a 55 member State Consultative Council was created to increase participation by the Omani people in the country's politics. This Council was then replaced in 1990 by the *Majlis ash-Shura*, an elected assembly which convened for the first time in January 1992. Ultimate power still lies in the hands of the Sultan, who makes all the final decisions and can negate election results, but an elected assembly is a first – be it minor – step towards a more democratic government. Suffrage is restricted to about 50,000 Omanis selected by the government to vote in elections for the Majlis ash-Shura, which only has advisory powers. Political parties are not permitted. The country's first written constitution was drawn up in November 1996 and outlines the basic system by which the Sultanate is governed.

Despite the somewhat autocratic nature of his rule Sultan Qaboos has shown that he only has his country's best interests at heart and has successfully modernised Oman without loosing sight of its history and tradition.

Geographical Information

Area and Main Physical Features

The Sultanate of Oman covers a land area of 212,460 square kilometres and has a coastline stretching 2,092 km along the Indian Ocean and the Arabian Gulf. It is situated on the south-eastern tip of the Arabian peninsula bordered by the Kingdom of Saudi Arabia to its west and the Republic of Yemen to its south. To the north-west of Oman is the United Arab Emirates and to the east is the Arabian Sea and Gulf of Oman.

Oman is mainly a low-lying country comprising a vast central desert plain with rugged mountains in northern and southern regions. Its highest peak is 2,980 m at Jabal ash Sham. The northern coastal strip is separated from the rest of Arabia by the Hajar mountains beyond which lies the Empty Quarter desert.

Population

The population of Oman is currently estimated at 2,363,591 of which the majority are Omani nationals and about 26.6 per cent are expatriates from other Arab countries, Baluchi, South Asia (India, Pakistan, Sri Lanka, Bangladesh), Africa and western countries (Europe, America, etc.). Population growth is 3.45 per cent per annum. 75 per cent of the population are Ibadhi Muslim, the remaining 25 per cent are from other faiths mainly: Sunni Muslim, Shi'a Muslim and Hindu.

The official language of the country is Arabic but English, Swahili, Farsi, Baluchi, Urdu and other Indian dialects are widely spoken. Nearing 80 per cent of the population (aged 15 and over) are functionally literate.

Climate

Oman experiences a typical desert climate with sweltering hot summers (April to October) and pleasantly cooler and sunny winters (November to March). In the summer temperatures can reach an uncomfortable 49 degrees celcius with humidity levels reaching 90 per cent. The interior areas tend to be less humid than coastal regions but equally hot. In the far south of the country there is the risk of a south-west summer monsoon occuring in May to September and the effects of the summer winds can also incite large sandstorms and dust storms in the interior from December to March. Additionally, periodic droughts are a prominent feature during the summer. Rainfall is infrequent and sporadic except in Salalah and the southern province of Dhofar where light showers occur from June to September/October.

Weather Chart

Average temperature (Celcius), rainfall (mm), sunshine in hours per day, humidity percentage.

Muscat	Jan	Feb	Mar	Apr	May	Jun	Jul	Aug	Sep	Oct	Nov	Dec
Max	25	25	28	32	37	38	36	33	34	34	30	20
Min	19	19	22	26	30	31	31	29	28	27	23	20
Rainfall	26	20	8	10	0	0	0	0	0	0	5	20
Rainy Days	2	1	1	1	0	0	0	0	0	0	1	2
Sunshine	9	10	9	11	12	12	9	10	11	10	10	9
Humidity	72	73	71	66	59	72	77	81	76	72	71	71

Regional Guide

The majority of Oman's population live on the Batinah Coastal Plain where 40 per cent of arable land is located. However, the urban population is growing at an estimated 17 per cent a year as people move away from agricultural rural areas towards the cities and towns. 622,506 people live in the capital Muscat, 538,763 in Al Batinah and 85,000 in Salalah and its suburbs. Oman is divided into five municipalities for administrative purposes: Greater Muttrah (referred to as the capital or capital area), Bowsher, Seeb, Amerat and Quriyat. Greater Muttrah is the most populated area and the location of the political capital Muscat, the modern port of Muttrah and the commercial and residential area of Ruwi.

Information Facilities

There is no official Omani tourist office as such but information about the country can be obtained either from your local embassy (see addresses below) or from the *Directorate General of Tourism*, Ministry of Commerce and Industry, PO Box 550, Muscat, Postal Code 113, Sultanate of Oman; tel +968 7717085; fax +968 7714213; e-mail tourism@mocioman.org Website www.mocioman.org. Other sources of information are the local hotels such as the *Crowne Plaza Muscat* (PO Box 1455, Ruwi, Sultanate of Oman; tel +968 560100; fax +968 560650; e-mail mcthc@interconti.com Website www.crowneplaza.com) and the *Hamdan Plaza Hotel* (PO Box 190, Salalah, Postal Code 211, Sultanate of Oman; tel +968 211025/6/7; fax +968 211187), or from local tour operators such as those listed below or found in the local yellow pages (www.omanyellowpages.com):

Al-Ghadeer Tours & Services: PO Box 103, PC 111, Airport, Sultanate of Oman; fax +968 590558; e-mail alghadeertours@hotmail.com
National Travel and Tourism: tel +968 566046; fax +968 566125. Long established company offering city, dhow, cultural and camel tours.
Oman Tourism and Travel Agencies: PO Box 2246, Ruwi 111, Sultanate of Oman; tel +968 704003; fax +968 790882.
Oman Travel and Tourism Bureau: tel +968 789845; fax +968 789843. Short and long tours covering most of what is on offer in Oman.
Zubair Tours: PO Box 833, Ruwi, P.C. 112, Oman; tel +968 708081; fax +968 787564; e-mail toursinb@alzubair.com Website www.alzubair.com

The following websites also provide handy notes on the country, what it has to offer, how to get there, etc.:

World Travel Guide: www.wtg-online.com
Excite Travel Pages: www.excite.com/travel
Oman Infoworld: www.Home.InfoRamp.Net/~emous/oman/govn.htm
Oman on the Net: www.members.tripod.com/~RUSTAQ/omanlinks.html
US Consular Information: www.travel.state.gov/oman.html
Oman Tourist Pages: www.nwet.co.uk
Oman Net: www.omanet.com

Useful Addresses

Embassy of the Sultanate of Oman: 167 Queen's Gate, London SW7 5HE; tel 020-7225 001; fax 020-7589 2505.
British Embassy: PO Box 300, P.C. 113, Muscat, Sultanate of Oman; tel +968 693077; fax +968 693087.

Embassy of the Sultanate of Oman: 2535 Belmont Road, NW, Washington, DC 20008, USA; tel +1 202 387-1980/2; fax +1 202 745-4933.
Embassy of the United States of America: PO Box 202, Medinat Al-Sultan Qaboos, P.C. 115, Muscat, Sultanate of Oman; tel +968 698-989; fax +968 699-771; e-mail aemctcns@gto.net.om Website www.usia.gov/posts/muscat

GREATER MUTTRAH

Muscat/Ruwi/Matrah (Muttrah)

The capital of Oman and the hub of its political, economic and commercial affairs, Muscat is also the site of the Sultan's home palace. It is in fact not just one city but rather an amalgamation of three urban regions (Muscat, Ruwi, Matrah) and a number of districts covering a 130 square kilometre (80 sq. mile) area. Due to the hills dispersed throughout the area, the three towns have maintained their own distinct entities. Muscat is the old port region and the location of the Sultan's palace. Matrah (or Muttrah) is the chief trading and residential port area. Ruwi is the capital's up-to-date commercial district.

Of the three towns, Muscat has perhaps the most to offer visitors. It lies on a crescent-shaped bay with a backdrop of jagged mountains. Its original city walls are still intact and its ancient souq is renowned for being one of the most interesting in the Gulf States. There are plenty of forts and museums to visit, in addition to the Alam Palace and the Zawawi Mosque. Within just half an hour's drive can be found excellent beaches.

Ruwi is situated inland and is the commercial headquarters of the country. Most business trips to the capital will be centred here.

Matrah has a large harbour (which has one side for modern ships and the other for traditional dhows) and acts as the main port of the capital region.

NORTH OF MUSCAT

Buraimi is an oasis town famous for its spices and palm products and formerly used as a vital stop along a caravan route. It is situated 290 km (180 miles) north-west of Muscat and now shares the oasis with the UAE's town, Al-Ain. The primary purpose of travelling here is to cross the border into the United Arab Emirates and compare the two nation's cultures. Al-Ain is more prosperous than Buraimi and offers its visitors a mixture of both modern and ancient in its attractions: old forts, museums, shopping (traditional and modern), and a zoo.
Musandam Peninsula is 400 km (250 miles) north-west of Muscat and about a three day drive from the capital. It was formerly a military zone and has only lately been open to tourist visits. The region is cut off from the rest of the country by the poorer coastal emirates of the UAE. Here, on this wild and barren land of ochre mountains, reputedly can be found the most breathe-taking scenery in the Arabian Peninsula. Not easy to get to but definitely worth all attempts to make it there.

SOUTH OF MUSCAT

Ibri situated 220 km (140 miles) south-west of Muscat is well-known for its indigo dyeing and weaving industries. Nearby is the deserted village of Sulaif worth visiting because of its town's traditional architecture.
Nizwa has become one of Oman's leading tourist centres renowned for its eight kilometre long palm oasis and its souq specialising in daggers, silver and brass items. Other attractions include its seventeenth century tower and well-preserved irrigation system (*falaj*). Surrouding villages are also worth seeing for their preservation of the traditional. Nizwa is situated 125 km (80 miles) south-west of Muscat.

Sur is located 160 km (100 miles) south-east of Muscat and is best reached from there by dhow. Alternatively a four-wheel-drive vehicle could be used to drive along the coastal road, which takes you through mountains, river valleys and along glorious empty beaches. Sur is a sea-faring town, a fishing village and a trading port where visitors can still observe the construction of traditional dhows by hand.

Wadi Nakh Gorge located 140 km (90 miles) south-west of Muscat, is an enormous gorge that is comparable in beauty to the Grand Canyon in the USA. The country's highest mountains and sheer cliffs are located here and the view overlooking the rocky river valley is truly amazing. For those willing to brave it, they can take a four hour hike down past cliff dwellings and terraces crammed onto narrow ledges halfway down the gorge.

Wahibah Sands are a collection of rolling desert sand dunes situated 135 km (85 miles) south of Muscat and covering a large part of north-eastern Oman. Bedouins are the only inhabitants of the area but their camels have mostly been traded in for four-wheel-drives.

DHOFAR

The region of Dhofar is located in the far south of Oman, 740km (460 miles) south west of Muscat by sea and 1,040 km (646 miles) south of Muscat by road and 1 hour 15 minutes by air from Seeb International Airport. The area comprises the coastal plain, the mountains and the desert and is renowned for its green valleys, tropical plantations and verdant wooded mountains. This region is also the home of the legendary Queen of Sheba. Thousands are drawn to this area every year not only to marvel at its natural beauty but to soak up the welcoming atmosphere of the people and discover the wealth of history that is harboured here.

Salalah the second largest of Oman's cities, is the capital of the Dhofar region of Oman and the birthplace of Sultan Qaboos. The city was once known as Zufar and was an important centre on the trade route between the 10th and 15th centuries. Its coastline runs along the Indian Ocean and its superb beaches have attracted many tourists to the area. Salalah is renown for its water sports and high quality seafood restaurants. It is a tropical city, verdant and peaceful with banana plantations surrounding it inland and stretches of sandy beaches on its shores. It makes a perfect base for those wishing to explore the neighbouring mountains and/or see the nearby excavation of an eleventh century village. Other attractions the city has to offer include a fantastic incense market, ruins of forts and the ruins of the Queen of Sheba's Palace at Khawr Rhori (also known as Sumhurram). Salalah is connected to Muscat by high standard modern roads.

Marbat. The town of Marbat was once the capital of Dhofar and is situated 66 km (40 miles) east of Salalah on the coast. It reputedly derived its name from *Marbat Al Khali* which literally means a place where horses are tied. Formerly famous for breeding and exporting horses as well as for the export of frankincense, the place is now famed for its export of dried fish and abalone (dried molluscs). Both a modern and ancient harbour can be found in the town reflecting the mix of old and new found within the area.

Taqah. Located 30 km (19 miles) from Salalah on the coast this town is the third largest in size in Dhofar after Salalah and Thumrayt. Taqah is well-known for its sardines which are sun-dried and used as cattle fodder and fertilisers.

Wadi Darbat. A natural park situated 32 km (20 miles) from Taqah, Wadi Darbat is famous for its awe-inspiring waterfalls, lakes and mountains, caves and wildlife. The largest natural cave in Oman is considered to be located here.

Mughsayl. 40 km (24 miles) west of Salalah, Mughsayl has some of the most beautiful beaches in Oman outlined by sculptured cliffs and blow holes formed in the limestone rocks where water plumes can reach a height of 98 feet (30 metres) or more. Khawr Mughsayl lies close by and is famed for its bird life.

Thumrayt is situated about 80 km (49 miles) from Salalah on the main road connecting Dhofar to the rest of Oman. It was once a major centre for those on caravan routes through the Arabian Peninsula and frankincense trees used to flourish here.

Sadh is a fishing village located 135 km (83 miles) east of Salalah. It is a popular site for camping and boating. An old fort can be found in the village and nearby stand the ruins of the ancient town of Muhalia.

Halaaniyaat Islands (or Juzor Al Halaaniyaat) lie about 50 km (31 miles) off the coast of Hasik. Located in the heart of the group of islands is the largest in size, Al Halaaniyah. These islands attract visitors for their beaches and extensive range of bird life.

Getting to Oman

Air

Flying is probably the easiest option of getting to Oman. The country operates two national airlines: *Gulf Air (GF)* which is co-owned with the governments of Abu Dhabi, Bahrain and Qatar, and *Oman Air*. *British Airways, Emirates, KLM, Kuwait Airways*, and *Lufthansa* are among the other airlines that service the region. The flight from Muscat to London lasts about 8 hours. Oman's international airport, *Seeb International Airport*, is situated 40 km (25 miles) west of Muscat. There are plans to establish another international airport in Sohar.

Sea

Sultan Qaboos and Mina Raysut are the country's major ports but traffic is mainly commercial.

Road

Land travel into Oman is only permitted with prior government consent. The favoured route is the north-south road from Muscat to Salalah, a journey of about 10-12 hours. Road travel through Saudi Arabia and the UAE is extremely restricted.

Useful Numbers

Airlines
British Airways: 0345-222111.
Emirates: 0870-2432222.
Gulf Air: 020-7408 1717.
KLM: 0990-7509000.
Kuwait Airways: 020-7412 0006.
Lufthansa: 020-8750 3500.
Oman Air: +968 707222/705140.

Insurance

All visitors to Oman are strongly recommended to take out comprehensive travel insurance. A list of addresses for some of the major insurers offering reasonable and flexible premiums can be found in the *Getting to Bahrain* chapter under 'Insurance.'

Useful Publications

Insight Guide: Oman and the United Arab Emirates, 1998, £16.95, ISBN 962-421-418-2.

Lonely Planet: Middle East on a Shoestring, 1997, £13.99, ISBN 0-86442-407-8.

Residence and Entry Regulations

The Current Position

With the exception of other GCC nationals, all individuals entering the Sultanate of Oman must be in possession of a valid visa and 'No Objection Certificate' (NOC) available from the Royal Oman Police Immigration Department (tel +968 569606). Those who wish to enter the country by road can only do so if their visa or NOC details such validity and a specific point of entry. Foreign nationals who have lived in one of the other GCC states for a minimum of one year and possess a valid residence permit and labour card can acquire a tourist visa on arrival as long as they meet the required conditions concerning professional status. Further details can be obtained from your local Omani Embassy/Consulate.

Israeli nationals and those holding passports with a valid or expired visa for Israel will not be granted entry into or transit through Oman.

Tourist Visas

Tourist visas can be applied for at the Omani Embassy/Consulate in your home country. They are valid for a one month period from the date of issue which can be extended if needed. Costs vary according to nationality. Generally it takes about five working days to process an application. All applicants need an Omani sponsor (either a tour company or hotel in Oman or Omani resident), and evidence of return or onward tickets in order to have their request for a tourist visa processed. You may not take up employment in Oman during your stay on a tourist visa. To apply for a tourist visa you must submit to the Embassy/Consulate the following documents: a typed application form, completed and signed; a full passport with at least six months validity remaining; two passport-sized photographs; a fee; details of travel plans; proof of employment or evidence of sufficient funds to cover your visit; a stamped self-addressed envelope if applying by post.

Business Visas

Applications for business visas are similar to those for tourist visas but in addition to the above documents required by the Embassy/Consulate you must present a business letter or employer's certificate. Business visas allow the holder to carry out business during their stay in Oman and are valid for up to three months after the date of issue. They take about a week to process. However, you can obtain an express permit visa specifically designed for business visits only that can be issued more quickly and are valid for just two weeks.

Residence & Work Permits

Obtaining a labour clearance card (work permit) from the Ministry of Social Affairs and Labour is a prerequisite to working in Oman. The work permit is renewable annually for an unlimited period. Employers are responsible for arranging the issue of both work and residence permits. Residence permits are valid for a period of two years.

Registering with your Embassy/Consulate

On arrival in the Sultanate of Oman, expatriates should ensure that they register with the regional Embassy or Consulate of their home country. This registration enables the home country's authorities to keep emigrants up to date with any information they need to be informed of as foreign nationals resident overseas and also enables them to trace individuals in the event of an emergency. The Consulates can also assist with information concerning an emigrant's status overseas and advise on any diplomatic or passport problems. They may also be able to help in an emergency e.g. in the unfortunate event of the death of a relative abroad. However, the Consulates do not function as a source of general help and advice, nor act as an employment bureau and they make this quite evident in response to any such enquiries.

Useful Addresses

The above regulations concerning visas for Oman detail the latest information however due to small changes constantly being introduced you should always check the most recent facts by contacting one of the addresses listed below:

Embassy of the Sultanate of Oman: 167 Queen's Gate, London SW7 5HE; tel 020-7225 001; fax 020-7589 2505.

British Embassy: PO Box 300, P.C. 113, Muscat, Sultanate of Oman; tel +968 693077; fax +968 693087.

Embassy of the Sultanate of Oman: 2535 Belmont Road, NW, Washington, DC 20008, USA; tel +1 202 387-1980/2; fax +1 202 745-4933.

Embassy of the United States of America: PO Box 202, Medinat Al-Sultan Qaboos, P.C. 115, Muscat, Sultanate of Oman; tel +968 698-989; fax +968 699-771; e-mail aemctcns@gto.net.om Website www.usia.gov/posts/muscat

Ministry of Social Affairs & Labour: PO Box 560, Muscat, Oman; tel +968 602444.

Setting Up Home

Only Omani nationals and other GCC nationals are permitted to own property in the Sultanate of Oman. Consequently all other foreign nationals must rent housing. Many of the large companies and employers arrange accommodation for their employees or offer a specific housing allowance for you to seek your own home. Rents vary according to which city you are looking to live in and the standard of the accommodation which is generally quite high. Compared to the other Gulf States, the cost of living in Oman is quite steep. For example in Ruwi an apartment costs about OR 150 per month and the monthly cost of a villa ranges between OR 500 to OR 1,000. It is advisable to contact a real estate agent to assist you in finding housing such as the *ATC Apartment Service* (PO Box 129, Azaibah, Oman 130; tel/fax +968 605-091) or *Al Habib* (PO Box 2663, Postal Code 112, Sultanate of Oman; tel +968 701866; fax +968 707237; e-mail wilaya@ gto.net.om). Other agents can be found in the local yellow pages or by searching the directory on-line www.omanyellowpages.com. Friends or work colleagues can also advise you on your move and housing notices can be found in local papers. Additionally you may try contacting the Ministry of Housing (PO

Box 173, Muscat; tel +968 703366) for further details on expatriate accommodation in Oman.

Utilities

Electricity & Water

To have your home connected to the electricity and water mains you need to contact Oman's Ministry of Electricity and Water (MEW – address below). The water consumption charge for residential users is 2 baizas per gallon, for electricity it is from 10-30 baizas per kilowatt per hour dependent on the quantity consumed, the greater amount, the higher the charge. Monthly bills are issued detailing methods of payment. The MEW recommend that you clean your air conditioner regularly in order to save on electricity.

Water running from taps in domestic homes is safe to drink although buying bottled water for drinking is probably a much more palatable option. A 24 hour hotline (153) has been established by the MEW to handle any emergencies or complaints and to ensure continuing water supplies.

The electricity voltage in Oman is 220/240V AC. British style three pin plugs are used.

Gas

Gas is widely used in homes for cooking appliances and cylinders can be bought from and delivered by local gas companies (see list below or consult your regional yellow pages www.omanyellowpages.com).

Telephones

Oman Telecommunications Company (OMANTEL) operates the Sultanate's wide range of up-to-date telecommunication services full details of which can be accessed on their website (see address below). To obtain a residential telephone line you must submit a completed application form (available from OMANTEL), a contact telephone number, a copy of your identity/Labour card or passport, and a guarantee letter from your sponsor undertaking to settle outstanding bills in case of default *or* a deposit of OR 400; for internet services a deposit of OR 100 is required.

For more information see the *Telephones* section in *Daily Life* chapter.

Useful Numbers

OMANTEL Switch Board	696844
International Directory Enquiries	143
National Directory Enquiries	198
OMANTEL Customer Care	699910
GSM Customer Care	196
Internet Customer Care	693379
Billing Enquiries	194
Telephone Faults/Complaints	192
Mobile Telephone Faults	593960

Useful Addresses

Ministry of Electricity & Water (MEW): PO Box 1491, Ruwi 112; tel +968 603800; fax +968 699183.

Oman Telecommunications Company (OMANTEL): Ministry of Posts, Telegraphs

& Telephones, PO Box 789, Ruwi, PC 112, Sultanate of Oman; tel +968 696844; fax +968 691338; telex 5400 OMANTELON; Website www.gto.net.om.

Gas Companies

Al Kindi Gas – Abdul Hamid Al Kindi: PO Box 500, Muscat 113, Sultanate of Oman; tel +968 706226/709836.

National Gas Company SAOG: PO Box 95, Rusayl 124, Oman; tel +968 626073; fax +968 626307.

Dhofar Gas Filling Co LLC: PO Box 1843, Salalah 211, Oman; tel +968 210882; fax +968 210813.

Muscat Manufacturers Co. for Industry & Cooking Gases: PO Box 2918, Ruwi 112, Oman; tel +968 626030/1; fax +968 626032.

Daily Life

The purpose of this chapter is to provide all the necessary practical information to successfully cope with a range of aspects of life in Oman so that armed with this knowledge your move to this unfamiliar country may be made that little less daunting.

Schools and Education

In Oman the education of both girls and boys is of great importance. Over the last 30 years the number of state schools has risen from just three to over 958 with the further development of over 100 schools underway. In 1997 five new private schools were opened making a total of 111 private schools in Oman regulated by the Ministry of Education (PO Box 3, Ruwi; tel +968 775209). The standard of education in both the public and private sectors is very high.

State schools offer free education to Omani nationals. Lessons are taught in Arabic with English taught as a second language. Such schools are segregated and teach children from the ages of six to seventeen preparing them for further education or advanced training at specialised colleges or at the Sultan Qaboos University. Pre-1970 there were no schools for girls, today girls comprise 48.6 per cent of the student population and in the private sector 41 per cent of the students are female.

Private schools cater for the children of expatriates from India, Pakistan, Arab and Western countries. The curriculum taught in these schools corresponds to that found in the child's home country so that the transition from studying in an international school in Oman to an institution in one's home country, or vice versa, is relatively easy with children being prepared for further education if that is what they wish to do. Contact individual schools for more details.

Useful Addresses

American International School of Muscat (ages 4-17): PO Box 202, Muscat 115, Sultanate of Oman; tel +968 600374; fax +968 697916; e-mail taism@gto.net.om

American-British Academy (ages 3-19): PO Box 372, Medinat Al Sultan Qaboos, PC 115, Sultanate of Oman; tel +968 603646; fax +968 603544; e-mail abaadoman@gto.net.om

The British School – Muscat (ages 3-18): PO Box 1907, Ruwi, PC 112, Sultanate of Oman; tel +968 600842; fax +968 601062; Website www.ecis.org/bsmuscat

Muscat Private School (ages 3-18+): PO Box 1031, Ruwi, PC 112, Sultanate of Oman; tel +968 565550; fax +968 560957.

The Sultan's School: PO Box 665, Seeb Code 121, Sultanate of Oman; tel +968 536777; fax +968 536273.

Further information on international schools and education in Oman can also be obtained from *The British Council* (PO Box 73, Postal Code 115, Madinat Al Sultan Qaboos, Sultanate of Oman; tel +968 600548; fax +968 699163; e-mail Colin.Hepburn@om.britishcouncil.org Website www.britishcouncil.org).

The Media, Post and Telecommunications

The Media

All printed matter, films and videos displaying scantily-dressed women, sexual contact between men and women, religious propaganda or politically-sensitive matter will be seized by the Ministry of Information (PO Box 600, Muscat 113; tel +968 603222/603888; fax +968 601638). Any books or personal videos discovered in luggage coming into the country will be reviewed by the Information Ministry to be returned (or not) to the owner in due course.

Television

An English news programme is broadcast daily on Omani television at 8pm and English language films are shown two or three nights a week generally at about 11pm. Satellite TV is available upon subscription and offers its viewers a range of programmes including the BBC World Service Television, entertainment and sports channels.

Radio

To find out the frequencies for the BBC World Service in Oman contact: tel 020-7557 1165; e-mail worldservice.letters@bbc.co.uk Website www.bbc.co.uk/worldservice. A monthly international programmes guide, *BBC On Air*, which includes information on World Service Radio, BBC World and BBC Prime television services can be obtained by contacting the BBC at tel 020-7557 2211; fax 020-7240 4899.

Books and Newspapers

Oman's main daily newspapers are: *Oman* (except Fridays), *Oman Arabic Daily*, and *Al Watan* – all in Arabic, and *Times of Oman* and *Oman Daily Observer* – both published in the English language. Foreign newspapers and magazines can be bought from the bookshops in Muscat's five star hotels and in certain supermarkets and other bookshops, e.g. the Family Bookshop in Qurm. Outside Muscat it is more difficult to find foreign papers with the possible exception of at the Salalah Holiday Inn and Salalah Family Bookshop. A magazine-cum-handbook, *Oman Today* is published every two months and contains comprehensive listings of restaurants, clubs and activities for expatriates. It is widely available throughout the Sultanate at a cost of 500 baisa.

Bookshops do exist in Oman but outside of the capital are quite rare and do not stock much in the way of English language books. It is better to look for books in the bookstalls of the major hotels but paperbacks can be quite expensive, even double the price that they would cost if bought in your home country.

In Muscat there are three public libraries: the Oman Chamber of Commerce and Industry (tel +968 707674), the Public Technical Library (tel +968 773111), and the United States Information Service (+968 698989).

Post

Ordinary and registered air mail is received by and sent from Muscat daily. Surface mail from Muscat to Europe and North America takes from two to three months. Usually post offices are open Monday to Wednesday 8am to 1pm and 4pm to 7pm. They close at 11am on Thursdays and remain closed on Fridays. The General Post Office at Ruwi and the branch post office in Muscat both offer poste restante services by which you can receive mail.

Sending postcards within Oman costs 30 baisa, to other Gulf and Arab countries 50 baisa and to Europe and North America 150 baisa. Letters weighing less than 20 grammes cost 50 baisa to send within Oman, 80 baisa to other Gulf states, 100 baisa to other Arab countries and to everywhere else in the world there is a postal charge of 200 baisa for the first 10g, 350 baisa for 20g and OR 1 for post weighing anything between 20g and 50g. Stamps can be bought at post offices and yellow posting boxes are found in several shopping areas. Courier services are widely available.

Useful Addresses

DHL International: Rumaila 106, Sultan Qaboos Street, Wattayah, Muscat, Oman; tel +968 563599; fax +968 564179.
Fedex (Federal Express): Sinau House, Ruwi, Muscat, Oman; tel +968 7933111; fax +968 7735554.
Ministry of Posts, Telegraphs and Telephones: PO Box 338, Ruwi 112; tel +968 697888/698931; fax +968 696817/696670.

Telephones

The international dialling code for Oman is +968. There are no area codes in the country. Central public telephone offices can be found in both Muscat and Salalah in addition to a few smaller cities and towns. Card phones are commonly in use and pay phone cards are readily available at shops and supermarkets in OR 1, 3 and 5 denominations. Direct-dial charges are 25 baisa for 3 minutes locally, 300 baisa a minute to other GCC states, 600 to 750 baisa a minute to most other Arab countries, and OR 1 per minute to Europe and North America. International calls are at a discount rate between 10pm and 7am, all day Friday and some public holidays.

Useful Telephone Numbers

Emergencies	999
Water Emergencies	153
Police	560099
International Directory Enquiries	143
Internal Directory Enquiries	198
Faults & Complaints	192
Talking Pages	600100
Speaking Clock	140
Weather Information	1103

Cars and Motoring

The network of roads in Oman is of a relatively high standard and the quality of driving although not great is not as poor as in the other Gulf countries. However, driving at night between cities can be hazardous due to little or no lighting, roaming goats and camels and speeding drivers.

Driving Regulations

Driving is on the right hand side of the road and the speed limit on major roads is 120 kmph. Those caught drinking and driving will incur severe penalties and it is prohibited to drive on the beaches. All passengers in the front seat of cars must wear seat belts or pay a fine of OR 10. Car insurance is required by all drivers and can be arranged through local insurance companies (see local yellow pages for addresses www.omanyellowpages.com), travel agents and car hire firms (if renting vehicles). Make sure that you take out fully comprehensive insurance, never settle for just third party.

Visitors can drive on a valid international licence or their home country's licence but residents must apply for a valid Omani licence. You should carry your driving licence and other documentation such as car ownership details, insurance, etc. at all times. In the event of an accident you must not leave your vehicle or attempt to move it until the police (tel +968 510228/7) have assessed the situation.

Purchasing a Car

Purchasing a car in Oman is relatively easy and cost-effective compared to prices you would find in your home country. You may decide to either buy a new car (addresses of car dealers listed below) or if you want to be more economical, a second hand car. Advertisements for the sale of second hand cars can be found in the Classified section of local papers or on supermarket notice boards. Information on cars, as well as advertisers selling models can also be found on the internet at www.omanauto.com.

Useful Numbers

Al Hashar & Co.: +968 702555.
Arabian Car Marketing: +968 561377.
Bahwan Automotive Centre: +968 561377.
OMASCO: +968 560752.
Wattaya Motors: +968 562729.
Zubair Automotive: +968 590430.

Car Rental

To hire a car in Oman when staying on a business or tourist visa you must be in possession of a driving licence issued in your home country or an international driving licence valid for three months. Resident expatriates need to apply for an Omani licence. Generally this can be obtained on the strength of a foreign driving licence without any further test being required. The majority of hotels have self-drive car hire facilities. Car rental costs from about OR 75 to OR 100 per week for a saloon car, OR 180 to OR 260 for a 4WD vehicle. It is worth shopping around for the best deal as prices can vary greatly at different companies.

Useful Addresses

Avis: PO Box 833, Ruwi 112; tel +968 601224; fax +968 694885.
Budget Rent-A-Car: tel +968 794721; fax +968 794723.
Europcar: PO Box 3275, Ruwi 112; tel +968 700190; fax +968 794061.
Hertz: PO Box 962, Muscat 113; tel +968 566208; fax +968 566125.
Thrifty Car Rental: Al Haditha LLC, PO Box 198, Muttrah 114; tel +968 604248.

Transport

Air

Oman has six civil airports serviced by *Oman Air*, the national domestic carrier. There are daily scheduled flights to Salalah Airport and daily charter flights to Fahud and Marmul. Flights are also available to the Musandam Peninsula, Buraimi, Sur and the island of Masirah. You should book all flights well in advance and confirm that you are travelling on the day before departure.

Buses

Local bus services operate in the capital, Muscat and there are national services (twice daily) to Salalah by luxury coach from the bus stations at Ruwi and the Muttrah Corniche. The major centres of population are also connected by a superb network of minibuses which operate as 'service' taxis. For further details contact the *Oman National Transport Company (ONTC)*, PO Box 620, Muscat, Oman; tel +968 590046; fax +968 590152.

Taxis

Taxis are plentiful in Oman and are recognised for being orange and white saloon cars or mini-buses with an orange light on the front. However, by Gulf standards taxis in Oman are not cheap and although there should be some scale of charges most taxis do not have meters and all fares should be agreed upon in advance of travelling. Taxi fares from the airport to hotels in the centre cost from about OR 8. Courtesy pick-up services are arranged by some hotels and limousines can also be hired through certain hotels at a rate of approximately US$30 per hour.

Banking and Finance

The Omani Riyal is a convertible currency with no restrictions on its import or export. Banks and moneychangers will change currency and are situated throughout Oman in Muscat and major towns. Cash card machines abound in banks and shopping areas. Hotels, restaurants and larger shops all accept major credit cards. Moneychangers tend to be open from 9am to 1pm, and 4pm to 7pm, Saturday to Thursday, and on Fridays 4.30pm to 8pm. Banks offer a wide range of services comparable to those that you would find in a branch in your home country and are generally open from 8am to 12pm, Saturday to Wednesday and on Thursdays from 8am to 11.30am.

Offshore Banking

If you are working for a large company in the Gulf you are likely to be earning quite substantial amounts of money some of which you will undoubtedly be looking to invest. One of the primary financial advantages of being an expatriate is that you can invest this money offshore in tax havens such as the Isle of Man, the Channel Islands, Gibraltar and Bahrain, thus accruing tax-free interest on your savings. Many such facilities are as flexible as UK high street banking and range from current accounts to long-term, high interest earning deposits. For more details and addresses of offshore banking units see *Offshore Banking* section in 'Bahrain Daily Living' chapter.

Tax and the Expatriate

There is no income tax or social security for expatriates to pay in the Sultanate of Oman nor do any other taxes exist for foreign nationals resident in the country. As a non-resident of your home country (i.e. for UK nationals spending fewer than 183 days in aggregate in Britain) you will not be subject to your home country's tax on earnings either. For more details on what you may or may not be entitled to or subjected to regarding tax regulations (on earnings, relocation expenses, investments, etc.) as an expatriate you should consult a specialist tax advisor. Useful contacts can be found in magazines such as *The Expatriate* and the large accounting/financial advisory companies like PriceWaterhouseCoopers (Plumtree Court, London EC4A 4HT; tel 020-7583 5000; fax 020-7822 4652) publish handy booklets giving detailed information on the tax implications for foreign nationals working in other countries.

Health Care in Oman

Health care is provided free of charge to Omani citizens but foreign nationals have to pay for treatment which can be quite expensive. Local medical treatment varies in quality and can be inadequate so taking out health insurance to cover the cost of private medical care is vital. Although hospital emergency service is available there is no ambulance service in Oman as such. Malaria is a concern in the interior and on the Batinah Coast. More information on vaccinations and health precautions can be obtained by visiting the Center for Disease Control and Prevention's website www.cdc.gov.

Useful Addresses & Telephone Numbers

Ministry of Health: PO Box 393, Muscat, Oman; tel +968 602177; fax +968 601430.
Adam Hospital: +968 434055.
Al Buraimi Hospital: +968 650033.
Al Nahda Hospital: +968 707800.
Ibra Hospital: +968 470535.
Khoula Hospital: +968 563625.
Quriat Hospital: +968 645003.
Sultan Qaboos Hospital: +968 211151.
Royal Hospital: +968 592888.
Rustaq Hospital: +968 875055.
Sohar Hospital: +968 840299.

Private Medical Insurance

Private medical care in the Sultanate of Oman is of a very high standard but it is also by no means cheap. Taking out the proper health insurance cover for you and your family is essential when moving out to the Gulf.

BUPA International (Russell Mews, Brighton, BN1 2NR; tel 01273-208181; fax 01273-866583; e-mail advice@bupa-intl.com Website www.bupa-intl.com) has designed its own Lifeline scheme that offers maximum choice and flexibility. There are three levels of cover: Gold, Classic and Essential, all of which provide full refund for hospital accommodation and specialists' fees so you never need to be concerned about unexpected bills for in-patient treatment such as an operation. Cover for emergency ambulance charges and sports injuries is also standard. The Gold and Classic schemes offer out-patient treatment which may be a very wise precaution in Oman. The most comprehensive cover is available with the Gold scheme which includes the cost of primary care treatment and home nursing. BUPA International has a 24 hour multi-lingual service centre dedicated to their expatriate members with an experienced team on hand to deal with any queries. Claims are paid promptly in any currency that you require, and you are covered anywhere in the world. For more information call +44 (0) 1273-208181.

For more details on other international health insurance schemes available to the expatriate and contact addresses see *Private Medical Insurance* in 'Bahrain Daily Living Chapter.'

Omani Law

The legal system in Oman is largely based on English common law and Islamic law (see *Shari'a law* in Gulf States' 'General Introduction' chapter). In the business world, modern commercial law is employed based on legal systems in use in other parts of the Middle East and Europe. The Sultan holds ultimate authority in all cases.

Social Life

Oman has so much to occupy its visitor or expatriate resident in the way of sporting activities, clubs, museums, and other sights and attractions. Additionally, there are numerous very sociable expatriate associations and societies covering a wide range of interests to also keep you busy.

Entertainment

The nightlife in Oman is not exactly electrifying but there are still plenty of things you can do even if somewhat limited in their range. In Ruwi there are two cinemas showing English and Hindi films, and local language centres often hold weekly screenings of foreign language films. The larger hotels throughout the country also provide lively and varied programmes including discos, nightclubs and live music events. Details are advertised in the local press.

Sports

Oman is particularly noted for its extensive choice of water sports – scuba diving, snorkelling, wind surfing, etc. There is also an abundance of opportunities to pursue land sports such as rugby, football, squash, tennis, running, cycling, golf, etc., and of course desert driving (see *Desert Driving* in Gulf States' 'General Introduction' chapter). Most resident expatriates are members of health and fitness clubs at the large international hotels which have excellent facilities although can be quite expensive.

Useful Telephone Numbers
Blue Zone Watersports: +968 737293.
Capital Area Yacht Club: +968 560345.
Gulf Divers: +968 692217.
Oman Dive Centre: +968 950261.
Sunny Day Water Sports: +968 700712.

Museums and Parks

The many historical sites and amusement parks located throughout the Sultanate include the following:

Museums

Bait Fransa. (tel +968 736613) Omani French Museum situated in Muscat. Opened in 1992 to commemorate links between Oman and France from the end of the seventeenth century to the present day. Exhibits include jewellery, costumes, chests, maps and navigational equipment.

Armed Forces Museum. (tel +968 312654) Military museum housed in a building once used as a fort in Ruwi. Recreates a picture of the major military events in Oman's history.

Bait Al Zubair. (tel +968 736688) Museum located in old Muscat, displaying a private collection of the Zubair family that includes weapons, jewellery, costumes and photographs.

Children's Museum. (tel +968 605368) A 'hands-on' museum for young people located near Al Qurm Park.

Marine Science and Fisheries Centre. (tel +968 740061) Displays living examples of much of Oman's marine life and vast collection of shells.

National Museum. (tel +968 701289)

Natural History Museum. (tel +968 605400) Creates a picture of Oman's wildlife. Exhibits include displays on the Arabian Oryx, Tahr, Lynx, etc. as well as a large whale/dolphin hall and national herbarium.

Oman Museum. (tel +968 600946) Small museum located in Muscat giving an overview of Oman's history.

Petroleum Development Exhibition Centre. Located in Qurm this centre provides a comprehensive history of the exploration and production of oil in Oman.

Parks

Qurm Natural Park. Constituting part of a large nature reserve, Qurm Natural Park covers an area of 1,476 square km (570,000 square miles) making it one of the largest in the Greater Muttrah municipality. Among its attractions are the tidal creeks of the mangrove forest situated in the grounds serving as the habitat for a wide variety of wildlife. There is also a boating lake with suspension bridge and fountain, as well as a newly opened fun fair offering rides and games for children and adults.

Wadi Kabir Park. Located in the Greater Muttrah municipality this small park offers visitors the chance to view a wide range of wildlife. The park also has a children's play area and fun fair.

Shopping

Oman is not a shopping haven like Dubai or Abu Dhabi in the UAE, but almost anything that you would want to buy is available if you know where to look. The shopping malls in Muscat sell nearly all the major international brand names and the larger supermarkets such as Al Fair, Spinney's and Prisunic, cater for most needs. The most economical way to buy fresh fruit, vegetables and fish is from the local souks. Souks are also great places to purchase local handicrafts and undergo a more traditional shopping experience. Shopping malls tend to open from about 9am to 1pm and 5pm to 10pm, Saturday to Thursday, and on Fridays 4.30pm to 9 or 10pm.

QATAR

Currency

The unit of currency is the Qatari riyal (QR) which is divided into 100 fils.
1 Qatari Riyal (QR) £0.1697; £1 QR 5.8924
1 Qatari Riyal (QR) US$0.2748; US$1 QR 3.6393

Introduction

Destination Qatar

The official name of Qatar is the State of Qatar with many simply referring to it as Qatar. The local long form is *Dawlat Qatar* and the short form, *Qatar* (pronounced *cat-ter*). Qatar is by no means top of anyone's Gulf destination list which may have a lot to do with its unfortunate reputation for being the dullest of the Gulf States. Admittedly the country does lack the lively expatriate night life found in either Bahrain or the UAE and yet it does offer more by way of evening entertainment than its neighbour, Saudi Arabia where even cinemas are non-existent.

Although local laws and customs are very much dictated to by conservative Islamic beliefs and practices, the atmosphere of Qatar is generally considered to be far more relaxed than that found in Saudi Arabia. Like the other Gulf states, Qatar is a mixture of the very old and the ultra-modern in terms of technology and architecture, etc. It is not yet as westernised as Bahrain and the UAE, nor is it as deeply rooted in its past as Saudi Arabia, but it is a country in transition that despite its modernisation will undoubtedly retain its traditional values, customs and culture. It may be a small quiet country but as this chapter will aim to show, it still possesses its own attractions that make it an exciting, challenging and engaging destination for anyone choosing to live in the Gulf.

Qatar's economy is still very much dependent on its limited oil reserves and like the other Gulf states the government is implementing a number of plans to aid the diversification of the economy. The proposed measures involve the further development of new industrial and residential centres such as Al-Khor and Ras Laffan Industrial City. Despite moves to replace the expatriate work force with Qatari nationals, the expertise of foreign workers is still very much in demand and with a greater emphasis being placed on the gradually emerging tourism sector, Qatar is definitely worth considering as a possible, and potentially very lucrative and interesting, destination for employment.

Pros and Cons of Moving to Qatar

It cannot be denied that the majority of expatriates who take up employment and residency in Qatar are initially drawn just by the excellent work opportunities and contracts that are available in the country. Employment contracts generally include not only a much higher wage than the equivalent which would be earnt in other countries but also accommodation or a housing allowance, utilities, travel to and from your home country once a year, and additional bonuses – both financial and otherwise, e.g. the handling of all paperwork involved in acquiring visas, etc., use of a company car, and so on. However, there is also the attraction of setting up a fresh life in a new environment in a country totally unfamiliar to what you are accustomed to.

Qatar may not be the most interesting of the states to live in and yet neither is it entirely without its good points. However, those of you who are single are strongly advised against coming here as the social life in the state is very much orientated around couples and families. Most socialising is within expatriate circles within private homes as opposed to public places as the choices are somewhat limited. There are an abundance of restaurants in the country serving good food from around the world, and there are hotels, bars and cinemas but apart from the numerous societies and sporting activities available there really is little else. Alcohol is available to residents with liquor licences but in restricted quantities from specified outlets.

The small size of the state makes Qatar feel to some a bit like living in a village atmosphere especially as the expatriate community is such a close network. You are unlikely to have much opportunity to become friends with any Qatari nationals but if you are lucky enough to do so, you will find, as with all other Gulf Arabs, that they are a particularly hospitable people who place great weight on the family unit and family honour.

Some of the positive aspects of living in Qatar are that it has a highly advanced and efficient telecommunications network, it has a number of very good international schools catering for the children of expatriates, the cost of living is relatively low and with no personal taxes to pay on your earnings you will have even more money spare to save or spend as you wish, and there is hardly any crime in the state. It may not have the abundance of natural beauty that somewhere like Oman does, and yet there are places of scenic brilliance that you can visit within the country and at the end of the day it is quite easy to visit the neighbouring Gulf states whenever you feel the need to do so.

From a Western perspective, the main pros and cons of living in Qatar can be summarised as follows:

Pros: High salaries, no personal taxes to pay.
Relatively low cost of living.
Low crime rate.
Excellent advanced telecommunications facilities.
High standard of education available to expatriates in international schools.
Wide range of leisure and social activities available.

Cons: Small country that can feel a bit confining.
Social life tends to revolve around married couples and families.
Scorching summer months.

Political and Economic Structure

Although archaeological findings have established that people did inhabit the Qatari peninsula in the Stone Age, there is virtually no evidence of habitation between that era up until about the mid-eighteenth century. It was at this time that the current ruling Al-Thani family began to rise to power. Originally a tribe of nomadic Bedouins, the Al-Thanis became pearl divers and fishers in the coastal regions of Qatar due to the extreme infertility of the inland areas.

Pearling, fishing and trade sustained the country's economy – such as it was – during this time. However, even before the collapse of the Gulf pearl in the world market, Qatar had never experienced much wealth or prosperity and

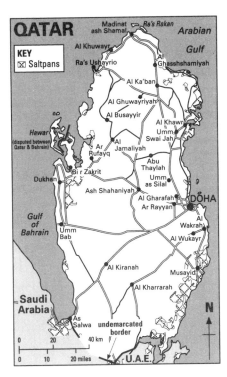

suffered a period of great poverty until the discovery of oil in the country in 1939.

For a more detailed history of the region see the *Reading List*.

The Economy

Oil is the mainstay of Qatar's economy accounting for about 75 per cent of its GDP (Gross Domestic Product). Due to the success of its oil industry Qatar has a per capita GDP comparable to the major West European industrial countries. However, Qatar's reliance on oil prices also means that its economy is particularly vulnerable to any changes that may occur in the world market so the country is working hard to capitalise on its assets, such as its proven natural gas reserves that have been rated third largest in the world, and to diversify its economy.

A promising tourism industry is currently under development in Qatar which brings healthy prospects for other sectors such as construction. With ongoing expansion plans in the oil, gas and petrochemicals industries as well, Qatar's economy appears to have a very bright and stable future ahead of it.

Government

Qatar is an independent, sovereign state presently ruled by the emir, Shaikh Hamad bin Khalifa Al-Thani. The Al-Thani family have officially been in power since the nineteenth century. The provisional Constitution of 1970 (known also as the Basic Law) inaugurated the emir as absolute ruler to abide by the tenets of justice, honesty, the Islamic religion, mutual respect and generosity. There are no political parties and no central government elections. The emir governs with the assistance of his Cabinet, the Council of Ministers, and a supreme legislative body, the Advisory Council. All 35 members of the existing Advisory Council are appointed by the emir. Ministers constitute the Council for the most part and can only advise on policy matters and legislation, the emir holds sole authority over any final decision-making.

Geographical Information

Area and Main Physical Features

Qatar is a peninsula, jutting out from the west coast of the Arabian Gulf, covering a land area of 11,437 square kilometres (including its islands and reefs). Approximately 160 kms in length and 80 kms in width at its widest point, the country mainly comprises very flat desert terrain, rising only to 110 m at its highest peak. The majority of the country is surrounded by water (its coastline is over 700 kms long), but Qatar does share with Saudi Arabia a land border of 60 kms. Coastal areas are generally characterised by salt flats (*sabkha*), whilst in the south-east of the country there are spectacular stretches of sand dunes rising to 60 m. Near the west coast are naturally eroded limestone plateaux that have left sphynx-like sculptures.

Several islands lie off the coast of Qatar, the most notable of these being Halul and the Hawar Islands. The former is situated 90 kms off the east coast and is used as an oil processing, storage and export terminal. The latter Islands are to the west and their ownership status is currently under dispute between Qatar and Bahrain. The International Court of Justice is to resolve the matter.

Population

Latest figures estimate that the population of Qatar is currently 697,126 only 20 per cent of which are Qatari nationals. The remaining 80 per cent of residents are expatriates mainly from the Indian sub-continent, other Arab countries (particularly Egypt, Jordan, Palestine and Syria) and the Philippines. Population growth is 3.82 per cent per annum. 95 per cent of the country is Muslim.

The official language of Qatar is Arabic but English is in common use. Approaching 80 per cent of the country are functionally literate.

Climate

Qatar experiences a typical desert climate. The winter seasons, usually from October through to April, are mild with very little (though sporadic) rainfall frequently in the form of tempestuous storms. Average temperatures at this time of year are from 20-30 degrees celcius, whilst in the sweltering summer months they can rise to over 40 degrees celcius. There is a high risk of sun stroke and heat exhaustion in the summer, not only due to the temperatures but also because humidity levels can reach 95 per cent. The lack of rain and consistent high temperatures give rise to poor soil conditions and sparse vegetation. When desert flora can be found it is quite amazing in its variety, especially just after a burst of rain which results in the desert 'coming alive' for a few days. Any agriculture in the country depends upon irrigation. Even the date palms found in the towns and 'farming' areas only survive due to continuous watering. The main source of water comes from desalination plants. Limited water can be irrigated from a restricted number of underground wells.

Weather Chart

Average temperature (Celcius), rainfall (mm), sunshine in hours per day, humidity percentage.

	Jan	Feb	Mar	Apr	May	Jun	Jul	Aug	Sep	Oct	Nov	Dec
Doha												
Max	22	24	28	31	36	39	40	40	38	34	30	24
Min	10	12	14	18	22	25	27	26	23	20	15	12
Rainfall	4	26	25	8	0	0	0	0	0	0	24	25
Rainy Days	2	2	1	1	0	0	0	0	0	0	1	2
Sunshine	8	9	8	10	11	11	11	10	10	10	10	8
Humidity	78	77	75	71	67	67	68	70	70	68	75	81

Regional Guide

An estimated 80 per cent of the population of Qatar live in its capital city, Doha. The remaining residents are situated in the smaller towns and major cities such as Al Rayyan, Ras Laffan Industrial City, Al Khor, Umm Said, Dukhan and Messaieed. Very few inhabit the rural areas.

Qatar does not as yet have an official tourist information office but you can find out more about the country by contacting either the *Qatar National Hotels Company* (PO Box 2977, Doha, Qatar; tel +974 495309; fax +974 436906) or one of the embassies listed below or by visiting one of the listed websites:

Useful Addresses

Embassy of the State of Qatar: 1 South Audley Street, London W1Y 5DQ; tel 020-7493 2200; fax 020-7493 2819.
British Embassy: PO Box 3, Doha, Qatar; tel +974 421991; fax +974 438692; e-mail british.embassy@doha.mail.fco.gov.uk
Embassy of the State of Qatar: 4200 Wisconsin Avenue, Suite 200, NW, Washington, DC 20016, USA; tel +1 202 274-1600; fax +1 202 237-0061.
Embassy of the United States of America: PO Box 2399, Doha, Qatar; tel +974 864701/3; fax +974 861669; e-mail usisdoha@qatar.net.qa Website www.qatar.net.qa/usisdoha/

Useful Websites

Arab Net: www.arab.net
Excite Travel: www.excite.com/travel
Internet Qatar: www.qatar.net
Middle East Travel: www.mideasttravelnet.com
Qatar Info: www.qatar-info.com
World Travel Guide: www.wtg-online.com

DOHA

Doha, once a scarcely populated fishing village, is now the location of Qatar's government, airport, seaport, hotels and recreational/sports facilities, major communications centres, and mostly everything with the exception of the oil and gas related industries. The hub of the city is its Corniche, a 7 km coastal causeway, along which the majority of the key structures are situated including the Emiri Diwan (royal palace), several ministries and three of the large hotels. Few old buildings remain standing in the capital but those that do can be found in the down town souk area or in the National Museum. Other tourist attractions include an Ethnographic Museum, Doha Fort, a Postal Museum, a zoo and amusement park. Doha is not known to be a particularly 'buzzing' place (in Western terms) but it offers a definite city atmosphere and there are of course always ample opportunities to pursue the traditional pastimes of wadi bashing and watching camel races, and exploring the rest of the country.

THE NORTH

Most of the country's historic sites can be found in the northern region including Umm Salal Mohammed and Zubara. Other significant towns in this area are listed below.

Al Rayyan.

Al Rayyan, situated 10 kms north of Doha, is currently the second most populated area outside the capital. It is the location of the Qatar Equestrian Federation which every year arranges over fifteen race meetings and an annual Arabian horse show.

Ras Laffan Industrial City.

Its prime location on the north coast of the Qatari peninsular and at the heart of the Arabian Gulf makes Ras Laffan Industrial city one of the world's most prominent and accessible emergent industrial export places. Development of this area is currently underway.

Al-Khor.

Al-Khor, situated on the north-east coast, is set to become the second largest urban area in Qatar. Plans are underway not only to develop it as an industrial complex and leading residential area, but to make it a major tourist spot. In addition to schools, hospitals, sports clubs, restaurants, etc. currently being built, large housing complexes (villas and apartment blocks) are also being erected. Not necessarily the place to be at this particular moment in time it is worth keeping an eye on this town's promising development.

THE EAST

Umm Said.

Umm Said, situated 32 kms south of Qatar on the east coast, has deep water facilities and is the site of Qatar's petrochemical and other industries.

THE WEST

Dukhan.

Dukhan, situated on the central west coast of Qatar, is the centre of its onshore oil and gas industry. Limestone rock formations and hillocks make the area's landscape slightly more interesting than the majority of the rest of the country. Additionally, some superb beaches are located here. Oil and gas personnel and their families mainly populate this region, with the majority working for QGPC, the national oil and gas company. Although there is not much on offer in Dukhan itself (apart from some restaurants and a social club for residents), it is only an hour's drive from the capital – an easy journey for those wanting to shop or pursue other leisure activities. Dukhan is a place for those seeking small town life.

THE SOUTH

Messaied.

Situated approximately 45 kms south of Doha on the south east coast of Qatar, Messaied is the hub of the oil processing and export industry. Several refineries, industrial plants and a commercial port are located here. Many of those who work in Messaied also live there but as it is such a small place, many decide to live in the capital due to the ease of commuting to work. However, despite its size, the fine sand beaches of Messaied make it one of the country's main tourist spots.

Getting to Qatar

Air

Qatar is very easy to travel to by air. The country's international airport, Doha International, is located 8 km (5 miles) south-east of the city centre. Among the airlines operating flights to Doha are: British Airways, Gulf Air, Qatar Airways, Emirates and Kuwait Airways. Flights from London to Doha last from 6 hours 55 minutes (Qatar Airways) to 8 hours 30 minutes (British Airways) and can be up to 13 hours 55 minutes if flying with one of the other airlines. There are no direct flights from the USA, a stopover occurs in one of the major European airports.

Road

Provided that you have arranged the necessary transit visas, driving to Qatar is perfectly feasible if you are prepared for the long journey ahead of you. The country is now linked to Europe via the Trans-Arabia Highway that runs through Saudi Arabia, and to the UAE and Oman via high standard hard-surfaced roads. However, it should be noted that the main international route from Saudi Arabia to Qatar is unreliable and commonly impenetrable during the rainy season.

Sea

Doha and Umm Said are the leading international ports where the traffic is mostly commercial but there are some passenger lines that stop at Doha.

Useful Telephone Numbers & Websites

Airlines
British Airways: 0345-222111; www.british-airways.com
Emirates: 020-7808 0033; www.emiratesairline.com
Gulf Air: 020-7408 1717; www.gulfairco.com
Kuwait Airways: 020-7412 0006.
Qatar Airways: 020-7896 3636/7514 9444.

Tour Operators
Explore Worldwide: www.explore.co.uk
Travelbag Adventures: www.travelbag-adventures.co.uk
Bales Tours: www.balesworldwide.com
Golden Hill Travel: www.goldenhilltravel.co.uk

Insurance

It is strongly recommended to take out comprehensive travel insurance when visiting Qatar. A list of addresses for some of the major insurers offering reasonable and flexible premiums can be found in the *Getting to Bahrain* chapter under 'Insurance.'

Residence and Entry Regulations

The Current Position

All visitors to Qatar require a visa with the exception of other GCC (Gulf Cooperation Council) nationals. Entry is refused to holders of Israeli passports and to those with Israeli stamps in their passport. An onward or return ticket in addition to proof of sufficient funds for the duration of your stay in the country must be presented. Types of Qatari visa include: business, visit, tourist, multiple entry, and resident. Sponsors are required by all applicants. Companies registered in the State of Qatar, hotels, or individual Qatari nationals can act as sponsors and must undertake responsibility for you during your stay in the country. Those with a healthy income and a valid residence permit can also sponsor dependents such as other family members and domestic servants.

The easiest way to obtain a visa is through a sponsor in Qatar but some Qatari embassies abroad do issue certain visas. Airlines destined for Qatar will not let you board their planes unless you are in possession of a valid Qatari visa.

Business Visa

These are the quickest to process of the visas and with the assistance of an efficient company can be issued within 3 days. Business visas are valid for a single trip to Qatar for a period of one week which can be extended for up to four weeks. The visa is valid for up to three months after the date of issue and must be used within that time. Once a business visa has been allocated the airport keeps a record of the original while a copy is sent to you. When you arrive at the airport you must hand over your copy for the immigration authorities to trace the original on their computerised files. Your passport is then stamped with a seven day validity visa.

Those in possession of a business visa can carry out their business in Qatar without having to undergo a medical examination or acquire an exit visa on departure.

Business visas can be issued by Qatari embassies overseas but due to the paperwork involved and extensive correspondence required with the sponsoring company it is much more convenient to let the relevant embassy and company in Qatar deal with the process.

Visit Visa

Visit visas can either be obtained by your sponsor within Qatar or issued by a Qatari embassy in your home country. They are valid for a single stay lasting any time from two weeks up to three months and can easily be extended. If a much longer period is required then you generally have to leave the country and return on a new visit visa. Those staying for a time over one calender month (30 days) are obliged to undergo a health examination (including X-ray and Aids test) and obtain an exit permit on departure. Individuals with a visit visa may work in Qatar but family members sponsored by foreign national residents in Qatar may not. Visiting dependents will also have to have a health check but do not require exit visas.

Tourist Visa

Tourist visas can only be arranged by hotels for tourists staying in the hotel for the length of their stay in Qatar. They are valid only for the period booked by the hotel, you must have proof of a return ticket out of the country and you will find it near impossible to extend your stay. Travel agents in your home country can make all the necessary arrangements for obtaining your tourist visa.

Multiple Entry Visa

With a multiple entry visa you are allowed to enter and leave Qatar as many times as you wish within the period of a year. Generally each visit must be under one or two months (as prescribed on the visa) with those staying over a 30 day period obliged to undergo a health check (involving X-ray and Aids test) and obtain an exit visa. Once you have acquired one of these visas you will find it easy to renew.

Exit Permit

Visitors who have been in Qatar for a period exceeding 30 days and chief holders of residence permits (i.e. not family dependents) must obtain an exit permit on departure. Your sponsor's representative normally handles the procedure and a permit can be issued within just a few hours (during a working day). Recently an office has been opened at Doha airport which can issue permits 24 hours a day. Family members of residents do not need exit permits and business travellers to-ing and fro-ing from Qatar can obtain easily renewable multi-exit visas, valid for a year.

Work and Residence Permits

Obtaining a residence permit in order to allow you to live and work in Qatar for long-term periods can be a lengthy, complex and tiring process but having undergone it once you will find it easy to renew an existing visa.

Employers normally sponsor only the salaried head of the household who then undertakes sponsorship of his/her dependents. A residence visa is applied for by the employer in Qatar before the intended date of arrival of the employee. Once it has been issued a copy is sent to the employee and the original held at the airport to be collected on arrival in the country. Prior to the residence visa being converted into the necessary residence permit several formalities have to be carried out by all applicants. Not only is a full medical check required (including X-rays and Aids test) but fingerprinting is statutory for all with the exception of girls under the age of 18 and boys under the age of 12 if they are on their father's or mother's sponsorship. Similarly, young children do not need to take an Aids test. Original certificates of education and professional qualifications attested by your home country embassy for a substantial fee must also be submitted with your application for a residence permit.

At a push, a very efficient and influential company could ensure that your residence permit is issued within about three weeks of your arrival in Qatar but more commonly permits can take up to three months to be processed. Before they can sponsor dependents the head of the household needs to secure their own residence permit and then go through the same process for additional family members. Original attested marriage certificates need to be provided by all married couples and all children must have a birth certificate. Additionally, immigration authorities must be presented with proof of villa or apartment rental before a visa for your spouse can be issued. The paperwork becomes even more complicated when trying to obtain residence permits for step-children and adopted children – it is possible but extremely wearing.

Once acquired, residence permits are valid for between one and three years and are relatively easy to renew. To maintain their validity the holder must *not* remain outside the country for a period exceeding six months. You can come and go from the country on your residence visa as much as you like provided that the head of the household obtains an exit permit for each departure.

Registering with your Embassy/Consulate

On arrival in Qatar, expatriates should ensure that they register with the regional Embassy or Consulate of their home country. This registration enables the home country's authorities to keep emigrants up to date with any information they need to be informed of as foreign nationals resident overseas and also enables them to trace individuals in the event of an emergency. The Consulates can also assist with information concerning an emigrant's status overseas and advise on any diplomatic or passport problems. They may also be able to help in an emergency e.g. in the unfortunate event of the death of a relative abroad. However, the Consulates do not function as a source of general help and advice, nor act as an employment bureau and they make this quite evident in response to any such enquiries.

Useful Addresses

Embassy of the State of Qatar: 1 South Audley Street, London W1Y 5DQ; tel 020-7493 2200; fax 020-7493 2819.

British Embassy: PO Box 3, Doha, Qatar; tel +974 421991; fax +974 438692; e-mail british.embassy@doha.mail.fco.gov.uk

Embassy of the State of Qatar: 4200 Wisconsin Avenue, Suite 200, NW, Washington, DC 20016, USA; tel +1 202 274-1600; fax +1 202 237-0061.

Embassy of the United States of America: PO Box 2399, Doha, Qatar; tel +974 864701/3; fax +974 861669; e-mail usisdoha@qatar.net.qa Website www.qatar.net.qa/usisdoha/

Setting Up Home

Real estate in Qatar can only be owned by Qatari or other GCC citizens so all foreign nationals have no choice but to rent housing. In some cases furnished accommodation or a housing allowance is provided by employers as part of their employment packages. If you do decide to seek your own accommodation then it is wise to contact a local real estate agent who can handle all the necessary paperwork for you. Assistance can be sought by contacting either the *Ministry of Labour, Housing and Social Affairs* (PO Box 201, Doha; tel +974 321934) or the *Arabian Tour Bureau Apartment Service* (PO Box 15224, 49 Gulf Street, Doha, Qatar; tel +974 410-730; fax +974 435-277). Addresses of other agents and property owners can be found in the local Yellow Pages or State of Qatar Business Directory, or by looking in regional newspapers.

Housing can be found within compounds (areas that are enclosed by walls and in which expatriates live) or outside the compounds. The benefits of living in a compound are the facilities that it offers, e.g. swimming pool, and the community lifestyle of which you immediately find yourself a part but equally you may decide that the 'small-town' community life that develops within the compounds is somewhat restrictive. However, whether you choose to live inside or outside a compound the quality of accommodation in apartments or villas is generally quite reasonable ranging from the basic to the very luxurious.

Homes are available unfurnished, semi-furnished or fully furnished. Unfurnished accommodation is basically offering you the four walls and the roof over your head. Semi-furnished villas or apartments provide any combination of air-conditioning facilities, carpets, light fixtures, wardrobes, curtains and appliances. If you decide to semi-furnish an average three bedroom villa with air conditioning, curtains, carpets and appliances you could be looking at spending between QR 27,000 to QR 40,000 whereas if you take out a one year contract on a villa that has already been kitted out if would in the long run be far cheaper and much less hassle. The average monthly rent charge of an unfurnished three bedroom villa is QR 7,500-10,000. Comparable semi-furnished to fully furnished accommodation would cost from QR 12,000 monthly. Fully furnished accommodation is as variable as semi-furnished housing and is priced accordingly.

Maintenance is not automatically included in your rental agreements and if it is the standard of service varies enormously. If you decide to carry out your own maintenance it can be costly so always check the terms of your rental contract.

Utilities

Water, Electricity & Gas

Water and electricity fees are normally charged on top of your monthly rent. A refundable deposit of QR 2,000 should be paid to the *Ministry of Electricity and Water* (PO Box 41, Doha; tel +974 410613/423251; fax +974 440048) in order to be connected to the mains. The deposit is returned upon the termination of your lease and once the balance of your account has been cleared. Billing depends on individual consumption rates but on average a family of four living in a three bedroom villa is charged about QR 300 a month.

The electricity supply is 220-240 volts, 50 cycles, and three pin plugs such as those found in the UK are commonly in use. Piped water is found in most homes in Doha and although drinkable, bottled water is probably a much more palatable choice.

Gas for cooking appliances can be bought in 25 pound bottles at a charge of QR 100 for a new bottle and QR 10 for a refill.

Telephones

Telephone line installation in domestic homes costs QR 200 and quarterly line rental is currently QR 100. Local calls are free but international calls can be expensive so most expatriates rely on the internet and e-mail service to stay in touch with friends and family overseas. The *Qatar Public Telecommunications Corporation* (PO Box 217, Doha; tel +974 400333; fax +974 413904) handles all installation and other telecommunication enquiries.

Domestic Help

The average monthly wage for a live-in helper is QR 800-1,500. Local staff are generally male and foreign domestic workers can be hired through several agencies who will handle all the necessary paperwork.

Daily Life

When embarking on relocating to a foreign country, especially one such as Qatar that is culturally so different to life in Western countries, all the countless duties involved can appear somewhat daunting. The aim of this chapter is to provide all of the practical information needed to cope successfully with a range of aspects of life in Qatar. By rising to meet the challenge posed by living in a society so steeped in Islamic customs you will find the experience exciting and rewarding and far less frightening than you may first have envisaged.

Schools and Education

Before the discovery of oil in Qatar, there were very few schools in existence just a handful of religious ones specifically for boys. Since that time a concerted effort has been made to ensure free public schooling to all Qatari and other GCC children resident in the country.

Foreign nationals have to pay for their children's schooling in Qatar although some major employers may cover the costs in their employment packages. Every leading ethnic community is represented by its own school offering the equivalent education that would be provided in the child's home country. Schools can cater for children from Kindergarten through to secondary school (or the end of High School) or only teach until primary school level. The standard of the international schools is generally considered to be quite high and fees are accordingly expensive ranging from QR 1,800-3,050 per term for nursery years, QR 3,500 to over QR 10,000 per term for primary and secondary/high school years, costs rising as your child enters the more senior classes. Additional expenses may include a registration fee and refundable deposit. All students wear school uniforms and all the British schools are gender mixed.

More detailed information about schools and education in Qatar is available from the British Council (PO Box 2992, Doha, Qatar; tel +974 426193/4; fax +974 423315; e-mail Usha.Khanna@britishcouncil.org.qa Website www.britishcouncil. org) and individual institutions should be contacted to discover more about what education system/s and facilities they provide.

Useful Addresses

Ministry of Education & Higher Education: PO Box 80, Doha; tel +974 333444; fax +974 413954.

Preparatory Schools
International School of Choueifat: PO Box 22085, Doha; tel +974 650053; fax +974 650057.
American International School: PO Box 22090, Doha; tel +974 421377; fax +974 420885; e-mail asdoha@qatar.net.qa
Central English Speaking Kindergarten: tel +974 672570; e-mail cesk@iname.com
Doha English Speaking School (DESS): PO Box 7660, Doha; tel +974 870170; fax +974 875921; e-mail dess@qatar.net.qa
Doha Independent School (DIS): PO Box 5404, Doha; tel +974 684495; fax +974 685720.
Doha Montessori: tel +974 691635; fax +974 691633.
English Modern School: PO Box 875, Doha; tel +974 672406/670829; fax +974 672405.
Gulf English School: PO Box 2440, Doha; tel +974 873865; fax +974 863947.
Park House English School: PO Box 102, Doha; tel +974 423343; fax +974 438896.
Qatar Academy: PO Box 1129, Doha; tel +974 803434; fax +974 809566.
Qatar International School (QIS): PO Box 5697, Doha; tel +974 690552; fax +974 690557; e-mail info@qis.org

Secondary Schools
American International School: PO Box 22090, Doha; tel +974 421377; fax +974 420885; e-mail asdoha@qatar.net.qa
Doha College: PO Box 7506, Doha; tel +974 687379; fax +974 685720.
English Modern School: PO Box 875, Doha; tel +974 672406/670829; fax +974 672405.
Qatar International School (QIS): PO Box 5697, Doha; tel +974 690552; fax +974 690557; e-mail info@qis.org

Qatar Academy: PO Box 1129, Doha; tel +974 803434; fax +974 809566.

Further Education
Qatar University: PO Box 2713, Doha; tel +974 892091; fax +974 835111.

The Media, Post and Telecommunications

The Media

All printed matter, films and videos displaying scantily-dressed women, sexual contact between men and women, religious propaganda or politically-sensitive matter will be seized by the Ministry of Information and Culture (PO Box 1836, Doha; tel +974 831333). Any books or personal videos discovered in luggage coming into the country will be reviewed by the Information Ministry to be returned (or not) to the owner in due course.

Television

Programmes in English are broadcast on Qatar's channel 37 (UHF) from late afternoon through to about midnight daily. English stations broadcasting from Abu Dhabi, Saudi Arabia, Dubai and Bahrain can be picked up with a good antenna. Additionally, cable satellite TV is available upon subscription and offers a range of over 20 channels including BBC World Service, CNN and many sports, films and entertainment channels.

Radio

To find out the frequencies for the BBC World Service in Qatar contact: tel 020-7557 1165; e-mail worldservice.letters@bbc.co.uk Website www.bbc.co.uk/worldservice. A monthly international programmes guide, *BBC On Air*, which includes information on World Service Radio, BBC World and BBC Prime television services can be obtained by contacting the BBC at tel 020-7557 2211; fax 020-7240 4899.

Newspapers and Magazines

There are five daily newspapers in Qatar, three in Arabic and two in English, *Gulf Times* and *The Peninsula*. Several international newspapers and magazines are also widely available one or two days or more after publication from local supermarkets or the Family Bookshop. There are a few English language magazines published in Qatar of which *Marhaba* and *Qatar Today*, both quarterly publications are among the best. They provide extensive information on local events and activities and feature articles of regional interest. Copies are distributed through large companies and residential compounds as well as in supermarkets.

Post

Qatar has a reasonably efficient postal service although it is not particularly quick. However, courier services are available. All post offices provide a *poste restante* service on application. The General Post Office in Doha is open from 7am to 8pm daily, with the exception of Fridays when it is open from 4pm to 6pm. Registered letters and parcels sent to Doha can be collected from here.

Useful Addresses
Department of Post: PO Box 713, Doha; tel +974 835555; fax +974 837777.

DHL Qatar Limited: PO Box 9520, Doha; tel +974 621202; fax +974 622020.
Falcon Express (Fedex): PO Box 4803, Doha; tel +974 434409; fax +974 424884.
TNT Express Worldwide: PO Box 1277, Doha; tel +974 412999.

Telephones

Local and international telecommunication facilities in Qatar are of a high standard with automatic telephone and fax dialling available to over 150 countries worldwide and internal calls made from landlines free of charge. The international dialling code for Qatar is +974. There are no local area codes. Qatar's telephone network is operated by Qatar Public Telecommunications Corporation (*Q-Tel*, PO Box 217; tel +974 400333; fax +974 413904) which is also the sole internet service provider in the country.

Mobile phone connection costs QR 500 and monthly rental is QR 60. Calls are charged at QR 0.45 per minute. Installation of internet services is QR 200, monthly rental is QR 50 and there is an on-line charge of QR 6 per hour.

Useful Numbers

Emergency Services: Police, Fire, Ambulance	999
Water Emergency	+974 325959
Electricity Emergency	+974 435704
Directory Enquiries	180
Telegrams	130
Speaking Clock	140
Q-Tel General Enquiries	+974 400400
Qatar Cablevision	177
Internet Qatar	+974 329999

Cars and Motoring

As a resident in Qatar, it is more or less essential to own a car if you want to be mobile as the country's public transport is so limited. The network of roads in the country is of a high standard linking all the main points of the peninsula. Speed limits are 60 kmph in cities and 100 kmph on highways. Traffic drives on the right hand side of the road and all cars are left hand drive. It is now compulsory to wear seat belts on roads outside the major towns.

The price of petrol in Qatar is one of the lowest in the world and despite the high fees of major service garages, small repair and service shops throughout the country offer very reasonable charges so that the overall cost of running a car in Qatar is extremely reasonable.

Driving Licences

In Qatar you can drive on a valid Western or international licence for up to seven days after which a local licence is required. A temporary licence, valid for 30 days, can be obtained by submitting a foreign or international licence together with a letter from your Qatari sponsor and your passport to the Traffic Department within a week of your arrival. Those who have gained residency in Qatar and hold driving licences from America, Canada, Australia or the European Union can easily obtain full Qatari licences on production of their national licence, a letter from their sponsor and a passport. An eye test and proof of familiarity with some basic road signs have to be passed before being given a Qatari licence and it is strongly advised that you leave all the paperwork to your sponsor. Once a local licence has been secured it is valid for five years and is simply renewed by taking more eye and road signs tests.

Car Rental

For the short term visitor to Qatar, hiring a car as opposed to buying one is the most economical option. A wide range of cars from compact saloons to four wheel drives can be rented from a selection of major international or local car hire firms. Third party insurance is compulsory for all drivers.

Useful Numbers

Avis: +974 622180.
Budget: +974 419500.
Euro Dollar: +974 321313.
Europcar: +974 438404.
Hertz: +974 621291.

Purchasing a Car

Almost all the leading models of cars are available in Qatar at prices much lower than those in Europe and the USA. Vehicles are specially customised for Middle Eastern driving conditions, for example more powerful air conditioning than normal is installed and tinted windows. No purchase tax on cars in Qatar, competitive prices, and very low running costs ensure that owning a car is a viable option for most residents in the country. Provided that you are on a fixed contract with a healthy income, obtaining a bank loan to cover the cost of buying a new car is quite easy.

If you would rather purchase a second-hand car to a brand new one then you will find plenty on offer at very reasonable prices. Advertisements for second-hand cars can be found in local daily newspapers and on supermarket notice boards or you may prefer to visit one of the local second-hand car dealers. When buying a previously owned car it is essential to check the service record to ensure in what condition the car is being handed over to you.

Importing Cars

Importing a car into Qatar probably causes more hassle and more expense than it is worth. Shipping is a long and complicated procedure that involves reams of paperwork. Regulations that must be attended to include ensuring that your car has a tinted windscreen, *no* catalytic converter, and be less than two years old. A tax of four per cent is levied on imported cars.

Car Registration and Insurance

All vehicles must be registered by their owners with the traffic police. The procedure involves completing lots of forms and going to the Police Traffic Division in Medinat Khalifa (PO Box 8989, Doha; tel +974 86800; fax +974 872624). It is advisable to get help with the process, most major car dealers will help with this and if buying a second-hand car you may get assistance from the previous owner. When the necessary registration papers have been received they should be kept with you in the vehicle at all times.

Car insurance – fully comprehensive or third party – is obligatory in Qatar and must be obtained before registering your vehicle. Costs range from approximately QR 300 to QR 2,000 according to type, size, age, etc. of vehicle.

Accidents

Road accidents are a common occurrence in Qatar due to the poor quality of driving in the country. If you are unlucky enough to be involved in an accident under no circumstances should you be tempted to move your car until the police have inspected the scene and verified the situation. An incident report will be written up by the police which you will then have to collect from the relevant police station before you can proceed with any vehicle repairs. When going to the police station it is essential to take an Arabic speaker along with you as few Qatari police speak English and you will need someone to represent your interests and make sure that you are being justly treated.

The best advice to avoid an accident – short of not driving at all – is to drive extra carefully yourself and be ever vigilant of fellow drivers on the road.

Transport

Taxis

Taxis are basically the only form of public transport in Qatar and are generally either orange and white painted saloon cars or limousines. The orange and white taxis can be hailed on the street or in fact anywhere including at roundabouts. Fares are very cheap – a journey within Doha costs on average about QR 9 – and the use of meters ensures that your fare is set at the right price. However, if you catch a taxi at the airport the driver is not likely to use a meter and will most probably charge you about QR 30 no matter where your destination. To avoid inflated prices like these you need to make your way to the nearby main road and hail a taxi there.

Despite its convenience and good value for money qualities, there can be a few minor hazards involved in taking a taxi such as actually making it to your destination and arriving there in one piece – although knowing the region that they are driving in well, the level of English language understanding among the taxi drivers varies substantially and driving is of a questionable standard. Nevertheless, travelling by taxis is on the whole relatively safe and you will nearly always make it to where you were intending to go.

Limousines have to be pre-booked and are notably dearer to travel in than the orange and white taxis (average journeys within Doha cost QR 25). They offer a reliable 24 hour service and are recommended for travel to the airport and late night journeys. To ensure punctuality it is advisable to book your limousine a day in advance as waiting time for a vehicle can be anything from 20 minutes to 2 hours according to how busy the company is.

Buses

As yet there is no organised public bus service in Qatar but a limited bus transport system operates between Doha and neighbouring towns.

Motorcycles and Bicycles

Only the extremely confident and competent should even dare to ride a motorcycle in Qatar as the roads may look perfect to cruise down at high speeds but the hazard of other drivers on the road and of sand makes motorcycling very dangerous. Desert cycling is definitely only for the fit and adventurous and cycling on public roads – for the same reasons motorcycling is highly risky – is strongly advised against.

Banking and Finance

The Qatar Central Bank (QCB), established in 1993 as the successor to the Qatar Monetary Agency, oversees the banking sector in Qatar, controlling the country's monetary policy, regulating interest rates, monitoring the commercial banking system, acting as the government's banker, and issuing currency notes and coins. Fifteen commercial banks are currently in operation in Qatar, seven of which are Qatari, two Arab, and the others foreign. The Qatar National Bank (+974 362449) is the oldest of the Qatari banks with its equity base managed equally by the government and by private sector shareholders.

A full range of banking services, Islamic and non-Islamic, is offered by the well-structured network of branches of foreign and local banks in Qatar. Foreign residents can open a bank account in Qatar as long as they are in possession of a current resident's permit, have the written permission of their sponsor, and earn a minimum salary (levels vary according to individual banks). A number of different accounts to suit all needs are available comparable to banks in the west and interest rates on accounts are very generous.

ATM facilities, with the appropriate bank cards, in addition to credit card services, etc. are provided by all the major banks and recent measures have ensured that you can use the ATMs of other banks to access your money. Numerous 'hole-in-the-wall' machines can be found throughout the country, many located in shopping centres as well as outside bank branches. A new system for paying for goods in certain retail outlets has also lately been introduced, NAPS, which allows you to use your bank card like the 'Switch' system in the UK. Although cheque books are issued by banks many retail outlets do not accept payment by cheques.

There are no restrictions on transferring funds into or out of the country and a variety of currencies are held in all the major banks in Qatar, so buying foreign currency and travellers cheques can be carried out with relative ease. Investment advisory services are offered by certain banks (see also below), and loans (usually for vehicle purchases) can be obtained (after the standard reams of paperwork have been processed). Additionally personal loans and if required, overdraft facilities can be arranged.

Typically banks in Qatar are open from 7.30am to 12pm, Saturday to Wednesday, and on Thursdays from 7.30am to 11am, although hours may vary. All banks are closed on Fridays.

Useful Telephone Numbers

Al Ahli Bank of Qatar: +974 326611.
ANZ Grindlays Bank: +974 418222.
Arab Bank Ltd: +974 437979.
Bank Saderat Iran: +974 414646.
Banque Paribas: +974 433844.
British Bank: +974 335222.
The Commercial Bank of Qatar: +974 490222.
Standard Chartered Bank: +974 414252.
United Bank Ltd: +974 438666.

Offshore Banking

If you are working for a large company in the Gulf you are likely to be earning quite substantial amounts of money some of which you will undoubtedly be looking to invest. One of the primary financial advantages of being an expatriate is that you can invest this money offshore in tax havens such as the Isle of Man, the Channel Islands, Gibraltar and Bahrain, thus accruing tax-free interest on your savings. Many such facilities are as flexible as UK high street banking and range from current accounts to long-term, high interest earning deposits. For more details and addresses of offshore banking units see *Offshore Banking* section in 'Bahrain Daily Living' chapter.

Tax and the Expatriate

There are no personal taxes, social insurance or other statutory deductions from salaries or wages paid in the State of Qatar. As a non-resident of your home country (i.e. for UK nationals spending fewer than 183 days in aggregate in Britain) you will not be subject to your home country's tax on earnings either. For more details on what you may or may not be entitled to or subjected to regarding tax regulations (on earnings, relocation expenses, investments, etc.) as an expatriate you should consult a specialist tax advisor. Useful contacts can be found in magazines such as *The Expatriate* and the large accounting/financial advisory companies like PriceWaterhouseCoopers (Plumtree Court, London EC4A 4HT; tel 020-7583 5000; fax 020-7822 4652) publish handy booklets giving detailed information on the tax implications for foreign nationals working in other countries.

Health Care in Qatar

Subsidised medical and dental treatment of a relatively high standard is available to both visitors and residents in Qatar. New residents should register as soon as possible with their nearest primary health care clinic. If more specialised treatment is needed, the patient will be referred to one of Qatar's four hospitals: the Hamad General Hospital, the Women's Hospital, the Rumailah Hospital, or the Psychiatric Hospital. A fifth state hospital is due to open shortly in the north of Qatar, specialising in general medicine and surgery. Private health care can also be sought with one of the many general practitioners, specialists and dentists located throughout the country. The cost of private health care is very high so health insurance is essential.

Health Cards

To receive any treatment in a clinic or hospital in Qatar requires the possession of a valid health card. Only Qatari residents are eligible to obtain a health card from their local health clinic. Annual health cards cost QR 200 for the first year and QR 100 per each subsequent year. This entitles the holder to mostly free care except for the more expensive treatments such as dialysis. Prescriptions carry a nominal charge.

Useful Telephone Numbers

Health Centres
Khalifa Town: +974 862655.
Al Rayyan: +974 803461.
Al Khaleej (West Bay): +974 837788.
Outpatient Clinic: +974 420444.
Al Jazira Polyclinic: +974 351155.
Al Mansoura Polyclinic: +974 883377.

Private Health Care
Al Mansoor Polyclinic: +974 823377.
Doha Clinic: +974 327300.
Dr John Heap (General Practice): +974 477475.
Dr Amal Badi (Gynaecologist): +974 324349.
Dr M Kayyali (Paediatric Consultant): +974 478555.

Dentists
Dr Odd Overoyen: +974 675225.
Dr Deborah Overoyen: +974 675995.

Family Dental Clinic: +974 442924.
Dr Sarah Aalders: +974 477175.
Queen Dental Clinic: +974 860024.

Private Medical Insurance

Private medical care in Qatar is of a very high standard but it is also by no means cheap. Taking out the proper health insurance cover for you and your family is essential when moving out to the Gulf.

BUPA International (Russell Mews, Brighton, BN1 2NR; tel 01273-208181; fax 01273-866583; e-mail advice@bupa-intl.com Website www.bupa-intl.com) has designed its own Lifeline scheme that offers maximum choice and flexibility. There are three levels of cover: Gold, Classic and Essential, all of which provide full refund for hospital accommodation and specialists' fees so you never need to be concerned about unexpected bills for in-patient treatment such as an operation. Cover for emergency ambulance charges and sports injuries is also standard. The Gold and Classic schemes offer out-patient treatment which may be a very wise precaution in Qatar. The most comprehensive cover is available with the Gold scheme which includes the cost of primary care treatment and home nursing. BUPA International has a 24 hour multi-lingual service centre dedicated to their expatriate members with an experienced team on hand to deal with any queries. Claims are paid promptly in any currency that you require, and you are covered anywhere in the world. For more information call +44 (0) 1273-208181.

For more details on other international health insurance schemes available to the expatriate and contact addresses see *Private Medical Insurance* in 'Bahrain Daily Living Chapter.'

Qatari Law

A discretionary system of law controlled by the emir is operated in Qatar. Shari'a law (see Gulf States' 'General Introduction') is the primary legislation abided by in the country although both civil and shar'ia courts exist. However, only shari'a courts have jurisdiction in criminal matters. Generally most of the floggings prescribed by shari'a law are carried out but physical mutilation does not occur and no executions have been performed since the 1980s.

Social Life

Qatar is not known for its active night life and has certainly taken longer than other Gulf countries such as the UAE and Bahrain to cater for the social and leisure needs of its expatriate community. However, the country is in an ongoing state of development and there are plenty of activities in which the foreign resident can participate, alternatively Bahrain and the UAE are only short journeys away by land or air. Once a month a limited quantity of alcohol can be bought by non-Muslim residents in possession of a liquor licence (available through your embassy) from specified outlets. Alcohol is also available at licensed bars and hotels. Eating out in one of the many restaurants serving cuisines from all over the world is another option to occupy your leisure time.

There are a wide range of sports in which to take part and an abundance of expatriate clubs covering a limitless spectrum of interests (contact your local embassy for more details). *Marhaba*, a magazine published monthly, gives essential information on all the current events happening within Qatar as well as detailing contact numbers for all the various clubs from amateur dramatics to ballet and jazz dancing, chess, keep fit, tapestry, women's groups, and a variety of sports societies. For those seeking a more traditional experience of Qatar there are lots of natural history sites to visit such as forts, and museums (see *Regional Guide* for more detailed information) and there is also a Natural History Group.

Cinema

Qatar has three cinemas all run by the Qatar Cinema and Distribution Company (QCD). The Gulf Cinema and Doha Cinema show mainly Indian or Arabic movies with the intermittent screening of a year old Western family style blockbuster. Entry fees are well below those in Europe and America and listings can be found in local newspapers or by telephoning the cinemas on +974 671811. In 1998, a new cinema was opened in The Mall which screens mostly Western films five times a day. One show daily is reserved for families but the other four are open to the general public. Again listings can be found in local newspapers. Expect to witness censorship of scenes involving serious nudity and what is described as 'of an adult nature.' Violence and swearing do not undergo censorship. Films can also be viewed at a number of local clubs and cultural centres such as *The Doha Club* (+974 418822) and *The French Cultural Centre* (+974 671037). Additionally some embassies organise cultural weeks which involve film screenings details of which can be found in the local press.

Shopping

In Qatar you will find that you are always near a shop of some kind and that you will be able to buy just about anything that you want from somewhere whether it is the latest designer labels or perhaps some more traditional Arab jewellery or handicrafts. The country is host to both ultra modern air-conditioned malls and old souks (bazaars). Bargaining is a must when buying anything from the markets or souks.

The cost of daily living in Qatar is comparatively low and local produce – vegetables, meat and fish – are best bought at the local markets, both for the reasonable prices and the freshness of the goods. Imported items are very costly. Shops are typically open from Saturday to Thursday, 9am to 10pm and on Fridays from 3.30pm to 10pm, although hours vary.

SAUDI ARABIA

Currency

The unit of currency is the Saudi riyal (SR) which is divided into 100 halalah.
1 Saudi Riyal (SR) £0.1647; £1 SR 6.0724
1 Saudi Riyal (SR) US$0.2666; US$1 SR 3.7505

Introduction

Destination Saudi Arabia

The official name of Saudi Arabia is the Kingdom of Saudi Arabia with many referring to it simply as the Kingdom. The local long form of the name is *Al Mamlakah al Arabiyah as Suudiyah* and the short form *Al Arabiyah as Suudiyah*. Saudi Arabia is a country of extremes and contrasts. It covers the largest land area of the Gulf States, is arguably the most insular in modern cultural thinking, upholds the strictest laws of the area and enacts the harshest punishments and yet is simultaneously the most up-to-date technologically and culturally in terms of shops, telecommunications, trade and industry, etc. On the surface the Kingdom is ultra modern but the reality behind this facade is that the rationale of the country's people and culture is deeply entrenched in the seventh century era of Mohammed.

Saudi Arabia has a strong and prosperous economy very much dependent upon its oil industry which began in the 1930s. Although the government is currently implementing a process of 'Saudisation' in its workforce – the replacement of expatriates with Saudi citizens at all levels of employment – the skills and expertise of foreign nationals, in particular from the West, is still very much in demand and will continue to be for many years to come.

Pros and Cons of Moving to Saudi Arabia

For the majority of individuals the primary motivation for choosing to work in Saudi Arabia is the money. Salaries for skilled workers are extremely generous especially compared to the equivalent for the same position in a person's home country. There are no personal taxes to pay and employment contracts tend to include all sorts of extra benefits such as accommodation or a housing allowance, use of a company car or a chauffeur, schooling fees for children, etc. and all major employers are required to provide medical care for their employees.

But beyond the lure of the money what does the Kingdom, notorious for its inhospitable attitude towards tourists who might 'pollute' its society, have to attract the expatriate worker? Many find that the challenge of acclimatising to life in a country so different in so many ways to what they are familiar with is what entices them to this region where the enforcement of Islamic laws is the most stringent of all the Gulf states.

From a Western perspective women are on the whole treated as second class citizens in Saudi Arabia – more so than anywhere else in the Gulf – although the reasons for the many restrictions placed on females, such as not being allowed to drive in the Kingdom, are strongly justified by many Saudis as rules to protect the female role and position in society (see *Women in the Gulf* in the Gulf States' 'General Introduction' section). However, within the compounds – walled residential areas designed to isolate the expatriate community from the Islamic community in general – women will find that they can lead their lives as freely as they are used to in their home countries as can all individuals, e.g. children can ride bicycles on the streets whereas outside the compounds the speeding traffic makes it extremely dangerous, certain liberties can be taken such as the discreet manufacture and consumption of alcohol within private homes, no restrictions on dress code within the compound areas, etc. The downside of living on a compound is that due to the small size of the communities everyone soon knows everyone else's business and the atmosphere can be quite claustrophobic but equally when you first move to a country such as Saudi Arabia, living on a compound is the ideal way to meet new people who can help you settle in, find out 'what's on', immediately make friends and begin enjoying an active social life.

There are no cinemas, theatres or clubs as such in the Kingdom but there are plenty of good restaurants and hotels and the opportunities for pursuing any kind of sporting activity are endless from scuba diving and snorkelling in the Red Sea to desert driving and copious other sports: sailing, tennis, squash, swimming, horse riding, etc. The myriad of expatriate clubs covering all sorts of interests from languages to Scottish dancing and Cubs and Brownies for children, additionally provide ample scope for you to occupy your spare time.

The cost of daily living in the Kingdom is pretty much standard with a full range of food and goods available. Fresh grown local produce is relatively cheap and of a good quality whilst imported goods are very expensive. A single person is estimated to spend about SR 1,500 a month on food while a married couple would spend about double this. All pork products and its derivatives are banned but you will have no problem purchasing beef or lamb. Other prohibited products include alcohol and any products containing traces of it. Recently, a Filipino worker was caught bringing two liquor-flavoured chocolate bars into the country and was sentenced to four months in prison and 75 lashes.

Some of the Saudi laws and penalties for infractions (see *Shari'a Law* in the Gulf States' 'General Introduction' section) may seem somewhat extreme and severe by Western standards but on the positive side the Kingdom has a very low crime rate. Punishments include spells in jail, lashings and executions and expatriates incur the same full penalty for any offence that they might commit as a Muslim offender would. Provided that you are careful and respect the local laws you should hopefully avoid any run-ins with the police that could result in any of these penalties.

Due to the numerous Saudi visa restrictions you may find yourself quite cut off from your friends and family at home as 'tourist visas' do not as yet exist as such and unless you have a multi 'exit and re-entry' visa you could experience problems trying to come and go as you please (see *Residence & Entry Regulations* chapter). However, fortunately due to the advanced systems of communications available today you can maintain regular and relatively efficient contact with your friends and family at home by e-mail.

At first Saudi Arabia can appear quite a daunting place and somewhat unfriendly but if you are lucky enough to break through the initial barriers that distance you from Saudi nationals, you will find that they are in fact a very welcoming, loyal and generous people. Once you have lived in the Kingdom for a while you will come to know the many attractions of the country that outweigh the negative aspects and like many other expatriates you may find yourself happy to stay for several years.

From a Western perspective, the main pros and cons of living in the Kingdom of Saudi Arabia can be summarised as follows:

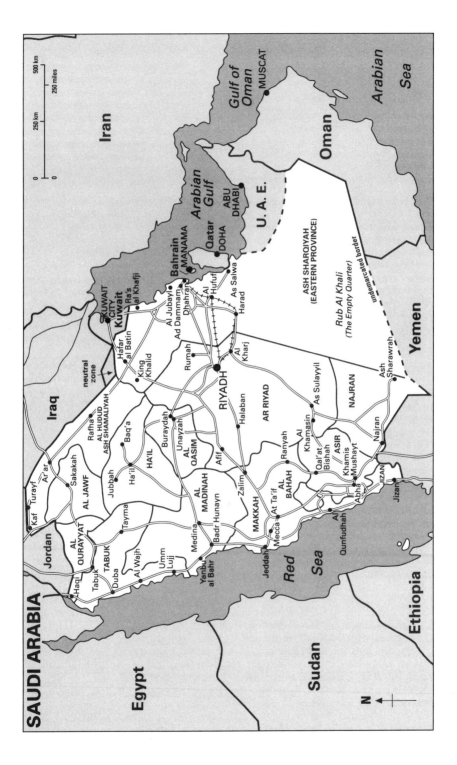

Pros: High salaries. No personal taxes to pay.
From 60 days holiday with some contracts.
Relatively low cost of living and good quality produce.
Hospitable nationals.
Very sociable expatriate community.
Accommodation of a high standard.
Low crime rate.
High standard of education in international schools.
English widely spoken.
Public transport convenient and inexpensive.
Exciting range of land and water sports.
Extraordinary natural beauty of the country.

Cons: Strict laws and harsh punishments for offenders.
Restrictions placed on women in work and daily life.
Public practice of religious faiths other than Islam is forbidden.
Consumption of alcohol illegal.
No bars, clubs, cinemas, theatres, concerts or public libraries.
Compound living – confining and claustrophobic.
Education and hospital fees expensive.
Very hot and dry summers.

Political and Economic Structure

The Abyssinians held sway over the Arabian Peninsula until about AD576 when they were conquered in the southern areas by the Persians. In AD622 the Prophet Mohammed fled from his home in Makkah to Madinah where he gathered together followers before returning to Makkah and recapturing the town. The year of his flight has been established as the start of the Muslim era. For more information on the inception and spread of Islam see the *Reading List* and *Islam* sections in the 'Gulf States General Introduction' chapter.

During the sixteenth century Arabia came under the rule of the Turkish Ottoman Empire subsequent to the Turks' capture of Makkah in 1517. However, local leaders still maintained much of their authority and under Turkish surveillance successive Sherifs of Makkah ruled the Hijaz region comprising the western area of the peninsula including the Red Sea coast as far south as Yemen.

In 1920 the Kingdom of Hijaz was declared an independent state after the Sherif of Makkah made a pact with the British agreeing to support their military campaign against the Turks in return for guaranteed independence. At this time the other side of the peninsula, the Najd, was under the rule of Abdul Aziz Ibn Abdar-Rahman better known as 'Ibn Saud.' Clashes over who held decisive control of the peninsula began to escalate between the Hashemite King of Hijaz and Ibn Saud's Najd forces throughout the 1920s. Ibn Saud triumphed and in 1926 was established as ruler of the Kingdom of Hijaz and Najd. In 1932 the Hijaz and Najd became known as the United Kingdom of Saudi Arabia. Having been driven out of the Hijaz the Hashemites settled with the thrones of Iraq and Transjordan (now Jordan).

Explorations for oil began in 1933 and substantial deposits were found in the eastern part of the country. With the resulting revenues Ibn Saud, King until his death in 1953, introduced a national infrastructure and basic state services. The discovery of oil dramatically transformed the country from a barren, impoverished desert state to a lucrative and modern economy although politically and socially (by western standards) progress is notably lacking. The ruling family and most Saudis are strict adherents to Sunni Muslim doctrine and Islamic laws are enforced by the *muttawa* (religious police). While eagerly drawing on western advancements in modern technology and economic drives, Saudi Arabia is equally fervent at keeping its nation 'untainted' by western cultural influences. A prominent feature of this ideology is the common practice of housing nearly all expatriates in compounds walled off from Saudi nationals. Despite its outward appearance of modernity the Kingdom still remains – in many ways – in the seventh century age of Mohammed.

The Economy

The pilgrimage to Makkah and Madinah and the export of dates together once formed the backbone of Saudi Arabia's economy. However, despite the Kingdom continuing to be a global leader in the production of dates, its economy is now highly dependent upon its oil and petroleum industry. The state has the largest proven reserves of petroleum in the world and is rated as the largest exporter of petroleum. Its petroleum sector accounts for approximately 75 per cent of budget reserves, 35 per cent of GDP (Gross Domestic Product) and 90 per cent of export earnings. The private sector accounts for about 35 per cent of Gross Domestic Product. Saudi Arabia ranks 20th globally in the size of its economy.

The rapid and successful development of the country's economy since the discovery of oil has allowed Saudi Arabia to establish a comprehensive social and physical infrastucture in terms of roads, air and sea ports, telecommunications, housing, schools and hospitals. In order to develop their economy even further the government are currently channelling their energies into ongoing projects such as: diversifying the economy to relieve the country's reliance on oil; improving economic efficiency via management of public sector activity and spending, and greater incitement of private sector initiatives; proposals for increased privatisation; restructuring of the agricultural sector.

Saudi Arabia's economy may be mostly reliant upon the strength of its oil sector but it is in a very healthy position nonetheless with future growth supported not only by an oil sector that can produce substantial revenue but also by an extensive physical and social infrastructure and a financial system with high liquidity levels. Additionally, there are increasingly more opportunities opening up for industrial development and for growing manufacturing output and non-oil exports, plus government incentives to encourage greater private sector activity.

Government and Politics

The Kingdom of Saudi Arabia is an absolute monarchy headed by King Fahd bin Abdul Aziz who came to office in 1982. Shariah (Islamic) law (see Gulf States 'General Introduction') dictates the king's mandate and duties to his subjects. God is the supreme authority but it is the responsibility of King Fahd to enforce Shariah law throughout the Kingdom. The King also holds the position of Custodian of the Two Holy Mosques in Makkah and Madinah highlighting the fundamental importance attached to the Islamic religion in the country.

A Council of Ministers established in 1953 are appointed every four years by the ruler to manage day-to-day affairs. It offers advice to the King and is responsible for government ministries and agencies. However, any decisions made by the Council through a majority vote will only take effect with the sanction of the King. The Prime Minister leading this Cabinet is the Custodian of the Two Holy Mosques, King Fahd, and his brother, Crown Prince Abdullah bin Abdul Aziz is the deputy premier and Commander of the National Guard.

In 1993 a 60 member Consultative Assembly (*Majlis as-Shura*) was created to act as a public forum for debate, meeting periodically to put forward recommendations to the King by majority decision. The Assembly has no official powers and in 1997 its body was increased to 90 chosen members from the religious, business, government and academic communities to carry out four year terms of office. Eight committees constitute the Assembly each with its own area of responsibility including foreign affairs, economic and financial affairs, health and social affairs. Political parties are prohibited within the Kingdom.

The justice ministry puts forward questions to an eleven member judiciary, the Supreme Council of Justice, which also oversees the work of the lower courts. The lower courts are made up of the general courts and summary courts, and the Court of Cassation comprising the Chief Justice and other judges, which arbitrates in penal suits. The Supreme Council of Justice may also recommend that specialised courts be set up by royal decree.

International Relations

The Kingdom of Saudi Arabia is a founding member of the United Nations, the Organisation of Petroleum Exporting Countries (OPEC), the Gulf Co-operation Council (GCC), and several other international and Arab organisations. In 1978 Saudia Arabia acquired a seat on the board of executive directors of the International Monetary Fund (IMF) and plans are currently underway for the country to join the World Trade Organisation (WTO).

Geographical Information

Area and Main Physical Features

The Kingdom of Saudi Arabia is the largest country in the Middle East occupying four fifths of the Arabian peninsula. Its land area is estimated at 2,331,000 sq km (900,000 sq miles), approximately nine times the size of the UK. The Kingdom is situated in south west Asia in a location where three continents meet: Europe, Asia and Africa.

It is bordered by: the Red Sea to the west (with a coastline of about 1,900 km); the Arabian Gulf to the east (with a coastline of about 610 km); Yemen and the Sultanate of Oman to the south; the United Arab Emirates, Qatar and the island of Bahrain to the east; Kuwait, Iraq and Jordan in the north. Only its borders in the north, with Qatar and a part of its border with Yemen are exactly demarcated, hence the estimate of its land area can only ever be an estimate.

The country's vast expanse of land gives scope for a varied topography. Although most of the Kingdom comprises vast stretches of sand – the largest continuous desert in the world, the Rub Al Khali otherwise known as the Empty Quarter covers the southern part of Saudi (approximately 640,000 square kilometres) and joins the Nafud desert in the north of the Kingdom – there are also some areas of vegetation and mountains. Situated alongside the Red Sea is the Tihama coastal plain, which is 1,100 kilometres long and 60 kilometres wide in the south, narrowing to the north as it approaches the Aqaba Gulf. To the east of the Tihama plain lie the Sarawat mountains rising to about 2,743m (9,000 feet) in the south and falling to 914m (3,000 feet) in the north. Large valleys slope eastward and westward from Sarawat. These valleys lead eastward onto the central region of Saudi known as the Najd Plateau. This region is mainly desert but some mountains can be found here such as the Tawabek, Al Aradh, Aja and Salmah. The Plateau is bordered by the Samman Desert and Dahnaa Dunes to the east, the Najd Plains to the north, and the Empty Quarter to the south. The east coast stretches for 610 kilometres and consists of vast sand areas. The Asir mountains rising to over 2,740m (9,000 feet) are located in the south-west of the country where rain is not uncommon and temperatures are much lower than in other regions.

A neutral zone exists between Saudi Arabia and Iraq of 7,000 sq km (2,700 sq miles) split equally between the two countries according to a pact made in 1975. In this region no fixed structures or military establishments can be constructed; Bedouin from both countries have access to the area. Saudi Arabia also shares a neutral zone with Kuwait of 5,770 sq km (2,230 sq miles). Saudi Arabia governs the southern half but the oil revenues from the area are divided between the two countries.

Population

The population of Saudi Arabia is currently over 20.7 million, of whom over 5.2 million are foreign nationals. Most of this population is concentrated in the major cities: Riyadh (3 million), Jeddah (3 million), Dammam/Khobar/Qatif (1.2 million), Madinah (900,000), Abha and Khamis Mushayt (900,000), Taif (600,000). Population growth is about 3.4 per cent per year and the projected population for the year 2010 lies in the region of 29.7 million. 90 per cent of Saudi citizens are Arab the other 10 per cent are Afro-Asian. Many foreign nationals come from Egypt, the Philippines, Sri Lanka, and Pakistan. These people are known as Third Country Nationals (TCNs) and are employed for all the menial jobs in the country.

All Saudis are Muslim. Open practice of any other religion is forbidden. Those found in contravention of this dictate will be imprisoned and deported. Renunciation of the Muslim faith by a Saudi national can result in public execution. Saudi Arabia's official language is Arabic but English is widely spoken as it is the Kingdom's language of commerce. 62.8 per cent of Saudis (aged 15 and over) are functionally literate.

Climate

Saudi Arabia is a country that mainly experiences sweltering summers and cold winters with the little rainfall that does occur being in the winter months (November to March). In the west and south-western part of the Kingdom, where the region tends to be more mountainous, the climate is reasonably moderate compared to the central desert areas, where Riyadh is located, which are subject to very dry hot summers and cold winters. The coastal regions, including Jeddah in the West and the Eastern Province on the Arabian Gulf, suffer high temperatures and oppressive humidity from April to October with only light relief offered by a moderate wind coming in from the sea. For the remainder of the year temperatures are still warm and the humidity much more tolerable.

For those unused to living in hot climates extra precautions need to be taken to avoid sunburn, heat exhaustion or heatstroke. Newcomers are advised not to spend prolonged periods in the sun, to protect their skin with sunscreen and to drink plenty of water.

Natural Hazards frequent sand and dust storms.

Weather Chart
Average temperature (Celcius), rainfall (mm), sunshine in hours per day, humidity percentage.

	Jan	Feb	Mar	Apr	May	Jun	Jul	Aug	Sep	Oct	Nov	Dec
Riyadh												
Max	21	23	28	32	38	42	42	42	39	34	29	21
Min	8	9	13	18	22	25	26	24	22	16	13	9
Rainfall	22.4	0.0	38.3	22.7	0.3	0	0	0	0	28.9	192.8	3.5
Rainy Days	9	0	18	11	7	0	0	0	0	18	32	5
Sunshine	7	8	7	8	9	11	11	10	9	10	9	7
Humidity	57	50	51	49	41	39	26	27	33	36	47	64

Jeddah

Max	29	29	29	33	35	36	37	37	36	35	33	30
Min	19	18	19	21	23	24	26	27	25	23	22	19
Rainfall	13	0	0	0	0	0	0	0	0	26	6	3
Rainy Days	0.8	0.0	0.0	0.0	0.0	0.0	0.0	0.0	0.0	2.0	3.0	2.0
Sunshine	7	8	7	8	9	11	11	10	9	10	9	7
Humidity	56	52	52	54	53	56	53	55	63	61	57	55

Regional Guide

Western expatriates living in Saudi Arabia settle mainly in the capital, Riyadh, in the centre of the Kingdom (the location of all foreign embassies), and the commercial city and port of Jeddah on the west coast. Other areas where expatriates live are on or near the Gulf coast where the Kingdom's oil is extracted and exported. In the Eastern Province, in a triangle of townships comprising Dhahran, Dammam, and Al Khobar, several thousand British people reside. Expatriates also live in Tabuk in the far north west of the Kingdom, Taif in the mountains surrounding Makkah, and Abha and Khamis Mushayt in the lofty mountains of the south west. The industrial cities of Jubail (approximately 80 kilometres north of Dammam on the Gulf) and Yanbu (400 kilometres north of Jeddah) are also attracting expatriate residents.

Information Facilities

Saudi does not actively encourage non-Arab or non-resident expatriate tourism to the country however, a recent development has been the establishment of a British tour operator, *Bales Worldwide Tours* (tel 01306-885991) offering ten day trips to the Kingdom. The tours are restricted to men, and women over 40 unless accompanied by a close male relative. Other than this information on the country can be sought by contacting one of the addresses or websites listed below.

Useful Addresses

Saudi Hotels and Resort Areas Co (SHARCO): PO Box 5500, Riyadh 11422, Saudi Arabia; tel +966 1 465-7177; fax +966 1 465-7172.

British Embassy: PO Box 94351, Riyadh 11693, Saudi Arabia; tel +966 1 488-0077; fax +966 1 488-3125.

British Consulate-General: PO Box 393, Jeddah 21411, Saudi Arabia; tel +966 2 654-1811; fax +9662 654-4917.

Foreign and Commonwealth Office: Middle East Department, Downing Street West, London SW1A 2AL; tel 020-7270 2996; fax 020-7270 3370; Website www.fco.gov.uk

Royal Embassy of Saudi Arabia: 30 Charles Street, London W1X 8LP; tel 020-7917 3000; fax 020-7917 3255; Website www.saudiembassy.org.uk

Saudi Arabia Information Centre: Cavendish House, 18 Cavendish Square, London W1M 0AQ; tel 020-7629 8803; fax 020-7629 0374; Website www.saudinf.com

Royal Embassy of Saudi Arabia: 601 New Hampshire Avenue, NW, Washington, DC 20037, USA; tel +1 202 342-3800; fax +1 202 337-4084.

Embassy of the United States of America: PO Box 94309, Riyadh 11693, Saudi Arabia; tel +966 1 488-3800; fax +966 1 488-7360.

Useful Websites

Arab Net: www.arab.net

Arab World Online: www.awo.net

Arabia Online: www.arabia.com
Saudi Pages: www.saudi-pages.com

Useful Publications

Guide for Living in Saudi Arabia, Middle East Editorial Association, Washington, 1984.
Riyadh Handbook, Ionis Thompson, Shell Publishing.
Saudi Arabia, Dr Muhammed Abdul Nayeem.
Saudi Arabia – A MEED Practical Guide, 1993.
The Saudis – Inside the Desert Kingdom, Sandra Mackey.
Travelling the Sands – Sagas of Exploration in the Arabian Peninsula, Andrew Taylor.

THE CENTRAL REGION

Situated in the heart of Saudi Arabia is the capital, Riyadh and several other important towns north and west of it such as Buraidah, Unaizah and Ha'il. Riyadh (which derives its name from the plural of an Arabic word meaning garden) lies in the central plateau, the Najd. Bedouin nomads still inhabit the Najd outside the towns although they are increasingly moving into centres of population. Dispersed across the Najd are countless oases in many of which modern agricultural measures have been initiated.

The central region is famously the most traditional and on the whole the most religiously conservative area of the Kingdom. In the town of Buraidah even foreign women are required to be veiled although this is the only place in the country which has such a ruling. Due to the lack of westerners in towns and villages of the Najd outside the capital any visitors to these areas will find themselves markedly objects of interest.

Despite Riyadh always technically being the country's capital it was not until the early 1980s that all the ministries and embassies were relocated there from Jeddah. All the embassies are now situated in an area called the Diplomatic Quarter. Prior to the relocation only one airline, *Saudia*, was permitted to fly into the capital, now Riyadh – as well as Jeddah and Dhahran – is served by many international carriers.

The discovery of oil has dramatically transformed the capital from what it once was. In 1932 Riyadh had a land area of just 8.5 square kilometres, by 1994 it was over 1,600 square kilometres. The majority of buildings within the city are less than 20 years old and very few date back beyond 50 years.

In order to visit any of the archaeological sites and forts within the region, except Dir'aiyah (the oasis town and ancestral home of the Al-Saud), the Najran Fort and those located in the Eastern Province, a special permit must be obtained from the Riyadh Museum (tel +966 1 402-0303). There is no cost for the permit on production of your passport or *igama* (residence permit).

THE EASTERN PROVINCE

The Kingdom's first discovery of oil took place in the Eastern Province in the 1930s. The region lies on the Arabian Gulf and is the location of the towns of Dhahran, Al-Khobar, Dammam, Qatif, Hofuf and Jubail. Dhahran did not even exist before the discovery of oil and Dammam and Al-Khobar were just small fishing and pearling villages. Dammam is now the administrative centre of the area and is linked to the capital by railway. The Dammam-Riyadh line passes through Abqaiq and Hofuf, the main town in the Al-Hasa oasis, and the journey takes about four to five hours.

Al-Khobar, whose first recorded settlement was in 1923, is in many ways more advanced than Dammam. Situated by the ARAMCO camp it developed very quickly and was once used as a major port for shipping oil to Bahrain to be processed. One end of the King Fahad Causeway linking Saudi to Bahrain is located here.

Dhahran, built by ARAMCO, is the site of the ARAMCO compound, an airport, the US Consulate and the King Fahad University of Petroleum and Minerals.

Qatif is situated about 13 km north of Dammam and is one of the centres of the Eastern Province's large Shiite Muslim communities. First settled in 3,500 BC, Qatif acted for centuries as the main town and port in the region.

Jubail is located about 90 km north of Dammam and was a small fishing village until the mid-1970s when it developed into one of the Kingdom's two newly-formed industrial cities accommodating an iron works, petrochemical plants, other smaller businesses and a Royal Saudi Naval Base. The other new city created was Yanbu situated on the Red Sea Coast.

Hofuf, famous for its old fort and fascinating souks, is the centre of one of the largest oasis' in the world, Al-Hasa. It is also one of the most verdant areas in the Kingdom and one of the world's greatest producers of dates.

THE SOUTH WEST

The south-western corner of Saudi Arabia where there are mountains, rainfall, verdancy and cooler temperatures than those inland and on the coastal areas, is known as the *Asir*. The mountains in this area lie along the same geological fault as the Great Rift Valley in Africa. Abha is the administrative centre of this region and is situated close to the Jebel Soudah peaking at approximately 2,910 metres (9,547 feet), the highest point in the Kingdom.

Asir was once an independent kingdom until 1922 when King Abdul Aziz conquered it. Local customs and architecture reveal the influence of neighbouring Yemen on the area. The capital of this region, Abha is a favoured weekend resort due to its temperate climate and incredible setting. Stretching from the Red Sea to the desert east of the mountains is the Asir National Park which divides naturally into the mountainous area north-west of Abha and the plains to the south-east.

THE WESTERN REGION

Saudi Arabia's western region is known as the *Hijaz*. Located here are some of the most important cities to both Muslims and non-Muslims alike. About half way down the west coast is the city of Jeddah, the foremost entry point for almost one million foreign pilgrims to Makkah once a year for the annual *Hajj*, in addition to the 3 million pilgrims who visit Makkah throughout the year to perform *Umra* (see section on *Islam* in the 'General Introduction to Living in the Gulf States').

In the sixteenth century the area came under nominal Turkish rule although local leaders maintained most of their authority and influence. During the first half of the nineteenth century the first foreign consuls began to arrive in Jeddah and in 1925 King Abdul Aziz assumed sovereignty over the region. From then until the mid-1980s foreign representatives were based in Jeddah rather than the country's capital Riyadh where they are now situated. Despite the major embassies moving to Riyadh there still remains a great number of foreign consulates within Jeddah as it is still regarded as the commercial centre of the Kingdom in addition to its role as the main port of entry for pilgrims to Makkah and Madinah.

Jeddah

Jeddah's old city region, whose walls were destroyed in the late 1940s and which is now a protected area where old buildings cannot be torn down unless beyond all repair and replaced with a comparable structure, is host to a number of worthwhile sights. Here can be found the restored traditional homes of two of Jeddah's merchant families, Sharbatly House and the Naseef House. There is also the Municipality Museum which can only be visited by those in possession of a permit from the Jeddah Municipality (+966 2 669-5556) and who have made an appointment with the curator of the museum. One other place that should be visited is the Christian cemetry whose existence is unknown to many Saudis and where the last burial occurred in the early 1950s. The cemetry is walled and entered by a large gate.

The historic area of Jeddah is in the Al-Balad district where houses have been reconstructed to their original state of 100 years ago. Many of the houses here belonging to old Jeddah families are open to tourists.

Makkah (Mecca)

Situated about 70 km east of Jeddah is the Holy City of Makkah where Prophet Mohammed was born in the sixth century AD. Makkah is where the prophet first began his preaching and to where he returned shortly before his death in AD632. Non-Muslims are strictly prohibited from entering the city and check points are situated on all roads leading into the city.

Makkah is Islam's holiest city to where all Muslims worldwide aim to visit at least once (the *hajj*) in their lifetime. At the heart of the city is the Grand Mosque placed alongside the sacred Well of Zamzam. In the main courtyard of the Grand Mosque is the *Kaaba* to which all Muslims turn when praying. According to Islamic tradition the first prophet Abraham built the Kaaba with his son Ishmael.

Al Madinah (Medina)

The second holiest city in Islam after Makkah, Madinah was the first place to accept the Prophet Mohammed's message. In AD622 the Prophet fled to this city then called Yathrib. The most revered place in the city is the Prophet's Mosque where he is now buried. Non-Muslims are forbidden to enter any of the historical or religious areas of the city but can visit the outskirts and Madinah's airport. Non-stop flights between Madinah and several other Saudi cities are operated by Saudia, the national airline, and international non-stop flights between Madinah and Cairo, Damascus and Istanbul are also available.

Getting to Saudi Arabia

Air

Saudia (SV) is the Kingdom's national airline. Free advice on air travel from the UK to Saudi Arabia can be obtained by calling the Air Travel Advisory Bureau on 020-7636 5000 (London) or 0161-832 2000 (Manchester). Saudi Arabia has three international airports at Riyadh (35 km north of city centre), Dhahran (13 km south-east of Dhahran), and Jeddah (18 km north of Jeddah). The flight from London to Riyadh takes about 6 hours 25 minutes, to Dhahran about 6 hours 25 minutes, and to Jeddah just under 6 hours.

Sea

The country's major international passenger ports are Dammam (on the Gulf), and Jeddah and Yanbu (on the Red Sea).

Road

The foremost principal international routes from Jordan are Amman to Dammam, Madinah and Jeddah. Roads also lead to Yemen (from Jeddah), Kuwait, Qatar and the UAE. Bahrain is linked to Al Khobar in Saudi Arabia by the King Fahad Causeway.

Useful Telephone Numbers

Airlines
Saudia: 020-7995 7755.
British Airways: 0345-222111.
Emirates: 0870-2432 222.
Gulf Air: 020-7408 1717.
KLM: 0990-750900.

Insurance

It is strongly advisable to take out comprehensive travel insurance when visiting Saudi Arabia. A list of addresses for some of the major insurers offering reasonable and flexible premiums can be found in the *Getting to Bahrain* chapter under 'Insurance.'

Residence and Entry Regulations

Saudi Arabia is notoriously an extremely difficult country to visit unless you are a Muslim. To enter the Kingdom a visitor must have a valid and relevant visa or expect to be sent straight home again. Unlike in the other Gulf States, hotels cannot sponsor visitors and in practice a tourist visa is virtually non-existent. However, recently a British Tour Operator, *Bales Worldwide Tours* (01306-885991) has introduced ten day trips to the Kingdom which incorporate the management of all the red tape involved in entering and exiting the country for short visits. But in general, for non-Muslims there are just three forms of visa: visitor, residence, and transit. For whichever type of visa is held, the bearer must have a Saudi sponsor, either an individual or a company, to vouch for the individual's conduct while he is in the country. Muslims can enter the Kingdom on a comparatively easy to obtain *hajj* or *umrah* visa (see section on *Islam* in the 'General Introduction to the Gulf States' chapter).

Visitor visas

To obtain a visitor visa an individual requires a formal invitation from the company or person sponsoring him or her. In effect the visitor visa is a business visa. A visa number accompanies the invitation which denotes that the sponsor has procured the authority to issue a visa for the invited person at the appropriate Saudi embassy. Individuals take this number to their nearest Saudi embassy and should receive their visa within a day. Visas are issued only by number and not by name, therefore: no number, no visa.

Transit visas

Airport transit visas

For those travelling by air who have no choice but to make a transit stop in Saudi Arabia, 24 hour and 48 hour transit visas can be issued at their local Saudi embassy. If a visa of this kind is obtained, the individual must surrender their passport to the immigration authorities at the Saudi airport they are passing through and reclaim it on their departure.

Road transit visas

Those driving between Jordan and either Yemen or Kuwait can usually obtain three-day transit visas issued only by the Saudi embassies in Amman or Sana'a. The visa and carnet of the destination country must be shown. Seven-day transit visas are frequently assigned for those driving between Bahrain, Qatar or the UAE and Jordan. Those driving between Oman and Jordan need to procure their transit visa in Abu Dhabi, the UAE.

Residence visas

To obtain a residence visa for Saudi Arabia initially takes about six weeks of paperwork to be completed by both the sponsor and the sponsored party. Copies of the employment contract, academic or professional qualifications of the individual seeking residency must be shown. Additionally, a comprehensive medical examination must be taken which includes an AIDS test to ensure the participant is HIV negative. Once all the forms have been successfully filled out, a visa number will be assigned which can be taken to the nearest Saudi embassy and exchanged for a visa. Once in the Kingdom this visa will be upgraded to a residence visa with the added provision that the owner surrenders his/her passport to the sponsor. The residence permit (*igama*), must be carried at all times.

To leave the Kingdom on a holiday requires an exit/re-entry visa arranged by the sponsor who will return the passport to its owner in return for the residence permit of the individual. The passport will only be valid for travel outside Saudi Arabia if it has been stamped with an exit/entry visa. An exit-only visa is issued to those leaving the country and not returning.

As all government business in Saudi Arabia follows the Islamic calendar, any Gregorian (western) date written on official documents is purely there for the ease of the Westerner and should by no means be taken as official. The official date will be the Islamic one. The Islamic year is eleven days shorter than the Gregorian year and so those with a one month visa must remember that it is only valid for an Islamic month not a Gregorian one. Oversight of this can result in outstaying the designated time period and incurring difficulties with the authorities on departure from the Kingdom.

Visa extensions can only be obtained by an indivdual's sponsor.

Registering with your Embassy/Consulate

On arrival in Saudi Arabia, expatriates should ensure that they register with the regional Embassy or Consulate of their home country. This registration enables the home country's authorities to keep emigrants up to date with any information they need to be informed of as foreign nationals resident overseas and also enables them to trace individuals in the event of an emergency. The Consulates can also assist with information concerning an emigrant's status overseas and advise on any diplomatic or passport problems. They may also be able to help in an emergency e.g. in the unfortunate event of the death of a relative abroad. However, the Consulates do not function as a source of general help and advice, nor act as an employment bureau and they make this quite evident in response to any such enquiries.

Useful Addresses

The visa information above describes the most up-to-date regulations, however, it is important to double check the details with a Saudi or British embassy in case of minor changes.

British Embassy: PO Box 94351, Riyadh 11693, Saudi Arabia; tel +966 1 488-0077; fax +966 1 488-3125.

British Consulate-General: PO Box 393, Jeddah 21411, Saudi Arabia; tel +966 2 654-1811; fax +966 2 654-4917. A Consular Officer is also resident in the Eastern Province: tel +966 3 857-0595 ext. 1443; fax +966 3 857-0643.

Foreign and Commonwealth Office: Middle East Department, Downing Street West, London SW1A 2AL; tel 020-7270 2996; fax 020-7270 3370; Website www.fco.gov.uk

Royal Embassy of Saudi Arabia: 30 Charles Street, London W1X 8LP; tel 020-7917 3000; fax 020-7917 3255; Website www.saudiembassy.org.uk

Royal Embassy of Saudi Arabia: 601 New Hampshire Avenue, NW, Washington, DC 20037, USA; tel +1 202 342-3800; fax +1 202 337-4084.

Embassy of the United States of America: PO Box 94309, Riyadh 11693, Saudi Arabia; tel +966 1 488-3800; fax +966 1 488-7360.

Passport Office: PO Box 171, Jeddah 21115, Kingdom of Saudi Arabia; tel +966 2 631-8177; fax +966 2 631-6690.

Passport Office: PO Box 6440, Dammam 31442, Kingdom of Saudi Arabia; tel +966 3 832-2577; fax +966 3 834-0936.

Setting Up Home

Even though only Saudi nationals and other GCC nationals can own property in the Kingdom of Saudi Arabia, which has traditionally forced expatriates of other countries to rent accommodation on a compound or 'off-compound,' recent developments and draft regulations by the Supreme Economic Council have hinted at a change to the legal requirements as far as investment in Saudi Arabia and ownership of property is concerned.

However, it is advisable as a first time resident in the Kingdom to live on a compound. Compounds are built with a Western independent lifestyle in mind. The accommodation units vary from large 3-4 bedroom villas with private gardens to town house style units or apartments. Sporting and leisure facilities are a very prominent feature in compounds. It is not a primary purpose of compounds to isolate Western and Saudi communities from each other, although it is recommended to choose a compound that has maintained an exclusively Western residential mix. This is mainly to avoid a problem with the clash of completely different cultures that would lead to mutual discomfort due to the different lifestyles. Saudisation (the replacement of foreign workers with skilled Saudi nationals) has resulted in more and more companies cutting back on their expatriate staff levels. Consequently, some compounds that were exclusively Western, just a year ago, have been compelled to accept local residents as tenants in order to stay in business.

Behind compound walls Westerners can on the whole continue their 'normal' lives and lifestyles with few or no restrictions imposed on them as far as dress

The Lifestyle

*"Elegant well appointed homes,
a superb environment, impeccable service
and superior facilities"*

Arabian Homes

codes, safety, and personal esteem is concerned. Western women can feel intimidated around swimming pools or recreational areas in mixed compounds where Arab/Muslim nationals enforce adherence to the strict Islamic rules on conservative dress codes, and the place and role of women in the family. This is not a deliberate ploy by the local community to intimidate, but the sheer unnaturalness of the situation is really what enhances the feeling of intimidation. What Westerners normally cannot understand is why Muslim women put up with this seemingly foreign practice because it is so alien to a Western mind (see *Women in the Gulf*, Gulf States' 'General Introduction' chapter). To avoid situations like this it is highly recommended to choose a compound that has maintained its largely Western mix and in this way to build up contacts and friends that can assist in making the integration into the larger Saudi community a more pleasant and enjoyable process. Living off-compound, unless you have established lots of contacts within the country and know your way around, can leave you very isolated from other people and struggling to discover what is going on around you.

Generally accommodation is included in an expatriate's contract and the employer is responsible for furnishing and equipping your home. Otherwise you may be given a housing allowance with which to find your own accommodation. To do this it is strongly recommended to go through a real estate agent (a list of which can be found in the local yellow pages or on the website www.ksayellowpages.com) who can keep you updated with the property market and help you through the leasing process. Local newspapers are another source of property information.

Leases

The following is a checklist of things to watch out for before signing any rental agreement:

Price. Get a clear understanding of what is included in the price and what items/services are deemed extras for which you will be charged separately.

Terms. Contracts are all for one Hejira year (eleven days shorter than the Gregorian calender), but due to the competitiveness of the market, compound managements are becoming more flexible as far as payment terms are concerned. Six monthly or even quarterly terms are acceptable if requested.

Small print. Make sure you check the details of the lease contract if you are personally responsible for the lease to ensure that there are no hidden surprises later on.

Paperwork. Always cover your own tracks and protect your position by even requiring the person who takes a cheque from you to acknowledge that they have done so by signing for the receipt of the cheque on a photocopy (even if you do not get offered an official receipt).

Negotiate. Standard process in the Middle East, especially in the light of the competitiveness of the market, but do not take a polite refusal to negotiate on the price of the accommodation personally.

Notice. Check the lease carefully as different terms and notice periods apply depending on compound management.

Lease period. Generally for one Hejira year. If you wanted to move out before the expiry of your lease that is fine, but do not expect to have an easy time in trying to get your money back. Therefore, once signed up, you are 'locked-in' to the contract for the entire year.

These comments on leases are to act as a guideline for prospective Western renters in order to safeguard themselves as far as possible as Shari'a Law operates in Saudi

Arabia, and its workings and processes are very foreign, confusing, and fraught with difficulty for someone used to European/American legal practices. The importance of understanding whatever contract into which you are entering cannot be overstated, and if in doubt contact a local solicitor (list of addresses can be found under *Accountancy & Legal Advice*, at the end of the *Starting a Business* chapter).

Compound Living

If your employer includes accommodation in your contract you may be offered a choice of compounds or be placed with other employees of the same company. If you have been given a housing allowance and want to live on a compound you will need to decide which one best suits you. Lower priced compounds of between SR 45,000 and SR 80,000 per year provide the basic necessities: furnishings, utilities, maintenance and a range of services and facilities such as swimming pools, playgrounds, school and shopping bus services. Those costing between SR 80,000 and SR 85,000 per year, provide the same services and facilities plus additional extras such as satellite TV, and are usually of a higher quality and standard.

The company, *Arabian Homes*, whose head office is located in Jeddah and branch offices in Riyadh and Yanbu, specialises in providing first class homes with superior services and facilities. Many top international organisations and leading local business establishments choose this company to house their senior personnel. Residents have the option of living in either an apartment, penthouse, townhouse or family villa within Arabian Homes' villages that are each specifically designed to create the feel of an exclusive and private community with a genuine village atmosphere. Residential properties are informally grouped around individual pool areas with easy access to sports and leisure facilities. Arabian Homes has more than seventy swimming pools, all with spacious sundecks and comfortable poolside furniture so that each is shared between just a few families. Additionally, numerous tennis courts, squash courts, and children's playgrounds are conveniently situated around the villages.

Arabian Homes ensures that all its residents are provided with a safe and secure environment in which to live by employing security personnel to closely monitor access to the villages and patrol the perimeter at all times. Every village is maintained to a very high standard with pools cleaned every morning and the water checked regularly. Whatever type of housing you choose to settle in you will find fully furnished and equipped to a superior level with silent running split system air conditioning and high quality double glazed windows to create cool and dust free interiors. Other luxury and convenience features include entryphones, multichannel satellite and cable television services, and international direct dial telephones are connected to every home.

High class restaurants can also be found in the Arabian Homes' villages in addition to superb sports facilities and well-stocked supermarkets, and – according to the size of the village – a range of other shops including travel agents, boutiques, sports shops, ladies and gentlemens hairdressers, beauty salons, dry cleaners and medical clinics. Day care nurseries are available for the very young and pre-schools with qualified teaching staff for the 3 to 5 year olds. All the villages are serviced by regular bus services and exclusive limousines available 24 hours a day. For more details contact:

Arabian Homes:
Head Office, PO Box 11326, **Jeddah** 21453, Kingdom of Saudi Arabia; tel +966 2 682-2201 ext. 752; fax +966 2 683-4560; e-mail sales@arabian-homes.com.sa Website www.arabian-homes.com

PO Box 85839, **Riyadh** 11612, Kingdom of Saudi Arabia; tel +966 1 4541888; fax +966 1 4546420

PO Box 727, **Yanbu**, Kingdom of Saudi Arabia; tel +966 4 3225007; fax +966 4 3221055

High standard expatriate accommodation is also provided at the Binzagr Villa Compound in Jeddah. Housing to suit all needs is available from three or four bedroom detached and semi-detached villas, to three bedroom town houses, and one or two bedroom apartments. All come with fully fitted kitchens and built in cupboards in all bedrooms. The larger villas include enclosed gardens and splash pools, as well as separate maids/drivers quarters.

All residents at the Binzagr Villa Compound have access to a wide range of recreational facilities including tennis courts, a squash court, 20 m swimming pool and children's pool with jacuzzi, barbecue areas, snooker and pool room, multi-purpose/function room, exercise room, darts room, and sauna. Regular school runs and other services are also provided. Further information can be obtained by contacting Rohan Badenhorst at Binzagr Villa Compound, PO Box 22719, Jeddah 21416, Saudi Arabia; tel +966 2 667 1254; fax +966 2 667 1181.

Off-Compound Accommodation

If you are given a housing allowance by your employer and choose to live off-compound then you should definitely contact an estate agent (a list of which can be found in the local yellow pages or on-line www.ksayellowpages.com) to assist you in your search for accommodation. The pros of not living within a compound include: it is much cheaper to live off-compound, not living with the people you work with, greater privacy for families, no involvement in compound gossip. The cons include: being responsible for your own maintenance which can prove to be very expensive, greater difficulty with getting 'out and about' as women have to organise their own taxis or lifts for transport if they are not serviced by a driver, social activities are not on your doorstep as they are in compounds, children cannot freely play out on the streets, Arab neighbours are well-known to be somewhat noisy especially during the night-time. Other factors to bear in mind when choosing housing off-compound is whether you are moving into furnished or semi-furnished accommodation – the cost of secondhand furniture and fittings is not cheap but then again does not lose its value either.

The cost of off-compound villas range from SR 30,000 to SR 120,000 per year with the more expensive ones being the more luxurious. Prices for apartments start at about SR 14,000 and rise to SR 30,000 per year according to the quality, number of rooms, type of furnishing and facilties of the apartments. Fully carpeted and furnished apartments in newer blocks cost between about SR 40,000 and SR 50,000 per year. It is always worth trying to negotiate the price and terms of your lease before signing anything.

Utilities

Electricity & Water

Electricity is billed monthly; water annually. The *Hejira* calender dictates the year and all bills are written in Arabic. Generally the cost of utilities is included as part of the rental contract. The basic prices of water and electricity are low due to government subsidies but charges increase according to consumption levels.

Both 110 volt and 220 volt AC, 60 cycles, with two-pin European-style plugs and three pin UK plugs are in common use. Bayonet and screw light fittings can be found.

The water in residential homes is officially suited for cooking and drinking purposes but in reality it depends on the quality of your pipes. Bottled water is widely available and can be delivered to your door in 19 litre bottles or you can fill up large containers for free at fill-up points.

Telephones

Most apartments and villas have phone lines already installed but if this is not the case then it could take months or even years to have a line connected dependent on the demand in your area. Applications should be made at the Saudi Telephone Office and your name will be added to a waiting list. The process costs a few hundred riyals. If you want a line installed quickly there are alternative services available but the charge can be some several thousand riyals.

For further information see the *Telephone* section in the 'Daily Life' chapter.

Useful Addresses

Ministry of Agriculture & Water: PO Box 2639, Riyadh 11195; tel +966 1 4012777; fax +966 1 4044592.

Ministry of Communications: PO Box 3813, Riyadh 11178; tel +966 1 4043000; fax +966 1 4062146.

Ministry of Industry & Electricity: PO Box 5729, Riyadh 11127; tel +966 1 4776666; fax +966 1 4775488.

Ministry of Public Works & Housing: PO Box 56059, Riyadh 11151; tel +966 1 4058300; fax +966 1 4022723.

Daily Life

When embarking on relocating to a foreign country, especially one such as the Kingdom of Saudi Arabia that is culturally so different to life in Western countries with far more rules and regulations that must be adhered to, the numerous duties involved can appear somewhat overwhelming. The aim of this chapter is to provide all of the practical information needed to cope successfully with a range of aspects of life in Saudi Arabia. By confronting head-on the challenge posed by living in a society so steeped in Islamic customs you will find the experience exciting and rewarding and far less frightening than you may have initially foreseen.

Schools and Education

State education in the Kingdom for Saudi nationals has undergone tremendous changes over the last 30 years in terms of numbers with the number of schools increasing from 3,283 in 1970 to a recorded total approaching 22,000 in 1995. Saudi citizens receive free state education at all stages. In the Saudi education system, which has not altered so dramatically over the past three decades, all subjects are mainly taught in Arabic with the Islamic ethos all pervasive. Those Muslims who wish to attend a non-Islamic international school in order to receive an education less overshadowed with religious dogma and more suited to training for employment in the global workplace require special permission from the Ministry of Education.

There are several schools throughout the Kingdom that cater primarily for the children of expatriates. Many of them follow an American style curriculum but schools teaching British and European curricula are also present. The majority of the international schools enrol children only up to the age of 14 after which children are usually sent to boarding school either back in their home countries or in neighbouring Bahrain. Alternatively they may continue their studies by correspondence. Private education is not cheap and it is well worth finding out whether your employment contract includes the payment of school fees. Children wear a uniform at all the schools in the country and the school week is typically Saturday to Wednesday with Thursdays/Fridays treated as the weekend.

SCHOOL PROFILES

Below is given a brief outline of just some of the international schools situated in Saudi Arabia. For more detailed information you should make direct contact with the schools themselves. Entry into these schools is highly competitive so it is advisable to begin arranging your child's schooling as early on in your preparations for moving as you can.

The British School in Riyadh comes under the umbrella of Saudi Arabian International Schools (SAIS). It follows a British National Curriculum and has a student body currently totalled at 1,100. Of this number about 60 per cent are British passport holders and the remaining percentage are children of some 40 different nationalities. The school is co-educational and caters for children from Nursery to Year 9 (ages 4-14 years old). Class sizes are small, on average about 16 in Nursery years and 20 in all other years. The standard of teaching is rated very high. Fees range from SR 15,000 per annum for Nursery years to SR 27,000 per annum for the senior years.

The British International School in Jeddah takes children from the ages of 3 to 16 and prepares students to sit either GCSEs, IGCSEs, International Baccalaureates

(IB) or the PSATs if they wish to enter the American education system after leaving the school. Additionally SATs and TOEFL examinations can be sat at a local centre. Fees range from SR 3,500 per term for those in the Nursery years to SR 9,400 per term for those in the upper school (Y7-Y11); a non-refundable registration fee of SR 200 and one-off entrance fee of SR 3,000 also needs to be paid.

Dhahran British Grammar School is one of nine schools enrolling children from the ages of 4-15, that form the International Schools Group in the Dhahran District. Two follow the British National Curriculum, five follow an American Curriculum and two provide an International Curriculum. All the schools within the group teach students to a very high standard and prepare them for an easy transition to a school back in their home country where relevant. Fees range from SR 26,300 per annum for the junior years to SR 30,250 per annum for the senior years; additionally, a building fee of SR 3,000, registration fee of SR 200 and one-off enrolment fee of SR 7,000 is payable.

Al Khobar British International School is a co-educational school which teaches a British National Curriculum to pupils from the ages of 3 to 14 (UK pre-school to Y9). Children of about 30 different nationalities attend the school. Academic standards are high. Fees are about SR 22,000 per annum (£3,640).

Asir Preparatory School in Khamis Mushayt is only for the dependents of the British Aerospace workforce (UK and Australia). Children are either British or Australian and mainly from ex-RAF and ex-RAAF families. The school teaches a British National Curriculum to pupils from the ages of 4 up to 11 years after which they are expected to attend boarding schools or other private sector schools. The school is co-educational and the average size of a class is 16 pupils. Schooling is free to the first two children of any British Aerospace (BAe) family, but third children and dependents of MOD and BAe sub-contractors' families have to pay SR 18,000 per annum (approximately £3,000).

Asir Academy is the only other school apart from the Asir Preparatory School in the south-western region of Saudi Arabia teaching a Western style education. It is part of the Saudi Arabian International Schools (SAIS) group and follows an American curriculum. The majority of its 280 pupils are dependents of McDonald-Douglas workers although it welcomes any English speaking students in the area. Fees are approximately SR 40,000 per year.

Useful Addresses

Riyadh

SAIS (Saudi Arabian International Schools): British Section, PO Box 85769, Riyadh 11612; tel +966 1 248 2387/0386; fax +966 1 248 0351; ages 4-14.

Jeddah

British International School (The Continental School): PO Box 6453, Jeddah 21422; tel +966 2 699 0019; fax +966 2 699 0163; ages 3-16; Website www.BISJeddah.com or www.continentalschool.com

Jeddah Preparatory & Grammar School: c/o British Consulate General, PO Box 6316, Jeddah 21442; tel +966 2 693 7380/8019; fax +966 2 693 7380; ages 3-14; Website jpschool.homestead.com

Medical City Primary School: King Khalid National Guard Hospital, PO Box 9515, Jeddah 21423; tel +966 2 665 3400; fax +966 2 685 2864; ages 4-11.

Taif

Taif Academy: Unit 61206, APO, AE 09802-1206; tel +966 2 725 4666 ext. 2286/5; fax +966 2 725 4666 ext. 2285.

Yanbu

Yanbu International: PO Box 30039, Yanbu Al-Sinaiyah; tel +966 4 392 1088/9; fax +966 4 392 1075.

Eastern Province

Abqaiq Academy: tel +966 3 566 0410; fax +966 3 566 2337.

Dhahran British Grammar School: PO Box 677, Dhahran 31932; tel +966 3 891 9555 ext. 2005; fax +966 3 891 5107; e-mail Ken_Battye@macexpress.org; ages 4-15.

Al Khobar British International School: PO Box 4359, Al Khobar 31952; tel +966 3 895 1404; fax +966 3 894 2312; ages 3-14.

Jubail British Academy: PO Box 10059, Madinat Al Jubail, Al Sinaiyah 31961; tel +966 3 341 7550; fax +966 3 341 2808; ages 4-13.

Jubail International: tel +966 3 341 7550/7681; fax +966 3 341 6990.

Western Province

Asir Academy: Consulate General Box R, Unit 61901, APO, AE 09809-1901; tel +966 7 223 3961 ext. 4086; fax +966 7 223 3961 ext. 4083.

Asir Preparatory School: PO Box 34, Khamis Mushayt; tel +966 7 222 0545; fax +966 7 223 8991; ages 4-11.

Further information on international schools in Saudi Arabia can be obtained either by visiting the website www.livingabroad.com/education or by contacting:

The British Council Riyadh: tel +966 1 462 1818; fax +966 1 462 0663; e-mail simon.chambers@bc-riyadh.bcouncil.org

The British Council West Saudi Arabia: tel +966 2 672 3336; fax +966 2 672 6341; e-mail neville.mcbain@bc-jeddah.bcouncil.org

The British Council Eastern Province: tel +966 3 826 9036/9831; fax +966 3 826 8753; e-mail allen.swales@bc-dammam.bcouncil.org

More details on the British Council in Saudi Arabia can also be downloaded from their website www.britishcouncil.org.

The Media, Post and Telecommunications

The Media

All printed matter, films and videos displaying scantily-dressed women, sexual contact between men and women, religious propaganda or politically-sensitive matter will be seized by the Ministry of Information (PO Box 843, Riyadh; tel +966 1 4068888; fax +966 1 4050674). Any books or personal videos discovered in luggage coming into the country will be reviewed by the Information Ministry to be returned (or not) to the owner in due course.

Television

Saudi Arabian TV's Channel 2 widely available throughout the Kingdom, broadcasts primarily in English with a French language news report broadcast nightly at 8pm. The programmes are a combination of old and extremely edited North American shows, locally made documentaries and talk shows. An English news broadcast is shown at 9pm every evening. Dhahran, in the Eastern Province, is the base of Aramco TV shown on Channel 3 which broadcasts comparatively up-to-date American programmes, including plenty of sport. About half of the population can also receive Kuwait TV and those living in the Eastern Province can pick up broadcasts from Bahrain, Qatar and the UAE.

Radio

To find out the frequencies for the BBC World Service in Saudi Arabia contact: tel 020-7557 1165; e-mail worldservice.letters@bbc.co.uk Website www.bbc.co.uk/worldservice. A monthly international programmes guide, *BBC On Air*, which includes information on World Service Radio, BBC World and BBC Prime television services can be obtained by contacting the BBC at tel 020-7557 2211; fax 020-7240 4899.

Radio broadcasts can also be received from Bahrain and Qatar by those in the Eastern Province of Saudi Arabia.

Books and Newspapers

The Kingdom's English language dailies are the *Arab News*, *Saudi Gazette*, and *Riyadh Daily*. All these papers generally have a good coverage of foreign news. *Arab News* has the largest readership amongst the three. The leading foreign newspapers and magazines can be bought in the chief cities normally at the major hotels and the big western-style supermarkets. Be warned though as all literature undergoes rigorous censorship before it reaches the shelves for purchase – pictures of scantily dressed women are adapted with a black felt pen to look modest, what is considered politically sensitive material will be ripped out of the publication as will any advertisements for alcoholic beverages. It is worth checking before buying any foreign magazine or newspaper just how much content has escaped unscathed.

A few bookshops and hotel bookstalls can be found in the larger cities in Saudi Arabia. However, the range of English language books available is somewhat limited.

Post

Airmail to Europe and North America takes about a week to arrive from Saudi Arabia. For letters sent by airmail to addresses outside the Arab world postage costs SR 1.5 for the first 10g and SR 1 for each extra 10g. Postage for mail sent within Saudi Arabia and the Arab world is 75 halalahs for the first 10g and 50 halalahs for each extra 10g. Sending postcards to addresses outside the Arab world is charged at SR 1 and within the Kingdom and other Arab countries 50 halalahs. Items sent by registered post cost SR 3 worldwide and SR 2 within the Arab world.

There are no poste restante services in Saudi Arabia and no mail is delivered to residential addresses. Most people receive mail through the post box number at their place of work or via their sponsor's address. Post offices are situated centrally in the large cities however, few post boxes will be found. Generally people tend to have mail posted from their place of work and pay the relevant postage cost. Courier services are widely available although quite expensive.

All incoming and outgoing mail is subject to censorship so remember to warn your friends and relatives not to send any controversial material or you will suffer the consequences such as a spell in prison or in extreme cases deportation.

Useful Addresses

DHL: FNAF Worldwide Express, PO Box 22199, Riyadh 11432; tel +966 1 4621919; fax +966 1 4620371.

Fedex: PO Box 63529, Riyadh 99997; tel +966 1 4654220; fax +966 1 4630075.

Ministry of Posts, Telegraphs and Telephone (PTT): Riyadh 11112; tel +966 1 4634444; fax +966 1 4637072.

Telephone

Saudi Arabia has a very efficient and reliable telephone service with direct dialling to almost every country in the world. In addition to offices and residential accommodation having direct telephone lines, nearly every town in the Kingdom has a telephone office through which international calls can be made. Calls to Europe from Saudi Arabia are charged at SR 8 per minute but from 2300 to 0300 hours there is a 20 per cent reduction on calls and from 0300 to 0900 hours a 40 per cent reduction. Fax, telex and/or telegraph services are also widely available. The international dialling code for Saudi Arabia is +966. The area codes for major Saudi cities are:

01	Riyadh
02	Jeddah, Makkah, Taif
03	Dammam, Dhahran, Al-Khobar, Jubail, Hofuf
04	Madinah, Yanbu, Tabuk
06	Buraidah, Qassim, Hail
07	Abha, Al-Baha, Jizan, Najran

Emergency numbers

Police	999
Ambulance	997
Fire	998
Road Accidents	993

Other useful numbers

International Information	900
Directory Assistance	905
Telephone Maintenance	904

Cars and Motoring

In Saudi Arabia cars are driven on the right side of the road. On open highways the speed limit is commonly 120 km/hour and 50 or 60 km/hour in towns. Petrol is cheap and most expatriates have the use of a company car or can easily purchase a car from other expatriates. The cost of buying a new British or Japanese model is far less than comparable prices in the West.

Driving Regulations

It is illegal for women to drive in Saudi Arabia (although there are currently rumours that the government may be reviewing this policy shortly). For alternative travel arrangements see the 'Transport' section below. Male residents wishing to drive in Saudi Arabia require a Saudi driving licence. Those caught driving without one can be landed with a fine of £150 and a 24 hour spell in jail. Saudi licences are normally obtained by employers when they obtain work and residence permits for their staff. If visiting the country or waiting for a Saudi licence to be processed non-Saudis can drive using an International Driving Permit or preferably a full Western home country licence, for up to 3 months as long as the Permit or licence is brought to the Traffic Police and a covering certificate (in Arabic) is procured. It is essential while driving to always carry a licence as failure to do so could result in a £50 fine and confinement in jail for 24 hours.

It is worth paying close attention to the table below for a comprehensive list of penalties prescribed for motoring offences. Most of the offences carry imprisonment as well as monetary fines and in some cases lashes. Even if you are only a passenger in a car being driven recklessly you can receive a £250 fine and 20 lashes. Those stopped with even the slightest hint of alcohol on their breath will be taken to a Government Hospital for a blood test which, if positive, can result in arrest, possible criminal charges being held against them and automatic expulsion from the country.

Fines, jail, lashes: The offenders' tariff*

Type of violation	Fine	Jail/lashes
Going through a red light	£150	3 days
Driving in wrong direction	£150	3 days
Speeding	£150	3 days
Illegal Paking	£80	3 days
Parking on sidewalk	£80	–
Not carrying driving licence	£50	24 hours
Driving Licence expired	£50	24 hours
No driving licence	£150	24 hours
Road licence expired	£80	3 days
Leaving the scene of an accident	£150	3 days
Ignoring traffic police instruction	£50	3 days
Exceeding pedestrian crossing line	£150	3 days
Reckless driving and skidding	£250	20 days/20 lashes
Accompanying reckless drivers while skidding	£250	20 lashes

Car Rental

Cars can be hired from any of the major international car rental companies with branches throughout the Kingdom. Those wishing to hire a car must be over 25 and can drive on their own national driving licence for up to three months provided that they have an officially-sanctioned Arabic translation with them. An international driving permit (with translation) is also useful but not obligatory.

Useful Numbers

Avis: +966 1 222639.
Hertz: +966 1 220-2678.

Accidents

Traffic accidents are one of the primary causes of death amongst British expatriates in Saudi Arabia. Traffic is very fast and the hot temperatures of the climate put an enormous strain on tyres which can unexpectedly disintegrate at speed resulting in fatal loss of control. Drivers should always wear a seat belt and ensure that their tyres are kept in good condition.

Drivers may not leave a scene of an accident until permitted to do so by the police. Where damage or injury has occurred, the driver(s) considered responsible are imprisoned straight away regardless of any injuries that they may have sustained. If a driver has accidentally been the cause of a death or injury of another driver or pedestrian they will still have to pay compensation or 'blood money' on a varying scale to the relatives of the deceased or to the injured party. Currently, a Muslim man's life is valued at 100,000 Saudi riyals (about £16,650), Christian lives are rated at only half this.

*Reproduced by kind permission of *Overseas Jobs Express*, 15/11/99

Insurance

Motor insurance, including third party cover, is obtainable in Saudi Arabia. It is not compulsory but is strongly recommended. Some Muslims have doubts about the policy of insurance and so expatriates driving their employer's vehicle on business should not take for granted that he is covered for third party claims. Drivers should always check what their insurance covers them for prior to driving.

Transport

Air

The most convenient way of travelling around the Kingdom is by air. There are nineteen domestic airports in the country and Saudia (SV) links all main centres. Jeddah is connected to Riyadh and Riyadh with Dhahran by 'Arabian Express' economy class. A boarding pass should be acquired the night before departure. During the Hajj there are special flights for pilgrims arriving at or departing from Jeddah.

Sea

Dhows can be chartered for trips on both coasts.

Rail

Saudi Arabia is the only Gulf country with a railway system. The functioning line links Riyadh to Dammam via Dhahran, Abqaiq, Hofuf, Harad and Al Yamamah. The air-conditioned trains run daily except Thursdays. Under four year olds travel free. Unfortunately, the railway line on the west coast made famous by Lawrence of Arabia's raid has for a long time been left to the desert. Further information can be obtained from the *Saudi Railways Organisation*, PO Box 36, Dammam 31241, Kingdom of Saudi Arabia; tel +966 3 832-2042; fax +966 3 834-0936.

Buses

SAPTCO (*Saudi Arabian Public Transport Company*, PO Box 10667, Riyadh 11443; tel +966 1 4545000; fax +966 1 4542100) have recently introduced inter-urban and local bus services using modern vehicles some of which have air-conditioning. Female passengers have designated areas to sit in cordoned off from male passengers.

Taxis

All cities offer taxi services but prices should always be negotiated before travelling anywhere as fares can be expensive and few taxis have meters (or if they do, rarely use them). Taxis are recognisable by their yellow colour.

Limousines

A number of companies operate white American air-conditioned saloons mostly used for journeys to and from the airport but also for travel within the cities. Fixed tariffs for certain trips (average SR 50) are prominently featured at airports and can be requested from drivers.

Banking and Finance

Banking in Saudi Arabia is relatively straightforward with commercial banks located throughout the country as well as money-changers in foreign currencies which offer banking transactions. No restrictions are in place on converting the riyal or transferring money outside the country. In general banks are open from 8am to 12.30pm and 5pm to 7pm, Saturday to Wednesday, and 9am to 12.30pm on Thursdays. The Saudi Arabia Monetary Agency (SAMA, PO Box 2992, Riyadh 11169, Kingdom of Saudi Arabia; tel +966 1 463-3000; fax +966 1 466-2966) operates as a central bank that regulates all financial activities. Several specialised banks have also been set up by the government to aid the finance of various activities in their particular sectors.

Useful Addresses

Riyadh
Arab National Bank: PO Box 56921, Riyadh; tel +966 1 4029000; fax +966 1 4027747.
Al-Rajhi Investment & Banking Corporation PO Box 28, Riyadh 11411; tel +966 1 4601000; fax +966 1 4600922.
Riyadh Bank: PO Box 22622, Riyadh 11416; tel +966 1 4013030; fax +966 1 4042707.
Saudi British Bank: PO Box 9084, Riyadh 11413; tel +966 1 4050677; fax +966 1 4050660.
Saudi Investment Bank: PO Box 3533, Riyadh; tel +966 1 4778433; fax +966 1 4776781.
United Saudi Commercial Bank: PO Box 25895, Riyadh; tel +966 1 4784200; fax +966 1 4783197.

Jeddah
Bank Al-Jazira: PO Box 6277, Jeddah; tel +966 2 6518070; fax +966 2 6532478.
Islamic Development Bank: PO Box 5925, Jeddah 21432; tel +966 2 6361400; fax +966 2 6366871.
National Commercial Bank: PO Box 3555, Jeddah; tel +966 2 6493333; fax +966 2 6446468.
United Bank: PO Box 11222, Jeddah; tel +966 2 6822500; fax +966 2 6821605.

Offshore Banking

If you are working for a large company in the Gulf you are likely to be earning quite substantial amounts of money some of which you will undoubtedly be looking to invest. One of the primary financial advantages of being an expatriate is that you can invest this money offshore in tax havens such as the Isle of Man, the Channel Islands, Gibraltar and Bahrain, thus accruing tax-free interest on your savings. Many such facilities are as flexible as UK high street banking and range from current accounts to long-term, high interest earning deposits. For more details and addresses of offshore banking units see *Offshore Banking* section in 'Bahrain Daily Living' chapter.

Tax and the Expatriate

There are no personal taxes levied on residents in the Kingdom of Saudi Arabia. Expatriate and local employees have a 2 per cent social insurance tax imposed on their gross salaries and housing benefits paid by all resident companies which the employer administers to and can treat as a valid business deduction. No other taxes exist for expatriates living in the Kingdom. As a non-resident of your home country (i.e. for UK nationals spending fewer than 183 days in aggregate in Britain) you will not be subject to your home country's tax on earnings either. For more details on what you may or may not be entitled to or subjected to regarding tax regulations (on earnings, relocation expenses, investments, etc.) as an expatriate you should consult a specialist tax advisor. Useful contacts can be found in magazines such as *The Expatriate* and the large accounting/financial advisory companies like PriceWaterhouseCoopers (Plumtree Court, London EC4A 4HT; tel 020-7583 5000; fax 020-7822 4652) publish handy booklets giving detailed information on the tax implications for foreign nationals working in other countries.

Health Care in Saudi Arabia

Medical care, both public and private, in the Kingdom is of a very high standard with the ratio of hospital beds per person being one of the lowest in the world. Centres and clinics throughout the country provide preventive, prenatal, emergency and basic health services. Additionally a fleet of mobile clinics routinely visit the more remote villages, dispensing vaccines and performing basic medical services. Advanced hospitals and specialised treatment facilities also exist in the major urban areas throughout the Kingdom. Major employers of foreign nationals are legally obliged to provide comprehensive health cover for all their employees.

The Ministry of Health provides 63 per cent of hospital beds, followed by the private sector with 13 per cent, the Ministry of Defence and Aviation with 8 per cent and the Ministry of Higher Education with 7 per cent, the National Guard with 3 per cent, and the General Organisation for Social Insurance, the Royal Commission and the Ministry of the Interior with 2 per cent each. The government is the major provider of financial support to health services at all levels.

Some Saudi hospitals are internationally famous, such as the King Khaled Eye Specialist Hospital and the King Faisal Specialist Hospital and Research Centre. These two hospitals employ approximately 40 per cent and 50 per cent Western staff respectively, and many other hospitals such as those of the National Guard and the Ministry of the Interior employ similar proportions of health professionals from Western countries.

Useful Telephone Numbers

Jeddah
Dr Ghassan N. Pharaon (GNP): +966 2 682 0289; medical and dental care.
Jeddah Maternity & Children's Hospital: +966 2 6652600.
King Fahad Hospital: +966 2 6656436.

Riyadh
Al Hamadi: +966 1 462 2000.
GNP Polyclinic: +966 1 478 4691.
Consulting Clinics: +966 1 465 9100.
King Faisal Specialist Hospital & Research Centre: +966 1 4647272.
King Khaled Eye Specialist Hospital: +966 1 4821234.
King Khaled University Hospital: +966 1 4670011.
King Fahad National Guard Hospital: +966 1 2520088.
Riyadh Royal Armed Forces Hospital: +966 1 4777714.
Security Forces Hospital: +966 1 4774480.

Al Khobar/Dammam/Dhahran
Al Mana General: +966 3 826 2111.
Al Thomairy General: +966 3 857 1700.

Al Mouwasat: +966 3 841 4444.
Dammam Central Hospital: +966 3 8427777.
Dammam Maternity & Children's Hospital: +966 3 8426666.

Abha
Abha General Hospital: +966 7 2240019.
Asir General Hospital: +966 7 2240726.

Private Medical Insurance

Private medical care in the Kingdom of Saudi Arabia is of a very high standard but it is also by no means cheap. Taking out the proper health insurance cover for you and your family is essential when moving out to the Gulf.

BUPA International (Russell Mews, Brighton, BN1 2NR; tel 01273-208181; fax 01273-866583; e-mail advice@bupa-intl.com Website www.bupa-intl.com) has designed its own Lifeline scheme that offers maximum choice and flexibility. There are three levels of cover: Gold, Classic and Essential, all of which provide full refund for hospital accommodation and specialists' fees so you never need to be concerned about unexpected bills for in-patient treatment such as an operation. Cover for emergency ambulance charges and sports injuries is also standard. The Gold and Classic schemes offer out-patient treatment which may be a very wise precaution in Saudi Arabia. The most comprehensive cover is available with the Gold scheme which includes the cost of primary care treatment and home nursing. BUPA International has a 24 hour multi-lingual service centre dedicated to their expatriate members with an experienced team on hand to deal with any queries. Claims are paid promptly in any currency that you require, and you are covered anywhere in the world. For more information call +44 (0) 1273-208181.

For more details on other international health insurance schemes available to the expatriate and contact addresses see *Private Medical Insurance* in 'Bahrain Daily Living Chapter.'

Saudi Law

The legal system in the Kingdom of Saudi Arabia is mainly based on Islamic law (see *Shari'a Law* in Gulf States' 'General Introduction'), although several secular codes have been introduced, and commercial disputes are handled by special committees supervised by the Ministry of Commerce. Both Muslims and non-Muslims alike are subject to the dictates and penalties prescribed by Shari'a law. In 1997, 124 foreign offenders (none from western countries) were executed in the Kingdom.

There are over 300 shari'a courts throughout the Kingdom which include courts of first instance and courts of appeal. Minor civil and criminal cases are handled in the summary and general courts of first instance presided over by a single *qadi* (judge). In serious cases such as major theft, sexual misconduct, or murder, three qadis sit in judgement. Appeals are taken to the shari'a appeals courts, or courts of cassation, which consist of three departments: penal suits, personal status suits, and all other kinds of suits. The Chief Justice and a panel of several qadis preside over all cases in the appeals courts situated in Riyadh and Makkah. At the head of the justice system is the king, Fahd bin Abdul Aziz, who holds ultimate power to pardon accused offenders. All cases of capital punishment are automatically referred to the king for final review.

Mutawwa'iin (Religious Police)

The Mutawwa'iin (or *Matawa*) patrol public places throughout Saudi Arabia ensuring that residents and visitors abide by the strict Islamic codes of behaviour and dress requisite in the country (see *Islam* section in the Gulf States' 'General Introduction'). Those who are found in contravention of the local rules have been known to have been harassed, accosted or arrested by the Mutawwa'iin who work alongside uniformed police and possess police powers. Infractions include inappropriate dress, consuming alcohol, women accompanied by a non-relative male, signs of worship of another religion other than Islam e.g. carrying a cross or owning a bible. At best you will just be stopped by the religious police and for example if you are a woman who has not covered her head, will be told to put a headscarf on and allowed to move on, at worst you could be physically harmed or deported, or in very extreme cases sentenced to death.

The degree to which the Mutawwa'iin regulate public behaviour outside the compounds varies across the country and in some areas they attempt to enforce the rule that male and female adults should not mingle in public unless they are close relatives. Couples are often stopped and asked for proof of their relationship whether through marriage or close family ties. If a woman is caught socialising with a man not related to her she may be arrested and charged with prostitution. It is common for women not in the company of a close male relative to be refused service at certain restaurants in particular fast-food chains and many restaurants no longer have 'family sections' in which women are allowed to eat without being accompanied by male relatives – such places do not always inform the public of their restrictions and it has been known that women found contravening these policies have been arrested.

All homosexual activity is deemed a criminal offence and those found guilty of the act can incur severe penalties such as imprisonment and/or public flogging, or in extreme cases – be sentenced to death.

Other examples of religious police actions can be viewed in the *Personal Case Histories* section of this book under the 'Saudi Arabia' accounts. If you experience any trouble with the Mutawwa'iin you should report it directly to your embassy/consulate (see *Residence and Entry Regulations* chapter for addresses).

Saudi Regulations & Prohibitions

Under no circumstances should you attempt to import, manufacture, possess or consume any alcohol or illegal drugs in Saudi Arabia. Those caught in violation of these decrees face severe punishment such as jail sentences, fines, public lashing, and/or deportation. Convicted drug traffickers incur an indisputable death sentence. Customs carry out thorough inspections at all points of entry into the country.

Other items prohibited in the country include anything that Saudi customs and postal authorities consider opposed to Islamic principles including non-Islamic religious materials, pork products (and their by-products), and pornography (loosely defined). Fashion magazines, 'suggestive videos', Christmas decorations, certain books, etc. may be seized and the owner fined or penalised in some way (see also *The Media* section above).

Social Life

In public, dancing, music and films are prohibited – hence no cinemas or theatres will be found in Saudi Arabia but there are plenty of other activities in which expatriates resident in the country can participate, and within the compounds dance clubs do exist. Opportunities abound to pursue practically any sporting interest that you may have from scuba diving in the Red Sea to desert driving (see section under Gulf States 'General Introduction') to golf, fishing, tennis, squash, windsurfing, etc. However, it should be noted that many sporting activities are restricted to men only but there are plenty of other expatriate clubs and societies that welcome both men and women, and that incite active social lives, such as the *British Women's Group Jeddah* (c/o British Consulate General, PO Box 393, Jeddah 21411; tel +966 2 654 1811), and the *Corona Group* (PO Box 3843, Riyadh 11481). Details of other associations covering a wide range of interests can be obtained from your local embassy/consulate in the Kingdom (addresses can be found in the *Regional Guide* section). The American Community Services (ACS), a branch of the American Embassy, publish a monthly newsletter detailing forthcoming events and other useful information. You can contact ACS by e-mailing acs@zajil.net.

Video rental is widely available and there is an extensive choice of good restaurants to choose from representing a myriad of different countries' cuisines but bear in mind that unaccompanied single women may be refused service at these restaurants as well as at the fast food chains present in the Kingdom such as KFC, McDonald's and Pizza Hut.

Shopping

Saudi Arabia is not a shopper's paradise in the glamourous way that Dubai and Abu Dhabi in the UAE are regarded, but you will find just about anything that you want to buy provided that you know where to look. There are both modern shopping malls selling the latest fashion, electronic, and household goods, etc. and traditional Bedouin souks where you can buy frankincense, Bedouin silver jewellery, craft items and camel saddles, etc. Due to the low taxes on goods many luxury items such as gold, French perfume and rugs, and electronic merchandise, such as radios and cameras, can be bought at very good prices. Bargaining is an intrinsic part of purchasing anything in the Kingdom.

You will find well-stocked supermarkets and grocery stores selling a comparable range of foods to that which you are used to in your home country. Basic foodstuffs such as bread, cheese, eggs, meats and vegetables are in abundance and reasonably priced but imported items such as American or European brand processed foods are much more expensive. Alcohol and pork and its by-products are prohibited in the country and so not publicly available.

THE UNITED ARAB EMIRATES

Currency

The unit of currency is the UAE Dirham (AED or Dhs.) which is divided into 100 fils.

1 United Arab Emirates Dirham (AED) £0.1682; £1 AED 5.9465
1 United Arab Emirates Dirham (AED) US$ 0.2723; US$1 AED 3.6727

Introduction

Destination the United Arab Emirates

The United Arab Emirates (commonly abbreviated to the Emirates or simply UAE) is known locally as *Al Imarat al Arabiyah al Muttahidah* and was formerly the Trucial States. The UAE comprises seven emirates: Abu Dhabi, Dubai, Sharjah, Ras al-Khaimah, Fujairah, Umm al-Quwain and Ajman. Within the last 30 years the country has transformed from being a remote, underdeveloped desert region once heavily reliant upon its pearl and fishing industries, to its present highly advanced oil-rich state.

Tourism has become a major player in strengthening the UAE's economy and Dubai has been marked out as a twenty-first century hot spot. Amongst its visitor attractions include the luxury hotels, the stunning beaches and excellent watersport opportunities, golf, shopping and cultural sites. To give an idea of the wealth that can be found in the Emirates, one of the most expensive hotels in the world to construct – and the tallest, soaring higher than the Eiffel Tower – Burj Al Arab, has just been opened in Dubai with the cost of en suite rooms ranging from £560 per night to £9,400 (during the peak season, November to April). However, not all the emirates in the UAE operate on this scale (see *Regional Guide* below), in fact the individual emirates differ greatly from one another. For example, Sharjah prohibits alcohol whereas it is relatively easy to acquire in Dubai and Abu Dhabi.

The standard of living throughout the UAE is high and accordingly wages are generally much greater than the equivalent in other western countries. The expertise of foreign workers is constantly in demand especially as the native population constitutes less than 20 per cent of the total figure of UAE residents. Perhaps one of the most westernised of the Gulf states materially, the UAE still retains elements of its wealth of Arab history and culture, providing its foreign worker with plenty of opportunities to experience a lifestyle quite unlike that with which they may be familiar in their home country.

Pros and Cons of Moving to the United Arab Emirates

The UAE offers a vast scope of employment opportunities to those with professional skills looking to earn high salaries and enjoy added bonuses such as accommodation or a housing allowance, payment of school fees, etc., as well as paying no personal taxes on income which means more money to spend or save. Although the majority are drawn here primarily for the financial benefits and with a view to saving substantial amounts, many find that the range of outdoor and social activities in the country often alters the flow of their money from investing to spending. Unless you plan to spend your days working and simply lazing by the pool, living in the UAE is not cheap. Alcohol and imported goods are particularly expensive although you can get bargains on local produce and electrical items.

Foreign nationals resident in the UAE comprise over 80 per cent of the population. The expatriate communities within the country tend to be extremely sociable although mainly mix within their own ethnic groups. Unfortunately, prejudice and discrimination against foreigners from certain countries such as the Philippines, India, and Pakistan, is rife and these workers, widely known as TCNs (Third Country Nationals) are generally assigned to all the menial jobs while the high-paid positions are filled by qualified westerners.

The nightlife in Dubai is considered to be one of the most 'buzzing' in the Gulf region and Abu Dhabi also has a very lively atmosphere for its expatriate residents to enjoy. Although neither emirate offers the full range of evening entertainments on a scale that can be found in major western cities, what they do offer can sometimes make you feel that you are in some colonial outpost of the EU rather than in an Arab Gulf country. To obtain an authentic feel for traditional Arab culture you may be better off visiting one of the UAE's neighbours such as Saudi Arabia or Oman.

On account of its ultra modern appearance it could easily be forgotten that the UAE is fundamentally an Islamic country and as such upholds certain standards and rulings as dictated by Shari'a law (see Gulf States' 'General Introduction'). Muslims and non-Muslims alike are subject to the prescribed penalties. Recently, two UK teachers were given heavy fines and sentenced for four and a half years in prison for unconsciously bringing three grammes of cannabis (enough for two joints) into the country in a camera case given to them by a friend. The upside to having such strict laws in the country is that the UAE has a very low crime rate. Although the atmosphere in the UAE is generally more relaxed than in some of the other Gulf States such as Saudi Arabia, especially as the number of foreign residents far outnumbers UAE citizens, care should still be taken over what clothes you wear, not eating or drinking in public during daylight hours in Ramadan, etc. (see *Social Customs and Practices*, 'General Introduction').

From a Western perspective, the main pros and cons of living in the United Arab Emirates can be summarised as follows:

Pros: High wages, no personal tax to pay.
Ability to practice non-Islamic faiths within certain compounds.
Alcohol can be widely purchased in Abu Dhabi and Dubai.
Lively night life; very sociable expatriate community.
Extensive and exciting range of land and water sports.
Excellent tax free shopping opportunities.
Very low crime rate.

Cons: Expensive rental and daily living costs.
Major cities lack traditional Gulf Arab culture.
Harsh penalties for offenders – imprisonment, flogging, etc.
Prejudices and racism evident.
Sweltering summers.

Political and Economic Structure

Traces of man's existence in the area now known as the UAE date back approximately nine or ten thousand years. Hence, there is not enough room to do the area's history full justice here. Suffice to say that from its early beginnings trade by sea and over land with neighbouring and overseas countries played an important role in the UAE's political and economic development as it continues to do so today. For more in-depth studies, see the *Reading List*.

Due to its prime location as a major trade route through the Gulf, the land which the UAE now occupies has been much fought over. From 1515 to 1633 the Portuguese inhabited the area until they were driven out by attacking tribes on land and British and Dutch onslaughts from the sea. The Al Ya'ribi imams of Oman then assumed control of the lower Gulf region until Persia obtained dominance in the mid-eighteenth century.

At that time, the British fleet continued to assert its powerful force in the Indian Ocean but its strength was rivalled by the local Qawasim (or Qassimis), whose descendents presently hold sway over the Emirates of Sharjah and Ras al-Khaimah. During the first two decades of the nineteenth century, these two powers encountered numerous conflicts. A treaty signed in 1798 between the British and the Al Busaids, whose descendents today rule Oman, incited the Qassimis to raid British vessels. The justification for this action being that the Al Busaids were the Qassimis chief rivals for regional governance and so in the Qassimis' opinion the British had just allied themselves with their enemies. From the British viewpoint the agreement was purely a defence tactic to avoid French presence in the Gulf and retaliated in force. They labelled the Qassimi raids as acts of piracy from which the area became known as 'The Pirate Coast.'

By the beginning of 1820 the British had all but completely destroyed the Qassimi fleet consequently establishing their authority in the Gulf. General Treaties of Peace were then imposed on nine individual emirates. These treaties permitted the sheikhdoms to continue warring with each other and so in 1835 the Maritime Truce was drawn up to control this. Modifications of this truce occurred until 1853 when it was replaced by the Treaty of Peace in Perpetuity. This treaty acknowledged British jurisdiction over resolving disputes between the sheikhs. As a result of this, the area became known by Europeans as 'Trucial States' until the British departed in 1971.

During the nineteenth and early twentieth centuries the region's pearling industry flourished providing the inhabitants with a strong economy, supported by fishing on the coast and simple agriculture inland. However, this phase of prosperity came to an abrupt end with the collapse of Gulf pearls in the world market in the early 1930s. The region was to undergo many years of extreme poverty for although oil prospecting began in 1939, it was not until 1958 that the first oil strike was made and in 1962 exports began. Since the discovery of oil the country has continued to rise from strength to strength.

Economy

The UAE has been established as the world's third largest holder of proven oil reserves behind Saudi Arabia and Kuwait. Due to the enormous revenues resulting from oil exports and the support of growing non-oil sectors such as manufacturing, tourism and transport, the UAE has become one of today's wealthiest countries with one of the most stable economies in the Middle East and Asia. In 1999 its per capita income was estimated at US$16,892 and in the face of comparatively low oil prices throughout the 1990s its economic growth has maintained a steady rate of approximately 4.7 per cent per annum.

The focus of the country's economic policy is diversifying sources of revenue and developing the growth rates of the non-oil sectors. The increase in spending of the expatriate population has played a large part in the overtaking of government expenditure by private expenditure at almost double the rate. This has assisted the government with its ongoing plans to improve medical, educational and cultural services for citizens and residents.

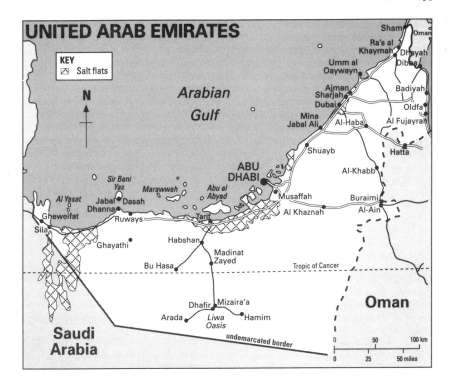

Economic growth in the non-oil sector, estimated at a rate of 8 per cent per annum between 1993-98, has generally been uniform across the services with the exception of the hotel business which has rocketed. Predictions forecast that trade and the tourism/hotel industry will be the fastest expanding areas within the non-oil sector which will result in an increasing demand for labour. Due to the recent drop in oil prices exports and re-exports are likely to decline in value but import demand is to stay constant.

As the GDP (Gross Domestic Product) contributed by non-oil sectors continues to rise and the UAE gradually moves from being wholly dependent upon its oil reserves (which currently supply a third of the GDP), the country is fast establishing itself a resilient economy able to withstand the unpredictable vicissitudes of the international oil markets.

A more detailed country economic review can be found in the *Regional Employment Guide* in the second section of this book, 'Working in the Gulf States.'

Government

On 2 December 1971, the British withdrew from the area then known as the Trucial States comprising the seven emirates: Abu Dhabi, Dubai, Sharjah, Ras al-Khaimah, Fujairah, Umm al-Quwain and Ajman. On this date six of those emirates joined together to form a federal state, the United Arab Emirates (UAE). Ras al-Khaimah entered the union the following year.

The UAE is a sovereign State with a federal system of government consisting of a Supreme Council of Rulers, a Cabinet, or Council of Ministers, a parliamentary body, the Federal National Council, and an independent judicial council headed by the Federal Supreme Court.

The highest ruling body is the **Supreme Council**, which is presided over by the President, Sheikh Zayed bin Sultan Al Nayhan, also Ruler of Abu Dhabi, and the Vice President, Sheikh Rashid bin Saeed Al Maktoum, Ruler of Dubai. The rulers of the other emirates constitute the remaining members of the Council. Within the Council an election for President and Vice President takes place every five years. The current President has been in office since the Council's inception in which he played a major role. General policy matters concerning education, foreign affairs, communications and development, and defence are dealt with by this Council, as well as the regulation of federal laws.

The **Council of Ministers**, is a twenty one member Cabinet, lead by a Prime Minister elected by the President with advice from fellow Supreme Council members. The Prime Minister, at present the Vice President, then elects the Ministers from among the federation's constituent emirates. This Cabinet working under the Supreme Council, acts as 'the executive authority' as written in the Constitution, for the UAE.

The **Federal National Council (FNC)**, consists of forty members chosen from the individual emirates in measure with their population figures: Abu Dhabi and Dubai are represented by eight members each, Sharjah and Ras al-Khaimah have six, Fujairah, Umm al-Quwain and Ajman have four. The FNC has the authority to regulate all proposed federal legislation, to question any Federal Minister over Ministry performance and to review the annual budget. Due to the demands placed on the FNC, a Research and Studies Unit and various sub-committees have been established.

The **Federal Judiciary**, is an independent ruling body incorporating the Federal Supreme Court and Courts of First Instance. Five judges chosen by the Supreme Council of Rulers comprise the Federal Supreme Court which reviews the constitutionality of federal laws and adjudicates intra-emirate conflicts and conflicts between the federal government and the emirates.

The individual emirates still retain a degree of **local government**, its structure and influence varying according to factors such as size and the level of development of each emirate. Local laws that affect everyday life can be decided by the regional authorities such as the legal purchase of alcohol in Abu Dhabi and Dubai that is considered an *illegal* activity in Sharjah.

International Relations

In 1971 the UAE joined the United Nations and the Arab League and today continues to be an active participant in both organisations working towards global peace. It is also a key member of the Arab Gulf Co-operation Council (AGCC or GCC) and is affiliated to the International Monetary Fund, the Organisation of Petroleum Exporting Countries (OPEC), and the World Trade Organisation. The UAE is host to sixty-two embassies and has established diplomatic relations with one hundred and forty-three countries. Amidst its campaigns for a more peaceful world presides its ongoing work towards Arab unity.

Geographical Information

Area and Main Physical Features

The UAE, which includes 200 islands off the coast, covers a land area of about 83,600 square kilometres. The Emirate of Abu Dhabi, the largest of the seven comprising the UAE, takes up 86 per cent of this land, 67,000 square kilometres. Second in size to this is the Dubai emirate with an area of 3,885 square kilometres.

The United Arab Emirates is situated in the northeastern region of the Arabian Peninsula with the Arabian Gulf lying to its north, the Gulf of Oman and Sultanate of Oman to its east and north, the Sultanate of Oman and Saudi Arabia to its south, and Qatar and Saudi Arabia to its west.

Stretching over 700 kilometres (of which 100 kilometres run alongside the Gulf of Oman), the UAE coastline encompasses offshore islands, coral reefs, salt-flats (*sabkha*) and lengths of gravel plain and desert. For the most part the UAE is characterised by the flatness of its desert topography. The well-known Empty Quarter or Ar-Rub Al Khali Desert, also found in Saudi Arabia and Oman, covers much of the Abu Dhabi Emirate with only the odd oasis interspersed among the expanse of sand dunes. However, the UAE is not all desert and there are the Hajar Mountains located in the east of the UAE near to the Gulf of Oman running from the Mussandam Peninsula in the north, through eastern UAE and into Oman. The Hajar Mountains date back over 200 million years making them the oldest rock formation in the Arabian Peninsula.

As recently as under 50 years ago, the Abu Dhabi Emirate was virtually uninhabited and uninhabitable but since the development of the federal capital, Abu Dhabi, and other major cities such as Al-Ain, the second city of the Emirate, 'greening' programmes have been underway to encourage verdancy in otherwise arid and barren areas.

Population

The population of the United Arab Emirates is currently over 2.2 million which includes over 1.5 million non-nationals. Population growth is 1.79 per cent per annum. Only 19 per cent of the population are UAE citizens, 23 per cent are of other Arab and Iranian descent, 50 per cent are South Asian (Indians and Pakistanis) and the remaining 8 per cent are expatriates from other countries (including Westerners and East Asians). 96 per cent are Muslim (Shi'a 16 per cent), the other 4 per cent are Christian, Hindu and of other faiths.

The official language of the UAE is Arabic, although English is widely spoken in the commercial world and Persian, Hindi and Urdu are also spoken to a greater extent than Arabic in certain areas. 79.2 per cent of the population (age 15 and over) are functionally literate.

Climate

The UAE's climate is similar to the other Gulf States on the Arabian Peninsula – sub-tropical and arid with high temperatures and sunny blue skies for the most part of the year. Summer is from June to September with humidity levels reaching their height in July and August. The humidity has been known to peak at 100 per cent and is such that it can be very wearisome to go anywhere and muster energy to do anything other than stay indoors with air-conditioning. Risk of sunstroke and heat exhaustion is particularly high during this time especially for those unused to living in hot climates. The importance of drinking plenty of water cannot be overstated as so much is lost through perspiration. November through to April are the most favourable months with cloudy skies and infrequent, irregular rainfall occurring from December to March.

Towards the end of the summer and throughout the winter, huge sandstorms can occur whipped up by hot desert winds, *shamal*. Heavy rainfall with loud thunder storms normally follow these sand storms.

Weather Chart

Average temperature (Celcius), rainfall (mm), sunshine in hours per day, humidity percentage.

	Jan	Feb	Mar	Apr	May	Jun	Jul	Aug	Sep	Oct	Nov	Dec
Sharjah												
Max	23	24	27	30	34	36	38	39	37	33	31	26
Min	12	14	16	18	22	25	28	28	25	22	18	14
Rainfall	24	24	5	2	0	0	0	0	0	0	5	26
Rainy Days	2.0	2.0	1.0	0.3	0.0	0.0	0.0	0.0	0.0	0.0	0.2	2.0
Sunshine	8	9	8	10	11	11	11	10	10	10	10	8
Humidity	71	72	68	65	62	65	64	65	69	70	69	72

Regional Guide

The majority of foreign nationals resident in the UAE settle in the two largest of the emirates, Abu Dhabi and Dubai. These are the most modern and highly-developed areas in the country offering both the business worker and tourist a comprehensive range of opportunities, attractions and activities to ensure a very busy, profitable, rewarding and enjoyable stay. The remaining emirates do not match up to the scale of development undergone in these regions over the last forty-odd years but each individually has something to offer either the prospective business worker or visiting tourist: from promising investment opportunities to relaxing, scenic and traditional sights, and an unlimited scope for pursuing sporting activities.

English is widely spoken throughout the UAE and the standard of accommodation is generally very high although accordingly expensive.

Information Facilities

There is no official UAE tourist office as such – or indeed for that matter, individual tourist offices for the separate emirates. However, most tour operators can provide information on the regions you plan to visit and arrange hotel reservations as well as local excursions and sporting activities. For more details on available tours, flights, etc. it is worth contacting the Emirates own DNATA Travel (UK branch: 27/43 Grosvenor Gardens, London SW1W 0BP), which has won a total of forty major awards in just the last ten years for its outstanding global travel services in both the tourism and business industries (for a list of other tour operators in the UK look under the 'Getting There' section at the end of this chapter, for tour operators in the UAE see below). In Abu Dhabi, the Abu Dhabi National Hotels Corporation (ADNHC – PO Box 46806, Abu Dhabi; tel +971 2 447228; fax +971 2 448495) in conjunction with Sunshine Destinations Management, handle all aspects of the country's tourist industry from promotion to organising specialised tours and meeting with tourists face-to-face (see website www.emirates.org/ tourism/abu_dhabi.html). Dubai, Sharjah and Fujairah have also set up tourist information servers that provide the low-down on everything you need to know about the areas whether you are planning a casual visit or a longer term stay. The best way to access this information is by visiting the respective websites:

Dubai Department of Tourism and Commerce Marketing: www.dubaitourism.com
Sharjah Commerce and Tourism Development Authority: www.sharjah-welcome.com
Fujairah Tourism Bureau: www.fujairah-tourism.com

The most comprehensive list of websites and links providing details on every aspect of life in the UAE can be found at www.uaeforever.com/TheList.html. The Emirates Center for Strategic Studies and Research provides a similar service at www.ecssr.ac.ae. For a more general country profile and links to other sites visit www.arab.net.welcome.html. To locate specific addresses within the UAE search the country's Yellow Pages site: www.uae.ypages.com/html/1.htm.

Useful Addresses

Embassy of the United Arab Emirates: 30 Prince's Gate, London SW7 1PT; tel 020-7581 1281; fax 020-7581 9616; e-mail embcdep@cocoon.co.uk

Government of Dubai Department of Tourism and Commerce Marketing: **UAE:** PO Box 594, Dubai; tel +971 4 223 00 00; fax +971 4 223 00 22; e-mail info@dubaitourism.co.ae Website www.dubaitourism.com; **UK & Ireland:** 125 Pall Mall, London SW1Y 5EA; tel 020-7839 0580; fax 020-7839 0582; e-mail dtcm—uk@dubaitourism.co.ae; **France:** 15 bis rue de Marignan, 75008 Paris; tel +33 1 44 95 85 00; fax +33 1 45 63 13 14; e-mail dtcm-france@wanadoo.fr; **USA (East & Central):** 8 Penn Center, Philadelphia, PA 19103; tel +1 215 751-9750; fax +1 215 751-9551; e-mail dtcm—usa@dubaitourism.co.ae; **USA (West Coast):** 901 Wilshire Boulevard, Santa Monica, CA 90401; tel +1 310 752-4488; fax +1 310 752-4444.

Tour Operators in the UAE

Abu Dhabi Travel Bureau: PO Box 278, Abu Dhabi; tel +971 2 338700.

Al Amaan Travels and Tourism: PO Box 1615 Al Ain; tel +971 3 655777; fax +971 3 655572.

Al Dhafar Tours and Travels Agencies: PO Box 866, Fujairah; tel +971 9 232550; fax +971 9 232551.

Al Zora Travel, Tours & Cargo: PO Box 13020, Dubai; tel +971 4 823990; fax +971 4 923988.

Arabianlink Tours: PO Box 821, Sharjah; tel +971 6 373000; fax +971 6 524095.

Dubai Travel & Tourist Services: PO Box 2533, Dubai; tel +971 4 515153; fax +971 4 527692.

Orient Travel &Touring Agency: PO Box 772, Sharjah; tel +971 6 357323.

Umm Al Quwain National Travel Agency: PO Box 601, Umm Al Quwain; tel +971 6 656615.

ABU DHABI

The largest of the seven emirates comprising the UAE and home to the federal capital, Abu Dhabi city, Abu Dhabi emirate has much to offer its visitor by way of modern and traditional culture. The capital lies at the head of a T-shaped island, 30 km from the regional airport located on the mainland. Al-Ain, the second largest city of the district and acting local capital for the eastern region is situated on the border between Oman and the UAE, 148 km from Abu Dhabi city. The Rub al-Khali or Empty Quarter desert covers a substantial part of the Abu Dhabi emirate.

Abu Dhabi

Most government offices and the headquarters for a number of international companies can be found in this city that is renown for its impressive modern architectural high-rise structures. Despite the aridity of the area, concerted efforts to encourage the growth of grass, palm trees and flowers, have earned it its reputation as a garden city. Amidst all this modernity can be found Al Husn Palace also known as the White Fort dating back to the late nineteenth century and situated in the grounds of the Cultural Foundation. The Foundation also houses an extensive library and museum for Islamic art and local history for those who wish to discover more about the traditional side of the city. The two hundred year old Al Maqta Fort is the other notable historic structure in the city where few sights date back beyond thirty to forty years ago.

The oil, banking and commerce industries dominate the feel of this blossoming place that has been developed over only the last forty odd years from being a non-descript fishing village to the prosperous metropolis it is today.

Al-Ain

Al-Ain was founded around the Buraimi oasis, the largest natural oasis in the UAE. Consequently its dairy and arable farms make it an agricultural centre of the emirates. The Ruler of the UAE was born here thus many Gulf Arabs are drawn to the place that is also the location of the oldest university in the UAE. Additionally, tourists may be attracted to the area's outstanding natural beauty and the empty dunes which surround the city making it an ideal starting point for sand dune expeditions. Among the sights to see are: the Al-Ain Museum that exhibits old photographs of Al-Ain and Abu Dhabi; the camel market; the Eastern Fort, birthplace of the UAE's President, Sheikh Zayed; the Jebel Hafit summit; the livestock souk; the Muraijib Fort and Park; Al-Ain's zoo and aquarium.

Al-Ain is a favourable weekend destination from both Abu Dhabi and Dubai, being only one and a half and little over one hour's drive from each location respectively. In the summer, the area's dry air makes it an ideal escape site from the humidity of the coast.

Liwa Oasis

This region is renowned for its incredible scenery that makes it a magnet for the weekend tourist. As the ancestral home of Abu Dhabi's ruling family, it attracts both expatriates and Emiratis. Liwa is located on the edge of the Rub al-Khali desert and possesses some of the most impressive sand dunes in the country. Hidden just below the arid surface are reserves of water that are responsible for the area's interspersed spots of verdancy. The most common way to explore Liwa is by desert driving (see 'Desert Driving' in the first section of this book, *Living in the Gulf States: General Introduction*.)

DUBAI

Dubai traditionally, and today still, thrives on trade in addition to its very healthy tourist industry that has developed considerably over the last thirty or so years. The city more than adequately caters for both business visitor/resident and tourist being the commercial capital of the UAE and home to the World Trade Centre, and one of the most progressive of the emirates. Hotels, clubs, sporting activities, shopping, and tourist attractions abound in the city and the surrounding area provides ample opportunities for desert driving and wadi bashing (see chapter on 'Desert Driving' in the first section of this book, *Living in the Gulf States: General Introduction*.) The city is renowned for its welcoming and relaxed atmosphere.

The Dubai Creek (*al-khor*) divides Dubai city into two towns: Bur Dubai to the west and Deira to the east. The Creek can be crossed either by taking: the Shindagha Tunnel that runs under the Creek at its northern end; the Al-Maktoum Bridge or Al-Garhond Bridge; or by an open water taxi (*abra*). Like Abu Dhabi, Dubai has become a very modern city in a very short time with few buildings and sights dating back beyond forty years. The oldest building in Dubai is reputedly the Al-Fahidi Fort, built in the early nineteenth century and converted from royal residential and later governmental use to a museum in 1971. The best way to find out more about

Dubai is to contact the Government of Dubai Department of Tourism and Commerce Marketing (address above).

SHARJAH (Ash-Sharqa)

What Sharjah may lack in terms of modern culture and glamour compared to Dubai and Abu Dhabi, it more than makes up for in its adherence to the past and tradition. In 1998, this emirate – third largest of the seven, was declared the Arab Cultural Capital by the United Nations Educational, Scientific and Cultural Organisation (UNESCO) because of its cultural foundations in arts, literature and heritage areas. In keeping with its observance of the traditional, Sharjah maintains a ban on all alcohol in the emirate.

To gain an insight into what life was like in the Arabian Peninsula before it began to be overrun by skyscrapers, hotels, and an influx of foreign nationals, Sharjah is the place to visit. Old buildings in the centre of the city have been restored to re-create how it must have looked in former times. Renovated structures accommodate the Art Centre, Art Galleries and Arts Café. The Sharjah Art Museum is in a building recently constructed.

The Sharjah Fort, first built in 1820, was left in virtual ruins in 1969 but has since been restored with the help of old photographs and documents so that it now has three towers (as opposed to the one it was reduced to) with rooms and halls linking them around a substantial courtyard. Additional attractions include an Islamic Museum, a Heritage Museum, an Archaeological Museum, and a Natural History Museum, located in the grounds of Sharjah Desert Park which lies 25 km outside the city.

Despite its strong ties with the past, Sharjah is by no means stuck there as it is the site for two-thirds of the UAE's manufacturing base, a fast developing International Airport, two active ports, and an Industrial Free Zone. In the 1980s, Sharjah was the main point of entry for UAE tourists on package tours.

AJMAN

Located on the coast between Sharjah and Umm al-Quwain, Ajman is the smallest of the emirates in size but the fourth largest emirate as far as number of industrial plants manufacturing consumer products is concerned.

For the visitor here there is little to see apart from the museum situated in the old police fort, dated late eighteenth century and formerly the ruler's palace before becoming a police station and subsequently, a museum in 1981. Ajman is only an hour's drive from Dubai and its museum ranks as one of the most interesting in the UAE. The characteristic UAE beaches and souks can also be found here but little else by way of tourist attractions.

UMM AL-QUWAIN (Umm al-Qa(i)wain)

Situated north of the main road connecting Dubai and Sharjah with Ras al-Khaimah, Umm al-Quwain is a small and comparatively isolated emirate which has remained unspoilt by Western influence. There are no skyscrapers to be found here and only three hotels to choose from if planning to stay in the area. the fort, mosque and watch towers and indeed everything in the town are all within easy walking distance of each other as the place is so modest in size.

RAS AL-KHAIMAH

Abundant in scenic beauty and greenery, the northernmost of the emirates Ras al-Khaimah lies on the Gulf Coast, with open sea on one side and desert and salt flats on the other and with mountains providing a magnificent backdrop to the view. The setting combined with the hassle free atmosphere of the region makes Ras al-Khaimah a popular weekend retreat for Dubai residents.

Similar to Dubai, a creek bisects Ras al-Khaimah into Ras al-Khaimah proper and Al-Nakheel. The former represents the old town and the latter, the more modern business area. To cross the Ras al-Khaimah Creek is a bridge and further south another road that runs along the brink of the water. The old town is the site of the region's museum housed in Ras al-Khaimah's old fort. Other than offering this attraction, the old town area remains more or less untouched by tourism. It welcomes visitors but has not yet been overrun with hotels and beach resorts, remaining – for the time being – a relatively quiet retreat from the business district located on the other side of the Creek in Al-Nakheel. Agriculture and mining are the main industries of the emirate.

FUJAIRAH

Fujairah is situated on the east coast of the UAE by the Gulf of Oman. It is the only emirate that does not have land overlooking the Arabian Gulf. It is considered to be one of the most scenic of the emirates (aided by its comparatively high annual rainfall) attracting many tourists who wish to explore the east coast area. Among its sights are two museums – one in a modern structure, the other recently set up in a renovated old building – the re-creation of a traditional mud-brick village, and the old Fort.

Fujairah was the last of the emirates to establish itself as an individual entity having been under Sharjah rule until 1952.

Getting to the United Arab Emirates

With the ongoing development of improved communications and transport, travel to anywhere in the world is getting easier and easier and flying to the UAE is no exception. There are six international airports in the UAE, the main ones situated in Abu Dhabi and Dubai and the others, catering for charter flights and smaller airlines, placed in the other major international centres as listed below. To find out the latest and best value for money flight information visit the following websites:

1Travel.com: www.1travel.com
Bargain Holidays: www.bargainholidays.com
Cheap Flights: www.cheapflights.co.uk
Internet Air Fares: www.air-fare.com
Lowestfare.com: www.lowestfare.com
TravelHub: www.travelhub.com

For those wishing to explore what the UAE has to offer its visitor contact one of the tour operators listed below. A comprehensive list of UAE hotels and additional tourist information can be found on the website www.hotelstravel.com/uae.html.

Airports in the UAE
Abu Dhabi International Airport, PO Box 20, Abu Dhabi, UAE; tel +971 2-757500; on the outskirts of the city, 37 kilometres away.
Al-Ain International Airport, PO Box 1554, Al-Ain, UAE; tel +971 3-855555; west of the city, 20 kilometres.
Dubai International Airport, PO Box 2525, Dubai, UAE; tel +971 4-245555; 20 minutes drive from the city, 4 kilometres.

Sharjah International Airport, PO Box 8, Sharjah, UAE; tel +971 6-581111; 10 kilometres from Sharjah, near to Dubai.
Ras al-Khaimah International Airport, PO Box 501, Ras al-Khaimah, UAE; tel +971 7-448111; 15 kilometres from the city.
Fujairah International Airport, PO Box 977, Fujairah, UAE; tel +971 9-226222; 5 kilometres from the city.

Air Services
British Airways: tel 0345-222111; www.british-airways.com
Emirates Airline: tel 0870-2432 222; www.emiratesairline.com
Gulf Air: tel 020-7408 1717; www.gulfairco.com
KLM: tel 0990-7509000; www.klm.com

Tour Operators
Arabian Odyssey: tel 01242-224 482.
British Airways Holidays: tel 01293-723171.
Golden Joy Holidays: tel 020-7794 9767.
Gulf Connections: tel 020-8715 1323.
Hayes & Jarvis: tel 020-8222 7822.
Kuoni Travel Ltd: tel 01306-743000
Orchid Tours: tel 01582-883377.
Somak Holidays: tel 020-8423 3000.
The Destination Group: tel 020-7400 4586.
Thomas Cook Holidays: tel 08705-133102.
Unijet: 01444-255600.

And specially for the sports' enthusiasts:

Eagle Gulf Tours: tel 01273-749661.
Golf and Leisure Breaks: tel 01491-576861.
Horse Racing Abroad: tel 01444-441 661.
Longshot Golf Holidays: tel 01730-268621.
Sports Tours International: tel 0161-703 8161.
Worldwide Fishing Safaris: tel 01733-849244.

Insurance

It is strongly recommended to take out comprehensive travel insurance when visiting the United Arab Emirates. A list of addresses for some of the major insurers offering reasonable and flexible premiums can be found in the *Getting to Bahrain* chapter under 'Insurance.'

Useful Guides

Abu Dhabi, Dubai: Explorer Guides (updated annually). In depth and well-informed. See website www.The-Explorer.com
Arab Gulf States: Lonely Planet Travel Survival Kit (1996). Features profiles on all the Gulf States. Website www.lonelyplanet.com
Off Road in the Emirates: Motivate Publishing. For those wanting to find out more about 4 Wheel Driving in the UAE.
UAE – MEED Practical Guide: MEED Publications. Comprehensive guide to the Emirates particularly useful for resident expats.

Residence and Entry Regulations

The Current Position

All individuals require a visa to enter the UAE with the exception of other GCC nationals, expatriate residents of the GCC, and transit passengers who do not leave the airport. In general visas are relatively easy to acquire provided that the applicant is not Israeli and has no Israeli stamps in their passport. Most visas are valid for periods of 30 or 60 days dictated by the Islamic calender not the western Gregorian calender. Failure to keep a close eye on dates could lead to overstaying the visa allowance. A ten day grace period in which to leave the emirates is granted to holders of 30 day visas (not for 60 day visa holders). Beyond this time a Dhs. 100 fine is imposed and a further daily charge of Dhs. 100 until departure.

Visit Visas

British nationals with residency in the UK can obtain visit visas on arrival in the UAE which entitle them to remain in the emirates for up to 60 days. Those travelling from other European countries, America, South Africa, and Australia, must procure their 30/60 day visas before departure from the UAE embassy in their 'home' country. The visit visa currently costs Dhs. 110 and can be extended.

Transit Visas

These visas are specifically for business trips, short breaks, and those travelling through the emirates. They cost Dhs. 120 and are valid for 14 days with no possibility of extension. To obtain these visas a UAE sponsor – either a business, hotel or individual resident in the UAE – needs to make the necessary arrangements. If lacking a sponsor a visa agency may act as a substitute but will charge highly for the privilege (up to Dhs. 2,000). Transit visas are processed more quickly than visit visas and do not require photographs. The visa itself awaits collection at the destination airport but it is important to ensure that the sponsor faxes a copy to the traveller before he/she departs as airports often request confirmation that a visa has been arranged before check-in at the airport of departure.

Single Women Travellers

All single women travelling to the emirates require sponsorship from a company, hotel or tour operator, or UAE resident. Even females who are resident British citizens may be denied a visa on demand at a UAE airport. It takes at least 24 hours for a visa application to be processed but could take longer so it is advisable to apply for a visa from a UAE embassy well in advance of the travel date. The following documentation is necessary for the application: a passport with a minimum of six months validity remaining; two photographs; a letter from the applicant's employer with an additional photocopy; proof of sponsorship – generally a fax of invitation sent direct to the embassy from a sponsor in the UAE; a copy of the application form obtained at the time of application. The cost of this at the UAE embassy in London is currently £20 to be paid in cash.

Renewing Visas

The Immigration Departments in Abu Dhabi (tel +971 2-462 244) and in Al-Ain (+971 3-510 000) can renew visit visas at a cost of Dhs. 500 for one month's extension. This can be done twice per visa but for the subsequent third month a visitor must leave the emirates and either fly back to their 'home' country to arrange a new visit visa or simply fly to a neighbouring country and collect a new visit visa on their return to the UAE. The latter is commonly known as a 'visa run.' The visa run simply involves obtaining an exit and new entry stamp in the individual's passport. Gulf Air (+971 2-332 600) offers a special visa run flight to Doha or Muscat from Abu Dhabi that returns passengers to the UAE capital after just an hour or so. The cost is a mere Dhs. 350 return but is applicable only to those travelling to the respective neighbouring countries to renew their visas. A perk of doing the visa run is great value duty free shopping to be found in the departure and arrival halls of the airports.

Residence Visas

A residence visa can be acquired either through the sponsorship of an employer or through the sponsorship of family. The obtainment of a health card (see below) is the first stage towards securing a residence visa. To retain residency status once it has been granted, the holder must not leave the UAE for a period exceeding six months. Children studying overseas but registered on their parents' sponsorship should remain mindful of this.

Those whose residency is being arranged for them by their employer should be spared the reams of paperwork involved in the process. However, they will need to provide their sponsor with the following documents: two passport photocopies, two passport size photographs and education/degree certificates validated by a solicitor and then the Foreign Office, who are required to attest the authenticity of the solicitor.

For those who are arranging sponsorship for family members (because their employers will not do so) or for those being sponsored by family the process is long and slow. First an application form acquired from the Immigration Department in Abu Dhabi needs to be typed out and sent with two passport photocopies, two passport size photographs, a medical certificate and Dhs. 100 worth of stamps. Application approval may take up to a month, after which a permit of entry for the UAE is issued and the holder must exit and re-enter the country. On re-entry to the UAE, the entry permit should be passed on to Immigration who will then stamp the holder's passport. Following this, the passport should be handed over to the Immigration Department in addition to a medical certificate, four passport size photographs and Dhs. 300. Finally, a permanent residency stamp should be issued. Generally, this process takes 1-2 months but a six month waiting period is not unheard of.

A minimum salary of Dhs. 3,500 is required to sponsor a spouse. Europeans sponsoring children do not need to earn a specified wage but other nationalities must receive a minimum salary of Dhs. 4,000. Constraints on sponsoring parents vary according to the sponsor's own visa status and occupation. Those with family sponsorship wishing to work need to obtain a labour card (see below) and undergo a second medical test.

Residence visas are valid for three years and are easily renewable.

Health Card

Health cards are imperative for those seeking residency and ensure free medical treatment at public hospitals for all residents. Medical standards in the public sector are considered high although private medical insurance (provided by some employers) is recommended as it will always rank superior.

Application forms for the health cards are available from the local Ministry of Health or from the regional government clinics. Submit the completed forms with two passport photocopies, two passport size photographs, a letter of employment and Dhs. 300. Those without employment seeking residency and a health card need to provide a tenancy contract, telephone and electricity bill (original and photocopies) in place of a letter of employment.

Initially a temporary health card is issued and a receipt for the Dhs. 300. This allows the holder to sit a medical test costing Dhs. 207. Both the temporary health card and the receipt for the Dhs. 300 are required in addition to two passport photographs. A medical examination and blood test for AIDS, Hepatitis, etc. will then lead to a medical certificate being issued.

A permanent health card can be collected on the date stated on the temporary health card which can be up to six months later, until which time the temporary card is a valid substitute.

Labour Card

A labour card is a prerequisite to all wishing to work in the UAE. It can only be acquired after residency has been secured.

After residency has been granted to an applicant being sponsored by their employer, the labour card should immediately follow in being processed with no further documents being required from the applicant.

For those with family sponsorship, a labour card must be applied for by their employer who will need a 'No Objection Certificate' (NOC) supplied by the sponsor, degree/further education certificates, two passport photocopies, two passport size photographs and commonly a photocopy of the sponsor's passport. A second medical test must also be taken.

For more information contact the Ministry of Labour and Social Affairs, PO Box 809, Abu Dhabi; tel +971 2 651890.

Registering with your Embassy/Consulate

On arrival in the United Arab Emirates, expatriates should ensure that they register with the regional Embassy or Consulate of their home country. This registration enables the home country's authorities to keep emigrants up to date with any information they need to be informed of as foreign nationals resident overseas and also enables them to trace individuals in the event of an emergency. The Consulates can also assist with information concerning an emigrant's status overseas and advise on any diplomatic or passport problems. They may also be able to help in an emergency e.g. in the unfortunate event of the death of a relative abroad. However, the Consulates do not function as a source of general help and advice, nor act as an employment bureau and they make this quite evident in response to any such enquiries.

Other Useful Addresses

Embassy of the United Arab Emirates, 30 Prince's Gate, London SW7 1PT; tel 020-7581 1281; fax 020-7581 9616; e-mail embcdep@cocoon.co.uk
Ministry of Health, PO Box 848, Abu Dhabi; tel +971 2 330000.

Embassies in the UAE:
British Embassy, PO Box 248, **Abu Dhabi**; tel +971 2 326600; fax +971 2 341744; PO Box 65, **Dubai**; tel +971 4 521070; fax +971 4 525750.

American Embassy, PO Box 4009, Abu Dhabi; Website www.usembabu.gov.ae
American Consulate General, PO Box 9343, Dubai; Website www.usembabu.gov.ae/CGDindex.htm

Setting Up Home

Renting Property

Those moving to the United Arab Emirates have no choice but to rent housing as UAE property or land can only be owned by UAE nationals or other GCC nationals. For many expatriates their accommodation may be included in their salary package. For those who must seek housing independently it is strongly advisable to rent from one of the numerous real estate agents in operation who will handle all the necessary paperwork rather than dealing directly with the landlord themselves. In Abu Dhabi help with renting property may be given by the Department of Social Services & Commercial Buildings, also known as the Khalifa committee (tel +971 2-563 3455), or local embassies may be able to offer advice.

Women should be aware that they are likely to incur far more difficulties renting property than a man and invariably have to put their employer's name on the lease. Only residents can take out a lease personally. They must supply their real estate agent with the following documents: a copy of their passport and visa, a 'No Objection Certificate' (NOC) from their employer, a copy of their salary certificate and the first signed rent cheque in addition (generally) to three post-dated cheques to cover any remaining lease payments.

Rent is always paid up front to the landlord usually to cover a six month period and sometimes a year's rental is demanded. It is more than likely that a bank loan will need to be taken out in order to meet the required sum. In some cases, the employer may help with the initial payment. Those renting through their company require a copy of the company trade licence, a copy of the passport of whoever is to sign the rent cheque and the cheque itself.

Estate Agents

Abu Dhabi:
Al Aman Real Estate & Commercial Estate, PO Box 47691; tel +971 2 795286; fax +971 2 795620.
Al Faris Real Estate Management, PO Box 8058; tel +971 2 777907; fax +971 2 774547.
Al Hijaz Real Estate, PO Box 43316; tel +971 2 327262; fax +971 2 348639.
Hana Real Estate, PO Box 4018; tel +971 2 217395.

Dubai:
Al Ali Real Estate, PO Box 5775; tel +971 4 277775; fax +971 4 278777.
Al Bayan Real Estate, PO Box 24229; tel +971 4 367999; fax +971 4 367500.
Better Homes, PO Box 2895; tel +971 4 447714; fax +971 4 496026.
Castles Plaza Real Estate, PO Box 25057; tel +971 4 551131; fax +971 4 553487.
Dream Land Real Estate, PO Box 22082; tel +971 4 246415; fax +971 4 280878.
Homes R Us Reality, PO Box 1219; tel +971 4 497774; fax +971 4 497787.

Sharjah:
Atlas Real Estate, PO Box 2881; tel +971 6 377171; fax +971 6 353440.
Court Real Estate, PO Box 392; tel +971 6 525515; fax +971 6 363311.
Deawel, PO Box 22836; tel +971 6 731121; fax +971 6 734424.

Kashwani Real Estate, PO Box 5163; tel +971 6 731133.

Ajman:
International Real Estate, PO Box 206; tel +971 6 446966.

Accommodation Options

There are four main choices of accommodation in the UAE: sharing a flat or villa, renting a fully furnished and serviced apartment, renting an unfurnished apartment, or renting a villa. Old style accommodation, including compounds have been, and continue to be, replaced with more modern and expensive housing.

Abu Dhabi boasts the highest rent prices with most of its residents living in high-rise apartment blocks and the more wealthy echelon of society leasing villas. Dubai is not as expensive as Abu Dhabi and there is greater opportunity to live in a villa although older, cheaper villas are gradually being replaced by more up-to-date, dearer ones and so living in an apartment is a more economical choice. To avoid the high costs of rent in Dubai centre many decide to live in the less costly neighbouring areas of Sharjah and Ajman, commuting into work. However, this is not a good idea if you have far to drive as the traffic around these areas is notorious for its hold-ups. Those living in Dubai and Sharjah must pay a municipal tax on rent of 5 per cent and 2 per cent respectively.

Sharing a flat or villa

The most economical option for accommodation is to flat/villa share with colleagues or friends. Advertisements can be found in the Classifieds section of regional newspapers or on notice boards in local supermarkets and sports clubs.

Furnished and Serviced Apartments

An expensive option for those wanting short-term, fully furnished accommodation and maid service. Serviced apartments usually include use of sports facilities and water and electricity connection fees. Daily/weekly/monthly or annual leases can be arranged.

In Abu Dhabi the current rental rates (Dhs.) per number of bedrooms are on average:

No. of bedrooms	1	2	3
Daily	330-550	605-825	770-1,045
Weekly	2,310-3,080	3,850-4,400	5,390-5,775
Monthly	8,250-9,350	11,000-12,100	13,200-14,300

Unfurnished Apartments

Apartments come with either central air conditioning (A/C) or window A/C. The former option is the more expensive and often included in the rental charge. The number and range of facilities that come with the apartment affects the rental fee accordingly: the more on offer, the costlier the rent. Flats can vary from being totally unfurnished to being semi-furnished (washing machine, cooker, fridge), with round-the-clock security, parking, sports facilities, satellite TV, etc.

In Abu Dhabi the rental rates per number of bedrooms are on average:

No. of bedrooms	Yearly Rent (in thousands of Dhs.)
1	30-38
2	36-45
3	50-60
4	75-120

Villas

Villas are the most costly accommodation option and like apartments vary in the facilities that they offer, with the more luxurious ones priced accordingly. In Abu Dhabi and Dubai average basic rental rates per number of bedrooms are:

Bedrooms	Yearly Rent (in thousands of Dhs.)
2	65-70
3	75-120
4	110-140

Additional Costs

Agent's Fee: normally a proportion of the rent (about 5 per cent).

Water and Electricity Department Deposit: currently a refundable cash amount of Dhs. 2,000 in order to be connected to the Mains, returned on cancellation of the lease.

Maintenance Fee: usually about 5 per cent of the annual rent.

Refundable Deposit: to be paid to the landlord to cover 'wear and tear', returned on completion of lease.

Hidden Costs: All leaseholders should double check what is and is not included in their rental fees, for example the high cost of A/C maintenance, repairs and energy bills in the summer, garden maintenance using costly water. Before a lease is signed, an agreement should be made as to whether or not the landlord is responsible for repairs.

Bills: If possible some old bills of the property should be reviewed to provide an idea of the cost of upkeep throughout the year. Tenants have to pay monthly electricity and water bills. Late payments can result in being cut off.

Furnishing Housing

Large companies may have a furniture warehouse from which employees can borrow, or they may pay for the removal of belongings from the 'home' country to the UAE, or they may provide a loan towards the cost of furnishing accommodation. Second-hand furniture shops are in abundance throughout the UAE but better value and quality items may be found through the Classifieds section in local newspapers or on notice boards in regional supermarkets. Large international furniture retailers such as Habitat can also be found in the UAE for those who can afford a more 'no expense spared' attitude.

Utilities

The Abu Dhabi, Dubai and Sharjah governments own the country's leading power plants for the supply of electricity and water. The federal Ministry of Water and Electricity's (MEW) production and capacity in its fourteen plants accounts for less than 15 per cent. Connection to the mains supply simply involves contacting the local Water and Electricity Authority (WEA or EWA) and paying a refundable deposit which lasts the duration of the tenant's lease.

Electricity

There is no shortage of electricity supply in the UAE which runs on 220/240 volts and 50 cycles. The three-point socket, as used in Britain, is in common use. Bills are issued monthly and are payable at the regional Water and Electricity Authority or at banks listed on the reverse of the bill. Bills are 'meter-read' and 'assessed' alternate months.

Water

In the emirates the cost of water is higher than oil. Filtered tap water is safe to drink but widely available bottled mineral water is a more palatable option. It is far more economical to purchase 20 litre water bottles in place of standard $1^1/_2$ litre bottles. Hand pumps, fixed pumps, and ceramic stands with taps are used for decanting the water from the large bottles. Refrigeration units can be bought at an average cost of Dhs. 700 but prices will vary according to different models. Delivery of the 20 litre bottles can be arranged with local water shops.

In the summer, those who have water tanks on the roof of their homes will find that hot water runs from the cold water tap and that in order to have a relatively cool shower they must ensure the immersion heater is kept off and use the hot water tap.

Payment of water bills is similar to that of electricity - monthly at the local Water and Electricity Authority or at banks listed on the reverse of the bill. Likewise, bills are 'meter-read' and 'assessed' alternate months.

Gas

Throughout the UAE, mains gas supplies do not exist but gas canisters can be bought from, and delivered by, the regional gas companies to fuel gas cookers. A central gas supply from rooftop storage tanks can be found in some of the most recently built homes.

Telephones

The telecommunication business in the UAE is controlled by one of the biggest and most prosperous companies in the Middle East, Emirates Telecommunications Corporation (ETISALAT). Since its inception in 1976, ETISALAT has worked hard to ensure that the UAE has one of the most highly-developed telecommunications services in the world. It provides the UAE with a number of telephone lines matching the highest international rate. Internet services were first introduced in August 1995 and there are plans to make the UAE a central base for internet services catering for the other Gulf States, East Africa, South-East and Central Asia and the Middle East. The use of mobile phones in the UAE rates greatest throughout the Middle East. This is mainly due to the low subscription fees.

To install a residential phone line a tenant needs to submit the following documents to their regional ETISALAT office: a completed application form (available from ETISALAT), a passport and residency visa photocopy, an NOC from their employer or copy of their tenancy agreement if the home is not registered under their name, in addition to Dhs. 250. Line installation will take place 2-5 days after the application has been received. Any extra phone sockets cost Dhs. 50 each. Monthly phone bills are issued (international calls itemised) and can be paid at ETISALAT branch offices or at certain banks (a list of which can be obtained from ETISALAT). If payment is not made within the first fourteen days of the month the line will be cut off. A billing enquiry service can be contacted by dialling 142. The quarterly rental charge for a telephone is Dhs. 45. Local calls made within each emirate are free. Cheap rates apply at the following times: for international calls

between 2100 and 0700 hours daily; for calls within the UAE from 1900-0700 hours; on Fridays and National Public Holidays.
For more information see the *Telecommunications* section in *Daily Life*.

Useful Addresses

Dubai Electricity & Water Authority: PO Box 564, Dubai; tel +971 4 348888; fax +971 4 348111.
Emirates Telecommunications Corporation (ETISALAT): PO Box 3838, Abu Dhabi; tel +971 2 2084753; fax +971 2 333753; e-mail ety2k@emirates.net.ae Website www.etisalat.co.ae

---

The 7-digit number scheme
ETISALAT are currently expanding their telephone networks which involves a scheme to change all 6-digit numbers in the UAE to 7-digits. This will affect all telephones, mobiles, fax machines, key systems and pagers. To obtain full details of the number changes either visit ETISALAT's website www.etisalat. co.ae/ 7digits/index.htm or contact the regional call centre:

Al-Ain: 03-506 1555.
Abu Dhabi: 02-332 999.
Dubai: 800-4627.
East Coast: (Fujeirah, Dibba, Kalba & Khorfakhan) 09-227 444.
Ras Al-Khaimah: 07-202 9444.
West Coast: (Sharjah, Ajman, Dhayd, Umm Al-Quwain, Abu Shagrah & Jubail) 06-561 1133.

Laundry

The larger supermarkets, some hotels and numerous small outlets provide laundry services at reasonable rates and next day delivery. Clothes can also be taken for an ironing-only service. Self-service launderettes are rare.

Domestic Helpers

Domestic helpers, generally from sub-continental countries such as India, are a common addition to most households. Residents must earn a minimum monthly wage of Dhs. 6,000 in order to employ a full-time live-in home helper as they must sponsor the worker and arrange their residency papers. The recommended way to go about hiring help is through an agency that invariably charges a small fee for their services. The cost of a residence visa for a domestic helper is about Dhs. 5,000 and the employer must agree to pay a monthly wage of at least Dhs. 750-1,000. Additionally, an airfare for the worker to return to their 'home country' once every two years must be paid.

Daily Life

The United Arab Emirates is generally considered to be one of the easiest states in the Gulf to acclimatise to due to its hospitable nation. However, living in the UAE will still be very different to what you may be familiar with in your home country. The purpose of this chapter is to provide all the necessary practical information to successfully cope with a range of aspects of life in the UAE so that armed with this knowledge your move to this country may be made that little less daunting.

Schools and Education

In a country whose population consists of far more resident expatriates than nationals perhaps it is not surprising to learn that its education system more than adequately caters for this. In addition to the state schools offering an Arabic curriculum mainly attended by UAE nationals and Arab expatriates, there are a number of private international schools that either specialise in offering an American or British or other European, Indian, Pakistani, etc. style education, or that can accommodate the teaching of all the different education systems. Those offering an American education attract not only western expatriates but Arab expatriates and UAE nationals as well; those with a British curriculum are mainly attended by Europeans but sometimes Arab and expatriates of other nationalities also attend.

The standard of teaching in the private schools is generally high. The British schools are all regularly inspected by the UK department of Education and Science and some receive OFSTED (Office of Standards in Education) inspections too. The UAE Ministry of Education ensures that only qualified teachers work in the system and schools undergo a check annually before receiving a licence. Parents are advised however, to additionally conduct their own research and ask friends and colleagues for more information on the schools and their reputation.

The majority of schools are segregated although co-ed schools do exist. All students are normally required to wear a uniform of some kind which takes into consideration the hot climate. Most schools run their own buses or parents can join a parent school run rota, details of which can be applied for from the individual schools. All schools in the UAE teach Arabic.

The international schools are fee-paying and expatriates working for large companies should find out whether or not their employer partially or wholly pays these fees.

The Structure of the Education System

Pre-school. Pre-schooling is available for children aged 3-4 1/2 years old and nurseries can take children from about one year old. For pre-schools, an interview is usually required before a child is accepted. English is generally the language used for teaching which normally occurs only in the morning. Fees range from about Dhs. 2,500 for five half-day-a-week terms but can differ considerably dependent on the standard of the school. Below is a list of useful telephone numbers of pre-schools and nurseries:

Abu Dhabi
Al Khubairat Community School: +971 2 462-280.
Cornerstones Pre-school: +971 2 462-734.
First Steps Kindergarten: +971 2 454 920.
Giggles: +971 2 215-255.
Humpty Dumpty: +971 2 652-650.
Sesame Street Private Nursery: +971 2 332-399.

Al-Ain
Al Juniors: +971 3 667-433.
Al Ain Little Flower School: +971 3 656-330.
Al Adhwa'a Private School: +971 3 667-667.

Dubai
Greenfield International Kindergarten: +971 4 550-551.
Happy Home Nursery: +971 4 518-228.
Kid's Island Nursery School: +971 4 448-272.
Little Flock English School: +971 4 448-044.
The British National Curriculum School: +971 4 441-614.
Tiny Home Montessori Nursery: +971 4 493-201.

Primary School Education. Children enter primary school at the age of at least four years old and leave when they are eleven years old. Due to the competition for places in the more popular nursery and primary schools parents are advised to investigate schooling when they are finalising other arrangements for their move to the UAE, and where required to pay deposits to ensure places for their children for the subsequent year. An additional deposit or debenture is also commonplace. Priority for places in the main English speaking schools is given to British, American, Canadian, Irish and Australian families and to siblings of children already in attendance at the school. Tuition fees range from about Dhs. 10,000-20,000 per year with potential additional charges – deposit, registration fee, application fee, debenture, books, etc.

Secondary Education. Secondary schools are attended by children aged from 11 to 17/18 years old. Most schools request proof of a child's prior school academic records and details of their education to date. In some cases a character reference is also required. Additionally, an entrance exam, comparable to the UK 11+ Common Entrance exam, may be sat, and a physical examination taken. A family interview may be necessary too.

Secondary schools teach syllabuses in line with the child's home country curriculum to ensure that he/she would be able, if the occasion arose, to successfully make the transition from a UAE school to a home school or vice versa. British schools prepare pupils for GCSEs and 'A' levels, while other schools allow students to sit French and International Baccalaureates or the American and Indian equivalents.

Tuition fees range from about Dhs. 15,000-43,000 a year with sixth form fees being the more expensive. As with primary school fees, extra charges may be incurred – deposit, debenture, registration fee, etc.

Special needs children. Special schools are provided for physically and mentally disadvantaged children from the age of 2 months to 20 years old. Contact the addresses below for more details.

Dubai Centre for Special Needs, PO Box 24921, Dubai, UAE; tel +971 4-449314/440966; fax 04-441861.
Al Noor Training Centre, PO Box 8397, Dubai, UAE; tel +971 4-3946088; fax 04-3946627.

Further Education. The majority of expatriate children who reach university level education return to their home country to enrol in further education. However, degree and diploma courses in Arts, Sciences, Engineering, Technology, Business and Management, etc. can be taken by expatriates in the UAE at most higher education institutes. This excludes the Higher Colleges of Technology and the Zayed Universities. Those considering such a move should remember that all teaching is segregated and men are taught by men, women by women. If women happen to need a male lecturer then lectures are conducted via the television screen.

For further details on higher education in the UAE contact the following addresses:

Ministry of Higher Education, PO Box 45253, Abu Dhabi, UAE; tel +971 2-65282; fax +971 2-775095.
Ministry of Education and Youth, PO Box 3962, Dubai, UAE; tel +971 4-691550.
National Admissions & Placement Office (NAPO), PO Box 45372, Abu Dhabi, UAE; tel +971 2-769400; fax +971 2-767172.
Central Services, PO Box 25026, UAE; tel +971 2-341153; fax +971 2-328074.

Universities

Ajman University College of Science & Technology, PO Box 346, Ajman, UAE; tel +971 6-455299; fax +971 6-446355.
American University of Dubai, PO Box 28282, Dubai, UAE; tel +971 4-3948889; fax +971 4-3948887.
American University of Sharjah, PO Box 26666, Sharjah, UAE; tel +971 6-5585555; fax +971 5585008/5585858.
UAE University: Al-Ain, PO Box 15551, Al-Ain, UAE; tel +971 3-642500; fax +971 3-645277; Website www.uaeu.ac.ae
University of Sharjah, PO Box 27272, Sharjah, UAE; tel +971 6-585000; fax +971 6-585186.

Other Useful Addresses

The British Council (e-mail information@ae.britcoun.org; Website www.britishcouncil.org):
PO Box 46523, **Abu Dhabi**; tel +971 2 659300; fax +971 2 664340.
PO Box 1636, **Dubai**; tel +971 4 3370109; fax +971 4 3370703.
Sharjah: tel +971 6 5722666; fax +971 6 5744788.

Private Schools

The following schools prepare pupils for local secondary schools' exams, Common Entrance exams, GCSEs and A-levels. All schools listed below are co-educational (unless otherwise stated) teaching children from a variety of nationalities, mainly British. There are 3 terms per academic year.

Ages from 2¹/₂-14:
The British National Curriculum School, PO Box 5760, Dubai, UAE; tel +971 4-441614; fax +971 4-497131.
English Speaking School, Dubai (DESS), PO Box 2002, Dubai, UAE; tel +971 4-3371457/3370973; fax +971 4-3378932.
Horizon English School, PO Box 6749, Dubai, UAE; tel +971 4-491442; fax +971 4-490514.
Jebel Ali Primary School, PO Box 17111, Dubai, UAE; tel +971 4-846485; fax +971 4-845373.
Jumeirah English Speaking School, PO Box 24942, Dubai, UAE; tel +971 4-3945515; fax +971 4-3943531.
Jumeirah Primary School, PO Box 29093, Dubai,UAE; tel +971 4-3943500; fax +971 4-3943960.
Ras Al Khaimah School, PO Box 975, Ras Al Kaimah, UAE; tel +971 7-352441; fax +971 7-362445.
Sharjah English School, PO Box 1600, Sharjah, UAE; tel +971 6-5522779; fax +971 6-5526921.

Victoria English School, PO Box 22549, Sharjah, UAE; tel +971 6-5350355; fax +971 6-5350344.

Ages from 3¹/₂-17/18:
Cambridge High School, PO Box 3004, Dubai, UAE; tel +971 4-824646; fax +971 4-824109.
Fujairah Private Academy, PO Box 797, Fujairah, UAE; tel +971 9-224001; fax +971 9-221710.
St Mary's Catholic High School, PO Box 52232, Dubai, UAE; tel +971 4-3370252; fax +971 4-3368119.

Ages 11-18:
Dubai College, PO Box 837, Dubai, UAE; tel +971 4-3999111; fax +971 4-3999175.
The English College, PO Box 11812, Dubai, UAE; tel +971 4-3943465; fax +971 4-3947242.
Jumeirah College, PO Box 29093, Dubai, UAE; tel +971 4-2947985; fax +971 4-3947731.
Latifa School for Girls, PO Box 11533, Dubai, UAE; tel +971 4-3361065/3361414; fax +971 4-3361462.
Rashid School for Boys, PO Box 2861, Dubai, UAE; tel +971 4-3361300; fax +971 4-3361407.

The following school teaches children, aged 4-18, an American curriculum. Terms are divided into two semesters and four quarters.

The American School of Dubai, PO Box 2222, Dubai, UAE; tel +971 4-440824; fax +971 4-441510.

The following schools prepare pupils, aged from 2¹/₂-17/18, for English, European International Baccalaureate and American High School exams:

Emirates International School, PO Box 6446, Dubai, UAE; tel +971 4-489804; fax +971 4-482586/482813.
International School of Choueifat, PO Box 1644, Ras Al Khaimah, UAE; tel +971 7-353446; fax +971 7-353447; e-mail iscrak@sabis.net
International School of Choueifat, PO Box 2077, Sharjah, UAE; tel +971 6-5582211; fax +971 6-5582865.
Al Ma'arifa Private School, PO Box 7190, Sharjah, UAE; tel +971 6-5544500; fax +971 6-5364441.
Sharjah International American School, PO Box 2501, Sharjah, UAE; tel +971 6-380000; fax +971 6-380099.

The Media, Post and Telecommunications

The Media

All printed matter, films and videos displaying scantily-dressed women, sexual contact between men and women, religious propaganda or politically-sensitive matter will be seized by the Information and Culture Ministry (PO Box 17, Abu Dhabi; tel +971 2 453000). Any books or personal videos discovered in luggage coming into the country will be reviewed by the Information Ministry to be returned (or not) to the owner in due course.

Television

Most terrestial television programmes in Abu Dhabi and Dubai are broadcast in Arabic but there is one English language channel that shows mainly imported American and British programmes. Terrestial channels with some programmes in English can also be viewed in Sharjah and Ajman.

The majority of the big hotels and serviced apartments throughout the UAE have satellite TV facilities and several apartment blocks have dishes installed so that residents need only purchase a decoder to subscribe. The main pay TV channels are Orbit (TV and radio services), Dubai Cable TV, DSTV, Panamsat 4, Showtime, Star TV and Star Select. A variety of programmes are available through these servers covering a range of interests and including BBC World and CNN.

Radio

To find out the frequencies for the BBC World Service in the UAE contact: tel 020-7557 1165; e-mail worldservice.letters@bbc.co.uk Website www.bbc.co.uk/worldservice. A monthly international programmes guide, *BBC On Air*, which includes information on World Service Radio, BBC World and BBC Prime television services can be obtained by contacting the BBC at tel 020-7557 2211; fax 020-7240 4899.

The Abu Dhabi English service, Capital Radio FM is on air for 18 hours a day, broadcasting news bulletins, music and requests, etc. The English service in Dubai, 104.8 Channel 4 FM, is on air for $17^1/2$ hours per day broadcasting similar programmes to Abu Dhabi FM with world news bulletins and news summaries issued ten times a day, headlines four times a day.

The UAE also has its own radio services on air 18 hours a day in Arabic and 24 hours in Asian languages.

Newspapers and Magazines

Newspapers and magazines are widely available in the UAE from hotel shops, supermarkets and bookshops as well as local corner shops and at major road junctions.

Foreign newspapers (mainly Asian, British, French and German language) can be bought at hotel bookshops and supermarkets although they cost more than in their home countries and are slightly dated. A wide range of magazines covering hobbies can also be found although many of the women's magazines may have pages missing due to censorship.

Daily English language papers produced in the UAE and available throughout the country include:

Emirates News, PO Box 791, Abu Dhabi.

Khaleej Times, PO Box 3082, **Abu Dhabi**; PO Box 11243, **Dubai** (www.khaleejtimes.com).

Gulf News, PO Box 6519, Dubai (www.gulf-news.com).

Gulf Today, PO Box 30, Sharjah.

These papers report on both local and international news, and come with weekly magazines, TV listings and very useful Classifieds sections. Subscription for a daily delivery can be arranged.

Books and Bookshops

A choice of English or European language books on a range of subjects are available from bookshops throughout the UAE including the following:

Abu Dhabi
Al Mutanabbi: tel +971 2 340 319.
All Prints: tel +971 2 336 999.
Book Corner: tel +971 2 315 323/7.
Spinneys: tel +971 2 212 919/660 200.

Al-Ain
Al Marifa Bookshop: tel +971 3 663 221.
The Box Bookshop: tel +971 3 643 754.

Post

Postal Services in the UAE are entirely run by the General Postal Authority (GPA) although both local and international courier services do exist alongside it (Aramex, DHL, Federal Express, TNT, etc.). An express mail service, *Mumtaz Express*, is also offered by the GPA and is cheap and dependable however it takes longer to deliver than the alternative couriers.

Delivery time within the UAE is usually 2-3 days. Mail to the USA and Europe takes about 10 days to arrive, to Australia: 8-10 days, to India: 5-10 days. Postage for airmail letters is approximately Dhs. 3-6, for postcards: Dhs. 2. Aerogrammes are available from post offices and cost Dhs. 2.

Post offices and certain shops sell stamps. Red letter boxes for outbound mail are located throughout the main cities at post offices and shopping centres. Generally, collections take place twice daily. Hotels may handle their resident guests' post.

All incoming mail arrives at the Central Post Office which then distributes it among centrally situated post office boxes. Residents can either have their mail directed to a company mailbox or rent a personal PO box. Application forms for PO boxes are available from the regional Central Post Office.

Useful Addresses:
General Postal Authority, PO Box 888, Dubai.
Central Post Office, PO Box 4444, Sharjah.
General Post Office, PO Box 760, Fujairah; tel +971 9 222235; fax +971 9 229011.

Telecommunications

For installation and billing of telephones look under 'Telephones' in the *Setting Up Home* section.

Public pay phones are widespread throughout the UAE with the majority using phonecards available from supermarkets, other shops and pharmacies; coin-operated pay phones are less common.

Mobile Phones
Mobile phones are available from ETISALAT, electronics shops or telecommunications shops and are in widespread use throughout the UAE largely due to the low subscription rates. On a quiet day application for a mobile phone can take just a couple of hours to process. Application forms are available from ETISALAT branch offices. The completed forms should be returned to the main regional ETISALAT office, in addition to your passport, a copy of your residence visa and Dhs. 340.

For those whose residency visa is still being processed or who only possess visit visas but want to use their mobile, ETISALAT can allot them a local mobile number and a number of call units to a SIM card which is then inserted into the mobile. A copy of your passport should be presented when applying for this service. The first card, valid for a month, costs Dhs. 300 (payable in advance) and the units are used up daily at a rate of Dhs. 10. To maintain this service for a period of up to a year, you need to 'refuel' the card with any number of units. To keep the same phone number your account must be credited before the end of the month or a new phone number will be allotted to your next SIM card. The quarterly rental fee for a mobile is Dhs. 90.

Useful Numbers

Directory Enquiries	180
Operator	100
Billing	142
Fault Report	170
Call booking	140

Area Codes for major cities

02	Abu Dhabi
03	Al-Ain
04	Dubai, Jebel Ali
06	Ajman, Umm al-Qaiwain
07	Ras al-Khaimah
09	Khor Fakkan, Dibba
085	Hatta

The Internet
ETISALAT controls all internet services through its UAE proxy server which regulates the sites which can be visited. As with connections worldwide, the Emirates Internet can be accessed from any standard telephone line using an appropriate modem. Requirements for connection are: a landline in your name or your company's name, a completed application form (from ETISALAT) and a passport copy. Registration costs Dhs. 200, monthly rental: Dhs. 85 per fourteen hours spent on-line and Dhs. 6 per extra hour. Optional software installation by an ETISALAT technician costs Dhs. 100.

Pagers
Pagers are available from ETISALAT, large supermarkets, electronics shops, etc. and are budget alternatives to mobile phones. Connection is made after application to ETISALAT and basic costs are Dhs. 80 per quarter for rental and a one-off connection fee of Dhs. 100.

Cars and Motoring

The high standard of the roads linking all the Emirates within the UAE does not, unfortunately, apply to the general quality of the driving you may witness on them. The UAE reportedly has the world's current highest death rates due to traffic accidents.

Cars should drive on the right side of the road – a rule that is not strictly adhered to by those who seem totally unaware of fellow drivers on the road. Speeding, swerving, lane drifting, pulling out suddenly and driving too close to the vehicle in front, are all frequent occurrences. Cyclists and pedestrians are not much better in matters of road safety – either cycling on the wrong side of the road, frequently without lights in the dark, or stepping out seemingly heedless of oncoming traffic.

That said, there are positive aspects to driving in the UAE. Petrol is far cheaper than most places in the world only costing on average Dhs. 3.65 per gallon/80 fils per litre, and re-fuelling is a relatively easy task as there are an ample number of petrol stations on the roads. The cost of buying and maintaining a car is also much lower than in most countries.

In a country where public transport is limited and there is no railway system, driving is the most favoured mode of transport.

Driving Regulations

Speed limits in towns are generally 60-80 kmph, on other major roads: 100-120 kmph. Speed cameras and other devices are in common use by the police to regulate speeding. On average speeding fines are Dhs. 200 but vary according to how fast the offender was travelling. Fines should be paid at the Traffic Police Department, Traffic Fines section.

Seat belts must be worn by both driver and passenger in the front seats of cars. In Abu Dhabi it has recently been made illegal to drive while using a hand-held mobile phone. This rule has yet to apply in the other emirates.

Renting/Leasing/Buying a Car

For those just on a short stay in the UAE, car rental is the best option. For those on longer visits, leasing or buying a car makes more sense.

Car Rental

All the major car hire companies have branch offices in Abu Dhabi and Dubai. Cars can be hired with or without a driver and must be rented for at least 24 hours. Costs are from Dhs. 140 per day for smaller cars, up to about Dhs. 1,000 for limousines. Prices vary considerably so it is a good idea to contact a few agencies to find the most competitive rate. The more established and reputable companies tend to have more dependable vehicles and can offer more invaluable assistance in an emergency. Comprehensive insurance is a definite must.

Temporary local driving licences will be arranged by the car hire company. The following documents are normally required in order to hire a car: passport, two photographs and either a valid international driving licence or a national licence from one of these countries: Austria, Belgium, Canada, Denmark, Finland, France, Germany, Greece, Holland, Ireland, Italy, Japan, Norway, Spain, Sweden, Switzerland, Turkey, UK and USA.

Leasing Cars

There are many benefits to leasing a car as opposed to purchasing one. Lease companies can provide a comprehensive range of services: insurance, registration, maintenance, replacement, 24 hour help and more or less take care of any problems that may arise – breakdowns, re-registration, etc. For those who are not staying for long periods in the emirates, it is a preferable choice to purchasing a car. Your employer may have contacts with a car rental company and be able to arrange a better rate than if you approach the company yourself.

Weekly, monthly or annual leasing is available with a range of cars, usually from Mitsubishi Lancers or Toyota Corollas to Mitsubishi Pajero 4 wheel drive (4WD) vehicles. The longer the lease the more the cost decreases, ranging from Dhs. 600 per week to Dhs. 2,500 dependent on car size. A passport copy, credit card and driving licence must be shown in order to rent any car.

Useful Addresses
Avis: PO Box 3237, **Abu Dhabi**; tel +971 2 323760; fax +971 2 312033; PO Box 6365, **Dubai**; tel +971 4 282121; fax +971 4 226908.
Budget: PO Box 3292, **Abu Dhabi**; tel +971 2 334200; fax +971 2 331498; PO Box 8323, **Dubai**; tel +971 4 823030; fax +971 4 823574.

For a more detailed list of car hire/leasing companies visit on-line the Hawk Business Pages (www.hawkuaebusinesspages.com) or the UAE Yellow Pages (www.onlineyellow.com) or the UAE Commercial Directory (www.u-net.com/projectp/blitz/rentacar.htm).

Purchasing a Car

It is obligatory to have a residence visa if wanting to buy a car in the emirates. Purchase, running costs and maintenance of a vehicle in the UAE is notably less expensive than in most other countries.

Foreign nationals wishing to buy a car in the emirates must have the following documents: application form from the Traffic Police, valid residence visa, original driving licence and copy, Emirati driving licence, copy of sponsor's passport, NOC from their company or sponsor and, copy of the company trade licence, vehicle transfer or customs certificate, copy of tenancy agreement, car insurance certificate, vehicle registration card.

Brand new cars can be bought from the local branch office of a wide variety of major dealers: Ford, Honda, Volvo, Jeep, BMW, Lexus, Toyota, Lexus, Mercedes-Benz, Mitsubishi, Range Rover, etc. Addresses can be found on-line at www.onlineyellow.com or www.hawkuaebusiness.com.

Second-hand car dealers can be found in abundance throughout the UAE due to the boom market for second-hand cars. A dealer will provide a limited warranty, insurance, finance and registration that does not come with more private sales but will also charge a premium of about Dhs. 5,000 for the privilege. Good deals on demonstration cars that have only been used for test-drives may be available at certain major dealers.

Bargains on second-hand cars may also be found through the Classified section in newspapers and supermarket/club noticeboards. Ensure that a second-hand vehicle is in good working order before purchase by having it checked over by a reputable garage for a cost of about Dhs. 300.

It is mandatory to direct all transactions and applications for vehicles through the Traffic Department or both buyer and seller can face a Dhs. 3,000 fine.

The following is a list of useful telephone numbers of second-hand car dealers in Abu Dhabi favoured by expatriates: *Obaid Mohd Trading*, +971 2 453 961; *Zakher Car Exhibition*, +971 2 451 450; *Zahrat Madeam Car Exhibition*, +971 2 451 909; *Reem Auto Showroom*, +971 2 463 343; and in Al-Ain: *Al Nuaimi Car Exhibition*, +971 3 656 345; *Al Wahda Exhibition*, +971 3 217 877; *Al Yazreb Cars*, +971 3 211 833. More addresses can be found by visiting the website www.hawkuaebusinesspages.com.

Importing a Car

Cars manufactured in 1997/1998 and imported by individuals or private car showrooms need an NOC from the official agent in the UAE or from the Ministry of Finance and Industry (if no official agent exists). The NOC is required to verify that the car is in line with GCC specifications and more probably to ensure that local dealers are not surpassed by their neighbouring competitors.

Even if the car is bought from an emirate other than the one in which you are resident, you need to import it. Much paperwork is involved in the process and the same documents listed under *Purchasing a Car* must be submitted to the Traffic Department along with the sale agreement, current registration and Dhs. 20. A set of temporary licence plates are then issued and are valid until a new registration application has been approved in the emirate in which you are resident.

Car Registration

Currently, annual car registration with the Traffic Police is obligatory. Either you handle the registration yourself which involves tackling reams of paperwork or some companies can provide a full registration service for you.

The process involves your car undergoing a technical inspection, checking lights, bodywork, emissions, fire extinguisher, etc. in order for it to be 'passed' by the Traffic Police. If the car receives the 'OK' then you are issued with a certification document. This document along with those listed under *Purchasing a Car*, should then be submitted to the Traffic Police in addition to insurance documents and Dhs. 360. All traffic offences and fines also have to be settled before registration can be completed.

Insurance

Car insurance is a prerequisite to car registration. Insurance companies will inspect the vehicle and need to know its date of manufacture. A copy of your regional driving licence, passport copy and copy of the existing car registration card must be submitted.

Cars receive a 13 month cover that costs on average 5-6 per cent of the vehicle value but rates vary according to age and model of the car and on the owner's prior insurance record. Always check that your insurance policy provides comprehensive cover. Those who plan to travel extensively around the emirates should also consider insurance cover for the Sultanate of Oman as you may find yourself occasionally straying onto Omani land, particularly if you are driving off-road near the border.

Breakdowns and Accidents

For an annual fee, the Arabian Automobile Association (AAA) (tel +971 2 4829 595) now offers a 24 hour breakdown sevice that includes help in minor mechanical repairs, a tow to the nearest garage if your car cannot be started, battery re-charging, or assistance if you run out of petrol, lock yourself out, or have a flat tyre. Additional services are also available such as off-road recovery, a rent-a-car service and vehicle registration.

If you experience a traffic accident of whatever magnitude, it is imperative not to move your car until the scene has been assessed by a traffic policeman who will apportion blame on the spot. In Abu Dhabi the numbers to dial at the scene of an accident are: 02 476 100 ext. 208/259 and in Al-Ain 03 828 200. In extreme cases dial 999.

Once blame has been apportioned an accident report is then documented by the police and a copy of it given to you. To have any repairs done to your car an accident report is a legal prerequisite. The form should be handed to your insurance company who will then arrange the necessary repair work. A green accident report signals that you are not at fault, a pink one means that you are. Your driving licence will be held by the police until they receive confirmation from your insurance company that the claim is being processed, after which you can retrieve your licence.

Transport

Air

A daily flight now connects Abu Dhabi and Dubai. A round trip ticket costs approximately US$250. If this service proves successful then it may be expanded to include other cities presently without domestic flights – Sharjah, Ras Al-Khaimah, Fujairah, Al Ain and Ruwais. Internal flights can also be chartered through certain tour operators and throughout the UAE there are small landing fields.

Sea

All coastal ports are served by commercial and passenger services. Water taxis travel between Dubai and Deira across the creek and there are plenty of opportunities to charter dhows, boats and charters for small trips either to nearby islands or along the UAE coast.

Useful Telephone Numbers

Blue Dolphin Speed Boat/Dhow Charters: +971 2 669392. Operates Barracuda speedboats and three traditional Arabian fishing dhows equipped with buffet, radio, shady deck areas and other amenities. Charter for the speed boats costs Dhs.1,000 for four hours or Dhs.300 per hour (minimum 2 hours). Charges for the dhows range from Dhs. 2,000 to Dhs.5,000/6,000 for a four hour trip dependent on size of the dhow and whether it is a weekend or not, or Dhs.600 per hour (minimum 2 hour trip).

Shuja Yacht Cruises: +971 2 742020. The yacht *Shuja* is a double-decker motor cruiser available for charter for private individuals or parties with a maximum capacity of 140 passengers. Charges range from Dhs.10,000 for five hours cruising including crew and a 50 per cent discount for the Forte Grand's exclusive catering service, to Dhs.20,000 for a full day's charter (9am to 11pm).

Al Dhafra: +971 2 732266. Operates four traditional dhows all available for charter. The dhows can accommodate a minimum of 10 passengers and a maximum of 90. Charges range from Dhs.150 per hour to Dhs.550 per hour.

Bus

Most towns in the UAE are linked by a limited bus service. Scheduled bus services are operated by most hotels to the airport, city centre and beach resorts.

Taxis

Taxis can be found in all towns in the UAE with urban journey fares metred in Abu Dhabi and for longer journeys fares should be agreed upon in advance. Air conditioned taxis cost more. Taxis are the favoured mode of public transport from Abu Dhabi to Dubai.

Banking and Finance

The UAE Central Bank regulates the well structured and ever developing network of local and international banks in the emirates that offer an extensive range of commercial and banking services equivalent to those found in western countries. The absence of an exchange control allows the easy transferral of funds into and out of the state and the UAE dirham is freely convertible. Typically, banking hours are from 8am to 1pm, Saturday to Wednesday, some also open from 4.30pm to 6.30pm, and on Thursdays 8am to 12pm. Exchange offices are generally open from 8.30am to 1pm and 4.30pm to 8.30pm.

To open a bank account in the UAE you need to present a banking advisor with your residence visa or show that your application is being processed, copies of your passport – personal details and visa, your actual passport, and an NOC (No Objection Certificate) from your employer/sponsor. On the whole most banks set a minimum account limit, commonly about Dhs. 2,000 for a deposit account and Dhs. 5,000 for a current account.

The preferred method of payment in the UAE is by cash although credit cards are becoming more and more accepted, particularly in larger shops and hotels. Cheques are not in common use and if insufficient funds are in your bank and the cheque bounces you are likely to incur a prison sentence. Automatic Teller Machines (ATMs), accepting all major cards, can be found throughout the UAE.

Useful Addresses

Abu Dhabi Commercial Bank: PO Box 5550, Dubai; tel +971 4 228141; fax +971 4 279632.

Arab Bank for Investment: PO Box 5549, Dubai; tel +971 4 212100; fax +971 4 234311.

Barclays Bank International: PO Box 1891, Dubai; tel +971 4 283116; fax +971 4 282788.

British Bank of the Middle East: PO Box 66, Dubai; tel +971 4 535000; fax +971 4 531005.

Emirates Bank International: PO Box 2923, Dubai; tel +971 4 256900; fax +971 4 268005.

Lloyds Bank International Ltd.: PO Box 3766, Dubai; tel +971 4 313005; fax +971 4 313026.

Offshore Banking

If you are working for a large company in the Gulf you are likely to be earning quite substantial amounts of money some of which you will undoubtedly be looking to invest. One of the primary financial advantages of being an expatriate is that you can invest this money offshore in tax havens such as the Isle of Man, the Channel Islands, Gibraltar and Bahrain, thus accruing tax-free interest on your savings. Many such facilities are as flexible as UK high street banking and range from current accounts to long-term, high interest earning deposits. For more details and addresses of offshore banking units see *Offshore Banking* section in 'Bahrain Daily Living' chapter.

Tax and the Expatriate

There is no income tax or social security for expatriates to pay in the United Arab Emirates nor do any other taxes exist for foreign nationals resident in the country. As a non-resident of your home country (i.e. for UK nationals spending fewer than 183 days in aggregate in Britain) you will not be subject to your home country's tax on earnings either. For more details on what you may or may not be entitled to or subjected to regarding tax regulations (on earnings, relocation expenses, investments, etc.) as an expatriate you should consult a specialist tax advisor. Useful contacts can be found in magazines such as *The Expatriate* and the large accounting/financial advisory companies like PriceWaterhouseCoopers (Plumtree Court, London EC4A 4HT; tel 020-7583 5000; fax 020-7822 4652) publish handy booklets giving detailed information on the tax implications for foreign nationals working in other countries.

Health Care in the United Arab Emirates

As part of the country's overall economic development in recent years, health care has advanced markedly and all members of the population now have access to a high quality of medical care often staffed by Western professionals, but with a growing body of highly trained native staff. Facilities are of a high standard but are very expensive so health insurance is essential.

The UAE Ministry of Health has plans to double the bed capacity of the nation's hospitals to 8,700 over the next ten years, a programme which would take current capacity to 6,000 beds by next year, 6,700 by 2005 and 8,700 by 2010. The aim is to ensure one hospital bed for every 300 people. 17 new hospitals are to be created in the northern emirates alone by 2005. In the same period there is also a plan to establish 25 new primary health centres in the UAE at a cost of Dhs. 100 million. As many as ten new Primary Health Centres (PHCs) are scheduled to open this year in the northern emirates with a target of serving the needs of 30,000 people each. The Ministry currently has a network of 97 PHCs in the country, including 22 in Abu Dhabi, 20 in Al Ain, 11 in Sharjah, 8 in Dubai and 16 in Ras Al Khaimah.

Useful Addresses

Dubai London Clinic: PO Box 12119, Dubai, UAE; tel +971 4 446663; fax +971 4 446191; e-mail dlc@emirates.net.ae

El Maghraby Eye & Ear Centre: PO Box 655, Abu Dhabi, UAE; tel +971 2 345000; fax +971 2 343940; Website www.elmaghraby.com

The Gulf Diagnostic Centre: PO Box 30702, Abu Dhabi, UAE; tel +971 2 658090; fax +971 2 658084; e-mail gdcmktg@emirates.net.ae

New Medical Centre Hospital Abu Dhabi: PO Box 6222, Abu Dhabi, UAE; tel +971 2 323296; fax +971 2 320878; e-mail nmc@emirates.net.ae

New Medical Centre Hospital Dubai: PO Box 7832, Dubai, UAE; tel +971 4 683131; fax +971 4 682353.

New Medical Centre Hospital Sharjah: PO Box 25262, Sharjah, UAE; tel +971 6 536936; fax +971 6 536378.

Tawam Hospital: PO Box 15258, Al Ain, Abu Dhabi, UAE; tel +971 3 677410; fax +971 3 671228.

Al Wasl Hospital: PO Box 9115, Dubai, UAE.

Private Medical Insurance

Private medical care in the UAE is of a very high standard but it is also by no means cheap. Taking out the proper health insurance cover for you and your family is essential when moving out to the Gulf.

BUPA International (Russell Mews, Brighton, BN1 2NR; tel 01273-208181; fax 01273-866583; e-mail advice@bupa-intl.com Website www.bupa-intl.com) has designed its own Lifeline scheme that offers maximum choice and flexibility. There are three levels of cover: Gold, Classic and Essential, all of which provide full refund for hospital accommodation and specialists' fees so you never need to be concerned about unexpected bills for in-patient treatment such as an operation. Cover for emergency ambulance charges and sports injuries is also standard. The Gold and Classic schemes offer out-patient treatment which may be a very wise precaution in the United Arab Emirates. The most comprehensive cover is available with the Gold scheme which includes the cost of primary care treatment and home nursing. BUPA International has a 24 hour multi-lingual service centre dedicated to their expatriate members with an experienced team on hand to deal with any queries. Claims are paid promptly in any currency that you require, and you are covered anywhere in the world. For more information call +44 (0) 1273-208181.

For more details on other international health insurance schemes available to the expatriate and contact addresses see *Private Medical Insurance* in 'Bahrain Daily Living Chapter.'

UAE Law

All the emirates operate systems of both secular and Islamic law in civil, criminal, and high courts. In 1971, a federal court system was initiated in all the emirates with the exception of Dubai and Ras al Khaimah. For more details see *Shari'a Law* in Gulf States' 'General Introduction' chapter, and UAE *Government* above.

Social Life

There are plenty of activities in which expatriates can participate in the UAE – sporting and non-sporting. You will find that your social life will be centred around other expatriates generally of the same nationality as yourself but due to the numerous expatriate clubs in existence and international churches where you can meet new people, the opportunities to mix with others are endless. UAE citizens, who are very much in the minority, tend to keep themselves to themselves.

Entertainment & Culture

Theatre.
Performances virtually always take place in one of the five-star hotels. Under the sponsorship of some international company, Western theatre companies often visit the UAE. Details of forthcoming plays can be found in the local papers or on fliers in the lobbies of the larger hotels.

Cinema.
Each of the main cities in the emirates tend to have their own cinemas mostly showing Indian and Pakistani films although Dubai has a cinema that shows recent English language films.

Nightlife.
Dubai is considered the centre of nightlife throughout the UAE. Despite Abu Dhabi, Fujairah, Al-Ain and Ras Al-Khaimah also offering discos and bars within their larger hotels, Dubai's 'buzzing' nightlife surpasses them all. Beware though, a night out on the town is invariably a very costly affair as it will be centred around expensive hotels where drinks, both alcoholic and non-, are fairly pricey due to the cover charges placed on top of the actual high cost of the drinks themselves. To find out the latest details on live acts and events consult the local newspapers and regional *What's on* magazine.

Restaurants.
Eating out is extremely popular throughout the Emirates and high standard restaurants abound serving cuisine from all over the world – Moroccan, American, European, Mexican, etc. There are also the usual range of fast food chains such as Kentucky Fried Chicken, McDonalds, Pizza Hut, etc. Despite opening from about 7pm, restaurants only tend to get busy from about 9pm. Generally, only restaurants and bars that are part of a hotel are licensed to serve alcohol although

there are a few exceptions to this rule in certain independent restaurants. Not surprisingly the mark up on alcohol, where it is available, is verging on the extortionate. A 15 per cent service charge is included in most bills regardless of the standard of the service that you receive. An optional 10 per cent tip can be added if you wish.

In Abu Dhabi taking a dinner cruise upon a dhow along the corniche is highly recommended to experience fantastic food and an exceptional view of the city.

Museums and Visitor Attractions.

The UAE may not be as rich in traditional cultural and heritage sites as its fellow Gulf countries and yet there are still plenty of things to do and see which will give you a feel for how the country operated before the discovery of oil. All the individual emirates have their old forts and examples of traditional architecture (be they somewhat overshadowed now by modern-day soaring skyscrapers). Among the museums to visit in Abu Dhabi are: the Cultural Foundation, Handicrafts Centre, Women's Craft Centre, Al Ain Museum, and Al Ain University Natural History Display. In Dubai there is Shaikh Saeed's House, the Dubai Museum and a range of ancient forts, mosques, palaces and other historic monuments to visit (see *Regional Guide* above for more details), and a new Wild Wadi Water theme park has just opened in Jumeirah Beach Resort, Dubai.

Liquor Licence

Alcohol can only be bought in the UAE from special licensed retail outlets by non-Muslim residents in possession of a liquor licence. The licence entitles you to purchase a prescribed amount of alcohol per month and can only be used in other emirates to that in which it has been issued, if it has been endorsed by the police of the other emirate(s). Sharjah does not permit the sale or purchase of alcohol within its borders. Applications for licences should be made at your local police headquarters and require the written approval of your sponsor/employer.

Sport

Dubai has acquired the reputation for being the 'sports capital of the Middle East' hosting top international sporting events in a wide range of fields including golf (for more details visit www.dubaigolf.com), tennis, horse racing (the Dubai World Cup is the richest horse racing event offering a prize money of £8 million), motor rallying, powerboat racing, football, rugby and sailing.

Throughout the UAE there are a multitude of opportunities to pursue any sporting interest that you may have on land or in/on water. From scuba diving, snorkelling, windsurfing, etc. to squash, golf, tennis, ice-skating, shooting, archery, go-karting, etc. Desert driving and safaris are also highly recommended and there are the usual range of traditional Arab spectator sports to observe – camel racing, falconry, bull-fighting, etc. (see Gulf States' 'General Introduction' for more details).

Shopping

Dubai has earned itself the reputation for being a shopper's paradise offering its residents and visitors a comprehensive range of tax-free shopping opportunities in both its ultra modern air conditioned malls and its ancient, traditional souks. In fact Dubai could easily be mistaken for one vast souk. Located by the Creek, the gold souk in Dubai is one of the largest retail markets for gold in the world. The cost of jewellery is dependent on the day's gold price (quoted in the local daily newspaper – for 22 carat gold jewellery, prices are presently about £6 a gram) with mark up for labour. It is the labour mark up which you must employ your negotiating skills to dispute and obtain a bargain price. Haggling in the souks is a prerequisite to purchasing anything from spices, to silks, other materials, Persian carpets, etc. Deira City Centre is renown for being 'Dubai's ultimate shopping experience.' Here can be found the major western stores such as the French hypermarket Continent, Ikea, Debenhams, etc. Across the Creek in Wafi are the designer shops: Chanel, Chopard, YSL, etc. and at the Bur Juman Centre you will discover Donna Karan, Christian Lacroix, etc.

Abu Dhabi and Sharjah are also known to have excellent shopping facilities, particularly if you want to buy electrical goods or carpets.

Typically shopping hours are from 9am to 1pm and from 4pm to 9pm or later, Saturday to Thursday. Most shopping malls open between 10am and 10pm. All shops are closed for prayers on Fridays from 11.30am to 1.30pm.

SECTION II

Working in the Gulf

Employment

Business and Industry Reports

Regional Employment Guide

Directory of Major Employers

Starting a Business

Employment

Overview

There are millions of expatriates and their families living and working in the Arabian Peninsula. The wealth accumulated in the region through the discovery of oil in the 1930s and culminating in the early 1960s has attracted major foreign companies to invest and set up business in the area, and vast numbers of professional, skilled and semi-skilled workers to cash in on the resultant numerous and prosperous employment opportunities available.

Once – only a few decades ago – the Gulf Arabs lived in mud brick houses with the most basic of amenities and were dependent upon the pearling, fishing, craft and trade industries. Now the nationals of the Gulf states, having found wealth, generally seek 'soft' government jobs and tend to regard other work, including the private sector, as being below their dignity. Hence the heavy reliance on a foreign work force.

Menial jobs and positions as house servants are carried out by Third Country Nationals (TCNs from the Philippines, Sri Lanka, Bangladesh, Thailand, India, etc.). Expatriates from Europe, North America and Australia are recruited for work requiring the expertise of highly skilled professionals. The pay for all employees is comparably much higher than that which they would receive in their home country especially when bonuses (such as accommodation or a housing allowance) and tax free wages are also taken into consideration. Westerners are not recruited for unskilled labour as they would expect to be paid far more than a TCN.

Despite low oil prices in the late 1990s that affected the buoyancy of the Gulf states' economies forcing local employers to cut down on their foreign work force, in addition to the plans to slowly but surely replace expatriate workers with Gulf citizens, foreign workers are still very much in demand in a range of fields throughout the Arabian Peninsula. In Oman 1998 figures show that the work force comprises about 61 per cent foreign nationals, in Kuwait 83 per cent, and in the UAE 91 per cent. However, according to Kuwait the six states of the GCC (Gulf Cooperation Council) intend to replace 75 per cent of the foreign work force with their own nationals by 2020. Evidence of this move was recently highlighted by the case of a banker who lost his £125,000 a year position with the Saudi International Bank when he was replaced by a junior who was less experienced than him but qualified for promotion because he was an Arab.

Nevertheless, it is widely believed among top recruiters for the region that expatriate expertise will always be sought after in the Gulf particularly in technical areas such as engineering. Despite the rise of training throughout the Arabian peninsula in specific skills required for banking, data processing, health, and tourism sectors, efforts to replace the foreign work force with local nationals has not been as successful as local governments may have hoped, either because their nationals have been poorly trained or the numbers of skilled local hands are simply lacking. In Bahrain, 33,996 new work permits were issued and 44,657 renewed in 1997, and in 1998, 35,718 new work permits were issued and 34,811 renewed despite the fact that 36,000 Bahrainis were trained to fill jobs traditionally held by foreign workers. In Oman, the issuance of private sector expatriate work permits is being restricted in cases where Omani workers possess the necessary skills to fill the position. Nevertheless, the most recent government figures reveal that while expatriate employment in the government sector fell by 1.2 per cent, expatriate employment in the private sector rose by 2.1 per cent. The employment opportunities are still there but are not necessarily as abundant as they once were and salaries – although still greater than those in most other countries – are gradually being reduced.

Throughout the Gulf the general attitude towards work is one of ease – *inshallah* (if God wills) – if something is meant to happen e.g. a business meeting, it will, if not, it will not. This may cause frustration amongst those who need to meet urgent deadlines but there really is nothing you can do but be patient and learn to adjust to the slower pace of life. One company in Oman recently cancelled a business conference on stress management because it was felt to be unnecessary as it was a non-existent problem in this company's work place.

In business it can take months for any transaction to reach a conclusion as there are so many committees and sub-committees and only one person holding the authority to actually approve anything. You will also soon learn that a 'Wasta' system is very much in operation throughout the Arabian Peninsula. Contacts are everything in getting things done. Knowing someone who has wasta (influence) is a tremendous advantage as they are generally considered as the individuals who have the power to accomplish deeds.

With oil prices now on the rise and the ongoing development plans in all the Gulf countries to diversify their economies, increase foreign investment, and encourage the establishment of new businesses, it is still a very good time for foreigners to take the pick of the lucrative opportunities now readily available.

Residence & Work Regulations

The Gulf states' visa systems are covered in detail in the individual country *Residence and Entry Regulations* chapters. A residence and work permit is a prerequisite to starting any job in the Arabian Peninsula and all the paperwork is usually handled by your employer prior to your entry into the Gulf.

Skills and Qualifications

Expatriates from the West seeking employment in the Gulf are generally expected to be highly qualified and in many cases have substantial experience in their profession, as jobs needing less skilled workers can easily be filled by those of other nationalities (e.g. Indians, Pakistanis, Filippinos, etc.) at a much lower rate of pay than an equivalent Western worker would expect for the same position. Many applications involve international recruitment tests and interviews are always required. For your work permit to be processed the presentation of certificates of skills and qualifications is necessary and their authenticity needs to be verified either by a member of your professional body (see list of addresses below) or by a registered lawyer whose practising status must in turn be verified by your embassy. RHR*Aspects of Employment

Aspects of Employment

Salaries & Employment Contracts

Throughout the Gulf you will find that the monthly wage for a skilled job will be far greater than you would receive in your home country for the equivalent position. Moreover, your earnings in the Gulf will all be tax free and the cost of living for daily items such as basic groceries – bread, cheese, vegetables, meat, etc. is relatively low so that you have even more money to spend on leisure activities or to save. For example, computer experts working in the Arabian Peninsula would expect to earn £25,000 to £60,000 per year, working a 44 hour week with 38 days holiday entitlement as well as accommodation or a housing allowance plus other benefits. According to CfBT, an organisation that recruits teachers for placements in Oman, educators there can earn between OR 800 to OR 1,500 (£1,284 to £2,406) per month again in addition to the provision of furnished accommodation or a housing allowance plus other benefits. Salaries for technical positions are dependent upon qualifications and experience and the job which you are offered and range from £20,000 to £120,000 tax free. The various other benefits included in your employment contract which some employers provide on top of accommodation or a housing allowance, can include school fees, health insurance, an end of contract gratuity and other bonuses, car loan, and sometimes air fares.

Most contracts require a minimum of a year's commitment although some are for two year placements, and some teaching contracts can be for just six months initially. Working hours are on average 40-48 hours per five day week or eight hours a day reduced to six hours a day during Ramadan, with Thursdays and Fridays generally treated as the weekend. The maximum overtime per week is 12 hours. School hours are commonly from 7.30am to 2pm; places of business are open either from 8am to 3.30pm Saturday to Wednesday or from 8am to 1pm and 3pm to 5.30pm; govenment offices open 7am to 2.15pm and 9.30am to 2.30pm during Ramadan. Banks' opening hours vary but are typically between 7.30am and 12pm and 3.30pm to 5.30pm Saturday to Wednesday and 7.30am to 11pm on Thursdays; during Ramadan, opening hours are from 10am to 1.30pm, Saturday to Thursday. Holiday entitlements can be anything from three weeks up to six weeks plus, as well as all public holdays. However, you should double check the details of your holiday allowance as some employers have been known to regard weekends as part of your holiday entitlement and/or dictate when you are permitted to take any vacation leave.

Conditions of a contract vary from job to job within different professions and from country to country within the Gulf. Never be afraid of negotiating the terms of your contract as bargaining is widespread throughout the Gulf at all levels. It is extremely important to check every single detail of your employment contract, not only your salary and benefits but what rights under law you will have if there are any changes made and what alterations your employer may be entitled to make during the agreement.

Once you have signed a contract you will find it next to impossible to legally argue against any of the stipulated conditions at a later date. Furthermore you need to ensure that what you sign is a clearly authenticated and accurate translation of the contract written up by your employer in Arabic as confusion can arise over just how much pay has been agreed upon and your holiday entitlement terms amongst other conditions. Gulf Arab employers are notorious for not always strictly honouring and adhering to the terms in your employment contract, much depends on your luck in finding the right employer. This is why you may be safer working for a well-known, large international company where the chances of unfair treatment are greatly reduced.

Amongst the most common disputes expatriate employees have with Gulf Arab employers are: unjustified dismissal, delay in salary payment, less wages paid than expected or salaries calculated at a lower rate of conversion than the market rate, unpaid overtime, longer working hours than agreed upon in the contract, end-of-term contract money not paid, annual leave denial or postponement, assignment to a different position than that described in the employment contract.

Early Contract Termination

Employers can legitimately sack you without justifying their action provided that they give you notice or pay in lieu of notice, or alternatively compensation for early completion of your contract. These terms should be clearly stated in your employment agreement. Under Labour Court law you are not entitled to anything else. However, you should not face too many difficulties in finding another position for which you are suitably qualified as long as you obtain a 'No Objection Certificate' (NOC) – letter of release – from your employer. Without this document you cannot be employed by another party.

After having signed a contract, withdrawing labour is illegal and so you need to double check that your agreement contains some acceptable break clause. If you do terminate your contract early you are likely to confront great problems as your employer is nearly always in possession of your passport which you hand over in return for your residence and working visa on arrival in the Gulf. Obviously you cannot return to your home country without your passport and you will not retrieve your passport until any labour dispute has been resolved. Moreover, you cannot find employment with any other organisation in the country unless your employer supplies you with an NOC which may not be very forthcoming if you break terms with them. You should also remember that if you have decided to return home early then you will undoubtedly have to pay for your own flight home plus other related costs for reneging on your contract. Your contract will detail just how much legal support you can expect to receive in your application.

Trade unions are illegal throughout the Gulf and your working conditions will have to be negotiated by yourself. Regional Labour Offices will adjudicate in any dispute between you and your employer. However, it is strongly recommended to try and resolve any disputes directly with your employer first as recourse to a Labour Office can entail lengthy and expensive legal procedures. Additionally, direct settlement with your employer can aid your application for your eventual exit visa for which only your employer can apply. Your Consul cannot involve itself in any contractual or labour conflicts.

Women at Work

It is estimated that over 90 per cent of international postings involve male employees and the workplace in the Gulf is undoubtedly dominated by men. However, there are plenty of women employed throughout the Gulf (the extent varying from state to state) and numerous opportunities do exist for women mainly in the areas of: health care, banking, education, food and beverage, and secretarial work. In Bahrain, Kuwait and the UAE women can be found in senior management roles more and more as their advancement is actively being encouraged by the emirs of these countries and throughout the Gulf many women are also beginning to run their own businesses. Generally women are allowed to work alongside men although in theory Saudi Arabia still strictly maintains its policy that they are not. Despite this Saudi ruling some women still reach relatively high positions of power within the work force and not all work places are segregated, for instance the American-Saudi company, Saudi Aramco.

However, the attitude that women are second class citizens is still pervasive in Gulf society and the majority of Arab men retain the view that a woman's place is in the kitchen at home with the family (see also *Women in the Gulf* in the Gulf States' 'General Introduction' chapter). Western women are particularly prone to criticism from Arab men who commonly look upon them as little more than sex objects or prostitutes. This is not reflective of all Gulf Arab men and is more evident in some states than others. Consequently, women need to be extra careful about any contact that they might have with men socially or in the work place as an innocent kiss on a man's cheek in greeting could be misconstrued by an Arab man as a come-on. No matter how brotherly or fatherly a woman may feel her relationship with a man to be she should refrain from any physical contact to avoid any possible confusion.

Sources of Jobs

A good starting point for seeking work in the Arabian Peninsula is to contact one of the countries' embassies in your home country. The embassies will not directly find employment for you but may suggest useful contacts and information resources to assist you in your search, and very occasionally opportunities do arise in certain government ministries for translators, teachers of English or management roles. Some of the Gulf states also have their own information centres which may be able to help or advise those wishing to work in their country. Other Middle Eastern associations listed below may also provide a similar advisory service.

Useful Addresses

Embassies

Embassy of the State of Bahrain: UK office: 98 Gloucester Road, London SW7 4AU; tel 020-7370 5132/3; fax 020-370 7773; e-mail information@bahrainembassy.org.uk Website www.bahrainembassy.org.uk. US office: 3502 International Drive, NW, Washington, DC 20008; tel +1 202 3420741/2; fax +1 202 362-2192.

Embassy of the State of Kuwait: UK office: 2 Albert Gate, London SW1X 7JU; tel 020-7590 3400; fax 020-7259 5042. US office: 2940 Tilden Street, NW, Washington, DC 20008; tel +1 202 966-0702; fax +1 202 966-0517.

Embassy of the Sultanate of Oman: UK office: 167 Queen's Gate, London SW7 5HE; tel 020-7225 001; fax 020-7589 2505. US office: 2535 Belmont Road, NW, Washington, DC 20008; tel +1 202 387-1980/2; fax +1 202 745-4933.

Embassy of the State of Qatar: UK office: 1 South Audley Street, London W1Y 5DQ; tel 020-7493 2200; fax 020-7493 2819. US office: 4200 Wisconsin Avenue, Suite 200, NW, Washington, DC 20016; tel +1 202 274-1600; fax +1 202 237-0061.

Royal Embassy of Saudi Arabia: UK office: 30 Charles Street, London W1X 8LP; tel 020-7917 3000; fax 020-7917 3255; Website www.saudiembassy.org.uk. US office: 601 New Hampshire Avenue, NW, Washington, DC 20037; tel +1 202 342-3800; fax +1 202 337-4084.

Embassy of the United Arab Emirates: UK office: 30 Prince's Gate, London SW7 1PT; tel 020-7581 1281; fax 020-7581 9616. US office: Suite 600, 3000 K Street, NW, Washington, DC 20007; tel +1 202 338-6500.

Information Centres and Middle East Associations

Anglo-Arab Association: 21 Collingham Road, London SW5 0NU; tel 020-7373 8414; fax 020-7373 2088.

Kuwait Information Centre: Hyde Park House, 60-60a Knightsbridge, London SW1X 7JU; tel 020-7235 1787; fax 020-7235 6912; e-mail kuwait@dircon.co.uk Website www.kuwait-information-centre.org.uk

Middle East Association: Bury House, 33 Bury Street, St James's, London SW1Y 6AX; tel 020-7839 2137; fax 020-7839 6121.

Middle East Centre: 66/68 Woodstock Road, Oxford; tel 01865 311469.
Saudi Information Centre: 18 Cavendish Square, London W1M 0AQ; tel 020-7629 8803.

Chambers of Commerce

Chambers of Commerce are geared to promote the interest of companies trading in the Gulf and the UK. As a rule, they cannot help you to find work, but they can be a useful source of information about companies in your region. Chambers of Commerce can supply directories of their members and you can then contact any companies that interest you. A detailed list of Chambers of Commerce in the Arabian Peninsula is given in the *Starting a Business* chapter.

Useful Addresses

Arab British Chamber of Commerce: 6 Belgrave Square, London SW1X 8PH; tel 020-7235 4363; fax 020-7245 6688.
Birmingham Chamber of Commerce and Industry: 75 Harborne Road, Birmingham B15 3DU; tel 0121-454 6171; fax 0121-455 8670; e-mail enquiries@birminghamchamber.org.uk
British Chambers of Commerce: 4 Westwood House, Westwood Business Park, Coventry CV4 8HS; tel 01203-694484; fax 01203-694690; e-mail enquiry@britishchambers.org.uk Website www.britishchambers.org.uk
London Chamber of Commerce and Industry: 33 Queen Street, London EC4R 1AP; tel 020-7248 4444; fax 020-7489 0391; e-mail lc@londonchamber.co.uk Website www.londonchamber.co.uk
Manchester Chamber of Commerce: 56 Oxford Street, Manchester M60 7HJ; tel 0161-236 3210; fax 0161-236 4160; e-mail recep@mancitecbl.org.uk
National US-Arab Chamber of Commerce: 1100 New York Avenue, NW, East Tower, Suite 550, Washington, DC 20005, USA; tel +1 202 289-5920; fax +1 202 289-5938; Website www.nusacc.org

EURES

EURES (short for Eurpoean Employment Service) is a computerised, pan-European and overseas job information network. The Overseas Placing Unit (OPU) of EURES regularly provides information on a variety of employment vacancies from hotel work to management throughout the Arabian Peninsula and can either be accessed at regional job centres in the UK or by contacting the Overseas Placement Unit (Level 4, Skills House, 3-7 Holy Green, Off the Moor, Sheffield S1 4AQ; tel 0114-2596051). The OPU can also provide advice and guidance on working abroad. A series of booklets is available at job centres, including *Working Abroad*, which offers practical help in finding work, and outlines the main considerations when seeking employment overseas.

Publications

Several newspapers in the UK carry advertisements for jobs throughout the Gulf region. *Overseas Jobs Express* is a particularly useful source of work opportunities in the Arabian Peninsula covering a wide range of fields from hospitality, teaching English, nursing to engineering and senior management roles. In addition to those newspapers listed below Britain's four major national daily broadsheet newspapers, *The Times*, *The Daily Telegraph*, *The Guardian*, and *The Independent*, also regularly advertise international appointments as do their Sunday counterparts: *The Sunday Times*, the *Sunday Telegraph*, *The Observer*, and the *Independent on Sunday*. For teaching positions, the *Times Educational Supplement* and the *Times Higher Educational Supplement* (both issued on Fridays) are fruitful sources; the former is good for ESL appointments too, as well as the *EFL Gazette*, which advertises courses more than actual positions, but is an excellent barometer of the global EFL scene.

Professional journals and magazines are another possible source of international job vacancies. The main UK trade publications include: *Architects' Journal*; *Building Engineer* (monthly), *Building Services and Environmental Engineering*, *Caterer and Hotelkeeper*; *Certified Accountant*; *Computing* and *Computing Weekly*; *Construction News* and *Contract Journal* (for the building and construction trades); *The Engineer*; *Flight International*; *The Lancet* (medical); *Nature* (science); *New Scientist*; *Nursery World*; *Nursing Times*; *The Stage*; *The Surveyor*; and *Press Gazette*. *News Expatriate Magazine* is another specialist publication containing many international job vacancies, as well as providing other valuable information for expatriates. It can be obtained from *Expat Network Limited* (International House, 500 Purley Way, Croydon CR0 4NZ; tel 020-8760 5100; fax 020-8760 0469; e-mail expatnetwork@demon.co.uk Website www.expatnetwork.co.uk).

Local daily newspapers in the individual Gulf countries may also carry advertisements for appointments. See separate country entries under the *Newspapers and Magazines* sections for details of regional publications.

An excellent guide to finding employment overseas is Elisabeth Robert's *Jobs and Careers Abroad* published by Vacation Work (9 Park End Street, Oxford OX1 1HJ; tel 01865-241978; fax 01865-790885; Website www.vacationwork.co.uk). This book provides essential information on global career opportunities and lists the professions and trades in demand overseas as well as detailing facts on different countries and careers.

UK Newspapers and Directories

Financial Times: 1 Southwark Bridge, London SE1 9HL. Carries advertisements for mainly senior business and executive positions, and has regular supplements and special reports on countries and sectors.

International Herald Tribune: 63 Long Acre, London WC2E 9JH; tel 020-7836 4802.

Middle East Economic Digest, MEED, 21 John Street, London WC1N 2BL. Weekly commercial business magazine.

Overseas Jobs Express: Premier House, Shoreham Airport, West Sussex BN43 5FF; tel 01273-440220; fax 01273-440229; e-mail editor@oje1.demon.co.uk Website www.overseasjobs.com. Published monthly. Invaluable source of international employment opportunities.

Major US Newspapers

Chicago Tribune: 435 North Michigan Avenue, Chicago, Il 60611, USA; tel +1 312 222-3232.

International Employment Gazette: 220 North Main Street, Suite 100, Greenville, SC 29601; tel +1 803 235-444. International recruitment newspaper.

Los Angeles Times: Times Mirror Square, Los Angeles, California, CA 90053, USA; tel +1 213 237-5000.

New York Times: 229 West 43rd Street, New York, NY 10036, USA; tel +1 212 556-1234; UK office: 66 Buckingham Gate, London SW1E 6AU; tel 020-7799 2981.

Wall Street Journal: Dow Jones Inc., 420 Lexington Avenue, New York, NY 10170, USA; tel +1 212 808-6700.

On-line Resources

Banking and Finance Jobs: www.cib.irg.uk/careers

Careermosaic: www.careermosaic.com
A very international website with branch sites focusing on various regions around the world.

Center for Global Assignments (CGA): www.contactCGA.com
Premier source of information and assistance concerning international assignments for companies and individuals. CGA engages in three primary activities: publishing, consulting, and research.

Escape Artist: www.escapeartist.com
Excellent international site which will lead you to the best recruitment sites for the country in which you are interested. Also provides other wide-ranging information.

Expats International: www.expats.co.uk
Offers information on jobs to its subscribers and vacancy advertising and applicant sourcing to employers and agencies on a global basis. The website is divided into five sections: Hot Jobs, Jobs, Applicants, Services and General Information. Expatriates of North American, British, Australasian and European nationality are targetted although the majority of jobs require interviews in the UK. However, for certain top managerial and executive positions major companies may cover your airfare expenses to the relevant country for interview.

Gulf Jobs: www.gulfjobs.com
Gateway to career opportunities in the Middle East.

Health Jobs Online: www.erol.users.netlink.co.uk/health.html
Medical, nursing, and therapy jobs internationally; as well as information on conferences and other links.

Healthcare Employment Resources: www.members.aol.com/pjpohly/links.htm

Information Technology Opportunities: www.it-opportunities.co.uk

International Staffing Solutions: www.iscworld.com
On-line weekly research and advertising clipping service. Subscribe to this service via the website, after which you will receive weekly updates on the latest job opportunities.

Legal Employment Search Site: www.legalemploy.com
Additionally, *The Lawyer's Guide to Jobsurfing on the Internet*, by William T. Barrett (published by Carrer Education Institutes, PO Box 11171, Winston-Salem, WC 27116, USA; tel +1 910 768-2999) is a very useful guide to finding international work via the web. Cost US$10 plus US$2 p+p.

New Boss: www.myboss.com
Good general recruitment gateway.

Offshore Technology: www.offshore-technology.com
The website for the offshore oil and gas industry.

Omancareers.com: www.ooline.com/ool/omani/main.html
This site gives up-to-date information on the latest vacancies for professional work in all fields throughout Oman.

OverseasJobs: www.overseasjobs.com
Leading source for information about international jobs. Expatriates and job seekers can search the job database by keywords or locations and post a resumé on-line for employers to view.

Reuters Business Briefing: www.reuters.com
On-line service giving access both to news and 2,000 business publications from around the world, including newspapers and trade journals. Information can be retrieved by word seacrh or selection lists for companies, countries and topics.

Applying for a Job

The best way to get a job in the Gulf is to apply through a recruitment agency (see *Directory of Major Employers* below) as most major companies in the Arabian Peninsula recruit their personnel through such organisations. Occasionally large companies place advertisements in the local and international press requesting direct applications for certain positions but on the whole firms prefer to use recruitment agencies to select appropriate applicants for their vacancies. An exception to this is international schools and other educational institutions which welcome direct applications from suitably qualified individuals.

Other advantages for the applicant using a recruitment agency is that there is no charge for the placement service as it is the employer who pays the recruitment fees. A recruitment agency will not only assist you in finding a suitable job but can advise you on your destination country and help you prepare for your move there. Due to the expense involved in the process (some companies pay for you to fly out to the Gulf for a face to face interview) and the nature of employment contracts which usually require at least a one year commitment, the selection process is thorough and potentially very time-consuming. For example, an agency like UltraFORCE (see below) insist on an initial telephone interview before pursuing your application any further. Face to face interviews and briefings follow with recruitment experts who will assess your suitability for working in the Gulf before matching you with an appropriate position for which they will help you in your application.

Apart from answering advertisements placed in the papers or applying to recruitment agencies by telephone or letter, there is always the option of placing your CV or resumé on the internet for prospective employers to view (see above *On-line Resources*). Several companies specialise in maximising your CV or resumé to its full potential, including *CV Special* (Dolphin House, Woodgreen, Witney, Oxford OX8 6DH; tel 01993-702040; fax 01993-702100; Website www.cvspecial.co.uk) and *Resumé Store International* (251 N. Dupont Highway, Suite 113, Dover, Delaware 19901, USA; tel +1 302 734-1283; e-mail resume@resumestore.com Website www.resumestore.com/oje.html); additional services offered can include briefing before job interviews, strategic mail shots overseas, and essential advice on careers and training.

Business and Industry Report

Overview

Oil plays a significant role in the stability and wealth of all the Gulf states' economies and the downturn in global oil prices in the late 1990s, which has since recovered, highlighted the need for the individual countries to attempt to lessen their dependence on oil-based industries by implementing measures to diversify their economies, and encourage privatisation and foreign investment. Economic diversification plans include the development of other sectors such as banking and finance, construction, aviation and airports, tourism, petrochemicals and refinery, re-export commerce, and telecommunications. IT is generally felt to be an essential component to economic growth throughout the Gulf region and analysts project that it will continue to be so for some years to come.

The following section provides a guide to the most important industries in the Gulf region. The current prosperity or otherwise of each industry is discussed with a view to its employment and business potential for the expatriate.

Agriculture

BAHRAIN

Agriculture accounts for only one per cent of Bahrain's GDP (Gross Domestic Product). The Island comprises mainly infertile desert land which receives minimal levels of rainfall. On the northern coast of Bahrain lies a three-mile wide strip of land, the only area in the country where fruits and vegetables can be cultivated naturally. The heavily subsidised agricultural sector produces some dairy products, poultry, and shrimp. Agricultural production has diminished due to lack of water resources although present rates of production from local farms still caters for approximately 50 per cent of the domestic demand for poultry, eggs, and fish.

Growth will continue in Bahrain's food processing industry providing export opportunities for semi-processed agricultural products. Beverage bases, vegetable oils, snack foods, and breakfast cereals comprise other major products in the agricultural sector whose production looks set to expand.

KUWAIT

Kuwait is almost wholly dependent on food imports as the country's harsh climate only allows for 0.3 per cent of the total land area to be used for crops. In 1997, agriculture and fishing accounted for just 0.5 per cent of the nation's GDP. Among the fruit and vegetables that are cultivated in Kuwait are tomatoes, cucumbers, and dates. The country's rich fishing resources, worth US$50.2 million in 1997, are nearly entirely consumed domestically.

OMAN

Despite efforts to become self-sufficient in leading staples, Oman's food supplies continue to be largely supported by imports. In order to create internationally competitive agriculture and fishing industries, the Omani government have introduced several incentives for foreign investors to enter these sectors, such as tax exemptions, soft (concessional) loans, utilities discounts, tariff protection, help with exporting products. The greatest potential is in the field of high-tech, high-yield agriculture. Other major issues in the agricultural industry include the rising salinity of the water table and water supply pressures.

The yearly fish catch is above 100,000 tonnes per annum, and current measures are underway to produce value added, manufactured fish products. Processing and packaging for export are primary concerns, as is the employment of improved technology on the sea.

QATAR

Qatar is not self-sufficient in food production, with agriculture accounting for only one per cent of the country's annual GDP. The state is heavily reliant upon raw and processed food imports. Grains, poultry, and eggs are among the few products that the country does produce for itself. Lately the demand for semi-processed foods (especially beverage bases and a selection of food ingredients) has risen with a recent growth in the food processing industry. In an attempt to strengthen the agricultural sector, the Qatari government is encouraging foreign investors by offering certain incentives, and a heightened awareness has been placed on the fishing industry, which is headed by the Qatar Fishing Company. About 7,000 tonnes of shrimps annually are handled by the company's processing plant.

SAUDI ARABIA

Saudi Arabia may be one of the most arid countries in the world, but despite the deficiency of adequate water supplies and arable land, the Saudi government continues to focus on plans to attain food self-sufficiency in order to reduce imports. In 1997, agriculture accounted for 6.1 per cent of the Kingdom's GDP and between five and six of the country's work force is employed in the agriculture sector.

There was a time when Saudi Arabia was the sixth largest wheat exporter in the world, and today it continues to produce substantial quantities of wheat and barley, although the government has introduced measures to limit domestic output and cease exporting wheat as it lessened subsidies. The state-run Grain and Flour Mills Organisation had been in charge of barley imports but in 1998, for the first time in 20 years, private importers were permitted to import the product. Among the products in which Saudi Arabia is self-sufficient are select fruits and vegetables, poultry, and eggs.

Expansion of the agriculture sector is wholly reliant on the efficient handling of Saudi Arabia's very limited water resources. In line with the Sixth Development Plan, which aims to diversify the sector's products, attention has been turned to crops grown with equipment requiring less water. A desalination programme has also been initiated by the government that includes a water pipeline from Hinni to Riyadh to provide rural areas with fresh water. The planned pipeline is to cost in the region of SR 590 million and to carry a capacity of 360,000 cubic metres of water per day. Resevoirs, pipelines, and purification plants are also being considered to provide Jeddah, Yanbu, and neighbouring areas with fresh water.

Saudi Arabia exports fish and fish products to surrounding Arab countries, the Far East, and the European Union. The Saudi Fish Company (SFC) operates and owns the largest network of fish orientated retail in the Middle East.

UNITED ARAB EMIRATES

Due to the country's scarce water resources, agriculture accounts for just three per cent of the UAE's GDP. Desalination plants rather than fresh water streams supply most of the nation's water. Date palms are the country's primary crop, and the UAE is self-sufficient in salad crops and poultry for most of the year. On average over 600,000 tonnes of produce are yielded in a farming season. Produce includes: certain fruits and vegetables, eggs, poultry, fish, and dairy products. Despite agricultural production having risen six-fold over the last ten years due to government investment through inputs and direct subsidies, the UAE is still dependent on food product imports such as fruits, frozen vegetables, vegetable oils, beverage bases, poultry parts, and snack foods.

Banking and Finance

BAHRAIN

Banking and finance has become the second largest sector of the Bahraini economy, making up over 26 per cent of the GDP. Bahrain has developed into one of the most varied and dynamic financial hubs in the Middle East, aided by the oil boom of the 1970s and the disappearance of Beirut as a leading banking centre during the 1980s. There are 180 financial institutions (investment, commercial and specialised banks, off shore banking units, money changing establishments) and over 100 insurance companies located on the Island representing a combination of local, regional and international firms which offer a diversity of financial services, products and activities. The Bahraini government is currently encouraging more foreign banks to set up in the country and pursuing other plans to strengthen its position against the potential competition from Dubai and a re-emerging Beirut.

In June 1989, the Bahrain Stock Exchange (BSE) was initiated to act as a securities regulator with management of the capital market, and to serve as a standard stock exchange. At the close of 1998, the market capitalisation of the BSE reached US$6.77 billion, and the index stood at 2,155.29 in mid-1999, with 41 listed companies. The BSE is looking to expand its services to local, regional, and international companies, and develop its strong ties with other GCC countries with a view to have their shares listed on the BSE.

KUWAIT

The Kuwaiti banking sector comprises seven commercial banks, held by the government and merchant families, making up a sum of 125 branches. The National Bank of Kuwait is the leading bank with 35 branches (1998 figure). Kuwait is also host to three specialised banks providing medium- and long-term financing, and four representative offices of foreign banks. The Kuwait Real Estate Bank aids in financing property lending, the Industrial Bank of Kuwait gives financial assistance with industrial and agricultural projects, and the Credit and Savings Bank helps Kuwaiti citizens financially with housing and personal residential development. The Central Bank of Kuwait has been regulating these institutions since 1984.

To attract investment a number of financial institutions are situated in Kuwait such as the Gulf Investment Corporation, which encourages direct investment by promoting joint ventures in the industrial sector with equity and debt funding, and Islamic investment groups: The International Investor (TII) and the International Investment Group, which provide foreign companies with customised financial services and products.

Currently three companies, Al-Ahlia, Warba, and the Kuwait Insurance Company, are in control of the insurance sector, although authority is to be passed over to foreign institutions.

In 1977, the Kuwait Stock Exchange (KSE) was initiated. During the Gulf War, the KSE was suspended, it reopened in September 1992. 65 Kuwaiti businesses, 10 foreign companies, and two mutual funds are currently registered on the KSE. Foreigners are not presently permitted to trade in the stock market, except through mutual funds, but the new parliament may lessen this restriction during its term.

OMAN

If the proposal put forward by the GCC to permit regional banks to cross borders is finally passed then the nature of commercial and retail banking in Oman could soon dramatically alter. The action could result in a consolidation within the Omani banking sector and an influx of foreign banks, in particular from the UAE and Bahrain. The merger between the Commercial Bank of Oman and the Bank of Oman, Bahrain, and Kuwait, which became entirely Omani-owned, acts as a precedent for future mergers, and will make the Commercial Bank of Oman the nation's largest bank.

According to appraisals revealed in mid-1998 from international assessors, overall Oman's investment climate appears relatively stable regardless of some internal trouble on the Muscat Securities Market.

QATAR

The Central Bank of Qatar monitors the country's banking sector which comprises fourteen banks, six of which are Qatari, two are non-Qatari Arab, and the remaining six are other foreign-owned. The Central Bank oversees the redemption of Qatar's currency, controls monetary policy, and regulates the banking system and interest rates on Qatari riyal funds. Banking activity mainly involves letters of credit and loans to private sector businesses for government projects. Total assets of the banking sector are estimated to be US$10.5 billion.

The Qatari government's increased privatisation measures, and foreign investment gains, should together help boost the country's stock market, the Doha Securities Market (DSM). In August 1998, the government revealed that 40 per cent of Qatar Public Telecommunications Company (Q-Tel) would be available via the DSM. By September 1998, Qatar's stock exchange the 19-share index stood at 141.4 points, an almost 42 per cent climb, with an overall capitalisation about US$4 billion. The addition of Q-Tel and the probable lisiting of other industries will not only raise the DSM's capitalisation, but it will also lessen the weight of the banking sector. Moreover, the addition of the Qatar Steel Company (Qasco) and Q-Tel will give some diversity to the Bourse which has up to this time been dominated by banking stock.

SAUDI ARABIA

There are a total of 1,229 banking branches in Saudi Arabia, possessing assets worth US$107.82 billion at the close of 1998, making the Saudi banking market one of the largest in the region. Commercial banks in the Kingdom operate traditional deposit taking and lending, inter-bank deposits, foreign exchange services, and government debt and equity. Five specialised credit institutions offer medium and long-term financing to the private sector and some public sector ventures. The Saudi Arabian Monetary Agency (SAMA) is the country's central bank.

A programme of restructuring and consolidation is currently underway in Saudi's banking sector. In 1997, Saudi Cairo Bank merged with the United Saudi Commercial Bank to form the United Saudi Bank (USB), which recently merged with Saudi American Bank (Samba) in mid-1999. Samba now represents the fourth largest banking network in Saudi Arabia, with 126 branches and a balance sheet of more than SR 77.2 billion (US$20.6 billion). In December 1998, UK-based Saudi International Bank (SIB) and Bahrain-based Gulf International Bank, revealed their plan to merge. SAMA is the sole largest shareholder in SIB and will receive shares in the new company in return for its stake. On completion of the merger, the company plans to create numerous new branches throughout the Arabian Peninsula, starting with Saudi Arabia.

In 1998, ten of Saudi Arabia's eleven commercial banks raised their third quarter profits, which, together were up 10.3 per cent in the face of the year's international economic crises. However, the country's stock exchange (the National Centre for Financial and Economic Information index, NCFEI), did not fare as well, and figures fell 28 per cent in 1998, although banking profits helped to stabilise the downturn near the close of the year. The NCFEI, set up by SAMA in 1990, is an over-the-counter market in which commercial banks purchase and sell shares through an electronic trading system. In February 1999, 74 companies were listed, and over the last decade the NCFEI has accomplished an average market capitalisation of US$43.88 trillion, making it the largest stock market in the Middle East. Despite the downturn in 1998, analysts predict that the Saudi market will be more prosperous in the future. The Saudi stock market is one of the chief stock exchanges by value amidst emerging markets, and is to be incorporated as part of the International Finance Corporation, a member of the World Bank Group.

UNITED ARAB EMIRATES

The UAE is currently in the process of establishing its own stock exchange, the Emirates Securities and Commodities Market. Abu Dhabi and Dubai are to have separate trading floors and a regulatory body, the Securities and Commodities Commission is to be in charge of drafting regulations to license brokers, determine audit and accounting standards, and draw up laws to protect investors against fraud.

There are 21 UAE-owned banks with over 200 branches, and 28 foreign banks with 119 branches in the UAE, all competing against one another, hence the need for regulation and the set up of common standards throughout the emirates, which will be in place once the stock market has been established.

Energy

BAHRAIN

Oil and gas still play a crucial role in Bahrain's economy despite the country's efforts to diversify. The late 1998 slump in global oil prices had its due effect on Bahrain by slowing its economic growth and in mid-1999, oil production stood at about 50,000 barrels per day (bpd) from its own oil fields as well as an additional 140,000 bpd from an off shore field shared with Saudi Arabia. Approximately 210,000 bpd are also imported from Saudi Arabia for refining. Oil accounts for 60 per cent of the government's revenue, but a mere 15 per cent of Bahrain's GDP.

Most of Bahrain's gas resources are used domestically although the country does export some gas-derived petrochemicals and liquefied petroleum gas (LPG). The state-owned Bahrain Petroleum Company (BAPCO) has recently been allocated US$16.2 million in order to transform Bahrain's only oil refinery into a manufacturer of unleaded fuel. However, it is dubious from where Bahrain will receive support for these plans.

A number of infrastructure development programmes instigated by BAPCO are underway, several with the assistance of American companies. For example, the Foster Wheeler Corporation has secured a US$15 million front-end engineering and design contract with BAPCO, while the American West Coast's Caltex has provided technological advisory services for the installation of new computer systems for the company. Furthermore, a contract of US$500 million has been issued for the expansion of BAPCO's refinery in the Awali Field.

KUWAIT

In 1998, Kuwait was estimated to possess 96.5 billion barrels of proven oil reserves, over nine per cent of the world's total. An additional five billion barrels of reserves, half of which are owned by Kuwait, are located in the Neutral Zone area that Kuwait shares with Saudi Arabia. The majority of Kuwait's oil reserves are situated in the 70 billion barrel Greater Burgan region, believed to be the world's second largest oil field. In the first half of 1999, oil production averaged 1.836 million barrels per day (bpd) and is set to retain this level through March 2000 in accordance with the output cuts introduced by the Organisation of Petroleum Exporting Countries (OPEC) aimed to strengthen oil prices and shoreup revenues. In 1998, 60 per cent of Kuwait's oil was exported to Asian countries, in particular Japan, other exports are shipped to Europe and North America. Kuwait accounted for 2.8 per cent of America's total oil imports in 1998.

Despite Kuwait's oil sector suffering greatly from the Iraqi occupation in 1990/1991, most of the production and refinery industry has now been restored. The country currently has the capacity to produce above 2.5 million barrels per day (bpd) of crude oil and the government plans to increase this figure to 3.5 bpd in 2010 by creating northern oil fields. In 1997, Kuwait's in-country refineries were operating near to their pre-Gulf War capacity of approximately 886,000 bpd which the government aims to increase to one million bpd in 2005 by raising capacity at the Mina al-Ahmadi complex and establishing a fourth refinery. Furthermore, Kuwait Petroleum Company (KPC) has invested in refineries in foreign nations and is developing its international downstream interests with a view to running a combined European and Asian refining capacity of 700,000 bpd. Additionally, the KPC is looking to construct a US$2 billion, 184,000 bpd refinery in the eastern Indian state of Orissa and a 300,000 bpd facility in Thailand.

OMAN

The US$3-US$5 billion liquefied natural gas (LNG) plant in Sur is key to Oman's plans to reduce its dependence on oil for export revenue. Purchasers for the 6.6 million tonnes of yearly output have already been secured through three contracts with Korea Gas Corporation (4.1 million tonnes per annum for 25 years), US-based Enron (1.6 million tonnes per annum), and Osaka Gas (700,000 tonnes per annum).

The Sultanate has proven natural gas reserves of over 25 trillion cubic feet, and a 1,000 km LNG pipeline is already complete. The Omani government and Royal Dutch Shell hold the two largest stakes in the LNG project at 51 per cent and 30 per cent respectively. Amongst the remaining stakeholders are TOTAL of France, Korea LNG, and Mitsubishi.

Over 90 per cent of the country's oil reserves, and almost 95 per cent of production, is handled by the Petroleum Development of Oman, a consortium between the Omani government (60 per cent), Shell (34 per cent), TOTAL (4 per cent), and Partex (2 per cent). Yibal, Oman's largest oil field, makes up 120,000 of the nation's estimated 900,000 barrels per day (bpd) production. Fresh reserves have been discovered in recent years, and several concessions are held to agreements for further exploration. This includes TOTAL's 1998 commitment to spend a minimum of US$66 million for exploration prior to 2005.

Currently, refining activities are confined to Mina al-Fahal, where the 85,000 bpd output is employed to meet domestic demand. However, the government has looked into projects with Pakistan, India, and the Caspian Sea region with a view to expanding refineries within its borders.

Oman's aging oil infrastructure looks set to undergo a revamp, and the drop in oil prices in the 1990s, which has since recovered, should lead to heightened competition to export more cheaply which means increased reliance on new technology to aid extraction, etc. Consequently, even more opportunities in the oil sector will abound in the coming years.

QATAR

Oil accounts for approximately 70 per cent of Qatar's government revenues. The country's proven oil reserves are currently estimated at 3.3 billion barrels. The state-owned Qatar General Petroleum Corporation (QGPC) monitors the pumping of oil from the onshore Dukhan field on the west side of the country and three off shore fields. The Dukhan site comprises four major hydrocarbon resevoirs: three oil-producing and one containing non-associated gas. Qatari plans for expanding the production capacity of facilities like the Dukhan site have been suspended indefinitely due to OPEC's international oil output cut. As of mid-1999, Qatar is on target to meet OPEC's production quota of 640,000 barrels of crude oil per day.

Qatar's oil income may look set to decrease but its liquefied natural gas (LNG) exports were predicted to increase twofold to above seven million tonnes in 1999. Qatar's LNG reserves are rated as the third largest in the world after the former Soviet Union and Iran. Ras Laffan LNG Company (Rasgas) revealed that it would begin exporting gas to South Korea's state gas company, Kogas, in mid-1999, and although confirmation is still pending, Rasgas was also awarded the international tender to provide a sum of 7.5 million tonnes of gas to India's state-owned Petronet LNG in 2002. Additionally, Qatar Liquefied Gas Company (Qatargas) is in the production stage of providing Japan with six million tonnes of gas annually.

Qatar has recently enlisted in the multi-billion dollar Dolphin gas project (see below *United Arab Emirates* 'Energy'), completing a distribution chain connecting Qatar with the UAE, Oman, and Pakistan. The UAE Offsets Group, acting as the trading hub, intends to purchase between 200 and 700 million cubic feet of Qatari gas per day. The gas is to be transported by pipeline to the UAE and distributed to Pakistan and Oman.

SAUDI ARABIA

In 1998, oil, natural gas, and refined products, accounted for 90 per cent of Saudi Arabia's total export earnings and 40 per cent of the Kingdom's GDP. Over one quarter of the global oil reserves are contained in Saudi Arabia's 77 oil and gas fields, with more than half of this concentrated in just eight fields. The Kingdom continues to be the leading oil supplier for the USA, Europe, and Japan. Current figures predict that the country's proven recoverable reserves of 261.5 billion barrels should last for almost a century, if the average 1998 crude oil production rate of 8.1 million barrels per day (bpd) is maintained. Some believe that there may even be a total of one trillion barrels of recoverable oil in Saudi land.

The slump in global oil prices in the late 1990s, which has since recovered, highlighted the need for diversification and privatisation in the Kingdom. However, it has yet to be conclusively decided whether foreigners will be permitted to invest in Saudi's upstream oil market although proposals from international oil companies who want to be involved in upstream ventures are being welcomed.

In the light of the mid-1999 OPEC (Organisation of Petroleum Exporting Countries) production quota cuts, Saudi Arabia has had to turn its focus on the creation of lighter crude reserves in order to maximise its petroleum income. A US$2-US$2.5 billion Shaybah venture is currently underway, with the involvement of two US companies, the Parsons Corporation and Bechtel, which aims to produce 500,000 bpd of crude oil and 870 million cubic feet per day of natural gas.

In February 1999, the first of five planned strategic reserve sites was inaugurated by the Crown Prince Abdullah. The multi-billion dollar site is set to have the capacity to store several million tonnes of refined products in the event of a war or natural disaster.

UNITED ARAB EMIRATES

Oil has been the mainstay of the UAE economy for the last forty years. 1998 figures reveal that the UAE is in possession of roughly 98 billion barrels of oil, 9.8 per cent of the world's reserves, most of which are located in Abu Dhabi, with 94 per cent of the country's total. Dubai's reserves are estimated at a total of four billion barrels, predicted to be exhausted in ten years. In 1998, Abu Dhabi produced an output of two million barrels per day (bpd), a level which is likely to remain constant throughout 2000 despite former plans for expansion, due to OPEC's restrictions placed on its members' output quotas to strengthen oil prices and shore up revenues. The Emirate's current oil reserves are projected to last for over 100 years.

The UAE's natural gas reserves, estimated at about 204.9 trillion cubic feet, are ranked fourth largest in the world after Russia, Iran, and Qatar. Approximately 92 per cent of the reserves are situated in Abu Dhabi, where the Kuff gas resevoir rates among the largest in the world. Present gas reserves are estimated to last for roughly 150 to 170 years. Due to the cuts on oil production quotas and the ever-increasing domestic demand for electricity, the UAE has shifted its focus onto developing its extensive gas reserves, expanding and modernising on-shore and off-shore gas extraction and distribution systems, and implementing other improvements within the industry.

An upstream gas development, transport, and marketing project, the Dolphin programme, worth US$8 billion to US$10 billion, started in 1999 and headed by the UAE Offsets Group (UOG), intends to import almost three billion cubic feet of gas per day from Qatar. The programme aims to establish one of the largest and most comprehensive gas supply infrastructures in the world and includes other projects such as the advancement of gas fields in Qatar, construction of a pipeline that will connect Qatar with the UAE and Oman, the set up of new industrial centres in the UAE, and the commencement of new power generator projects. The imported gas will help lessen shortages in Abu Dhabi and Dubai, places where the UOG projects demand to double by 2005. In June 1999, the UOG chose American-based Mobil as its technical partner to carry out the upstream part of the programme.

In 1998, the UAE's installed power generating capacity stood at about 6,850 megawatts. Population growth and new industrial expansions have attributed to an ever-increasing demand for electrical power that looks set to continue to rise sharply throughout the next decade. In response to this, a comprehensive restructuring in the water and electricity sectors has been called for and privatisation with minority interests held by foreign firms encouraged. The operator of Abu Dhabi's first Independent Power Project (IPP) secured US$556 million in commercial funding for the planned development of al-Taweelah cogeneration plant. CMS Energy, an American-based firm, was selected to handle the management, financing, construction, and running of the facility, and was awarded 40 per cent ownership in the project. The US$700 million development will add 710 megawatts of power and 50 million gallons per day of desalinated water to the UAE's supplies by August 2001. Other potential sites for a second 1,000 megawatt IPP are currently being investigated by Abu Dhabi Water and Electricity Authority (ADWEA).

Industry and Manufacturing

BAHRAIN

To aid economic diversification, Bahrain has invested in basic industries, such as ship repair, petrochemicals, and aluminium smelting. There are plans to develop the country's Arabian Ship Repair Yard (ASRY), already the largest in the Gulf, and establish a large petrochemical complex at Sitra as well as a sulphur derivative plant. The nation's aluminium sector has grown from basic smelting to a highly advanced variety of downstream operations that currently include a rolling mill, an extrusion plant, two automobile wheel factories, a factory manufacturing aluminium powder, and the largest single aluminium smelter. Aluminium Bahrain (ALBA), in which the Bahraini government holds a 77 per cent stake, regulates the country's aluminium sector. Saudi Arabia's Public Investment Fund and Bretons Investment of Germany are also major shareholders in ALBA.

ALBA, the largest aluminium producer in the Middle East, accounts for the leading share of non-oil exports out of Bahrain. In 1997, the aluminium production of ALBA reached 493,032 tonnes of the company's present total production capacity of 500,000 tonnes per annum. A number of plans to expand the corporation include a US$250 million, 20,000 tonne aluminium alloy facility in addition to a calcined coke plant that will allow Bahrain to produce its own calcined coke rather than depend on imports.

KUWAIT

Since the Gulf War, the manufacturing industry in Kuwait has been rebuilding itself at a rapid pace, far outstripping the finance, transportation, and construction sectors. The main products of the manufacturing industry are oil-related. Kuwait's Petrochemical Industries Company (PIC) has been known to primarily manufacture low-value products such as ammonia, urea, and fertiliser for exports, but recently the company has turned its production to higher-value products such as polypropylene.

The region's largest petrochemical project, the EQUATE joint venture, involving both PIC and American-based Union Carbide, is in operation at the US$2 billion industrial complex at Shuaiba which includes a 650,000 metric tonne per annum ethylene cracker, two polyethylene units with a capacity of 450,000 metric tonnes per annum, and a 350,000 metric tonne per annum ethylene glycol plant, all of which came on line in 1997. The products are exported in the main to Saudi Arabia, the United Arab Emirates, and East Asia.

OMAN

The manufacturing industry in Oman accounts for only approximately five per cent of the GDP. Products being manufactured are typically perfumes, oils, non-metallic and wood products, and detergents. Potential developers are being encouraged to invest in the light industry by several incentives being introduced by the Omani government. A high percentage of Omani exports to the USA are represented by textiles.

QATAR

The Qatari government has actively encouraged the advancement of both heavy and light industry that utilises domestic resources to their maximum. A steel and iron industry has been established to meet the demand of the energy sector, and healthy gas reserves have resulted in the set up of chemical, petrochemical, and fertiliser industries. A number of developing industrial projects in the industrial city of Messaieed are to receive US$110 million investment capital from the Qatari government over a five year period.

Qasco, the leading company in Qatar's steel industry, was started in 1978 under Japanese management but came under the supervision of the Qatari government in the 1980s. Its success is reflected by the fact that its net profit in 1997 was US$93.6 million, and according to the International Trade Commission (ITC), Qatar is the sole producer in the Middle East that has successfully exported a substantial amount of its steel production. Over the past ten years, 90 per cent of Qasco's concrete reinforcing bars have supplied 30 per cent of the GCC market.

Foreign investors have joined with state-owned companies in developing fertiliser and petrochemical plants in Qatar. At the head of the petrochemical industry in the country is Qatar Petrochemical Company (Qapco), which saw its profits fall by 52 per cent in 1998, but has continued to increase its industrial capacity by recently opening its fifth export-orientated petrochemical plant. Products are exported throughout the Gulf and the Far East. The Qatar Industrial Manufacturing Company (QIMCO), which has direct investment in eight projects across the region, has been set up to encourage private sector investment in small and medium-sized industrial projects.

SAUDI ARABIA

The Saudi government has actively been encouraging the development of heavy industry in the public sector in order to strengthen the country's non-oil industrial sector and diversify its industrial base. The 70 per cent government-owned Saudi Basic Industries Corporation (SABIC), the largest petrochemical company in the Middle East, which controls and operates 16 plants with international firms, producing petrochemicals, plastics, steel, and fertilisers, is playing a major role in the government's industrial diversifcation plans. SABIC annually generates over US$6 billion in revenues. The joint-venture holding company has increased production from 11.9 million tonnes per annum in 1990 to 25 million tonnes in 1998. In support of such development projects, the Saudi Industrial Development Fund was set up by the government and in February 1999, committed itself to SR 70 million (US$18.7 million) in new loans to aid start up and growth of industrial ventures. In March, five more loans were granted, raising SIDF's commitments to SR 32.99 billion, comprising 2,071 individual loans, of which 746 have been repaid in full.

Mining is another area where investment is being encouraged. Saudi Arabia holds the largest store of mineral deposits in the Gulf, including 20 million tonnes of gold ore, 60 million tonnes of copper, 10 billion tonnes of phosphate, and millions of tonnes of other elements. During mid-1999, investment in the mining sector came to approximately US$6.7 billion. It is hoped that mining will develop into the second largest source of government income over the next ten years, as yearly expansion in this sector was predicted to reach 9.9 per cent during the Fifth Development Plan. With this in mind, the government set up the Saudi Arabian Mining Company (Ma'adin) with a starting capital of US$1 billion in April 1997. The company manages the mineral sector and regulates its progress.

In 1998, construction accounted for about 9.3 per cent of Saudi Arabia's GDP, up from 8.6 per cent in 1997. The development of construction activity did slow in 1998 on account of budget cuts but recovery was expected in 1999. Potential mergers are under discussion among the eight major Saudi cement companies in order to protect themselves from a predicted slump in the industry. On the whole, privately-owned companies are involved in this sector, and the government actively supports international companies to join with Saudi investors in the set up of industrial ventures. Construction policy dictates that 30 per cent of any contract awarded to a foreign firm be sub-contracted locally.

The restructuring of Saudi's extensive power sector has been a major industrial project in recent years. Ten existing power companies merged to form the 85 per cent state-owned Saudi Electricity Company (SEC), which is responsible for generation, transmission, and distribution of the country's power. The development of the power sector has shown to be vital to meet the ongoing demand brought about by industrialisation and modernisation.

UNITED ARAB EMIRATES

In 1997 the UAE's industry (non-oil or gas related) sector accounted for 11.2 per cent of the country's GDP. In 1999, industry was rated second only to oil production in terms of contribution to GDP, compared to its fourth position in 1996 after oil, government services, and trade. Despite manufacturing continuing to be dominated by the production of chemicals and plastics, other sectors have developed. Free trade zones have aided industrial growth through the influx of international firms. Industries that are appearing to have healthy expansion potential are construction, cement, and aluminium, followed by food processing and re-exports.

With a view to strengthening the UAE's petrochemical infrastructure, the construction of the country's first major petrochemicals facility, the Abu Dhabi Polymers Company (Borouge) is underway, headed by the Abu Dhabi National Oil Company (ADNOC) in partnership with the European chemicals giant Borealis. The US$1 billion complex located at Ruwais, 60 miles west of Abu Dhabi, will comprise two polyethylene units with a capacity of 225,000 tonnes per annum. Output from the facilities will be aimed at the Far East and will operate on some of the lowest-cost energy feedstock in the world. Opportunities may result from this project for private investors to invest in a new downstream capacity, either directly or through joint-stock companies.

The Dubal Aluminium Company of Dubai, established in 1979, has always played a significant role in the Gulf's aluminium production. Producing 390,000 tonnes per annum in 1999, the company intends to increase its production capacity in 2000 to over 500,000 tonnes per annum. The EU has become a chief target for Dubal with sales to Europe rising 750 per cent between 1997 and 1998, from 10,000 tonnes to 85,000 tonnes, out of total sales of 402,000 tonnes.

Growth of the construction sector in the UAE has been aided by the expansion of the cement and building materials market. Construction activity slowed in the late 1990s but developments are underway in the emirate of Ras al-Khaimah, which has become the chief domestic reserve of building materials for the UAE. In summer 1999, production started at Ras al-Khaimah Cement Company's 550.5 million dirham (US$150 million) cement plant, which is to have a capacity of one million tonnes per year of Portland cement. Production capacity at other Ras al-Khaimah companies producing white cement, ceramics, and construction materials, is also planned to be increased.

Information Technology (IT)

Over recent years IT has made an enormous impact on economies worldwide and Canada's Nortel Networks predicts that the value of the global internet economy will reach US$2.8 trillion in 2003. In the Middle East the IT sector is currently exhibiting a 25 per cent annual growth which shows no signs of diminishing. Moreover, spending on IT products and services in the region is projected to increase at a rate of 14 per cent per annum, from US$17.8 billion in 1997 to US$34.9 billion in 2002; and over 500,000 computers are predicted to be purchased yearly during this period. In 1998, the International Data Corporation (IDC) revealed that five of the six Gulf states were among the world's fastest-growing PC markets: Kuwait, Oman, Qatar, Saudi Arabia, and the UAE. Bahrain was only just outside the top ten. From 1994-8, the GCC computer market grew by up to 60 per cent per annum, which slowed to 25 per cent in 1998 with the slump in oil prices. In 1999 the growth was expected to be 15-20 per cent.

The presence of IT in the Middle East is still at its beginning stages. Despite the numbers of internet subscriptions having risen twofold over the last year, there are still only 300,000 subscribers in an area of 200 million. Although, in the Gulf region other estimates vary wildy of between 230,000 and 700,000 internet users, predicted to increase to 2.5 million by 2002. Internet penetration in the GCC is growing by 100 per cent a year, compared to growth in western Europe of 30 per cent. The UAE has the highest ratio of internet users in the Arab world, followed by Egypt, then Bahrain, boosted by Batelco subscribers in Saudi Arabia's Eastern Province, then

Lebanon and Kuwait with up to 50,000 internet subscribers. Qatar has under 20,000 internet users connected to its national internet service provider (ISP), Q-Tel. Saudi internet penetration stands at below one per cent but is projected to quadruple by 2002. Internet growth has arrived late in Saudi Arabia, where authorities insist on screening residents' surfing habits, users are limited to sites that have been cleared by the authorities.

Only four per cent of the extensive market of internet users throughout the Middle East participate in any kind of e-commerce, much below the 15 per cent global average. This figure, in addition to the fact that there are still only 300,000 subscribers out of a potential 200 million, indicates the limitless scope for development in the Middle East IT sector. Lately an American company, Lucent Technologies, was awarded a US$35 million contract to expand Saudi Arabia's internet network.

Both education and training in the Middle East IT sector have become increasingly more imperative to a country's economic growth and stability as IT has infiltrated the infrastructure of all nations. It is a perfect time to invest now in a virtually untapped market with instantaneous growth potential where IT opportunities abound and regional support for the development of the industry is highly favourable. Arab IT companies are currently crying out for western technology and expertise to aid the fast-growing expansion of the sector.

Tourism

BAHRAIN

Bahrain is one of the most popular tourist spots on the Arabian Peninsula. In 1997, over three million visited the country mainly from neighbouring Gulf states. Increasing numbers of tourists from Europe, the Americas, and Asia are also being drawn to the Island. The opening of the 15 mile King Fahd causeway linking Bahrain to Saudi Arabia in 1986 had a significant impact on the rise of visitors to Bahrain. Hotel occupancy levels in the capital, Manama, rose from 58.9 per cent in 1997 to 63.3 per cent in 1998.

The Bahraini government is actively encouraging the growth of its tourist industry aiming to make it account for 10.5 per cent of its GDP, a rise of 1.3 per cent from its present level. The Bahrain Promotions and Marketing Board (BPMB) was established to promote all aspects of business and tourism in the country and since 1996 has been opening representative offices overseas. Among the many attractions established for visitors in Bahrain include global class exhibition facilities, five star luxury hotels, golf courses, an ice rink, a go-karting facility, and a Kids World fun centre.

OMAN

Tourism in Oman is a relatively new concept of which the government has only recently begun to encourage the development provided that it does not conflict with local custom. Over the next ten years hotel capacity is set to increase twofold. In Salalah, a previously untouched area in terms of global tourism on a major scale, a leading international chain is constructing a hotel resort. Furthermore, Radisson SAS Worldwide joined with locally-owned Global Development Company in a new US$15.6 million, 142 bedroom luxury hotel planned to open recently in Muscat. Most international visitors to the region are currently from Europe, in particular Germany. Other tourists come on day trips from the neighbouring UAE. By concentrating on the development of hotels and improved travel services, the Omani government is looking to assist in the expansion of its country's tourism sector seen as an important factor in aiding the diversification of the nation's economy.

The Directorate of Tourism within the Omani Ministry of Commerce and Industry plans to heighten Oman's international presence not only through the newly constructed and soon-to-be built hotels, but also through hosting large-scale attractions such as annual festivals, global dune rallies, and yacht races. Nine new tourism-related projects were revealed in October 1998, including the construction of over 200 new hotel rooms.

Since 1989 the number of tourists visiting the Sultanate of Oman has been increasing by a compounded yearly rate of 10 per cent. In 1997, visitors to the country reached a total of 361,000.

QATAR

Qatar's tourism industry, such as it is, is still very much at its early stages with the government currently implementing plans to encourage its growth, including a renovation of Doha International Airport and the erection of six major hotels, amongst which are the Hilton, Four Seasons, and Ritz-Carlton. Additionally, a US$250 million shopping centre in the West Bay district of the capital, Doha, is presently under construction. This site will include international clothing outlets, a multi-screen cinema, and an ice rink. A 350 room, four star hotel with health club and restaurants, as well as eight residential and commercial buildings are to also be built around the site.

Qatar's tourist attractions include: stunning beaches, a world-acclaimed golf course, plenty of opportunities to pursue any number of land and water sports such as scuba diving, sailing, motor boating, fishing, tennis, squash, horse riding, desert driving, etc. Furthermore, the country's very low crime rate makes Qatar a very safe country in which to reside or to visit.

SAUDI ARABIA

Tourism in Saudi Arabia falls into three main categories: the *Hajj* (see *Islam* in Gulf States' 'General Introduction'), business travel, and recreational tourism from within the country and other GCC states. A recent development has been the appointment of a UK tour operator, *Bales Worldwide Tours* (tel 01306-885991), that offers ten day trips to the Kingdom to men, and women over 40 (unless accompanied by a close male relative). But with the exception of this company recreational tourists from outside Saudi Arabia are not actively encouraged. Tourist visas as such do not in general exist, nevertheless the Kingdom still received a total of 3.5 million visitors in 1996, of which the majority were pilgrims in the *Hajj*, or visitors travelling to Saudi holy sites throughout the rest of the year.

In 1998, 1.13 million pilgrims travelled to Saudi Arabia for the *Hajj*, accounting for 66 per cent of the total of pilgrims that year. Due to Makkah's capacity to cater for only two million visitors the government requested that frequent Saudi pilgrims remain at home in order to allow more Muslim foreigners to participate. In 1997 the number of Saudi pilgrims fell dramatically to 500,000 from the previous year's figure of one million. Foreign pilgrims are encouraged as they help to boost the private sector investment in retail outlets in Madinah and Makkah due to their propensity to buy consumer products while travelling.

There are already 30 top class hotels in Saudi Arabia but plans to construct 21 more are currently underway. Additionally, a new city centre in Madinah is planned, a Four Seasons complex in Riyadh, and further projects in the Eastern Province and along the Red Sea Coast are being implemented to cater for the slowly growing tourist market. In the south-west of the Kingdom lies Asir where the local government is actively looking towards encouraging visitors from outside the GCC by investing in the growth of its tourism industry. In 1997, Asir gained over SR 2.2 billion (US$590 million) from tourism and over 70 per cent of its population are employed in this developing sector. The first private tourism and hotel management college in Saudi Arabia was established in this province.

UNITED ARAB EMIRATES

Tourism is a boom industry in the UAE with Dubai, the site of 70 per cent of the country's hotels, acting as the hub of this highly successful and ever-growing sector. Visitors from Russia have traditionally been the chief customers in the UAE's hotels but recently their decreasing numbers have been replaced with tourists from the UK and India. In 1998, the UAE received almost 2.2 million visitors. Dubai welcomed a total of 1.82 million foreign tourists in 1997, a figure predicted to increase by 63 per cent in this year, 2000.

Amongst the country's many attractions are its clean, sandy beaches, opportunities to watch first-class horse racing, participate in desert safaris, and play golf on high quality golf courses. Numerous luxury four and five star hotels are located throughout the country. Recently, the emirates of Sharjah and Fujairah have established their own tourism bureaus to encourage the growth of the industry in their regions. Development plans include the construction of more hotels and other visitor attractions such as golf courses.

Regional Employment Guide

In the first section of this book, *Living in the Gulf States*, the major regions of the Gulf states were discussed with a view to residence. In this section, the same regions are covered but with a view to the employment prospects available in the major industries in each country. The information provided will give some idea of the industries which are dominant and the types of jobs which are most readily available in each area.

Population figures for the major cities are given in brackets (1997 figures).

Bahrain

Capital: Manama (144,343).
Other Major Cities: Muharraq (76,222), Rifaa (49,014), Jidhafs (42,000), Isa (40,000).
Population: 607,000.
Labour Force: *total:* 140,000; *by occupation:* industry, commerce, and service 78 per cent, government 21 per cent, agriculture 1 per cent.
Unemployment rate: 15 per cent.
Main industries: petroleum processing and refining, aluminium smelting, off-shore banking, ship repairing, tourism.
GDP – composition by sector: services 61 per cent; industry 38 per cent; agriculture 1 per cent.

Bahrain initiated economic expansion programmes more than 20 years ago due to its awareness of its limited oil resources. Consequently, Bahrain now has one of the most diversified economies in the Arabian Peninsula with highly advanced communications and transport facilities. Comparatively the Island has one of the largest collections of manufacturing industries in the Gulf region and the biggest network of international bank branches. The Bahraini government is currently implementing privatisation plans and encouraging foreign investment to help further strengthen the country's economy.

In response to unemployment figures, the government has concentrated on its programme of Bahraini-isation – the replacement of foreign workers with local nationals. Added incentives are being offered to foreign companies recruiting Bahraini nationals. The education system in the state is also being improved to prepare young Bahrainis to fill job opportunities created. A quota system has been introduced to prescribe the number of Bahraini citizens that should be employed in certain sectors at a given time, and when awarding international bids, some regional companies take into consideration which bidders offer the greatest number of opportunities to nationals.

Kuwait

Capital: Kuwait City.
Other Major Cities: Hawalli, Farwaniya (1,154,503), Ahmadi (435,000), Al Jahra (150,000).
Population: 2.19 million.
Labour Force: *total:* 1.1 million; *by occupation:* government and social services 50 per cent, services 40 per cent, industry and agriculture 10 per cent.
Unemployment rate: 1.8 per cent.
Main industries: petroleum, petrochemicals, desalination, food processing, construction materials, salt, construction.
GDP – composition by sector: industry 53 per cent; services 47 per cent; agriculture 0 per cent.

Kuwait's oil wealth, which came into fruition in the 1950s, was such that the country was able to develop its basic infrastruture by the early 1980s, and to establish a highly advanced state with very generous domestic policies. The reconstruction costs of the 1990/91 Gulf War took their toll on the country's economy but it has since managed to recover and the government continues to offer its citizens free education, health care, and retirement.

The hydrocarbons sector dominates the Kuwaiti economy accounting for 95 per cent of export earnings. The manufacturing sector mainly comprises petroleum's downstream industries, such as oil refining and petrochemicals. Due to the country's dependence on its oil production, its GDP fell by 2 per cent in 1998 with the slump in the world's oil prices. In response to this, the government has turned its focus on to privatisation and foreign investment in order to aid economic diversification and expansion, and to maximise employment opportunities for Kuwaiti nationals. Proposals include the privatisation of the national airline, the telecommunications sector, and various aspects of the energy sector.

Foreign investment has been encouraged by the introduction of several government measures including allowing international companies to bid for the development of Kuwait's northern oil fields in 1999, and the opening of the Kuwaiti Stock Exchange (KSE) to foreign investors. In 1999, an emiri decree authorised the 100 per cent foreign ownership of new companies, a figure which had previously been restricted to 49 per cent. Additionally, a free trade zone was officially inaugurated at the Shuwaikh port in July 1999.

The sharp recovery of oil prices in 1999 should aid the government to pursue its other plans for economic growth which include development in the country's infrastructure, power generation, and oil industry.

Oman

Capital: Muscat (622,506).
Other Major Cities: Al Batinah (538, 763), Salalah and suburbs (85,000).
Population: 2.4 million.
Labour Force: *total:* 780,500; *by occupation:* agriculture 37 per cent.

Main industries: crude oil production and refining, natural gas production, construction, cement, copper.
GDP – composition by sector: services 54 per cent; industry 43 per cent; agriculture 3 per cent.

Oman's economy is highly dependent upon its oil industry but due to the country's limited proven reserves, only enough to last for about the next 20 years at present production levels, the Sultanate is now heavily concentrating on diversifying its economy. In 1997, Oman's re-export industry grew by 31 per cent and growth looks set to continue with the opening of a new container terminal at Port Raysut in November 1998. The fall in oil prices resulted in higher than predicted budget deficits, with expenditure surpassing revenue by US$263 million in 1998. The 1999 budget reviewed its oil price predictions from US$15 per barrel to US$9 per barrel which lead to an expected 1999 budget deficit of over US$1.5 billion. Nevertheless, the Omani government's skill in handling these shortfalls by revising the budget, aided by the current upturn in oil prices, is projected to prevent a devaluation of the Omani riyal and to encourage long-term stability.

Despite the fact that Oman's five year plan (1996-2000) involves increases in investment spending, the overall budget is aimed at reducing expenditures. All government ministries have been requested to sharply cut discretionary spending. At the same time, international private investment is being encouraged and the Oman Centre for Investment Promotion and Export Development (OCIPED) has recently been set up to assist private investors in obtaining licences and in other aspects of project implementation. Furthermore, revised ownership and tax laws should increase foreign investment in Omani companies, and Oman has officially applied for membership in the World Trade Organisation (WTO). The Omani economy has also been boosted by the active participation of non-GCC citizens in the Muscat Securities Market.

Other measures to aid economic expansion, improve services, and provide foreign and local private investors the opportunity to own equity in the nation's blue chip companies, include government plans to privatise, in part or fully, certain state-owned companies in Oman, such as the Global Telecommunications Organisation, which operates all telephone and internet services in the Sultanate, the national airport, and the Oman National Transport Company, which will allow up to 49 per cent foreign investment.

Qatar

Capital: Doha (380,000).
Other Major Cities: Rayyan (91,996), Umm Said (41,905), Al Khor (11,000), Al Wakrah (3,805).
Population: 625,0000.
Labour Force: *total:* 233,000.
Main industries: crude oil production and refining, fertilisers, petrochemicals, steel reinforcing bars, cement.
GDP – composition by sector: services 50 per cent; industry 49 per cent; agriculture 1 per cent.

The Qatari government's plans to diversify its economy and move away from its reliance on the oil sector lie mainly in developing the country's liquefied natural gas (LNG) sector and in encouraging foreign investment. The slump in world oil prices in the late 1990s, which has since undergone a marked recovery, led to a decline in oil revenue so that government expenditures fell marginally in the fiscal year

1998/99. Tens of billions of dollars have been invested by the government in advancing and marketing the state's gas reserves, an investment that is expected to culminate in a very healthy return.

The yearly revenue from LNG is projected to rise steadily, perhaps amounting to US$700 million in 2001, which will more than make up for any deficit suffered resulting from the fall in oil prices at the end of the last century, and will assist the stabilisation of Qatar's foreign debt level. In 1997, Qatar's GDP growth was estimated at 10 per cent, reflecting one of fastest expanding economies in the world. This rapid growth is largely due to the onset of Qatar's LNG exports and industrial developments.

The Doha Securities Market (DSM), established in July 1995, has fallen in line with emiri measures to highlight privatisation as central to the modernisation of the country's economy. By the close of 1998, 40 per cent of Qatar Public Telecommunications Company (Q-Tel) was floated on the stock market, and plans to add Qatar Steel, among other industries to be privatised, are under discussion. In the future, other GCC national companies may be added to the listings. The DSM is undergoing fast expansion with a strong capitalisation base of approximately US$4 billion.

Saudi Arabia

Capital: Riyadh (2.8 million).
Other Major Cities: Jeddah (2.5 million), Damman/Khobar/Qatif (1.2 million), Madinah (900,000), Abha and Khamis Mushayt (900,000), Taif (600,000).
Population: 20.6 million.
Labour Force: *total:* 7 million; *by occupation:* government 40 per cent; services 30 per cent; industry, construction, and oil 25 per cent; agriculture 5 per cent.
Main industries: crude oil production, petroleum refining, basic petrochemicals, cement, two small steel-rolling mills, construction, fertiliser, plastics.
GDP – composition by sector: services 48 per cent; industry 46 per cent; agriculture 6 per cent.

Throughout the 1970s and 1980s, Saudi Arabia's economy was wholly dependent upon oil exports, merchandise imports, foreign workers, and government spending. Nearing the close of the 1980s the Saudi government began implementing plans to diversify and expand its economy by focusing on the development of downstream oil industries, such as oil refining and petroleum. Economic diversification measures now also include the encouragement of foreign investment and drives towards privatisation in the public sector.

The slump in world oil prices during 1998 which resulted in heavy losses to Saudi government revenue, of which oil accounts for 75 per cent, highlighted the economy's vulnerability to oil price vicissitudes. Despite government spending being cut by 15.8 per cent in the 1999 budget, a 144 per cent increase in the fiscal deficit for that year was still projected.

Increasing the role of the private sector, as laid out in the country's Sixth Development Plan (1995-2000), includes the promotion of the financial sector, which additionally involves the creation of 500,000 new jobs for Saudi nationals. Ten national power companies, including the four Saudi Consolidated Electric Companies (SCECO), are also to be merged and privatised.

Saudi Arabia is currently in the process of applying to be a member of the World Trade Organisation (WTO) and in order to meet WTO requirements has promised to implement a number of changes in its policy such as reduced subsidies, accelerated privatisation, a new foreign investment code, alterations to present commercial laws and regulations, and the imposition of a tax on national corporations. Membership of the WTO will provide Saudi Arabia with more opportunities for expansion in worldwide trade, not only in petrochemicals, but for non-petrochemical products too.

United Arab Emirates

Capital: Abu Dhabi (798,000).
Other Major Cities: Dubai (501,000), Sharjah (314,000), Ras Al-Khaimah (130,000), Ajman (76,000), Fujairah (63,000), Umm Al Quwain (27,000).
Population: 2.5 million.
Labour Force: *total:* 794,400; *by occupation:* industry and commerce 56 per cent; services 38 per cent; agriculture 6 per cent.
Main industries: petroleum, fishing, petrochemicals, construction materials, some boat building, handicrafts, pearling.
GDP – composition by sector: services 55 per cent; industry 43 per cent; agriculture 2 per cent.

The UAE has the highest per capita income in the Arab world, aided by the fact that it holds the third largest proven oil deposits in the world. Over the last few decades the UAE has worked hard to diversify its economy with the result that in 1998, oil-based industry made up only one third of the country's GDP. A 20 year economic diversification plan is currently underway in the UAE to encourage economic development. US$13.4 billion has been set aside by the government for the advancement of the non-oil economy. A number of major projects are being implemented throughout the UAE in a variety of sectors, including aviation and airports, tourism, petrochemicals and refinery, re-export commerce, and telecommunications. In 1998, approximately 70 per cent of the UAE's non-oil trade was accounted for by trade and finance.

Abu Dhabi

Over 90 per cent of the UAE's oil reserves and output, 9.1 per cent of the world's proven oil reserves, are accounted for in Abu Dhabi. 4.5 per cent of the world's natural gas reserves, the third largest natural gas reserves found in the Middle East after Iran and Qatar, are also located in Abu Dhabi. However, these gas reserves – for the most part – remain untapped.

A major expansion programme run by the state owned Abu Dhabi National Oil Company (ADNOC) is in progress designed to meet the needs of the developing gobal market for petrochemical products. Furthermore, other industrial programmes such as ship building and aircraft maintenance, as well as water development and projects in electrical power and the electronics industry are underway promising to make Abu Dhabi central to trade and industry in the UAE.

Abu Dhabi is to be the site of the first independent water and power project in the UAE. This project, aimed at supplementing the UAE's power and water supplies with 580MW and 50 million gallons a day of desalinated water, costs US$700 million and takes the form of Taweelah A2 power station which is to be finished by April 2001. Abu Dhabi's offshore natural gas reserves are to generate the operational power.

Dubai

Dubai, the commercial capital of the UAE, is the sole Emirate whose economy would survive prosperously without its oil and gas revenue. This is due firstly, to its prime location as a commercial centre for import and export – it accounts for over 70 per cent of the UAE's imports and re-exports, and half of its non-oil exports, serving not only the Gulf but linking the Indian sub-continent, Africa, the Far East and the Commonwealth of Independent States (CIS). Secondly, to its aluminium exports, the largest contributor to exports after oil; and thirdly, to the wide range of industries in business in the emirate.

The greatest number of visitors to the UAE are found in Dubai with a yearly increase of 10-15 per cent, that includes both business travellers and leisure tourists. This rise in tourism has lead to more hotels being built and ongoing improvements being made to accommodation in the city.

Jebel Ali Free Zone (JAFZ)

The Jebel Ali Free Zone was established in 1985 to aid investment. Due to the comparatively easy procedures for setting up business here, over 1,000 foreign companies have situated their regional offices at JAFZ with about 100 of these being British. Businesses are drawn to the area because they are guaranteed: full foreign ownership; exclusion from all import duties provided the goods remain within the free zone; exclusion from corporate taxation with the additional incentive of a 15 year assurance in the free zone, and a 15 year corporate holiday.

Currently, a US$165 million fertiliser plant and a US$45 million unleaded petrol plant are being built in the free zone as well as a US$400 million condensate refinery that aims to produce jet fuel, diesel, naphtha, gasoline and liquefied petroleum gas (LPG).

Due to the success of this free zone others have been set up in Ajman, at Dubai International Airport, Fujairah, Sharjah International Airport, Umm al-Quwain and Ras al-Khaimah.

Fujairah

Fujairah port lies on the eastern coast of the UAE between the Far East and Europe. Due to this location it acts as a formidable rival to Dubai's transhipment operations, a position enhanced by the nearness of Fujairah International Airport, which in turn offers opportunities for sea-air trade. Business is also drawn to Fujairah because of its free trade zone.

Tourism is a major industry in Fujairah. Visitors are attracted by the region's beautiful landscapes and its flora and fauna generated by the annual rainfall being greater here than elsewhere in the emirates. Additionally, this rainfall allows the emirate to develop a realistic agriculture sector.

Ras al-Khaimah

Ras al-Khaimah's economy relies on the construction materials industry. The cement, pharmaceuticals, ceramic and mosaic tiles, and plastics sectors are the main contributors. Oil resources in the area are currently being utilised once again and the Ras al-Khaimah LPG plant is to treat natural gas extracted from Oman. The treated product is then to be exported through Ras al-Khaimah.

Ras al-Khaimah has one of the most prolific agricultural sectors in the UAE due to its high annual rainfall comparable to Fujairah. It also boasts the biggest dairy farm in the country with its own herd of cattle providing meat and milk. Additionally, the emirate is the location of one of the biggest poultry businesses. Government funding aids the efficient operation of many of the farms.

Tourism is set to become a fast-growing industry in the area as it is renowned for its impressive scenery, lofty mountains and natural hot springs. A tourist beach resort has just been established and plans for a five star hotel are under way.

Ajman

The number of industrial plants located in Ajman is such that it rates third among the emirates. The textile industry is very profitable here as well as food processing plants. Furthermore, Silent Night Beds and Gulf Craft luxury yachts are based here. Ajman tourism and agriculture sectors are currently being targetted for development.

Sharjah

About 60 per cent of the UAE's manufacturing output is accounted for by Sharjah, the third largest emirate. The most prominent of the regional industries are: chemical, metallic, beverage and tobacco. Within the private sector, building and construction play a leading role. Agriculture accounts for approximately 5 per cent of Sharjah's GDP, due to the use of saline water in irrigation in desert locations. Oil and gas resources continue to provide intrinsic support to the area's economy.

Directory of Major Employers

The following is a list of the leading employers of personnel for the Gulf region. The majority of addresses are those of recruitment agencies who specialise in placing suitably qualified individuals in top positions either throughout the Gulf or in one or two particular countries as specified.

General Professional

Anders Glaser Wills: Capitol House, 1 Handwell Place, Southampton SO14 1HU; tel 01703-223511; fax 01703-227911; Website www.cdi-agw.com. A UK leading human resources specialist which has just opened an office in Dubai, the UAE. Arranges positions for professional, technical and managerial personnel throughout the Middle East.

Anthony Moss & Associates: 173/175 Drummond Street, London NW1 3JD; tel 020-7388 0918; fax 020-7388 4973; Website www.amoss.com. Recruits international experts in banking, training, transportation, water, waste, agriculture, construction, oil and gas and manufacturing, at middle and senior management level throughout the Middle East.

Arabian Careers: 7th Floor Berkeley Square House, Berkeley Square, London W1X 5LB; tel 020-7495 3285; fax 020-7355 2562; e-mail recruiter@arabiancareers.com Website www.arabiancareers.com. Recruits professionals in all fields throughout the Gulf region.

Ashtead Management Consultants: Gothic Lodge, 11 Church Road, Great Bookham, Surrey KT23 3PD; e-mail royj@ashteadman.co.uk Website www.ashteadman.co.uk. Places qualified personnel in all areas throughout the Middle East.

Bilingual People: 18 Hanover Street, London W1R 9HG; tel 020-7491 2400; fax 020-7491 1900; e-mail admin@blpeople.demon.co.uk. Recruits bilingual individuals to work in all industry areas, provides interpreters and translators. Placements in Saudi Arabia and Kuwait.

Business Aid Centre: Dubai, UAE; tel +971 4 376467; Website www.bacdubai.com. Recruitment and training specialists in the United Arab Emirates.

CARE Institute of Educational & Management Services: PO Box 44393, Abu Dhabi, UAE; tel +971 2 317081; fax +971 2 336858; e-mail carefor@ emirates.net.ae Website www.carefor.com. Recruits professionals for work in a variety of fields, including the oil and petrochemicals industries, education, management, safety and security, in the UAE.

CCM Recruitment International: 64 Lower Gardiner Street, **Dublin 1**, Ireland; tel +353 1 836 6092; fax +353 1 836 6093; 258 Belsize Road, **London** NW6 4BT; tel 020-7316 1859; fax 020-7316 1895; e-mail info@ccmrecruitment.com Website www.ccmrecruitment.com. Places professionals throughout the Middle and Far East in the fields of engineering, medical and IT.

Delton Personnel Ltd: 14 Ribblesdale Place, Preston PR1 4NA; fax 01772 885 005; e-mail delton@provider.co.uk. Places language instructors in Abu Dhabi. Places skilled workers in all fields worldwide.

DLA Recruitment Consultants: 10 Bedford Street, London WC2E 9HE; tel 020-7420 8000; fax 020-7379 4820; e-mail info@dla.co.uk Website www.dla.co.uk. Recruits newly qualified ACAs seeking a move from practice into finance and business roles in some of the following sectors with several blue-chip organisations throughout the Middle East: Advertising, Media, FMCG, Leisure, Pharmaceuticals and Telecoms.

Grafton Recruitment Ltd.: 35-37 Queens Square, Belfast BT1 3FG; tel 028-9024 2824; fax 028-9024 2897; Website www.grafton-group.com. Ireland's leading consultancy group placing personnel in the following sectors: accountancy, catering, construction, electronics, IT, nursing, and sales and management, throughout Saudi Arabia.

Harrison Jones Associates Buckingham House East, The Broadway, Stanmore, Middlesex HA7 4EB; tel 020-8385 7881; fax 020-8385 7882; e-mail jobs@hja.co.uk Website www.hja.co.uk. Recruits skilled workers in all fields throughout the Gulf.

Joblink International Inc.: 3440 Wiltshire Boulevard, Suite 525, Los Angeles, CA 90010-2106; tel +1 213 388-4815; fax +1 213 388-5140; Website www.joblink2usa.com. Specialises in recruitment and permanent placement of foreign educated and trained professionals in the USA, as well as in the placement of US professionals to multi-national companies in the Middle East.

Kenneth Roberts & Associates Group: International House, 32 Greendale Drive, Middlewich, Cheshire CW10 0PH; tel 01606-834002; fax 01606-835007. Recruits financial experts for companies throughout the Middle East mainly for one-year renewable contracts.

Ministry of Foreign Affairs: PO Box 22711, Doha, Qatar; fax +974 353592; e-mail jobs@mofa.gov.qa. Applications always welcome from specialists in the following fields: Political Science, Translation (English/Arabic & Arabic/English), Political & Economic Research, IT.

Muscat Consultancy Services (MCS): PO Box 1676, Muttrah PC 114, Sultanate of Oman; tel +968 796636 ext. 317/323; fax +968 700124; e-mail mcs@tawoos.com Website www.tawoos.com/mcs. MCS is a Human Resources (HR) consultancy involved in all aspects of HR and recruitment. It is a wholly owned subsidiary of a large Omani owned company with strong connections to the Royal family. Personnel are recruited for senior and specialist positions primarily in Oman but on occasion in the UAE also. All applicants sit internationally recognised tests and psychometric assessments.

Network Overseas: 34 Mortimer Street, London W1N 8JR; tel 020-7580 5151; fax 020-7580 6242; e-mail overseas@networkoverseas.cc Website www. networkoverseas.cc. Agency recruiting highly qualified professionals throughout the Middle East in the fields of ancillary hospital services, engineering and construction, information technology, medical, nursing, teaching.

Technical Trading & Training Co (TTTC): PO Box 26, Mina Al-Fahal, Postal Code 116, Sultanate of Oman; tel +968 568040; fax +968 568820; e-mail tttco@omantel.net.om. TTTC is a limited liability company established in 1995 recruiting highly qualified individuals for jobs in the private and commercial sectors throughout Oman.

UltraFORCE UK Group: www.ultraforce.co.uk. Specialises in placing skilled workers throughout the Gulf in the leisure, technical, and hospitality industries. Comprehensive briefing and advice given on all overseas positions.

Construction, Industrial Resources, Engineering, and General Industrial

Abu Dhabi National Oil Company (ADNOC): PO Box 898, Abu Dhabi, UAE. Petroleum company recruits technical staff for onshore/offshore operations.

Al Wazan: PO Box 3994, Abu Dhabi, UAE; tel +971 2 223200; fax +971 2 223335; e-mail alwazan@emirates.net.ae. One of the leading oil and gas recruitment agencies in the Arabian Peninsula, covering all the Gulf countries.

Alba International: Alba House, Princes Street, Douglas, Isle of Man; e-mail alba@alba.net Website www.alba.net. International oil and gas recruitment company.

Assistance Teknica Ltd: York House, Borough Road, Middlesborough, Cleveland TS1 2HJ; tel 01642-224545; fax 01642-243514; e-mail Eng.ser@Teknica.co.uk. Recruits personnel in the areas of iron and steel, engineering, safety, associated training.

Contracts Consultancy: 162-164 Upper Richmond Road, Putney, London SW15 2SL; tel 020-8333 4141; fax 020-8333 4151; e-mail ccl@ccl.uk.com Website www.ccl.uk.com. Places qualified individuals (engineers, geologists, technicians) in the areas of construction and general industrial throughout the Gulf.

Corporate Resources (Hertford) Ltd: 28 Waterdale, Hertford, Herts SG3 8DU; tel 01992-422022; fax 01992-558661. Provides placements throughout the Gulf for professionals in construction, engineering, telecommunications, technical sectors.

Daulton Construction Personnel: 2 Greycoat Place, London SW1P 1SB; tel 020-7222 0817; fax 020-7233 0734; e-mail mike@daultonpersonnel.demon.co.uk Website www.daultonpersonnel.co.uk. Specialises in professional, managerial and technical appointments within the construction industry in all the Gulf countries. Provides advice and background information on countries to applicants travelling overseas.

EM Engineering Ltd: 44a Newtown Road, Denham, Uxbridge, Middlesex UB9 4BE; fax 01895-811533; e-mail EMEngineering@btinternet.com. Recruits qualified engineers for positions throughout the Gulf region.

Grove Personnel: 46/48 Southbourne Grove, Bournemouth, Dorset BH6 3RB; tel 01202-417533; fax 01202-421746; e-mail jobs@grovepersonnel.co.uk Website www.grovepersonnel.co.uk. Places professional British quantity surveyors, buyers, estimators, planning engineers, project managers, and civil engineers, throughout the Gulf region.

Hill McGlynn International: Prospect House, Meridiens Cross, Ocean Way, Ocean Village, Southampton SO14 3TJ; tel 01703-221122; fax 01703-220011; Website www.hillmcglynn.com. Recruits construction personnel for positions throughout the Gulf – project managers, quantity surveyors, engineers, planning engineers, plant managers.

International Staffing Consultants (Europe): PO Box 124, Eastleigh, Hampshire SO50 8ZE; tel 023-8065 1281; fax 023-8062 0877; e-mail isceurope@iscworld.com. The European office of the US recruitment company, *International Staffing Consultants (ISC)*. ISC are members of the largest and oldest network of employment agencies in the world, the NPA, and have over 1,000 recruiters in 400 affiliated offices around the world. Recruitment is usually for experienced and qualified engineers, as well as managers, sales and marketing, and IT professionals throughout the Middle East.

LA Recruitment Services: 173 Union Street, Aberdeen AB11 6BB; tel 01224-212929; fax 01224-573845. Recruits personnel for positions in the oil and gas industries throughout the Gulf.

Morgan-Bryant Personnel Ltd: 8 The Causeway, Teddington TW11 0HA; fax 020-8255 6248. Recruits technical, managerial and engineering staff for industrial positions throughout the Gulf.

NES Overseas Ltd: 6 Ambassador Place, Stockport Road, Altrincham, Cheshire WA15 8DB; tel 0161 929 1313; fax 0161 926 9867; e-mail nesoverseas@compuserve.com Website www.nes.co.uk. Places qualified engineering and technical staff in Abu Dhabi in the following industries: oil and gas, petrochemical, construction, power and telecommunications.

PGA (Peter Glaser & Associates): PO Box 55, Bodmin PL30 4YH; tel 07071-221155; fax 07071-221166; e-mail pglaser@pga.co.uk Website www.pga.co.uk. Specialises in the placement of qualified professionals in the fields of construction (civil and building), water, waste and environmental, and power sectors.

Precision Resources: London House, 100 New Kings Road, London SW6 4LX; tel 020-7371 7500. Technical recruitment consultancy with vacancies for suitably qualified and experienced staff in oil and gas refinery operations and maintenance.

Premier Personnel: 25-29 High Street, Leatherfield, Surrey KT22 8AB; tel 01372-379183; fax 01372-372301. Recruits staff for construction engineering positions.

Professional Management Resources Ltd: PO Box 23, Wadhurst, East Sussex TN5 6XL; fax 01892-784228. Recruits personnel from all engineering disciplines for placements throughout the Gulf in the civil construction, oil, gas, power, water and petrochemical industries.

Search Consultants International: 4545 Post Oak Place 208, Houston, TX 77027, USA; tel +1 713 622-9188; fax +1 713 622-9186; e-mail info@searchconsultants.com. Executive recruitment in oil and gas exploration and production, petrochemicals, contract engineering and project management.

Sherry Sherratt Technical Recruitment Ltd: PO Box 4529, London SW18 3XD; tel 020-8875 1849; fax 020-8875 1894. Places qualified technical staff in industrial positions throughout the Gulf region.

Taylor Recruitment: Hacros Building, 2 Chalk Road, Godalming, Surrey GU7 3HH; tel 01483 418383; fax 01483 418989. Places qualified engineers, technicians and managers throughout the Gulf region.

Woodridge Associates: The Ridge House, The Ridge, Broad Blunsdon, Swindon SN2 4AD; tel 01793-721500; fax 01793-721700; e-mail cv@woodridge.co.uk Website www.woodridge.co.uk. Recruits professionals (engineers, managers, technicians, etc.) in the industrial fields throughout the Gulf region.

Useful Publications

Construction News. Trade magazine published weekly or available on-line at www.emap.co.uk/construct/cn-jobs.htm.

Oil and Gas International Yearbook. Available in public reference and business libraries.

Oil & Gas Journal. Weekly publication available from Penn Well Publishing, PO Box 1260, 1421 South Sheridan Road, Tulsa, Oklahoma 74101, USA.

World Oil. Specialist 'downhole' magazine, dealing with exploration, drilling and production. Available from PO Box 2608, 3301 Allen Parkway, Houston, TX 77252-2608, USA; tel +1 617 848-9306; fax +1 713 520-443.

Health Professionals

AMI Middle East Services Ltd: 6th Floor, Byron House, 7-9 St James's Street, London SW1A 1EE; tel 020-7839 3812; fax 020-7973 0278. General health care recruitment throughout the Middle East.

Associates for Advanced Care International: PO Box 24077, Dubai, UAE; tel +971 4 314488; fax +971 4 311443; e-mail aacrecr@emirates.net.ae. Places qualified nurses in Saudi Arabia, the UAE, and Bahrain.

Athena Saudi Arabia: PO Box 61587, Riyadh 11575, Saudi Arabia; tel +966 1 4648245; fax +966 1 4615012. Recruits medical staff at various levels in all specialties at one of five hospitals in Saudi Arabia.

BML Recruitment Consultants: Mylen House, 11 Wagon Lane, Birmingham B26 3DU; tel 0121-742 7524; fax 0121-742 3512; e-mail info@bmlmed.co.uk Website www.bmlmed.co.uk. Places health professionals in hospitals in Saudi Arabia and Kuwait but currently expanding to incorporate other Middle Eastern countries. Provides full briefing on all aspects of living and working in the relevant country.

BNA International: 3rd Floor, 443 Oxford Street, London W1R 2NA. Recruits qualified health care staff for positions throughout the Gulf.

British Nursing Association: www.bnauk.com. Branches across the UK; addresses are available on their website. Appointments available for short or long term contracts throughout the Middle East.

Choice Personnel PO Box 7108, Cloisters Square 6850, Perth, West Australia; tel +11 61 8 9321 2011; fax +11 61 8 9321 1113; e-mail kjones@choice.net.au Website www.choice.net.au. Recruits health professionals for placements in Saudi Arabia and the UAE.

EHL Corporation: Edmonton, Canada; tel +1 708 413-9176; fax +1 780 413-9177; Website www.e-h-l.com. Professional medical search and placement services, with an emphasis on international relocation. Clients in UAE, Qatar and Saudi Arabia.

GAMA International Limited: 2nd Floor, Moreau House, 116 Brompton Road, London SW3 1JJ; tel 020-7581 5544. Saudi Arabian company providing health care management and related services within the Kingdom of Saudi Arabia. Recruits all types of qualified, experienced hospital staff to work in its general, psychiatric and other specialist hospitals.

O'Grady-Peyton International: 332 Congress Street, Boston, Massachusetts 02210, USA; tel +1 617 422-0300; fax +1 617 422-0399; Website www. opginc.com. Recruits medical staff at various levels for positions in Saudi Arabia.

PHP (UK) Ltd: The Stamford Hospital, Ravenscourt Park, London W6 0TN; tel 020-8686 9155; fax 020-8636 9154. Recruits health staff for hospitals in Saudi Arabia.

Professional Connections: 10 Stratton Street, Mayfair, London W1X 5FD; tel 020-7544 6848; fax 020-7544 6849; e-mail profcoldn@aol.com. Places qualified health care staff in hospitals in Saudi Arabia and the UAE.

Professional Connections Ltd: 5 City Gate, Bridge Street Lower, Dublin 8, Ireland; tel +353 1 679 2277; fax +353 1 679 2396; e-mail profconn@iol.ie. Recruits medical staff at various levels for positions in Saudi Arabia and the UAE.

Royal Embassy of Saudi Arabia: Medical Section, 119 Harley Street, London W1; tel 020-7935 9931. Provides advice on medical work in Saudi Arabia.

The Royal College of Nursing: 20 Cavendish Square, London W1M 0AB; tel 020-7409 3333. The world's largest professional union of nurses, offers an advisory service to members considering working abroad and provides information on finding employment abroad.

Saudi Medicare Company: PO Box 25639, Riyadh 11466, Saudi Arabia; tel +966 1 4540387; fax +966 1 456 1231. Recruits qualified staff for hospitals in Saudi Arabia and the UAE.

Worldwide Healthcare Exchange: The Colonnades, Beaconsfield Close, Hatfield, Herts AL10 8YD; tel 01707-259233; fax 01707-259223; e-mail wheuk@btinternet.com Website www.whe.co.uk. Recruits qualified nurses for hospitals in Saudi Arabia and the UAE.

Useful Publications

British Medical Journal, Website www.bmj.com. Includes classified section containing advertisements for a wide range of agencies recruiting medical staff for overseas positions.

Health Professionals Abroad, Vacation Work Publications, 9 Park End Street, Oxford OX1 1HJ; tel 01865-241978; fax 01865-790885; e-mail vacationwork@vacationwork.co.uk Website www.vacationwork.co.uk. Comprehensive guide to finding work overseas in all areas of health care.

Health Sevice Journal. Major professional health journal which includes employment advertisements. Available on-line at www.hsj.co.uk.

Nursing Standard. Carries international vacancies. On sale weekly through newsagents or accessible on-line at www.nursing-standard.co.uk.

Postgraduate Doctor Middle East. Published six times a year containing up to the minute articles specially commissioned for the region. Practising doctors or medical students living in Bahrain, Kuwait, Oman, Saudi Arabia and the UAE can receive a free sample copy and subscription details by contacting PMH Publications, PO Box 100, Chichester, West Sussex PO18 8HD; tel 01243-576444; fax 01243-576456; e-mail doctor@pmh.uk.com Website www.pmh.uk.com/health/docme/docme.htm.

Hotel & Catering

The Country Club: PO Box 5185, Manama, Bahrain. Often requires Food and Beverage staff at managerial level.

Dubai Creek Golf & Yacht Club: Dubai Golf Office, PO Box 24040. Dubai, UAE; fax +971 4 475393; e-mail executive@dubaigolf.com. Food and beverage personnel often required by this 5 star leisure complex in the UAE.

Oasis Beach Hotel: PO Box 26500, Dubai, UAE. Recently opened ten-storey four star deluxe hotel in Dubai recruits food and beverage staff.

Sheraton Abu Dhabi Resort & Towers: PO Box 640, Abu Dhabi, UAE; tel +971 2 6970200; fax +971 2 773894; e-mail Gary_Sharpe@sheraton.com. Recruits staff for all hotel positions in each of the six Gulf countries.

WIPS (Wermeille International Placement Services): Eggfluhstrasse 17, 4054 Basel, Switzerland; tel +41 61 422 06 55; fax +41 61 422 06 56; e-mail wips@access.ch Website www.access.ch/wips. Places staff in the hotel and catering industry throughout the Gulf at management level or highly skilled specialists.

Useful Publications

Caterer & Hotelkeeper, a monthly magazine incorporating international vacancies advertisements. Available from Reed Business Information, Quadrant House, The Quadrant, Sutton, Surrey SM2 5AS; tel 01444-445566.

Catering Today, magazine published fortnightly including overseas appointments. Available from Proteach Publishing and Communications, PO Box 222, Santa Claus, IN 47579; tel +1 812 937-4464.

IT & Computing

Al-Khaleej Computers: PO Box 16091, Riyadh 11464, Saudi Arabia; tel +966 1 463 3230; fax +966 1 463 3230.

Austin Knight Ltd.: Knightway House, 20 Soho Square, London W1A 1DS; tel 020-7437 9261. Offers positions to marketing executives, customer support engineers, computer engineers and field service engineers in Saudi Arabia and throughout the Middle East.

Computer 2000: 100 Walker Street, North Sydney, NSW 2060, Australia; tel +11 61 2 9964-0411; fax +11 61 2 9964-0488; e-mail jobs@comp2000.com.au. Specialises in the placement of permanent and contract IT professionals in Saudi Arabia, Australia and Asia with some placements in the UAE.

James Baker Associates: 105 Queens Road, Reading, Berkshire RG1 4DA; tel 0118-950 5022; fax 0118-950 5056; e-mail info@jba.clara.net Website www.jba.clara.net. Places experienced IT and computer specialists throughout the Middle East.

Useful Publications

Computer User's Yearbook. Available in most librairies, is a valuable source of information and contains useful lists and addresses of recruitment agencies throughout Britain, in addition to extensive lists of various training courses available at all levels, plus salary surveys for each job area.

Computing. Weekly journal includes advertisements for vacancies abroad, available from 32-34 Broadwick Street, London W1A 2HG; tel 020-7316 9818; Website www.vnu.co.uk/bc/ctg.

Computer Weekly. Reference point for IT employment opportunities overseas available from Quadrant House, The Quadrant, Sutton, Surrey SM2 5AS; tel 020-8652 8080; Website www.computerweekly.co.uk

Language Schools & Language Consultants/Services

Amideast: 1730 M Street, Suite 1100, Washington, DC 20036-4505, USA; tel +1 202 776-9620; fax +1 202 776-7020; e-mail dduncan@amideast.com. Specialises in placing US qualified EFL professionals in positions throughout the Middle East.

ELS Language Centers/Middle East: PO Box 3079, Abu Dhabi, UAE; e-mail elsme@emirates.net.ae. Employs EFL trained teachers throughout the Middle East.

International Schools Service (ISS): 15 Roszel Road, PO Box 5910, Princeton, NJ 08543, USA; tel +1 609 452-0990; fax +1 609 452-2690; e-mail edustaffing@iss.edu Website www.iss.edu. Places K12 teachers in international schools worldwide.

QTS International Education Consultants: Churchill House, 27 Otley Old Road, Leeds LS16 6HB; tel 0113-230 1141; fax 0113-230 0780; e-mail director@qts-worldwide.com Website www.qts-worldwide.com. International education consultants operating in the recruitment of school teachers, inspection of schools, schools' advisors. Places qualified individuals throughout the Gulf region.

Robaco Global: 8 Nesburn Road, Barnes, Wearside SR4 7LR; fax 0191-551 9102; e-mail Robaco@dial.pipex.com. Recruits teaching staff for positions throughout the Gulf.

TESOL (Teachers of English to Speakers of Other Languages): 700 S. Washington Street, Suite 200, Alexandria, Virginia 22314-4287, United States of America; tel +1 703 836-0774; fax +1 703 836-6447; e-mail career@tesol.edu Website www.tesol.edu. An international education association offering comprehensive support to its members in finding employment in the education field throughout the Middle East and elsewhere worldwide.

United States Information Agency (USIA), English Language Programs Division: Room 304, 301 4th Street SW, Washington, DC 20547, USA; tel +1 202 619-

5869; fax +1 202 401-1250; e-mail English@usia.gov Website www.usia.gov. Provides information on finding educator jobs throughout the Middle East in addition to country facts.

Bahrain

Bahrain Training Institute (BTI): PO Box 32333, Isa Town, Bahrain; tel/fax +973 683416.

Bahrain Computer & Management Institute (BCMI): PO Box 26176, Manama, Bahrain; tel +973 293493; fax +973 290358.

The British Council: PO Box 452, Manama 356, Bahrain; tel +973 261555; fax +973 241272; Website www.britishcouncil.org

Cambridge School of English: PO Box 20646, Manama, Bahrain; tel +973 532828; fax +973 530227.

Global Institute: PO Box 11148, Manama, Bahrain; tel +973 740940; fax +973 720030.

Gulf Academy: PO Box 10333, Manama, Bahrain; tel +973 721700; fax +973 722636.

Gulf School of Languages: PO Box 20236, Manama, Bahrain; tel +973 290209; fax +973 290069.

Kuwait

The British Council: PO Box 345, 13004 Safat, Kuwait; fax +965 252 0069; e-mail bckuwait@kuwait.net Website www.britishcouncil.org

ILC Recruitment: White Rock, Hastings, East Sussex TN34 1JY. Recruits highly qualified educators for the ILC school in Kuwait.

Institute for Private Education: PO Box 6320, 32038 Hawalli, Kuwait; tel +965 573 7811/2; fax +965 574 2924. Anglo-Kuwait joint venture under British management.

Language Centre: Kuwait University, PO Box 2575, 13026 Safat, Kuwait; tel +965 481 0325; fax +965 484 3824.

New English School: PO Box 6156, Hawalli 32036, Kuwait; tel +965 531 8060; fax +965 531 9924; e-mail admin@neskt.com Website www.neskt.com.

Oman

The British Council: PO Box 73, Postal Code 115, Madinat Al Sultan Qaboos, Sultanate of Oman; Website www.britishcouncil.org

Capital Institute: PO Box 936, Ruwi 112, Sultanate of Oman; tel +968 709336; fax +968 701070. One of the country's main English teaching centres.

CfBT: PO Box 2278, Ruwi, Postal Code 112, Sultanate of Oman; tel +968 604938; fax +968 692537; e-mail cfbtoman@omantel.net.om Website www.cfbt.com. Recruits education and training consultants, and project managers throughout Oman with current plans to operate in the UAE also.

College of Administrative Sciences: PO Box 710, Ruwi 112, Sultanate of Oman; tel +968 751572; fax +968 751570. Private college of higher education offering intensive English courses for students.

Educational Services Overseas Ltd: PO Box 2398, Ruwi 112, Sultanate of Oman; fax +968 565573.

Polyglot Institute: PO Box 221, Ruwi, Sultanate of Oman; tel +968 701261; fax +968 794602.

Qatar

Arizona English Language Center: PO Box 7949, Doha, Qatar.

The British Council: PO Box 2992, Doha, Qatar; tel +974 426193/4; fax +974 423315; Website www.britishcouncil.org

Language Institute: PO Box 3224, Doha, Qatar.
ELS Language Center: PO Box 22678, Doha, Qatar.

Saudi Arabia

The British Council (Website www.britishcouncil.org):
Riyadh: tel +966 1 462 1818; fax +966 1 462 0663; e-mail simon.chambers@bc-riyadh.bcouncil.org.
West Saudi Arabia: tel +966 2 672 3336; fax +966 2 672 6341; e-mail neville.mcbain@bc-jeddah.bcouncil.org
Eastern Province: tel +966 3 826 9036; fax +966 3 826 8753; e-mail allen.swales@bc-dammam.bcouncil.org
Elite Training Services: PO Box 11015, Jubail Industrial City 31961, Saudi Arabia; tel +966 3 341 5514; fax +966 3 341 1336.
English Language Center: King Fahd University of Petroleum & Minerals, Dhahran 31261, Saudi Arabia; tel +966 3 860 2395; fax +966 3 860 2341; e-mail elcrecru@kfupm.edu.sa
English Language Center: Hail Community Center: Hail Community College, Hail, Saudi Arabia; tel +966 3 860 2395; fax +966 3 860 2341.
European Centre for Languages & Training: PO Box 60617, Riyadh 11555, Saudi Arabia; tel +966 1 476 1218; fax +966 1 479 3328; e-mail anojaim@compuserve.com
Intertech Services: Rockville, MD 20852, USA; tel +1 301 984-7899; fax +1 301 984-7939. Specialises in placement in Saudi Arabia for a Saudi Army contract.
Riyadh Schools for Boys and Girls: PO Box 1541, Riyadh 11441, Saudi Arabia; tel +966 1 402 8411; fax +966 1 405 1944.
Saudi Arabian Defence Office: 22 Holland Park, London W11 3TD. Occasionally advertises for teachers with high academic qualifications.

United Arab Emirates

Academic Search Consultation Service: 1818 R Street, NW, Washington, DC 20009, USA; tel +1 202 332-4049; fax +1 202 234-7640. Recruits highly qualified professionals to work in women's universities in the UAE.
Al-Worood School: PO Box 46673, Abu Dhabi, UAE; tel +971 2 448855; fax +971 2 449732.
The British Council: PO Box 46523, **Abu Dhabi**; tel +971 2 659300; fax +971 2 664340; PO Box 1636, **Dubai**; tel +971 4 3370109; fax +971 4 3370703; e-mail information@ae.britcoun.org Website www.britishcouncil.org
International Language Institute: PO Box 3253, Sharjah, UAE.
Polyglot Language School: PO Box 1093, Dubai, UAE.
Higher Colleges of Technology: PO Box 47025, Abu Dhabi, UAE.

Useful Websites

Dave's ESL Café: www.eslcafe.com – for students and teachers offering links to training, placement, and many other resources.
English Expert: www.englishexpert.com – website includes up-to-date job boards advertising teaching vacancies throughout the Gulf and worldwide.
k12 Jobs: www.k12jobs.com – job search site for educators.
Search Associates: www.search-associates.com – one of the major international school placement organisations.
Teaching Jobs: www.teachingjobs.com – job search site for educators.

Useful Publications

Directory of Overseas Schools, International Schools Service (ISS), 15 Roszel Road, PO Box 5910, Princeton, NJ 08543, USA; tel +1 609 452-0990; fax +1

609 452-2690; e-mail edustaffing@iss.edu Website www.iss.edu

English Language & Orientation Programs in the US (ELOPUS): IIE Books, Institute of International Education, PO Box 371, Annapolis Junction, MD 20701-0371, USA; fax +1 301 206-9789; Website www.iie.org

The International Educator: The International Educator, 131 Main Street, Hatfield, MA 01038, USA; tel +1 413 247-3300; fax +1 247-5758.

Teaching English Abroad, Vacation Work Publications, 9 Park End Street, Oxford OX1 1HJ; tel 01865-241978; fax 01865-790885; e-mail vacationwork@ vacationwork.co.uk Website www.vacationwork.co.uk

Professional Associations

Professional associations can be a useful contact point for their members with regard to practising overseas as they may be able to provide helpful links with related companies abroad. Details of all professional associations in the UK can be found in the directory *Trade Associations and Professional Bodies of the UK* available at most UK reference libraries; the American equivalent is the *Encyclopaedia of Associations* (published by Gale Research Inc.). A selection of some of the exhaustive list of addresses of professional bodies follows below.

Hospitality and Catering

Hotel Catering and Institutional Management Association (HCIMA): 191 Trinity Road, London SW17 7HN; tel 020-8672 4251; fax 020-8682 1707. Provides useful brochures on the various career paths in the industry. They also have a website at www.hcima.org.uk, which includes membership information and professional development services.

Computing

Association for Computing Machinery: 11 West 42nd Street, New York, NY 10036, USA. Sets qualifying examinations for the computer industry in the USA, and can also supply information on careers in computing.

British Computer Society: 1 Sanford Street, Swindon SN1 1HJ; tel 01793-417417; Website www.bcs.org. Produces a useful booklet dealing with careers in computing and sets qualifying examinations.

Canadian Information Processing Society: 430 King Street West, Suite 205, Toronto, Ontario M5V 1L5.

Computer Services Association: 5th Floor, Hanover House, High Holborn, London WC1V 6LE; tel 020-7405 2171.

Information Technology Industry Training Organisation: 16 Berners Street, London W1; tel 020-7580 6677.

Institute of IT Training: Institute House, University of Warwick Science Park, Coventry CV4 7EZ; tel 01203-418128; Website www.demon.co.uk/ ittrain/index.html

Institution of Analysts and Programmers: Charles House, 36 Culmington Road, London W13 9NH; tel 020-8567 2118; Website www.CityScape. co.uk/users/ew73. Helps members and potential members with general advice on careers in computer programming and systems analysis.

International Computer Professional Association (ICPA): 2261 Market Street, Suite 309, San Francisco, CA 94114, USA; tel +1 415 252-7467; fax +1 415 252-5769. Provides a number of membership services to software professionals in all countries looking for work abroad, including a fortnightly newsletter *The Network*.

Medicine & Nursing

British Dental Association: 64 Wimpole Street, London W1M 8AL. Publishes *FDI Basic Facts – Dentistry Around the World*, which lists manpower statistics, education, licensing and legislation information on oral health care systems.

British Medical Association: Tavistock Square, London WC1H 9JP; tel 020-7387 4499; fax 020-7383 6400. The International Department gives advice and information to members wishing to work abroad.

Medical Women's Federation: Tavistock House South, Tavistock Square, London WC1H 9HX. Appointments Service circulates information on vacancies in Britain and overseas to interested members. They warn, however, that they hear of very few vacancies.

Royal College of Midwives: International Section, 15 Mansfield Street, London W1M 0BE; tel 020-7872 5100. Advises members who are interested in practising midwifery overseas or making study visits for short periods.

Royal College of Nursing: 20 Cavendish Square, London W1M 0AB; tel 020-7409 3333; fax 020-7495 0961. Has an International Office that provides an advisory service for members seeking employment overseas or planning electives or professional visits outside the UK. The International Office does not arrange employment but can provide information and contacts for most countries.

Royal Pharmaceutical Society of Great Britain: 1 Lambeth High Street, London SE1 7JN; tel 020-7735 9141; fax 020-7735 7629. Does *not* help find employment but overseas vacancies are advertised in their publication, the weekly *Pharmaceutical Journal*. Registered pharmaceutical chemists applying for a position abroad are advised to contact the Soicety for information on pharmaceutical practice in the country concerned.

Oil and Gas, and Engineering

The American Petroleum Institute: 1220 L Street, NW, Washington, DC 20005, USA. Regulatory and research organisation representing over 200 companies in the oil and gas industry. The institute can provide information on employment prospects in the industry.

Appointments Bureau of the Royal Institute of British Architects: 66 Portland Place, London W1N 4AD; tel 020-7580 5533. Handles UK and overseas appointments (often in the Middle East) for experienced architects and architectural technicians. Its *International Directory of Practices* gives details of British firms with overseas offices.

Association of Consulting Engineers: Alliance House, 12 Caxton Street, London SW1H 0QL; tel 020-7222 6557.

British Geotechnical Society: c/o The Institution of Civil Engineers, 1-7 Great George Street, London SW1P 3WA; tel 020-7665 2233.

The Institute of Petroleum: 61 New Cavendish Street, London W1M 8AR; tel 020-7467 7110; e-mail ip@petroleum.co.uk. This organisation gives advice to those intending to work in the oil industry in the UK, both upstream and downstream, onshore and offshore. The Institute produces a wide range of useful publications, career information booklets, and oil data sheets which are available to the public. *A Career in Oil* outlines careers opportunities for graduates and the different fields of work in the oil industry. *Working Offshore* is a useful information pack which is regularly updated, outlining training courses, the jobs available in North Sea operating companies, drilling companies and construction yards, and a list of recruitment agencies for such work. Membership of the Institute includes a subscription to the monthly journal, *Petroleum Review*. There is also a Library and Information Service at the above address.

Institution of Electrical Engineers (IEE): Michael Faraday House, Six Hills Way, Stevenage, Herts. SG1 2AY. Provides a professional brief for its members called *Working Abroad* containing general information on living and working abroad. Its fortnightly newspaper *IEE Recruitment* contains classified advertisements which sometimes include overseas positions, and is included as a supplement with *IEE News* and *IEE Review*.

Institution of Structural Engineers: 11 Upper Belgrave Street, London SW1X 8BH; tel 020-7235 4535.

The Petroleum Exploration Society of Great Britain: 17/18 Dover Street, London W1X 3PB.

The Royal Institute of Chartered Surveyors: Surveyor Court, Westwood Way, Coventry CV4 8JE; Website www.rics.org.uk. Has recruitment consultancy which can advise on overseas employment. Over 7,000 of its qualified members are serving in over 100 countries worldwide, including the Middle East.

UK Offshore Operators' Association: 3 Hans Crescent, London SW1X 0LN; tel 020-7589 5255.

UK Petroleum Industry Association (UKPIA): 9 Kingsway, London WC2B 6XH; tel 020-7240 0289.

Starting a Business

All the economies of the Gulf states are heavily reliant upon oil revenues. Although global oil prices have since experienced a healthy recovery, when they fell sharply in the late 1990s, all the Gulf economies were affected to a lesser or greater degree, and their vulnerability to the ongoing vicissitudes in oil prices was highlighted. With this in the forefront of the governments' minds, each country has been working towards diversifying, in order to strengthen, their economies. Drives towards privatisation and foreign investment are also much in evidence throughout the Arabian Peninsula – for example, the establishment of more free trade zones, which provide even more incentives than elsewhere for foreign investors and international businesses to set-up in these areas. For those considering exporting to the Gulf, the UK Department of Trade and Industry (DTI, www.gov.uk), and US National US-Arab Chamber of Commerce (www.nusacc.org), both provide invaluable information, advice, and support. Trade relations between the Gulf states and America, and the Gulf states and Europe, have always been, and continue to be, very strong.

Each Gulf country is very individual, with its own strengths and weaknesses, rules and regulations, and attitudes towards foreigners and women (for more details see separate country profiles in the *Living in the Gulf States* chapter). The laws governing foreign investment, and the incentives to the set-up of international businesses also differs from state to state (see *Choosing an Area* and *Investment Incentives* below). Carrying out thorough research on your prospective destination country and the market for your product, as well as attaining a sound understanding of both the major business practices and cultural differences between your home country and whichever Gulf state in which you intend to set-up, is vital for success.

As with any bureaucracy, but perhaps even more so in the Gulf, as Gulf Arabs will never say 'no' to anything outright and invariably you have to go through several other bodies before reaching the one who actually has the authority to agree to anything, a great deal of time can be wasted in talking to the wrong people. Much of the headache can be removed by employing a well established business relocation agency, or by becoming a member of the *Middle East Association* (see *Preparation from Scratch*, below for more details), which can greatly assist you in all aspects of setting up a new business venture in the Gulf region. There are also US and British trained lawyers and accountants on hand to ease the process of settling in.

When embarking on any new business venture, it is essential to have the right advice, and a detailed business plan. The Gulf is a tempting place to start business in the sense of the financial rewards that can result, but much careful planning is involved. This chapter can give some useful pointers, but there is no substitute for contacting the relevant organisations in the individual states that you have identified as possibilities, and accumulating your knowledge of the business environment from there.

Procedures Involved in Starting a New Business

Preparation from Scratch

Within the scope of this book it is not possible to detail all the preparation that is necessary before contemplating a business start-up. Each Gulf state has different laws and different incentives to offer prospective foreign investors. For more information on the advantages and disadvantages of each Gulf country see *Choosing an Area* below.

Assuming that you have decided on a country, one way to start is to source all your information from your own country. It is better to build up a client relationship with a firm that can then introduce you to associates in the Gulf than to contact Gulf firms direct. See *Accountants* below for a list of accountancy firms in the UK and USA. If you are in the UK, regional Chambers of Commerce (list of addresses in the *Employment* chapter) are a possible starting point. Bear in mind that they exist to promote trade between the UK and other countries, not to help people work and invest abroad, but can give limited advice to people wanting to set up business abroad. Regional Chambers in the Gulf (addresses below) are likely to be more fruitful sources of information. Having said that, the National US-Arab Chamber of Commerce (1100 New York Avenue, NW, East Tower, Suite 550, Washington, DC 20005, USA; tel +1 202 289-5920; fax +1 202 289-5938; Website www.nusacc.org) has a particularly informative website detailing contact names and information on companies active in specific industries in the Gulf, market information, economic data, and commercial regulatory information.

Another good starting point for all those considering setting up business in the Arabian Peninsula, is to contact *The Middle East Association*, (Bury House, 33 Bury Street, St James's, London SW1Y 6AX; tel 020-7839 2137; fax 020-7839 6121; e-mail mail@the-mea.co.uk Website www.the-mea.co.uk) established in 1961. The Association aims to promote trade between the United Kingdom and the Middle East (all Arab countries, Iran and Turkey, Ethiopia and Afghanistan) by offering its members practical help and advice towards expanding their business with these markets. Services include a comprehensive programme of seminars and discussions on market developments; individual confidential consultations, market briefings and a general enquiry service; provision of background material and general export information; business introductions in the Middle East and the UK, including government departments; a specialised reference library and information centre;

advice on legal services, advertising, printing, interpreting and translating. Additionally, the Association holds regular functions and meetings which provide a forum for the exchange of information and experience as well as the opportunity for networking with businessmen interested in the same markets. Further, the Association is also involved in sponsoring (with British Trade International financial support), organising and managing trade missions to the Middle East as well as UK participation in exhibitions in the region.

Invaluable assistance in establishing business in the Gulf can also be obtained from the Department of Trade and Industry (DTI, contact address below). The DTI aims to promote enterprise, innovation, and increased productivity, in particular by supporting potentially successful business start-ups, and by increasing the capacity of business, to grow, to invest, to develop skills, to adopt best practice, and to exploit opportunities abroad, recognising the development of the knowledge economy and taking account of regional differences.

Preparation for setting up business in the Gulf should include extensive visits to the area. Relocation agents and real estate agents can assist with all the necessary groundwork. Although it is theoretically possible to set up a branch or an export outlet solely through the medium of advisors this would be courting disaster. You should spend as long as possible getting to know the area and its business climate, and also meeting your advisors, who should be local nationals. The more familiar they are with your particular circumstances, the more efficiently they will be able to cater for your needs. Living in the Gulf, working with Gulf Arabs, and joining professional associations or service clubs, can provide you with indispensable advice, contacts, and allies.

Useful Addresses

Department of Trade & Industry: Arabian Peninsula Section, Bay 507, Kingsgate House, 66-74 Victoria Street, London SW1E 6SW; tel 020-7215 5000 (general enquiries); fax 020-7215 4831; Website dti.gov.uk; **Bahrain & Oman:** tel 020-7215 4388; e-mail sheila.towe@eirv.dti.gov.uk; **Kuwait & Qatar:** tel 020-7215 4811; e-mail jeff.alford@eirv.dti.gov.uk; **Saudi Arabia:** tel 020-7215 4839/4852; e-mail anita.kainth@eirv.dti.gov.uk; **United Arab Emirates:** tel 020-7215 4329; e-mail owen.o'connor@eirv.dti.gov.uk.

Trade UK Customer Services: The Dialog Corporation plc, The Communications Building, 48 Leicester Square, London WC2H 7DB; tel 020-7925 7810; fax 020-7925 7770; e-mail exports@dialog.com Website www.tradeuk.com

BAHRAIN

Embassies:

British Embassy: PO Box 114, Manama; tel +973 534404; fax +973 536109; e-mail britemb@batelco.com.bh Website www.ukembassy.gov.bh

Embassy of the United States of America: PO Box 26431, Manama, Bahrain; tel +973 273300; fax +973 272594; e-mail usismana@batelco.com.bh Website www.usembassy.com.bh

Chamber of Commerce:

Bahrain Chamber of Commerce & Industry: PO Box 248, Bahrain; tel +973 250369/233913/229555; fax +973 241294/224985.

Professional Institutes & Registration Bodies:

Aluminium Bahrain (ALBA): PO Box 570, Bahrain; tel +973 830000; fax +973 830083.

Bahrain Natural Gas Company (Banagas): PO Box 29099, Bahrain; tel +973 756222; fax +973 756991.

Bahrain National Oil Company (Banoco): PO Box 25504, Bahrain; tel +973 754666; fax +973 753203.

Bahrain Petroleum Company BSC (Bapco): Awali, Bahrain; tel +973 754444; fax +973 752924.

Gulf Petrochemicals Industries Corporation (GPIC): PO Box 26730, Bahrain; tel +973 731777; fax +973 731047.

Other Useful Addresses:

Arabian Exhibition Management: PO Box 20200, Bahrain; tel +973 250033; fax +973 242381.

Bahrain International Exhibition Centre: PO Box 11644, Bahrain; tel +973 550111; fax +973 553447.

Bahrain Monetary Affairs: PO Box 27, Manama; tel +973 535535; fax +973 534170.

Bahrain Promotions & Marketing Board (BPMB): PO Box 11299, Manama, Bahrain; tel +973 533886; fax +973 531117.

Bahrain Stock Exchange: PO Box 3203, Manama; tel +973 261560; fax +973 256362.

Central Statistics Organisation: PO Box 5835, Manama, Bahrain; tel +973 725725; fax +973 725507.

Directorate of Customs and Ports: PO Box 15, Manama, Bahrain; tel +973 727171; fax +973 727556.

Ministry of Commerce & Agriculture: PO Box 5479, Manama; tel +973 531531; fax +973 530455.

Ministry of Development & Industry: PO Box 1435, Manama; tel +973 291511; fax +973 290302.

Ministry of Finance & National Economy: PO Box 333, Manama; tel +973 530800; fax +973 532853.

Ministry of Foreign Affairs: PO Box 547, Manama; tel +973 227555; fax +973 210575.

Ministry of Interior: PO Box 13, Manama; tel +973 272111; fax +973 262169.

Ministry of Works & Agriculture: PO Box 5, Manama; tel +973 535222; fax +973 533095.

Ministry of Oil & Industry: PO Box 1435, Manama; tel +973 291511; fax +973 293007.

Useful Websites:

Business/travel information in Bahrain: www.bahrain.com/bahrain/bahrain.htm
Bahrain Stock Exchange: www.bahrainstock.com
Yellow Pages: www.bahrainyellowpages.com

KUWAIT

Embassies:

British Embassy: Arabian Gulf Street, Safat 13001; tel +965 2403334; fax +965 2407395; e-mail britemb@ncc.moc.kw or tradeukw@ncc.moc.kw

Embassy of the United States of America: PO Box 77, Safat 13001, Kuwait City; tel +965 5395307/8; fax +965 5380282; Website www.usia.gov/posts/kuwait

Chamber of Commerce:

Kuwait Chamber of Commerce & Industry: PO Box 775, Safat 13008; tel +965 2433864/6; fax +965 2433858/2404110.

Professional Institutes & Registration Bodies:
American Business Council (Kuwait): PO Box 29992, Safat 13159, Kuwait; tel +965 2430718; fax +965 2409450.
British Business Forum (BBF): PO Box 300, Safat 13003; tel +965 2405346; fax +965 2405348.
Kuwait Petroleum Corporation (KPC): PO Box 26565, Safat 13126, Kuwait; tel +965 2455455; fax +965 2467159/2423371.
Kuwait National Petroleum Company: PO Box 70, Safat 13001; tel +965 3262616/2420120; fax +965 3260280/2433839/2431678.
Kuwait Oil Company (KOC): PO Box 9758, Ahmadi 61008; tel +965 3989111/3984111; fax +965 3983661.
Petrochemicals Industries Company (PIC): PO Box 1084, Safat 13011; tel +965 2422141; fax +965 2405791.

Government Departments:
Central Tenders Committee: PO Box 1070, Safat 13011; tel +965 2401200; fax +965 2416574.
Ministry of Commerce & Industry: PO Box 2944, Safat 13030; tel +965 2480000; fax +965 2411089.
Ministry of Finance: PO Box 9, Safat 13001; tel +965 2468200/2480000; fax +965 243462.
Ministry of Oil: PO Box 5077, Safat, 13051 Kuwait; tel +965 2415201; fax +965 2417088.
Ministry of Social Affairs & Labour: PO Box 563, Safat 13006; tel +965 2480000; fax +965 2419877.

Useful Websites
Information on Kuwait's constitution: www.kuwait.org
Kuwait Information Office: www.kuwait-info.org
Red Pages (equivalent of UK yellow pages): www.kuwait1.net
Yellow Pages: www.kuwaityellowpages.com

OMAN
Embassies:
British Embassy: PO Box 300, Muscat 113; tel +968 693086; fax +968 693088.
Embassy of the United States of America: PO Box 202, Medinat Al-Sultan Qaboos 115, Muscat; tel +968 698989; fax +968 699771; e-mail aemctcns@gto.net.om Website www.usia.gov/posts/muscat

Chamber of Commerce:
Oman Chamber of Commerce & Industry: PO Box 1400, Ruwi 112; tel +968 707674; fax +968 708497.

Professional Institutes & Registration Bodies:
Petroleum Development Oman LLC: PO Box 81, Muscat 113; tel +968 678111; fax +968 677106.
Public Establishment for Industrial Estates: PO Box 2, Rusayl 124; tel +968 626080/626094; fax +968 626053.

Other Useful Addresses:
Ministry of Commerce & Industry: PO Box 550, Muscat, PC 113; tel +968 799500.
Ministry of Development: PO Box 881, Muscat, PC 113; tel +968 698900.
Ministry of Petroleum & Minerals: PO Box 551, Muscat, PC 133; tel +968

603333; fax +968 696972.
Muscat Securities Market: PO Box 3265, Ruwi 112; tel +968 7712607; fax +968 7712691.
The Omani Centre for Investment Promotion & Export Development (OCIPED): PO Box 25, Al Wadi Al Kabir 117; tel +968 7712344; fax +968 7717600.

Useful Websites
Yellow Pages: www.omanyellowpages.com

QATAR
Embassies:
British Embassy: PO Box 3, Doha; tel +974 421991; fax +974 438692; **Commercial Section:** tel +974 353543/356541; fax +974 356131; e-mail bembcomm@qatar.net.qa
Embassy of the United States of America: PO Box 2399, Doha; tel +974 864701/3; fax +974 865543 (Commercial/Consular section); e-mail usisdoha@qatar.qa Website www.qatar.net.qa/usisdoha

Chamber of Commerce:
Qatar Chamber of Commerce: PO Box 402, Doha; tel +974 423677/425131; fax +974 324338.

Professional Institutes & Registration Bodies:
Chartered Institute of Patent Agents: Staple Inn Buildings, High Holborn, London WC1V 7PZ; tel 020-7928 2345; fax 020-7928 5037.
Patent Office: Central Enquiry Unit & the Marketing & Information Directorate, Room 1L02, Concept House, Cardiff Road, Newport, South Wales NP9 1RH; tel 0645-500505; fax 01633-814444/813600; e-mail enquiries@patent.gov.uk

Government Departments:
Central Tenders Committee: PO Box 1968, Doha; tel +974 413089.
Department of Commercial Affairs: PO Box 22355, Doha; tel +974 432103; fax +974 431412.
Department of Economic Affairs: PO Box 1968, Doha; tel +974 416234; fax +974 415731.
Exhibitions Department: PO Box 1968, Doha; tel +974 834450; fax +974 834480.
Exploration & Development of New Ventures Department: PO Box 3212, Doha; tel +974 491288/833091; fax +974 831850.
Department of Financial Affairs: PO Box 83, Doha; tel +974 461444; fax +974 413617.
Department of Industrial Affairs: PO Box 2599, Doha; tel +974 832121/2/3/4; fax +974 832024.
Legal Affairs & Contracts Department: PO Box 3212, Doha; tel +974 491467; fax +974 831752.
Petroleum Engineering Department: PO Box 47, Doha; tel +974 402440; fax +974 402215.

Useful Websites
International Investment: www.iinv.com
US-Qatar Business Council: www.qatarbusinesscouncil.org
Business Brief Qatar: www.eyi.com/mideast/MEBBqatr.htm
Yellow Pages: www.qataryellowpages.com

SAUDI ARABIA

Embassies and Consulates:
British Embassy: PO Box 94351, Riyadh 11693; tel +966 1 4880088; fax +966 1 4882373.
British Consulate-General: PO Box 393, Jeddah 21411; tel +966 2 6541811; fax +966 2 6544917; e-mail commercial@jeddah.mail.fco.gov.uk
Embassy of the United States of America: PO Box 94309, Riyadh 11693; tel +966 1 4883800; fax +966 1 4887360.
Royal Embassy of Saudi Arabia, Economic Section: Liscartan House, 127 Sloane Street, London W1; tel 020-7730 8657.

Chambers of Commerce:
Council of Saudi Chambers of Commerce & Industry: PO Box 16683, Riyadh 11474, Kingdom of Saudi Arabia; tel +966 1 405-3200; fax +966 1 402-4747.
Riyadh Chamber of Commerce & Industry: PO Box 596, Riyadh 11421, Kingdom of Saudi Arabia; tel +966 1 404-0044; fax +966 1 402-1103.
Jeddah Chamber of Commerce & Industry: PO Box 1264, Jeddah 21431, Kingdom of Saudi Arabia; tel +966 2 651-5111; fax +966 2 651-7373.
Eastern Province Chamber of Commerce: PO Box 719, Dammam 31421, Saudi Arabia; tel +966 3 857-1111; fax +966 3 857-0607.
Federation of GCC Chambers: PO Box 2198, Dammam 31451; tel +966 3 8265943/8266794; fax +966 3 878883/8578130.

Professional Institutes and Registration Bodies:
Directorate General for Mineral Resources: Jeddah, Kingdom of Saudi Arabia; tel +966 2 478-0552/1980.
General Organisation for Social Insurance (GOSI): PO Box 2963, Riyadh 11461, Kingdom of Saudi Arabia; tel +966 1 477-7753; fax +966 1 476-5700.
High Commission for the Development of Ar Riyadh: PO Box 94501, Riyadh 11614, Kingdom of Saudi Arabia; tel +966 1 488-3331; fax +966 1 482-9331.
National Centre for Financial & Economic Information: PO Box 6902, Riyadh 11402, Kingdom of Saudi Arabia; tel +966 1 404-3945; fax +966 1 402-5605.
Real Estate Development Fund: PO Box 5591, Riyadh 11139, Kingdom of Saudi Arabia; tel +966 1 477-5120; fax +966 1 479-0148.
Royal Commission for Jubail & Yanbu: PO Box 5964, Riyadh 11432, Kingdom of Saudi Arabia; tel +966 1 479-4373; fax +966 1 478-3275.
Saline Water Conversion Corporation (SWCC): PO Box 5968, Riyadh 11432, Kingdom of Saudi Arabia; tel +966 1 463-1111; fax +966 1 463-1952.
Saudi Arabian Agricultural Bank: Riyadh 11126, Kingdom of Saudi Arabia; tel +966 1 405-362; fax +966 1 402-2359.
Saudi Arabian Basic Industries Corporation (SABIC): PO Box 5101, Riyadh 11422, Kingdom of Saudi Arabia; tel +966 1 401-2033; fax +966 1 401-2045/3831.
Saudi Arabian Monetary Agency (SAMA): PO Box 2992, Riyadh 11169, Kingdom of Saudi Arabia; tel +966 1 463-3000; fax +966 1 466-2966.
Saudi Arabian Standards Organisation (SASO): Riyadh 11471, Kingdom of Saudi Arabia; tel +966 1 452-0000; fax +966 1 452-0086.
Saudi Consulting House: Riyadh, Kingdom of Saudi Arabia; tel +966 1 448-4533.
Saudi General Organisation for Grain Silos and Flour Mills: PO Box 3402, Riyadh 11471, Kingdom of Saudi Arabia; tel +966 1 464-3500; fax +966 1 463-1943.
Saudi Industrial Development Fund (SIDF): Riyadh 11149, Kingdom of Saudi Arabia; tel +966 1 477-4002; fax +966 1 479-0165.

Other Useful Addresses:
The Saudi British Bank: PO Box 9084, Riyadh 11413, Kingdom of Saudi Arabia; tel +966 1 405-0677; fax +966 1 405-0660; Website www.sabb.com.sa
British Offset Office: UK MoD Team, PO Box1003, Riyadh 11431; tel +966 1 4655957; fax +966 1 4658469.
British Trade Office: PO Box 88, Dhahran Airport 31932; tel +966 3 8570595 ext 1443/1482; fax +966 3 8570634; e-mail btokhobar@atcworld.com
Saudi Information Centre: 18 Cavendish Square, London W1M 0AQ; tel 020-7629 8803.
Al-Harithy Co. for Exhibitions Ltd: PO Box 40740, Jeddah 21511; tel +966 2 6546384; fax +966 2 6546853.
Dahran International Exhibition: PO Box 7519, Dammam 31472; tel +966 3 8579111; fax +966 3 8572285.
Dammam Port: PO Box 28062, Dammam 31421, Kingdom of Saudi Arabia; tel +966 3 833-2500; fax +966 3 857-9223.
Jeddah Islamic Port: PO Box 9285, Jeddah 21188, Kingdom of Saudi Arabia; tel +966 2 647-1200.
Riyadh Exhibition Company Ltd: PO Box 56101, Riyadh 11554; tel +966 1 4541448; fax +966 1 4544846.
Saudi Railways General Corporation: PO Box 40471, Riyadh 11499, Kingdom of Saudi Arabia; tel +966 1 448-0000; fax +966 1 448-9400.
Saudi Ports Authority: PO Box 5162, Riyadh 11422, Kingdom of Saudi Arabia; tel +966 1 405-0005; fax +966 1 403-5072.

Useful Websites
Saudi Online: www.saudi-online.com
Yellow Pages: www.ksayellowpages.com

UNITED ARAB EMIRATES
Embassies and Consulates:
British Embassy: PO Box 248, Abu Dhabi; tel +971 2 326600; fax +971 2 341744; e-mail commercial@Abudhabi.mail.fco.gov.uk
British Embassy: PO Box 65, Dubai; tel +971 4 521893/524993 (Commercial Section); fax +971 4 527095 (Commercial Section); e-mail commercial@dubai.mail.fco.gov.uk
American Embassy: PO Box 4009, Abu Dhabi; Website www.usembabu.gov.ae
American Consulate General: PO Box 9343, Dubai; Website www.usembabu.gov.ae/CGDindex.htm

Chambers of Commerce:
Abu Dhabi Chamber of Commerce & Industry: PO Box 662, Abu Dhabi; tel +971 2 214000; fax +971 2 215867; Website www.adcci.com
Ajman Chamber of Commerce & Industry: PO Box 662, Ajman; tel +971 6 422177; fax +971 6 427591; Website www.ajcci.co.ae
Dubai Chamber of Commerce & Industry: PO Box 1457, Dubai; tel +971 4 221181; fax +971 4 211646; Website www.dcci.org
Federation of UAE Chambers of Commerce & Industry: PO Box 3014, Abu Dhabi; tel +971 2 214144; fax +971 2 339210.
Federation of UAE Chambers of Commerce & Industry: PO Box 8886, Dubai; tel +971 4 212977; fax +971 4 235498.
Fujairah Chamber of Commerce, Industry & Agriculture: PO Box 738, Fujairah; tel +971 9 222400; fax +971 9 221464.

Ras Al Khaimah Chamber of Commerce, Industry & Agriculture: PO Box 87, Ras Al Khaimah; tel +971 7 333511; fax +971 7 330233.

Exhibition Organisers:
The Dubai World Trade Centre: PO Box 9292, Dubai; tel +971 4 3064044; fax +971 4 318034.
Al Fajer Information & Services: PO Box 11183, Dubai; tel +971 4 621133; fax +971 4 622802.
Channels: PO Box 55254, Dubai; tel +971 4 824737; fax +971 4 825757.
Dubai Rai International Exhibition & Conference Organisers: PO Box 9225, Dubai; tel +971 4 319444; fax +971 4 319011.
Dubai Shopping Festival Secretariat PO Box 25425, Dubai; tel +971 4 235444; fax +971 4 235888.
Fairs & Exhibitions Ltd: PO Box 773, Dubai; tel +971 4 822855; fax +971 4 822866.
International Conferences & Exhibitions (Gulf): PO Box 29884, Dubai; tel +971 4 460503; fax +971 4 460498.
IIR Exhibitions Ltd: PO Box 21743, Dubai; tel +971 4 512777; fax +971 4 518604.
International Exhibitions Abu Dhabi: PO Box 5546, Abu Dhabi; tel +971 2 446900; fax +971 2 446135; Website www.adcc1-uae.com
Expo-Centre: PO Box 3222, Sharjah; tel +971 6 391888; fax +971 6 392888.

Other Useful Addresses:
American Business Council of Dubai & the Northern Emirates: 16th Floor, World Trade Centre, PO Box 9281, Dubai, UAE; tel +971 4 314735; fax +971 4 314227; e-mail amchamdx@emirates.net.ae
British Business Group: PO Box 43635, Abu Dhabi; tel +971 2 457234; fax +971 2 450605.
British Business Group of Dubai & the Northern Emirates: PO Box 9333, Dubai; tel +971 4 313144; fax +971 4 314155.
CERT Technology Park: Muroor Road, Abu Dhabi; Website www.britishbusiness.org
Department of Economic Development: PO Box 13223, Dubai; tel +971 4 2229921; fax +971 4 2225577.
Department of Tourism & Commerce Marketing (DTCM): PO Box 594, Dubai; tel +971 4 2230000; fax +971 4 2230022; e-mail dtcm_ho@dubaitourism.co.ae Website www.dubaitourism.com; **UK office:** 125 Pall Mall, London SW1Y 5EA; tel 020-7839 0580; fax 020-7839 0582; e-mail dtcm_uk@ dubaitourism.co.ae
Dubai Airport Free Zone: PO Box 2525, Dubai; tel +971 4 2027000; fax +971 4 2995500; e-mail freezone@dca.gov.ae
Dubai Municipality: PO Box 67, Dubai; tel +971 4 2215555; fax +971 4 2246666.
Dubai Ports Authority: PO Box 2149, Dubai; tel +971 4 451545; fax +971 4 452002; Website www.dpa.co.ae
Jebel Ali Free Zone Authority: PO Box 3258, Dubai; tel +971 4 815000; fax +971 4 815001.

Useful Websites
Kompass UAE: www.kompass-uae.com
UAE Yellow Pages: www.uae.ypages.com/html/1.htm
UAE Interact: www.uaeinteract.com
Dubai Business: www.dctpb.gov.ae/dctpb/business/business.html
Business Directory: www.hawkuaebusinesspages.com
Jebel Ali Free Zone: www.jafza.com

Ajman Free Trade Zone: www.ajmanfreezone.com
Hamriyah Free Zone: www.hamriyahfz.com
Ras al-Khaimah Industrial Free Zone: www.rakiftz.com
Sharjah Airport International Free Zone: www.saif-zone.com
Dubai World Trade Centre: www.dwtcuae.com

Online Resources

The following is a list of useful websites for all those doing business throughout the Gulf.

Arab Net. www.arab.net
Useful country information on all of the Gulf states.

Arab Online. www.arabia.com
Business news information on the countries throughout the Gulf as well as useful links to other relevant sites.

Arab World Online. www.awo.net
Country facts and figures, commercial directories, 'Best Opportunities for Investment and Export,' and useful business links, for all the states in the Arabian Peninsula.

Gulf Business Explorer. www.igulf.com/main.htm
Directory of businesses throughout the Middle East and Gulf region.

Middle East Business Information. www.ameinfo.com
Country facts and figures, up-to-date business information.

Useful Publications

In addition to those publications listed below it is well worth visiting your local reference and business libraries to obtain a copy of one of the *Kompass Registers* which list the major commercial enterprises across the world. They are classified by country and type of product. Another valuable collection of international trade and telephone directories is held at the *Export Market Information Centre (EMIC)* (Kingsgate House, 66-74 Victoria Street, London SW1E 6SW; tel 020-7215 5444/5; fax 020-7215 4231; Website www.dti.gov.uk). This organisation provides a self-help reference library for exporters and is open from 9am to 8pm Monday to Friday, 9am to 5.30pm on Saturdays. It holds market research reports, trade fair catalogues, and country profiles. A similar service is available at *The Middle East Association* (Bury House, 33 Bury Street, St James's, London SW1Y 6AX; tel 020-7839 2137; fax 020-7839 6121), open weekdays from 9am to 5.30pm.

A British Library/Lloyds TSB Bank Business Line is operated by the *British Library Business Information Service* (tel 020-7412 7454/7977; open Monday to Friday, 9am to 5pm) which provides useful information on international employment and trade to researchers and companies.

Thousands of useful business books are also listed on Amazon Books database. Visit their website www.amazon.com for more details.

GENERAL READING
Countertrade & Offset – A Guide for Exporters. DTI Publications, 1998, £20.
Don't They Know Its Friday? Book Representation & Distribution Ltd, 244A
   London Road, Hadleigh, Essex SS7 2DE; tel 01702-552912; fax 01702-

556095.

Gulf Spotlight Magazine, DTI Publications. Annual guide to doing business in the Arabian Peninsula.

Hints to Exporters Visiting the Arabian Peninsula. DTI Publications, 1999, £10.

Middle East Economic Digest (MEED). Weekly magazine featuring Middle Eastern business news. Available from MEED Subscription Services. Also published by MEED: *MEEDmoney, The Advertisers' Guide to the Middle East*, and *Finance Guide to the Middle East*.

Middle East and North Africa, Europa Publications. Yearbook source of highly detailed commercial and political information.

Middle East Monitor: The Gulf, Business Monitor International. Monthly magazine featuring detailed economic information and relevant news articles on each of the Gulf states.

Middle East Trade, Middle East Trade Publications Ltd.

Overseas Trade Magazine. Published 10 times a year providing export news and information on opportunities in foreign markets. Free of charge to UK exporters from *Overseas Trade*.

Websites for Exporters. DTI Publications, 1999, £10.

BAHRAIN

General Report – Government Ministries and Officials, British Organisations & Joint Ventures. DTI Publications, 1997, £20.

Project List – Construction; Electricity; Healthcare; Infrastructure; Tourism; Water & Sewerage. DTI Publications, 1998, £25.

Project List – British Organisations & Joint Ventures & Franchises. DTI Publications, 1999, £25.

Sector Report – Healthcare. DTI Publications, 1997, £30.

OMAN

Sector Report – Oil & Gas, Power Generation & Water. DTI Publications, 1998, £60.

QATAR

Sector Report – Oil & Gas. DTI Publications, 1999, £50.

SAUDI ARABIA

Project List – Airports; Chemicals; Defence; Electricity; Environment; Food; Health; Mining; Oil; Gas & Petrochemicals; Ports; Telecommunications; Tourism; Water. DTI Publications, 1998, £25.

UNITED ARAB EMIRATES

General Report – British & Associated Firms with Representatives in Abu Dhabi, Dubai and the Northern Emirates. DTI Publications, 1996, £50.

Sector Report – Oil, Gas & Petrochemicals in Abu Dhabi. DTI Publications, 1996, £30.

Sector Report – Agriculture & Fisheries in Dubai & the Northern Emirates. DTI Publications, 1997, £30.

Sector Report – Healthcare in Dubai & the Northern Emirates. DTI Publications, 1996, £30.

Useful Addresses

Business Monitor International: 179 Queen Victoria Street, London EC4V 4DU; tel 020-7248 0468; fax 020-7248 0467; e-mail subs@businessmonitor.com

Website www.businessmonitor.com
DTI Publications Orderline: Admail 528, London SW1W 8YT; tel 0870-1502 500; fax 0870-1502 333; Website www.dti.gov.uk/ots/publications/
Europa Publications: 18 Bedford Square, London WC1B 3JN.
MEED Subscription Services CENTROBE: PO Box 14, Harold Hill, Romford, Essex RM3 8EQ.
Middle East Trade Publications Ltd: 34 Percy Street, London W1.
Overseas Trade: Brass Tacks Publishing Co Ltd, 143 Charing Cross Road, London WC2H 0EE; tel 020-7478 4700; fax 020-7437 3591.

Business Practices in the Gulf

When preparing to do business in the Gulf it is very important to be aware of the customary practices involved in order to avoid unwittingly offending Arab sensibilities and harming your chances of securing your desired goal (see also *Social Practices in the Gulf* in the 'General Introduction to the Gulf States' chapter). You will soon realise that the key to successful business transactions in the Gulf is first and foremost patience. Securing a deal can take several months to achieve within which regular visits of at least one every two or three months should be maintained.

Business Calls

You should always ensure that you are prompt for any appointments despite the fact that invariably your meeting will be delayed or postponed. Seeing all the people you wish to see is very much dependent on how good your contacts are – as your own reputation develops you will find it increasingly easier to meet with those whom you want to. Hours of waiting is a matter of course at all levels of business and showing any signs of impatience is considered very bad manners.

Business Meetings

Business meetings initially involve finding yourself in a room full of other visitors who will only be seated after exchanging greetings with the host and as many of the others present as is appropriate. When directed to your seat you may find someone else already sitting there but they will move to make room for you. This is a sign that you are thought more important than the other person for the time being until another occasion when you will find yourself the displaced individual. Generally the most eminent visitor is seated on the host's right nearest to his desk. Only after you have undergone a group meeting and with any luck managed to arouse the interest of your host will you be able to arrange an exclusive interview for a future date.

Presentations

The key to giving a successful presentation lies in your ability to remain calm at all times. Speech and actions should be slow and deliberate. Showing any signs of anger or excitability is regarded as extremely ill mannered or vulgar as is launching straight into business matters before exchanging the habitual courtesies first (enquiring after your host's health and family, etc.). Developing a strong personal relationship and mutual trust with your host is of the utmost importance. Confidence and pride in your product will inspire like feelings in your audience.

As with giving any kind of presentation, the most effective approach is one of simplicity, clarity, and succinctness. A well-prepared speech of about 20-30 minutes should be comprised of short sentences, short words. You should avoid using abbreviations, slang, colloquial idioms and jargon. Ideally your presentation will involve lots of action-packed film in concise punchy pieces. The days of using slides are well and truly over. A copy of your presentation for your audience is an added bonus.

New business ideas and techniques stand a much better chance of success if you present them as running in conjunction with or alongside traditional beliefs rather than opposed to them.

Business Documents and Accessories

You should always remember and respect the fact that Arabic is the local language. Consequently, all presentations, visiting cards, brochures and contracts should be in Arabic in addition to English. The employment of an interpreter may be expensive but can be essential. Local business centres can generally supply able interpreters that speak the local dialect or classical Arabic.

A highly polished and expensive image is all-important in stimulating serious Arab interest in your business. This means that everything about your business should be well thought out; company literature should involve spending a lot of money to produce brochures, etc. of a rich professional looking appearance with plenty of glossy photographs. As with presentations, simple language (both in Arabic and English) should be used and overly technical or complicated terminology avoided. It will cost far more to stint at any stage in business terms than to spend that little bit extra financially and reap the merited rewards.

Business transactions

Building up a strong business relationship and trust with an Arab in order to secure business deals can take months if not years. When negotiating a deal you should bear in mind the following general points:

Oral commitments. Particular care should be taken over agreeing to anything orally as the spoken word in a traditional Muslim Shari'a court has greater significance than the written. Arabs are well-known for their exceptional memories and spoken agreements are considered as binding as any other type. Further, remember that you will be expected to honour every single detail of your contract to the very minutiae.

Bargaining. Securing the best deal is of supreme importance to an Arab not only for his own satisfaction but to gain the respect of his peers. Consequently, bargaining is inherent to any agreement that an Arab may make. Arabs are very shrewd businessmen so it is unwise to enter into any negotiations with an over-inflated price. Any reduction that you do agree to needs to be prudently justified otherwise you could rouse suspicion that you have been setting prices too high. It is wise to always keep something in reserve so that when you have arrived at your lowest price you can offer the interested party something else concerning another aspect of your contract, e.g. training or services. You should aim at making your customer feel and look as if he has attained the most favourable and profitable deal that was possible.

Arab etiquette. As they believe it to be somewhat rude to do otherwise, you are very unlikely to ever receive an outright 'no' to any business proposal that you might make to an Arab. Any hints you may take as indications that your product may be purchased could just be expressions of polite interest. However, if a proposal has been agreed upon it is extremely rare for an Arab to renege on a contract. Nevertheless, you should remain wary as there is never any fool-proof guarantee – cases of broken promises and bad debts are known.

Confidentiality. All discussions between you and an Arab, no matter how trivial or more relevant to subsequent negotiations and contract, should be regarded as strictly confidential. Any breach of this confidence will result in immediate termination of talks.

Contracts. These should be kept as straightforward as possible. The body of the text should comprise easily translated terms with additional details appended. Avoid, where possible, any amendments as they are considered dishonourable.

Accountants

The largest accountancy firms have branches in major cities throughout the Arabian Peninsula, and will advise individuals setting up business as well as large corporations. Additionally, they publish a selection of free books and materials on a wide range of business topics, from setting up business to import and export, and relocation. Price WaterhouseCoopers's series of *Doing Business in Bahrain/Kuwait/Oman, etc.* is particularly informative on the tax and employment aspects. Arthur Andersen is also active in this area.

The head offices of the largest accountancy practices in the UK and North America are as follows:

Horwath Clark Whitehill, 25 New Street Square, London EC4A 3LN; tel 020-7353 1577.
Robson Taylor Chartered Accountants, 1st Floor, Bradford House, St Stephens Avenue, Bristol BS1 1YL; tel 0117-927 9145.
Robson Rhodes, 186 City Road, London EC1V 2NU; tel 020-7251 1644.
PricewaterhouseCoopers, 1 Embankment Place, London WC2N 6NN; tel 020-7583 5000; **US Office:** 1301 Avenue of the Americas, New York, NY 10019, USA; tel +1 212 707-6000; fax +1 212 707-6886.
KPMG, 8 Salisbury Square, London EC4Y 8BB; tel 020-7311 1000; **US Office:** 345 Park Avenue, New York, NY 10154, USA; tel +1 212 758-9700.
Arthur Andersen, 1 Surrey Street, London WC2R 2PS; tel 020-7438 3000; **US Office:** 1345 Avenue of the Americas, New York, NY 10105, USA; tel +1 917 452-4400; fax +1 917 527-9915.
Ernst and Young, Rolls House, 7 Rolls Buildings, Fetter Lane, London EC4A 1NH; tel 020-7928 2000; **US Office:** 787 7th Avenue, F114, New York, NY, USA; tel +212 773-3000.
Deloitte and Touche, Hill House, 1 Little New Street, London EC4A 3TR; tel 020-7936 3000; **US Office:** 1633 Broadway, New York, NY 10019-6754; tel +1 212 489-1600; fax +1 212 489-1687.

Also contact the two major accountancy bodies the ICAEW (Institute of Chartered Accountants in England and Wales) and ACCA (Association of Certified Chartered Accountants).
ICAEW, PO Box 433, Chartered Accountants Hall, Moorgate Place, London EC2P 2BJ; tel 020-7920 8100; Website www.icaew.co.uk
ACCA, 29 Lincolns Inn Fields, London WC2A 3EE; tel 020-7242 6855; Website www.acca.co.uk

Language and Translation Services

Although English is widely spoken in business throughout the Arabian Peninsula, when conducting any business in the Gulf, the employment of translation services will be essential for all written transactions and communications. Embassies in the

Arabian Peninsula can advise on translators and interpreter services as well as the *Institute of Linguists* and *Institute of Translation and Interpreting*, which do not undertake translation work themselves but do provide the names of their members for translation services.

The Department of Trade and Industry (DTI), operate a National Languages for Export campaign, which aims to provide the exporter with details on how to take a strategic approach to language and cultural issues in international business, and can advise on selecting suppliers of language services. Four 'How to do it' guides are available covering translation, interpreting business language strategies, trading across cultures, and language training.

Further free information and advice on language training, cultural consultants, interpreters, and translators, can be obtained from the National Business Language Information Service (NATBLIS) database.

Dr. Ahmed A. Audhali Law Firm (PO Box 1158, Al Khobar 31952, Saudi Arabia; tel +966 3 864-3011/3793; fax +966 3 894 5837) not only handles a comprehensive range of legal matters for expatriates in Saudi Arabia, but also provides the translation services of highly qualified and experienced translators.

Useful Addresses

Institute of Linguists, 48 Southwark Street, London SE1 1UN; tel 020-7940 3100; fax 020-7940 3101; e-mail info@iol.org.uk Website www.iol.org.uk

Institute of Translation and Interpreting, 377 City Road, London EC1V 1NA; tel 020-7713 7600; fax 020-7713 7650; Website www.iti.org.uk

National Languages for Export, Bay 905, Kingsgate House, 66-74 Victoria Street, London SW1E 6SW; tel 020-7215 8146/8155; fax 020-7215 4856.

National Business Language Information Service (NATBLIS), c/o Centre for Information on Language Teaching and Research (CILT), 20 Bedfordbury, London WC2N 4LB; tel 020-7379 5131; fax 020-7379 5082.

Choosing an Area

The area you decide to live and work in will depend to a large extent on what kind of business you want to carry out. Each Gulf state within the Arabian Peninsula should be reviewed as a separate economic area, each with its own strengths and weaknesses. Regional development agencies and Chambers of Commerce will be able to provide you with detailed economic and business information on the advantages and disadvantages of investing or setting up in their countries. There are also free zones in some of the Gulf countries (not in Oman or Qatar), which offer added incentives for foreign investors (see below, *Investment Incentives*). Corporate tax levies also vary (see below, *Taxation*), which may influence your decision.

Further advice on which country would best suit your requirements can be obtained by contacting one of the organisations listed below.

Useful Addresses

American Business Council (Kuwait): PO Box 29992, Safat 13159, Kuwait; tel +965 2430718; fax +965 2409450.

American Business Council of Dubai & the Northern Emirates: 16th Floor, World Trade Centre, PO Box 9281, Dubai, UAE; tel +971 4 314735; fax +971 4 314227; e-mail amchamdx@emirates.net.ae

Bahrain Promotions & Marketing Board (BPMB): PO Box 11299, Manama, Bahrain; tel +973 533886; fax +973 531117.

British Business Forum (BBF): PO Box 300, Safat 13003, Kuwait; tel +965 2405346; fax +965 2405348.

British Business Group: PO Box 43635, **Abu Dhabi**, UAE; tel +971 2 457234; fax

+971 2 450605.

British Business Group of Dubai & the Northern Emirates: PO Box 9333, Dubai, UAE; tel +971 4 313144; fax +971 4 314155.

Department of Tourism & Commerce Marketing (DTCM): PO Box 594, Dubai, UAE; tel +971 4 2230000; fax +971 4 2230022; e-mail dtcm_ho@dubaitourism.co.ae Website www.dubaitourism.com

Exploration & Development of New Ventures Department: PO Box 3212, Doha, Qatar; tel +974 491288/833091; fax +974 831850.

Omani Centre for Investment Promotion & Export Development (OCIPED): PO Box 25, Al Wadi Al Kabir 117, Oman; tel +968 7712344; fax +968 7717600.

Saudi Information Centre: 18 Cavendish Square, London W1M 0AQ; tel 020-7629 8803.

Raising Finance

If you are intending to live abroad for a long-term period it is highly unlikely that you will be able to borrow start-up capital from a UK bank. This of course is dependent on a series of factors: your credit history, your standing with the bank, your business history, and the collateral that you can provide. If you are able to mortgage or sell your house in the UK, or provide it as collateral against a loan, that would be seen as sufficient by a UK bank. You would not be able to get a loan simply on the basis of a start-up in the Gulf. On the other hand, if you are opening a branch or distribution operation in the Gulf and using the parent company at home as a base, the best way to raise finance would be from a UK bank. It is unlikely that a Gulf bank would lend money to an unknown quantity with no trade record. Bank references would not count for much in this situation: the bottom line is that the bank does not know you.

If you are trying to set up in the Gulf with no umbilical cord to your own country, then the first port of call should be a state economic development office (addresses can be obtained from regional Chambers of Commerce, see *Preparation from Scratch* above). You will be advised on all aspects of business in the state, and will be put in touch with local banks. You should be aware that all banks advise on the difficulty of getting a loan for a business start-up. However, there are numerous state incentives (see below), that banks are using to increase their loans to this sector.

Investment Incentives

All the governments of the Gulf states are currently implementing plans to encourage foreign investment and foreign business, with a view to improving their local economic environments. The regional Chambers of Commerce (see 'Useful Addresses' above under *Starting from Scratch*) provide information on markets, financing, and other related areas, to foreigners intending to invest in the Gulf area. They will also put investors in touch with Gulf firms which are interested in opening up a joint venture, and will provide a list of state development agencies.

Among the investment incentives common to some or all of the states are various tax breaks (see *Taxation* below), and the set up of free trade zones – areas where imported and exported goods can move freely without paying duty: goods can be manufactured, stored, and transported, and duty is only paid when the goods enter the Gulf market, and then at preferential rates. This is very attractive to foreign importers: when goods enter the Gulf, the assessment for duty does not include the cost of processing and profit realised. More details can be obtained by contacting the free trade zone in which you are interested, either in Bahrain, Kuwait, Saudi Arabia, or the United Arab Emirates. Addresses can be obtained from regional embassies or from local Yellow Pages directories. It is also worth contacting the organisations listed under *Choosing an Area* for further information on Gulf country markets, financing, etc.

The following is an outline of what investment incentives the individual states offer the prospective foreign investor.

BAHRAIN

Bahrain not only offers its foreign investor a promising market place, economic freedom, and a mature commercial infrastructure, but also provides a very welcoming lifestyle, with first-class educational and health care facilities, a secure and cosmopolitan way of life in a virtually crime free environment, and an extensive range of social amenities for workers outside business hours.

The Island is strategically located halfway between east and west time zones, is at the heart of a 100 million people regional market with some of the highest incomes in the world, offers duty free access to the GCC states, is directly linked by road to the Eastern Province of Saudi Arabia, which has a 3.5 million population, and is a regional centre for air travel and distribution.

In Bahrain, there are: no personal, corporate, or withholding taxes payable; no exchange control restrictions on repatriation of capital, profits, and dividends; supportive government policies for overseas investors and government services to aid business planning; duty free zones at ports and industrial areas; duty free merchandise for re-export; duty free import of materials and machinery for manufacturing; a freely convertible and stable currency linked to the US dollar. 100 per cent foreign ownership of companies is allowed, as well as up to 49 per cent foreign ownership in joint ventures, and individual expatriates resident in Bahrain for over a year can purchase up to one per cent of any publicly-listed Bahraini corporation. The country also has an established legal system with highly developed and mature commercial laws. The state is not only the financial hub in the Middle East, but has one of the most advanced telecommunications systems in the region. Additionally, in Bahrain the costs are low for energy, utilities, rents, and labour.

There are two free trade zones in Bahrain, used for the temporary storage of imported goods marked out for re-export. Bahrain's chief port, Mina Sulman, offers a free transit zone to ease the duty free import of equipment and machinery. The North Sitra Industrial Estate is the site for the other free trade zone.

During the first quarter of 1996, nearly 70 new businesses registered in Bahrain.

KUWAIT

Kuwait is in the process of reviewing its laws and regulations concerning foreign investment in order to attract more foreign investors. Outside the free trade zones, joint ventures are presently restricted to 49 per cent foreign ownership, but discussions on opening up further to investors are believed to be underway, in particular to aid the advancement of the technology sector and the financial market. Additionally, tariffs in Kuwait stand at a flat rate of four per cent, although agricultural items, food, and basic consumer goods enter Kuwait duty free.

New legislation has also been introduced to ease Kuwait's way into the World Intellectual Property Organisation. In spring 1999, new copyright, patent, and trademark laws, which established lengthened terms and tighter penalties, were passed by the Kuwaiti government. This action ended a piracy dispute with the American authorities regarding the protection of video, audio, and pharmaceutical products, and will bring the state's regulations in line with global standards.

As a member of the World Trade Organisation (WTO), in 1999 Kuwaiti authorities requested that its grace period be extended until 2003 or 2004 for the finalising of reforms in the customs sector so that it totally complies with WTO stipulations. Officials are also hoping to establish a unified code of customs between the GCC countries so that they might unite to form a common market.

OMAN

In 1996 Oman's tax laws and regulations were greatly relaxed in order to encourage more foreign investment. For the first time, foreign investors were permitted to own majority stakes, up to 65 per cent, in large Omani industrial projects. Furthermore, in certain cases the Development Council allowed 100 per cent foreign ownership for projects capitalised above US$1.3 million. Taxation on foreign companies was also revised to treat foreign investors on a more equal footing with national investors (for details see *Taxation* below).

Import duties are roughly five per cent, except on necessities, which are exempt, and some protected locally produced products. Employers pay a tax on wages of seven per cent of basic salary for foreign workers and eight per cent for Omanis.

Oman's Tender Board, which handles assignments, purchases, and project implementation, with the exception of those related to defence and security, award tenders. In 1997, the board accepted 119 tenders for over US$500 million.

QATAR

Qatar offers ten to twelve years in tax holidays for foreign investors, as well as exemptions from taxes on income, electricity, water, and power facilities. 100 per cent foreign ownership of companies is allowed in the country. Joint ventures involving foreign partners always take the form of limited liability partnerships (see below *Business Structures & Registration*). Foreigners are not allowed to own property or invest in privatised public services, but foreign investors have been permitted to own up to 25 per cent stake in fertilisers, petrochemical, and steel industries. It is compulsory for all business to employ a local agent or representative to act as a sales channel for promoting products and services in the local market.

SAUDI ARABIA

The Saudi government actively encourages foreign investment, especially investment that is linked with joint ventures with Saudi partners. Three conditions for foreign investments are outlined in the Saudi foreign capital investment code: the venture must be a development project; the investment must generate technology transfer; a Saudi partner must own a minimum of 25 per cent equity (this can be waived). In a 1990 resolution, the Ministry of Industry and Electricity defined 'Development Projects' to include agriculture, contracting, health, industrial, and specialised service projects. Mostly high-technology projects are given priority, while projects in construction, general operations, and maintenance are discouraged.

The Ministry of Industry and Electricity's Foreign Capital Investment Board reviews all licence applications and counsels prospective investors. It also assesses applications and potential projects. Projects must encourage economic diversification, provide access to modern technology, and create more opportunities for Saudi employment. Joint ventures always take the form of limited liability partnerships.

100 per cent foreign-owned companies are entitled to a wide scope of investment incentives, including competitive utility rates, land in the industrial estates at nominal rents, treatment as domestic producers for government procurement contracts, and custom duty exemptions on raw materials and capital goods. However, joint ventures are favoured and only joint ventures with a minimum of 51 per cent of GCC ownership interest can export duty free to other GCC countries.

UNITED ARAB EMIRATES

Despite tariffs in the UAE standing at four per cent, more than 75 per cent of imports still enter the country duty free, and there are no tariffs on exports. Each emirate has its own customs authority, while a national committee formulates general policies. Outside the free trade zones foreign investors must work with a UAE sponsor, and to bid on federal projects, a company must be at least 51 per cent UAE-owned. These rules are not applicable to defence contracts or other projects where there is no local company to provide the necessary goods and services.

The establishment and development of free trade zones is key to the UAE government's plans to encourage foreign investment. The chief attractions of free zones is that they allow 100 per cent foreign ownership, and added incentives such as extended tax holidays, subsidised energy, and total repatriation of capital and profits. Additionally, the zones offer support services, for instance, sponsorship, housing for workers, dining facilities, recruitment, and security.

Copyright, trademark, and patent laws drawn up in 1992, are now being enforced by the UAE government. The UAE is acknowledged as a regional leader in fighting computer software piracy and has been successful in cutting its occurrence.

Relocation Agencies and Business Services

Relocation agencies provide a variety of different services, from advising and helping employees who are being relocated, either within the Gulf region or overseas, to advising companies and individuals who want to set up an office or business in a new area. See *Preparing to Go* and *Relocation Companies* in the Gulf States 'General Introduction' chapter for more details and contact addresses.

Real estate agents are useful sources on relocation. The large international accountancy firms, in particular Deloitte and Touche, Andersen Consulting, PriceWaterhouseCoopers, and Ernst and Young, also now advise on site selection and relocation. They have the advantage of being able to use their huge client bases, and their expertise in taxation, management consulting and real estate to give an all-round service. When dealing with firms of this size, it is worth bearing in mind that they would be charging around £200 per hour, and would farm out minor consultancy work to a smaller consultant. it is advisable to go to the small consultant first, who would charge an hourly rate of £50-£60.

Law firms offer advice on areas such as structuring business organisations, employment and labour matters, tax and real estate, and litigation, and arbitration.

Most of these services can be found in the regional Yellow Pages directories, or from regional Chambers of Commerce.

Business Structures and Registration

An important consideration for any company setting up in the Gulf is the choice of business entity. The three main structures are a commercial agency, a branch office, and a subsidiary. Each is subject to a particular tax regime, and affects the owner's legal liability in a different way.

Commercial Agency

In the GCC, a commercial agency is an entity where a foreign party appoints a GCC individual or company as the representative of any product or service of the foreign party. In all cases, whether the relationship is formed as a distributorship, sales agency, or otherwise, the relationship will be governed by local law. Appointing a commercial agent generally allows the foreign business person to attain a substantial market penetration without setting up a direct presence. Local law entitles the agent to certain rights that cannot be waived by contract.

BAHRAIN

In Bahrain, commercial agencies are governed by the Bahrain Commercial Agencies Law, which stipulates that all commercial agency agreements be registered with the Ministry of Commerce and Agriculture, and that the claims of unregistered agencies will not be heard. Once registered, the Bahrain Commercial Agencies Law grants certain statutory rights to the commercial agent that cannot be waived by contract. At the forefront of these rights is exclusivity within Bahrain for the relevant products or services. The commercial agent is protected against early termination by the foreign party, but the Law also allows for de-registration upon the expiry of the agent's agreed term. To qualify for registration, a commercial agent must be a Bahraini citizen or a validly incorporated Bahraini company that is a minimum of 51 per cent Bahraini-owned and that it has its head office in Bahrain.

KUWAIT

A foreign company is able to carry out business in Kuwait by appointing a Kuwaiti agent, which conducts business under its own trade licence and in its own name. The agent can be a Kuwaiti individual or company. If a Kuwaiti company, it need not be 100 per cent Kuwaiti-owned. Registration of the agency in the Agency Register at the Ministry of Commerce and Industry, gives the agent notable protection in line with the Laws of Commerce. However, the law does not oblige the foreign party to ensure that it is strictly upheld, and unlike in the other Gulf states, the registered agency contract is not legally required to be an exclusive agreement. Kuwait law also acknowledges 'distributorship' as a separate category of commercial agency. A distributor's activities are usually limited to promoting, importing, and distributing, the products of the foreign party, and do not include negotiation and performance of contracts on behalf of the foreign party.

OMAN

The Law of Commercial Agencies governs all commercial agencies in the Sultanate of Oman, and requires the registration of all commercial agency agreements with the Ministry of Commerce and industry. Upon registration, an agent gains certain rights of exclusivity for the marketing of the product in the region, and the award of compensation upon termination. However, lately, the Ministry has permitted some non-agents under special circumstances to import products into Oman which are the subject of registered agencies. Non-agent importers, just as registered agents, are still required to provide after sales service, and may do so through the set up of workshops or through consent with existing entities.

Registration as commercial agents used to be restricted to Omani nationals or companies with 100 per cent Omani-ownership, but recent developments in the regulations now entitles companies with up to 49 per cent foreign ownership to register and act as agents.

QATAR

The Commercial Agencies Law governs all commercial agencies in Qatar, and stipulates that all commercial agency agreements be registered with the Companies Control Department of the Ministry of Finance, Economy, and Commerce. Only Qatari nationals or 100 per cent Qatari-owned companies are eligible for registration. Once registered, the law gives a commercial agent certain statutory rights that cannot be waived by contract, such as exclusivity within Qatar for the relevant products and services, protection from termination, and compensation upon termination or non-renewal of the agency. More than one agent may be appointed by the same manufacturer to handle different product lines.

SAUDI ARABIA

All commercial agency agreements in Saudi Arabia are obliged to be registered with the Saudi Ministry of Commerce, although failure to register an agreement does not make it unenforceable. Furthermore, registration of the agreement does not necessarily grant the commercial agents rights beyond the terms of the contract. There are no specific laws that stipulate that the relationship must be exclusive, but the Ministry of Commerce normally refuses to register agreements that do not give the commercial agent an exclusive appointment in regard of either geographical scope or product line. Only Saudi nationals or 100 per cent Saudi-owned entities are eligible for registration.

UNITED ARAB EMIRATES

The Federal Commercial Agencies Law stipulates that all commercial agency agreements in the UAE should be registered with the Federal Ministry of Economy and Commerce, and that the claims of unregistered agencies will not be heard. Once registered, commercial agents are granted certain statutory rights that cannot be waived by contract, such as exclusivity within the region for the relevant products or services, and protection from termination. Outside free trade zones, commercial agents must be UAE nationals or 100 per cent UAE-owned companies to be eligible for registration.

A single agent for the whole of the UAE, or several agents for each emirate or groups of emirates, may be appointed by a foreign business. More than one agent may be appointed by the same manufacturer to handle different product lines.

Branch Office

With the exception of Kuwait and Oman, all GCC states allow foreign companies under certain conditions to set up local branch offices without any local equity participation. Branch offices can conduct business, hire staff, and operate local bank accounts in their own name. This structure gives the foreign party more control over local operations than an agency or subsidiary. Local law may also allow the establishment of a representative office, a specific type of branch office with limited activities.

BAHRAIN

The Bahraini Companies Law requires branch offices of a foreign company in Bahrain to appoint a Bahraini citizen as a sponsor. Generally the sponsor's compensation takes the form of either a flat fee or a percentage based on branch office revenues in Bahrain. However, exemptions to the sponsorship requirement were introduced in 1991 for a branch office that uses Bahrain as a regional centre or a representative office for its business activities in the Middle East. All applications for exemption are reviewed individually.

KUWAIT

Foreign companies are not permitted to establish their own wholly-owned branch offices in Kuwait.

OMAN

Foreign companies are generally not permitted to set up their own wholly-owned branch offices in Oman, although the same Foreign Investment Law that stipulates this ruling also marks out certain exceptions, such as banks and 'companies.which are engaged in activities in the Sultanate of Oman by virtue of agreements or special contracts concluded with the government of the Sultanate or its public institutions,' and 'companies ... which are engaged in a project declared to be an Economic Development Project.'

QATAR
Qatari law usually requires foreign companies conducting business in Qatar to do so in partnership with a Qatari individual or company, and does not permit branch offices of foreign companies. However, exemptions to the law exist which would allow a foreign company to set up a branch office to carry out a particular contract in Qatar. Applications by foreign companies for an exemption would involve the appointment of a Qatari Service Agent (similar to a 'sponsor' or 'national agent' in other Gulf states). The Qatar Ministry of Finance, Economy, and Commerce considers each application on a case-by-case basis.

SAUDI ARABIA
Despite the registration of branches of foreign companies in Saudi Arabia being allowed according to the Saudi Companies Regulations, approval for such a move must be sought from the Foreign Capital Investment Committee (FCIC) of the Saudi Ministry of Industry and Electricity. Historically, the approval of this authority has never been forthcoming and although policy has relaxed marginally over recent years, it is still relatively difficult for foreign companies to set-up branch offices in the Kingdom. Branches of foreign companies must currently gain the approval of the Ministry of Industry and Electricity (including the FCIC) and the Ministry of Commerce, and are not eligible for any tax holiday.

UNITED ARAB EMIRATES
A branch office of a foreign company is required to appoint a local national agent, sometimes referred to as a sponsor. Generally, the national agent assists the foreign company in licensing and immigration red tape. The national agent does not take part in any aspect of the foreign company's business in the UAE, unless otherwise specified in their contract. The national agent is only entitled to an agreed fee, and is not liable for any of the foreign company's obligations. Foreign companies can appoint more than one national agent to accommodate offices in more than one emirate.

Subsidiary
Commercial advantages in operating through a local subsidiary exist for certain businesses in the Gulf region. Local subsidiaries are different from the wide variety of structures known as contractual joint ventures.

BAHRAIN
The set up of Bahraini companies with majority or 100 per cent foreign ownership is allowed in Bahrain provided that such companies use the Island as a regional centre for their activities. The limited liability company is on the whole the most convenient structure for Bahraini subsidiaries of foreign companies. A limited liability company is required to have a minimum of two (but no more than fifty) shareholders, and can be incorporated with a capital as little as BD 10,000 (US$27,250). The liability of shareholders is restricted to the assets of the limited liability company.

The limited liability company provides a substantial degree of flexibility in management and distribution of profits. Such companies with majority Bahraini ownership may qualify for preferential treatment in government tenders and in tariff treatment on exports to other Gulf states, which is not likely to be extended to such Bahraini companies with majority foreign ownership.

KUWAIT

There are two types of corporate entity in Kuwait in which a foreigner may be a partner: the Limited Liability Company (known locally as a 'WLL'), and the Private Shareholding Company (also known as a 'closed joint stock company'). The latter is the only form of Kuwaiti company in which a foreign corporate party may hold shares (up to 49 per cent) in its own name. In practice, establishment of a Private Shareholding Company is not easy and there has been little foreign participation in such companies.

WLLs must be at least 51 per cent Kuwaiti-owned, and cannot be used as a vehicle for banking, insurance, or investment of funds belonging to third parties. There must be at least two shareholders in a WLL and at the most 30. WLLs may be incorporated with a capital of KD 7,500, but occasionally higher minimum amounts are required at the discretion of the relevant authorities at the Ministry of Commerce and Industry.

OMAN

Foreign ownership of up to 65 per cent in an Omani commercial company may be granted in the Sultanate. Such companies can carry out commercial activities in the fields of agriculture, construction contracting, industry, services, and tourism. However, foreign equity participation is restricted to 49 per cent if the company intends to engage in commercial agency activities, including import and export. A minimum of OR 150,000 is required to set up such Omani companies, although in certain circumstances this figure may be reduced to OR 30,000.

QATAR

In recent years there has been a growing interest among foreign companies in the establishment of Qatari subsidiary companies. Such companies are required to have at least 51 per cent Qatari-ownership, and at present there are limited fields of activity open to such mixed-ownership subsidiary companies, as trading activities are effectively reserved for Qatari nationals and Qatari-owned companies. Foreign party participipation in contracting companies must obtain approval from the Ministry of Finance, Economy, and Commerce, which up to date has proved hard to come by.

A limited liability company is one of the most convenient forms of corporate organisation for Qatari subsidiaries of foreign companies. A limited liability company may comprise a minimum of two shareholders and a maximum of 50. The capital requirement for such Qatari companies is set at a minimum of QR 200,000 (about US$55,000). The liability of shareholders is limited to assets of the limited liability company.

SAUDI ARABIA

Foreign parties are not allowed 100 per cent ownership in Saudi companies, but are permitted majority ownership, subject to certain conditions. In order to give approval to any application, the FCIC requires that all joint ventures have a minimum of 25 per cent Saudi ownership.

The limited liability company is the most convenient form of corporate organisation for Saudi subsidiaries of foreign companies, and requires at least two, and up to 50, shareholders, who may not be members of the general public. The minimum share capital is SR 500,000 (roughly US$133,000). Shareholders are liable for the debts of the company to the degree of the subscribed share capital. Such companies provide substantial flexibility in management.

UNITED ARAB EMIRATES

Outside the free trade zones, all companies established in the UAE must be at least 51 per cent UAE-owned. The most convenient form of corporate organisation for UAE subsidiaries of foreign companies is the limited liability company. A minimum of two and a maximum of 50 shareholders, who are not members of the general public, can form a limited liability company with a capital of Dhs. 150,000 (US $41,000). The liability of shareholders is restricted to the assets of the limited liability company. A substantial degree of flexibility in management and distribution of profits is offered by the limited liability structure, and such companies incorporated in the UAE may qualify for preferential treatment in government tenders.

Ideas for New Businesses

If you are thinking of setting up a business in the Gulf, the importance of thorough market research cannot be overstressed. The following factors need to be examined in detail: the size of the target market; the size of the niche that makes up the core of the market; the trends that are affecting the market at any one time; who exactly are the consumers, and what makes them tick – why should they buy your product? Who are the distributors, and what will it cost you to use them? What sort of price should your product be fixed at? What is the competition, and what are its strengths and weaknesses?

Manufacturing and finance are two of the leading sectors in terms of growth potential. Foreign investment is positively welcomed throughout the Arabian Peninsula. Tourism is also a developing industry in the Gulf region. The following is a list of the key target sectors in each country. More detailed information on the major sectors in each country can be found in the 'Employment' chapter under *Business & Industry Report* and *Regional Employment Guide*.

Prime Target Sectors

Bahrain

Aluminium Bahrain (ALBA) and its
  downstream activities.
Clothing.
Construction.
Creative and media.
Energy.
Environment.
Financial services.
Food and drink.
Gifts.

Health care.
Household items.
Metals.
Oil, gas, petrochemicals.
Power generation.
Telecommunications.
Textiles.
Tourism.
Training and education.
Water, sewerage.

Kuwait

Chemicals.
Consumer goods.
Education (equipment, supplies, universities).
Environment (equipment, pollution control, technology, waste management).
Health care.

Oil and gas.
Power.
Sports and leisure.

Oman

Aerospace
Clothing.
Construction.
Creative and media.
Education.
Energy.
Environment.
Financial services.
Food and drink.

Health care.
Oil and gas.
Petrochemicals.
Ports.
Power
Recreation.
Telecommunications.
Tourism.
Training.
Water and sewerage.

Qatar

Aviation (aerospace, airport development, airports).
Construction.
Consumer goods.
Oil and gas.
Petrochemicals.
Power.
Sports and leisure.

Saudi Arabia

Aerospace.
Construction.
Consumer goods.
Creative and media.
Education and training.
Energy.
Engineering.
Environment.
Financial services.

Health care.
IT and electronics.
Leisure.
Mining.
Oil and gas.
Petrochemicals.
Safety/security.
Telecommunications.
Textiles.

United Arab Emirates

Business services.
Clothing.
Construction.
Education.
Energy.
Environment.
Financial services.

Health care.
Household goods.
Oil and gas.
Petrochemicals.
Recreation.
Telecommunications.

Exporters

The Arabian Peninsula Desk of the Overseas Trade Services of the Department of Trade and Industry (DTI) in London (Bay 507, Kingsgate House, 66-74 Victoria Street, London SW1E 6SW) and the regional Business Link offices (see below) offer help and information specifically for exporters in a number of ways. They are able to provide basic market information, commission status reports on specific companies and find suitable representatives for UK firms as well as giving current information on tariff rates and import procedures. Fees are charged for most of these services. Although this service will only be of use to those considering exporting to the Gulf, the DTI also publishes several booklets focused on exporting and the Gulf region, including *Gulf Spotlight* and *Exporting – Overseas Trade Services*, both of which are free of charge from the DTI. It can also advise on small businesses thinking of venturing into the Gulf.

Additionally, the DTI's Export and Information Centre Library at Room 150, 1st Floor, Ashdown House, 123 Victoria Street, London SW1; tel 020-7215 5444, is worth a visit for anyone researching into business opportunities in the Gulf. the library boasts a mine of statistical information and business and industry reports, as well as an extensive supply of Gulf *Yellow Pages*. The library is open from 9.30am-5.30pm, Monday to Friday, visitors may use the library at any time within these hours (you will have to sign in with a business address).

An alternative to the DTI's Arabian Peninsula Desk in London are the Business Link offices set up around the country as one-stop-shops for businesses. They can also advise on exporting to other countries including the Gulf. To find your nearest, look up Business Link in the telephone directory, or ring the Business Link Signpost Line: 0345-567765, or visit the website www.businesslink.co.uk.

A further useful source of information for exporters can be obtained by contacting the law firm, Nabarro Nathanson (50 Stratton Street, London W1X 6NX; tel 020-7493 9933; fax 020-7629 7900; Website www.nabarro.com), who publish a booklet, *An Exporter's Guide to Trading in the Gulf*, detailing all the legal aspects involved in trading in the Gulf region.

Running a Business

Employing Staff

The work force throughout the Arabian Peninsula consists mainly of Arab expatriate workers and Third Country Nationals (TCNs) from countries such as India, Pakistan, and the Philippines. There are also a substantial number of Europeans and American nationals with specialised expertise working throughout the Gulf. All the Gulf countries are currently pursuing programmes of nationalising their work forces, i.e. replacing foreign workers with their own citizens. The process is slow as the numbers of skilled local nationals with the qualifications required by certain positions is still relatively small, and so dependence upon professional western workers is still very high. Foreign companies looking to set-up business in the Gulf will often find that their contract requires them to employ a minimum number of local nationals, or indeed for positions needing skilled workers, employ local citizens over expatriate workers wherever possible. For positions requiring non-skilled workers, a cheap work force is on hand in the form of the TCNs.

The following is only a guide to key factors to bear in mind when employing staff in the Gulf region. It must be stressed that Labour Laws and regulations vary considerably from state to state and that to receive more detailed information on exactly what is involved in employing staff in any of the Gulf countries it would be best to contact the relevant regional Ministry of Labour (see below), or contact the regional Chamber of Commerce (see 'Useful Addresses' under *Preparation from Scratch* above).

Wages. Wages and salaries are usually agreed upon between the employer and employees. There is no requirement to pay employees either an annual bonus, or a share of profit, or end of service benefits, unless these benefits have been included in the employment contract.

Working Hours. A typical working week consists of eight hours per day, six days per week. This is reduced to four and six hours per day in the public and private sectors respectively during the month of Ramadan. Overtime should be paid at a minimum rate of time and a quarter (time and a half being more common) except on Fridays and public holidays when the minimum is time and a half. Hours will vary from country to country, and from job to job.

Holiday Entitlement. A statutory minimum of two weeks paid annual leave is due to employees with less than five years continuous service. After this period the minimum is four weeks per annum. In practice the amount of leave granted in a year varies greatly depending upon the employer. The employer, usually being a sponsor, is liable to pay all expatriate workforce air fares to the home country on engagement and termination.

Trade Unions. No trade unions exist in any of the Gulf countries. Strikes and lockouts are prohibited. Any employer-employee disputes will initially be handled by the regional Ministry of Labour and Social Affairs. Appeals can then be taken to court if so desired.

Useful Addresses

General Organisation for Social Insurance: PO Box 5319, Manama, **Bahrain**; tel +973 532222; fax +973 530209.

Ministry of Labour & Social Affairs: PO Box 32333, Manama, **Bahrain**; tel +973 687800; fax +973 686954.

Ministry of Social Affairs & Labour: PO Box 563, Safat, 13001 **Kuwait**; tel +965 246 6300; fax +965 242 1412.

Ministry of Social Affairs & Labour: PO Box 560, Muscat 113, **Sultanate of Oman**; tel +968 602444.

Ministry of Labour, Social Affairs & Housing: PO Box 201, Doha, **Qatar**; tel +974 321955; fax +974 328666.

Ministry of Labour & Social Affairs: Riyadh 11157, **Saudi Arabia**; tel +966 1 477 1480; fax +966 1 478 3653.

Department of Economic Development: PO Box 13223, Dubai, **UAE**; tel +971 4 222 9922; fax +971 4 222 5577.

Taxation

The following is a guide to the taxation on corporate income and profits in the individual Gulf states. More detailed information can be obtained by contacting one of the accountancy firms listed below.

BAHRAIN

In the state of Bahrain there are no taxes on income, sales, capital gains, or estates. The only exception to this are some specific taxes levied on oil-producing and exploration companies. There are no taxes or withholding taxes on interest, dividends, fees, or other remittances. Companies can transfer accumulated profits and capital without restrictions.

A yearly commercial registration fee, which varies according to the business activity and the form of the company, is payable by all companies.

KUWAIT

Businesses in Kuwait that are 100 per cent Kuwaiti-owned are not liable to any corporate tax. Income tax is only levied on the profits and capital gains of foreign corporate bodies (which includes foreign partnerships, such as firms of lawyers or engineering or management consultants) carrying out business and trade in Kuwait, directly or through an agent, or conducting a business or trade in Kuwait as an agent of others. Carrying out trade or business includes: purchases and sales in Kuwait and maintaining a permanent place of business in the state where contracts for such purposes and sales are executed (other than just purchases of properties, goods or services in Kuwait); operation of any industrial or commercial project in Kuwait; rental of properties in Kuwait; provision of services in Kuwait.

Tax on corporate income is based on the 'slab' principle – the whole amount of profit is taxed at the highest rate. See table below for current rates.

Taxable Income (KD)

Above	Below	Percentage Rate
0	5,250	0
5,250	18,750	5
18,750	37,500	10
37,500	56,250	15
56,250	75,000	20
75,000	112,500	25
112,500	150,000	30
150,000	225,000	35
225,000	300,000	40
300,000	375,000	45
375,000		55

The law allows a degree of leeway when the taxable income is marginally over the preceding slab amount. Total profit for the year is taxed at a single rate applicable to the relevant taxable income band.

Other Taxes

Customs duties. The standard customs duty is 4 per cent on the c.i.f (cost, insurance, freight) value of goods. Occasionally a higher duty, generally 15 per cent, is imposed to protect local industry. Foreigners whose activity is confined to exporting goods to Kuwait are not subject to income tax.

Export Tax. An export tax of 4 per cent is charged on all goods that have not been subject to import duty.

Foundation for Scientific Research. A fee of 2 per cent of the net profit of Kuwait's shareholding companies is payable to the Kuwait Foundation for Scientific Research.

Deductions

All expenses other than capital outlays, incurred in the conduct of a business or trade, wherever incurred, are deductible, provided that the expenditure is supported by full documentation.

Tax Incentives

Inward investment. The following incentives may be granted to new and existing industries by the Industrial Development Committee of the Ministry of Trades and Commerce:

• Nominal taxes or no taxes for other than oil companies and tax holidays of up to ten years. This does not apply to contracting companies. It is aimed at encouraging companies introducing new technology to Kuwait.

• No restrictions on repatriation of profits, fees, capital, salaries, or other monies.

- Exemption from customs duties on machinery and raw materials required for approved projects.

Capital Investment. There are no particular incentives for capital investment other than those for inward investment detailed above.

Withholding Taxes

There are no withholding taxes. However, a Ministerial Order issued in 1985, dictates that the final payment due to a contractor or sub-contractor is withheld until presentation of a certificate from the Ministry of Finance confirming that the company concerned has settled all of its tax liabilities. The final payment should be no less than 5 per cent of the total contract value.

Tax Treaties. Kuwait has double taxation treaties with the People's Republic of China, Cyprus, Ethiopia, France, Germany, Hungary, Italy, and Romania. In 1999 treaties were also signed with Indonesia, Switzerland, and the United Kingdom. Some of these treaties exempt supplies in a supply and installation contract from Kuwait taxation and additionally provide for total tax exemption on construction-related contracts if the total duration is less than a stipulated period of 6 to 12 months.

OMAN

The Omani government have recently changed the rates of tax applicable to corporate entities, with a view to encouraging foreign investment. The new rates detailed below are applicable for the tax year 1999 and following years.

100 per cent Omani-owned companies, majority-owned Omani companies, investment funds set up under the Capital Market Law, and public joint stock companies listed on the MSM (Muscat Securities Market), will be liable to the following tax rates:

Net Income OR	Percentage Rates
First 30,000	0
Above 30,000	12

Companies with over 49 per cent but less than 100 per cent foreign ownership will be subject to the following rates of tax:

Net Income OR	Percentage Rates
First 30,000	0
Next 100,000	15
Next 150,000	20
Next 280,000	25

Companies with 100 per cent foreign ownership will be charged tax at the rates listed below. Tax is assessed either by applying the percentage relative to the bracket in which the taxable income falls, or by applying the percentage of the bracket for taxable income immediately below that in which the taxable income falls and adding the excess of taxable income to the result. The lower total is the tax payable.

Special provisions are applicable to the taxation of income derived from the sale of petroleum. The tax rate specified for such companies is 55 per cent. However, in practice the tax on such activities is governed by the individual Exploration and Production Sharing Agreement entered into between the Omani government and the company engaged in the sale of petroleum.

Taxable Income (OR)

Above	Under	Percentage Rate
0	5,000	0
5,000	18,000	5
18,000	35,000	10
35,000	55,000	15
55,000	75,000	20
75,000	100,000	25
100,000	200,000	30
200,000	300,000	35
300,000	400,000	40
400,000	500,000	45
500,000		50

Other Taxes

No other taxes are charged on sales or profits other than the withholding taxes covered below.

Tax Incentives

An amendment made in 1996, stipulates that companies engaged primarily in the following activities are exempt from tax: industry and mining; export of products manufactured or processed locally; promotion of tourism, including operating hotels and tourist villages other than under management contracts; agriculture and animal husbandry and the processing of agricultural produce; fishing and fish processing; implementation of public utilities projects other than under management or construction contracts.

The exemption is valid for a duration of five years form the date of start-up of production or the practice of activities and may be liable to such conditions as the Minister of Commerce and Industry may specify. The exemption is renewable for a period not in excess of five years, subject to approval by the Financial Affairs and Energy Resources Council.

Foreign companies engaged in oil and gas exploration activities, while subject to tax under the law, generally have their tax obligations discharged by the government under the conditions of the Exploration and Production Sharing Agreement.

Foreign companies employed in government ventures considered to be of national importance have been known to negotiate a tax protection clause whereby any tax paid by them is reimbursed by the government.

Withholding Taxes & Tax Treaties

Withholding tax was introduced under an amendment made effective from November 1996. Foreign companies that do not have a permanent set-up in Oman for tax purposes and that derive income from Oman by way of royalties, management fees, rental of equipment or machinery, transfer of technical expertise, or research and development, are now liable to withholding tax at 10 per cent of gross income from such sources. Such tax must be withheld by the Omani-based company and paid to the tax department within fourteen days of the end of the month in which tax is deducted or payments are due or made to the foreign company.

Currently, the Sultanate of Oman has a comprehensive double taxation treaty only with France, India, and the United Kingdom. Agreements relating to air transport income also exist with various other countries, including India, Jordan, Kuwait. Tax credit is permitted by certain countries, for instance, Germany, Italy, the United Kingdom, and the United States, in respect of tax paid by foreign business bodies in Oman.

QATAR

The income and profits of foreign corporations operating in Qatar and, in the case of a joint venture, the foreign venturer's share of the joint venture profit, are subject to taxation. Income and profits can be charged on the profits of any corporate entity, wherever incorporated, conducting a trade or business in Qatar, although in practice, tax is not presently levied on any corporate entity that is Qatari-owned. A partnership is deemed by the tax authorities to be a corporate entity. From March 1 1989, it was decided that all citizens from the Gulf Cooperative Council (GCC) countries were to be treated as Qatari citizens.

Current rates of tax are as follows:

Taxable Income (QR)

Above	Under	Tax on Upper Limit (QR)	Percentage Rate
0	100,000	–	0
100,000	500,000	50,000	10
500,000	1,000,000	150,000	15
1,000,000	1,500,000	300,000	20
1,500,000	2,500,000	625,000	25
2,500,000	5,000,000	1,500,000	30
5,000,000			35

Other Taxes

There are no other taxes, apart from customs duty charged on certain imports.

Tax Incentives

On the whole, there are no applicable tax incentives, however, the emir may grant certain tax exemptions. Applications for tax exemptions can be made to the Tax Exemption Committee. Factors taken into consideration which may influence the acceptance of an application include:

*   If the venture contributes to supporting agriculture, communications, industry, land reclamation, mining, oil, tourism, trade, or any activity or project needed by the state and is beneficial to the state economically or socially, regardless of whether the venture is wholly owned by individuals, companies or corporations, or whether it is owned by Qataris, by a joint venture, or wholly by foreigners.
*   If the venture is in line with the aims of the economic development plan and has gained the approval of the relevant governmental authorities.
*   If the venture contributes to national economic growth with due regard to the following: commercial profit; degree of integration with other projects; degree of reliance of the project on the production material available in the country; degree of its effect on the trade balance or the balance of payments.
*   If the venture is to result in the introduction of modern technologies.
*   If the venture is to result in the creation of employment opportunities for Omani nationals.

Withholding Taxes

None.

SAUDI ARABIA

Income tax in Saudi Arabia is only levied on foreign owned companies at the rates tabled below. Saudi nationals (and nationals of other GCC countries, who are deemed as Saudi nationals for Saudi tax purposes) are subject to Zakat, an Islamic direct tax on net worth. In cases where a company is owned by both Saudi and non-Saudi investors, the share of taxable income attributed to the non-Saudi interest is liable to income tax, and the Saudi portion undergoes Zakat taxation.

Taxable Income (SR)	Percentage Tax Rate
First 100,000	25
Next 400,000	35
Next 500,000	40
Thereafter	45

Taxes on imputed profits for non-resident payments. When companies registered in Saudi Arabia make payments to non-resident companies, the Saudi tax authorities usually hold the Saudi-based company responsible for taxes on such payments as agent of the recipient. This procedure is applicable to payments for plant and equipment rentals, insurance premiums, payments to sub-contractors, professional services, management fees, and royalties. Assessment of Saudi taxes on these payments is on an arbitrary basis, with the minimum profit imputed at 15 per cent of the payments. The 15 per cent imputed profit rate is usually applied for insurance premiums, but higher profit rates may be imputed on other forms of income, especially fees for consultants' services and management fees. Royalties are normally considered as 100 per cent taxable to the recipient. The domestic company is subject to taxes relating to these foreign payments even if it enjoys a tax holiday on its own Saudi profits (see 'Tax Incentives' below).

Other Taxes

No value added tax system exists in Saudi Arabia, nor is there any form of stamp, transfer, excise, sales, turnover, production, real estate, or property taxation except insofar as they may fall within the scope of Zakat, which is applicable only to Saudi companies and individuals.

Tax Incentives

Inward Investments. The following incentives may be granted to certain eligible companies which have gained the approval of the Saudi government:

* A ten year tax holiday for agricultural and manufacturing ventures, and a five year tax holiday for other economic ventures who have the approval of the Foreign Capital Investment Committee, provided there is a minimum of 25 per cent Saudi participation throughout the venture period.
* No limitations on repatriation of profits, fees, capital, salaries, or other monies.
* Low interest or interest free loans up to 80 per cent of fixed costs for agricultural ventures of less than SR 3 million, and up to 40 per cent for agricultural ventures in excess of SR 3 million.
* Sites for the construction of plant and industrial buildings and housing for the workforce at nominal rents.
* Exemption from customs duties on machinery and raw materials needed for approved projects.
* Tariff protection for local products.

Capital Investment. No particular incentives are available for capital investment other than those listed under 'Inward Investment' above.

Withholding Taxes & Tax Treaties

Officially no withholding taxes as such exist in Saudi Arabia. However, a company making certain kinds of payments (see 'Taxes on imputed profits for non-resident payments' above) is deemed to be responsible for the tax liability of the recipient and, accordingly, is obliged to retain the tax at the corporate rate on the deemed-profit element. This retained tax is due and payable at the time the company's own tax is due, namely, two and one-half months after its year-close. There is no requirement to withhold tax on payments of dividends.

Saudi Arabia has no double taxation treaties with other countries, with the exception of France with whom it shares a limited tax agreement.

UNITED ARAB EMIRATES

Despite the existence of income tax decrees in most emirates (including Abu Dhabi, Dubai, and Sharjah), these decrees have not yet been enforced. Corporate taxation is restricted to oil-producing companies and branches of foreign banks. The rulers of each emirate set the rates of taxation on oil-producing companies, and rates vary between emirates and between companies, according to the conditions of the different production concession agreements.

Foreign-owned banks are liable to tax, according to the type of licence under which they operate in the emirates of Abu Dhabi, Dubai, and Sharjah. The applicable rate of tax is 20 per cent of the profit earned in the respective emirate, as revealed by the audited accounts, adjusted, in the case of the Dubai emirate, to limit head office and regional office expenses to a maximum of 2.5 per cent of gross income, and to restrict allowances for loan losses to specific dubious items. General provision for loan losses is not a tax-deductible expense (this also applies in the case of the Sharjah emirate). There are limitations on the carry forward of losses for the branches of foreign banks. In Dubai and Sharjah, tax losses can be carried forward for only two years. In Abu Dhabi, losses can be carried forward and utilised against profits for one year in every five.

Useful Addresses

Coopers & Lybrand Jawad Habib: UGB Tower, 5th Floor, Diplomatic Area, Manama, Bahrain; tel +973 530077; fax +973 530088.

PricewaterhouseCoopers: KIC Building, Opposite Al Ahli Bank, Safat 13062, Kuwait; tel +965 2408844; fax +965 2408855.

Coopers & Lybrand: Hatat House, Suites 205-210, PO Box 3075, PC 112, Ruwi, Sultanate of Oman; tel +968 563717; fax +968 564408.

Al Juraid & Company: 10th Floor, North Tower, King Faisal Foundation Building, PO Box 8282, Riyadh 11482, Saudi Arabia; tel +966 1 465 4240; fax +966 1 465 1663.

PricewaterhouseCoopers: Suite 303, City Tower 2, Shaikh Zayed Road, PO Box 11987, Dubai, UAE; tel +971 4 321919; fax +971 4 321572.

Accountancy & Legal Advice

Accountants are well placed to offer a wide range of advice, and introduce you to Gulf firms with which they have made contact. Large accountancy firms will be able to advise you from scratch. What is the best vehicle for your business: should you set up a partnership, a corporation, a branch? They will take into account the size of the business that you wish to set up, and the nature of the product. They will advise on the best location, from the point of view of taxation regimes in different areas, infrastructure, and all the available regional and state grant funding and investment incentives. Any accountant advising on Gulf business should be well-informed on all the options for location and incorporation. Depending on your level of knowledge of the Gulf, there is no doubt that it is best to start with a firm in your own country (list of addresses under *Accountants* and *Taxation* above). Legal advice on all aspects of your set-up can be sought from regional or international law firms located in the Gulf.

Useful Addresses

British Law Firms with offices in the Gulf:
Allen & Overy: One New Change, London EC4M 9QQ; tel 020-7330 3000; fax 020-7330 9999; Dubai office.
Berrymans Lace Mawer: Salisbury House, London Wall, London EC2M 5QN; tel 020-7638 2811; Dubai office.
Clifford Chance: 200 Aldersgate Street, London EC1A 4JJ; tel 020-7600 1000; fax 020-7282 7071; Dubai office.
Clyde & Co.: 51 Eastcheap, London EC3M 1JP; tel 020-7623 1244; fax 020-7623 5427; Dubai office.
Denton Hall: 5 Chancery Lane, Clifford's Inn, London EC4A 1BU; tel 020-7242 1212; fax 020-7404 0087; Abu Dhabi, Dubai, and Oman, offices.
Hill Taylor Dickinson: Irongate House, Duke's Place, London EC3A 7LP; tel 020-7283 9033; fax 020-7283 1144; Dubai office.
Nabarro Nathanson: 50 Stratton Street, London W1X 6NX; tel 020-7493 9933; fax 020-7629 7900; Website www.nabarro.com. Publish *An Exporter's Guide to Trading in the Gulf: Legal Aspects.*
Norton Rose: Kempson House, Camomile Street, London EC3A 7AN; tel 020-7283 6000; fax 020-7283 6500; Bahrain office.
Richards Butler: Beaufort House, 15 Botolph Street, London EC3A 7EE; tel 020-7247 6555; fax 020-7247 5091; Abu Dhabi, Oman, and Qatar offices.
Simmons & Simmons: 21 Wilson Street, London EC2M 2TX; tel 020-7628 2020; fax 020-7628 2070; Abu Dhabi office.
Trowers & Hamlins: Sceptre Court, 40 Tower Hill, London EC3N 4 DX; tel 020-7423 8000; fax 020-7423 8001; Abu Dhabi, Bahrain, Dubai, and Oman offices.

Law Firms in the Gulf:
Afridi & Angell: PO Box 9371, Dubai, UAE; tel +971 4 310900; fax +971 4 310800. Offices also in Abu Dhabi and Sharjah, in the UAE, and New York City in the USA.
Al Mahmood & Zu'bi: Suite No 1, 3rd Floor, Bab El Bahrain Building, PO Box 502, Manama, Bahrain; tel +973 225151; fax +973 224744; e-mail almazubi@batelco.com.bh
The Law Office of Al-Essa, Al-Bader & Partners: PO Box 4207, Safat 13043, Kuwait; tel +965 243 8020/1/2; fax +965 243 2272.
Mansoor Jamal & Co.: Salalah House, 6th Floor, Muttrah Business District, PO Box 686, Ruwi, PC 112, Sultanate of Oman; tel +968 706612; fax +968 704579; e-mail mj-co@gto.net.om
Law Offices of Gebran Majdalany: PO Box 4004, Doha, Qatar; tel +974 428899; fax +974 417817; e-mail tariq@qatar.net.qa
Dr Audhali Law Firm: PO Box 1158, Al-Khobar 31952, Saudi Arabia; tel +966 3 864 3011; fax +966 3 894 5837.
Almihdar Law Firm: PO Box 1180, Jeddah 21431, Saudi Arabia; tel +966 2 687 4909; fax +966 2 687 9668.
Key & Dixon: PO Box 33675, Dubai, UAE; tel +971 4 590096; fax +971 4 590029; e-mail keydixon@emirates.net.ae

APPENDIX I

Personal Case Histories

BAHRAIN

Mary Sayer

Mary first arrived in Bahrain when she was 23, to work in the Regency Intercontinental hotel. At that time Bahrain's economy was strained and she was unfortunately made redundant 15 months later. She then changed her career and worked within a company that specialised in preparing and training young Bahraini nationals for the world of work. She worked as marketing manager before the company went bankrupt 18 months later. After that she worked very briefly for a bank as an Executive Secretary but did not enjoy it. She then trained to become a teacher of English as a Foreign Language. Five years later she is now employed as an educational advisor and teaches English on top of her normal working hours.

What were your first impressions of Bahrain?
I left London in the middle of February when it was cold, wet and generally miserable. I arrived in Bahrain in the middle of Ramadan but what first struck me was the weather. It was warm and dry. Bahrain is a small island and you are never very far away from the sea. I was made to feel very welcome in Bahrain within the first month. It was strange adapting to a different culture especially during Ramadan when everything is turned upside down. Initially I was surprised at how civilised Bahrain actually was, somehow I was expecting to arrive in the heart of the desert, in the middle of the 1950s. Bahrain is now a very modern state with everything you have in the western world. The layout of the shopping areas and souqs may be different but they are far more enjoyable to ramble around than the newer modern shopping malls that have developed in the last two years.

How are women treated in Bahrain?
One thing that I found strange was that women were treated differently here. I knew about Muslim culture before I arrived and did expect to find life a little difficult but I was surprised to find out that you are treated like a lady everywhere. There are separate queues in the post office, banks, etc. where you are served first. Working as a woman is different and you do have to forget the attitude you have in the western world, where we expect to be treated equally and there are laws for discrimination. Bahrain is probably one of the most liberal countries in the Gulf where women are able to work in almost all fields, however, do not expect to be sheltered from laws as companies do openly discriminate against sex, age, and race. I remember when I first started working in the hotel and I helped clear tables and take food orders out. I had men running from all angles to assist me and they thought it very strange indeed that a manager, let alone a female one, should be lifting their fingers to carry anything.

I came from a large London hotel where women were in key positions and arrived in Bahrain to find out that I was the only woman manager in the Food and

Beverage department and the youngest in the hotel. I am pleased to say that five years on more women are working and several of them hold senior positions in a variety of companies. It is very pleasing to see that daughters are being given the same opportunities for education and development as sons. The new emir is working to give women a greater role in society. However, working within Bahrain can be very frustrating as progression is not always on your ability to do the actual job but more on the length of service to the company. You often have to deal with people who are clueless about business but have been in the same position for 15 years.

What problems should those doing business in Bahrain anticipate?
Dealing with any government body does take time. Bahrain operates very much on a 'Wasta' basis (i.e. knowing someone with influence who can help you achieve what you want to achieve, someone with wasta is someone with power) and very often it is the only way to actually get anything done. In business it can take months for a decision to be made on anything – this is because there are so many committees, sub-committees and one person holding the actual power to approve anything, but once the decision has been made things move very quickly.

Have you faced any major difficulties since you have been in Bahrain?
The one major difficulty I had was within the first three months of arriving in Bahrain I was in the process of getting my residence and work permit. UK nationals in the past could get in and out of Bahrain without needing visas or entry certificates. I soon learnt that there are restrictions on how some countries view your nationality. I am half-Ugandan and was actually born in Uganda and was therefore Ugandan in the local authority eyes and not British. The fact that I have only ever held a UK passport and was brought up in England was irrelevant. This caused me a great deal of personal distress and changed my ability to get in and out of Bahrain. Since then I have changed my sponsorship several times with no difficulty. In addition to this *all* nationalities now have to have an entrance and exit visa for Bahrain.

What do you think of Bahrain and its people?
Bahrainis themselves are the most pleasant of people. They are genuine and very polite, although there is a very wide gap between those who have and those who have not. There is a high level of English spoken in Bahrain so it is possible to communicate with everyone. The social life in Bahrain is fantastic, because people do not pay taxes there is more money to spend on social activities. There are a hive of clubs to suit all tastes and so many restaurants and bars to choose from. Bahrain is very liberal and although it is a Muslim country, there are no constraints on drinking. People tend to make close friendships quickly here, as it is very much a transient society. Weekends can be a two-day, one and a half days or one-day affair, depending on whom you work for. The summer months tend to be *extremely* hot and outdoor activity is limited.

What is the accommodation situation like in Bahrain?
Accommodation is never a problem here. Often when you first arrive your company will provide you with accommodation or an agent to find suitable villas/houses or flats. Rents can be rather high in certain places but there is no shortage in finding excellent accommodation to suit every budget. Houses/flats tend to be more luxurious than those back in the UK and it does not take long to adjust to your new surroundings. Domestic help is very common and very cheap as well. Many families will employ someone to look after the house and the children while both

parents work. Settling into Bahrain does not take too long once you have found somewhere to live. Buying cars is easy, although the standard of driving does take some getting use to. Overall the standard of living is very high and hard to give up.

Is there anything that you dislike about living in Bahrain?
One thing even after five years that I dislike about Bahrain is the weekend visitor from Saudi Arabia. I am not talking about the expats taking a quick 'R&R' (rest and relaxation) but the Saudis who come over in their droves to hit the nearest liquor stores and buy copious amounts of Black Label and Bud then wander around the cheaper hotels leering at the stage acts. Even to this date I get frustrated with their horrendous driving ability, and the fact that they think any woman not in an *abaya* is a prostitute and will treat you as such. It is a saving grace that the Bahraini men accept Western women as part of the island and will respect you.

KUWAIT

Jane Thomas

Jane is 39, and has been living in Kuwait for the past six years. She came here with her husband and two sons. Her husband is in the oil industry. Initially, she did not work as the children were young when they arrived, but she was approached by one of the largest regional companies to do some writing for them. She had connections with this organisation in London when she had her own business in a different field. After a trial article, they retained her and as the children started playgroup and then school, she took on more and more work. She now works for one of the major five star hotels, and the original company in addition to advertising agencies and others. The work is mostly writing magazine articles and editing text translated from Arabic into English.

What are the main difficulties encountered in moving to Kuwait?
There is an amazing amount of red tape, and the rules and regulations seem to change and vary for no particular reason. Be prepared to spend up to a month completing spouse and children's paperwork. All potential residents will need to undergo an Aids test, chest X-ray for TB and blood group test in Kuwait. Most of these tests will be done at opposite ends of the city. Most companies employ a full time person who helps with this process. Drivers will need to be fingerprinted and take eye tests – but British nationals do not need to take a driving test. What is most frustrating is the constant waiting and standing in line before discovering that the formalities are no longer handled in a particular office. British nationals on the whole are processed quicker and more easily than Asian and Philippine nationals. There is still a feeling of gratitude for our part in the Gulf War and often – though *not always* – things can be done quicker for us. Be warned, if you arrive in June, July or August temperatures can reach around fifty degrees centigrade, but usually without humidity.

What is the situation like for women in Kuwait?
Women work, drive, and suffer little discrimination here. Many Kuwaiti women hold senior posts, and so there are no problems in the workplace. Women can choose their style of dress, and the majority respect local traditions and tend not to wear too short skirts or shorts in public places (other than beach clubs). Generally women keep their shoulders and tops of the arms covered, but not everyone does this. There are incidents of youths following western women in their cars, but this is rarely more than a game for bored youths and driving to a hotel or police station

or somewhere public usually ends the game. In the main, women are treated with respect and if you break down, cars stop immediately and mobile phones are offered to you. I have not heard of anyone experiencing anything but concern and help in this situation. Crime is low and generally women feel safe – of course like anywhere there are the occasional incidents. Kuwait allows Christians to worship in their own churches and there are a number of different churches. At Christmas and Easter the shops are full of Santas, Christmas Trees, etc./Easter eggs, bunnies etc. Learning Arabic would be useful, but is not at all essential and possibly most expats never learn more than a few words. English is widely used and many Kuwaitis have had a US/UK college education. There are two major English newspapers which provide good and relatively free coverage of local and international news.

How easy is it to find work in Kuwait?
For women accompanying their husbands, most end up as teachers or those unqualified, as teaching assistants. Others take secretarial posts. Finding work is not too difficult, but depends on qualifications. Many like myself work from home. For husbands accompanying wives (rare due to visa requirements here) many find work pretty quickly.

What is there to do socially in Kuwait?
Like many expat postings there is an active social life. Societies abound – Caledonians, Welsh, Australian, Indian, Philippine, theatre and choral groups, darts, etc. Scuba diving, sailing and other water sports are popular, and there are a couple of beach clubs with swimming pools and nice beaches. Most of the hotels have health clubs and tennis facilities. Many Kuwaitis and some of the companies have beach houses along the coast which are popular for weekends (Thursday and Fridays – most people have a two day weekend – though not all – and in the banking and certain international sectors the weekend is on a Friday and Saturday). Horse riding is also popular and many enjoy watching camel racing in the winter months. Many enjoy camping and days out in the desert or boating out on the Gulf or exploring the islands.

What do you like least and most about Kuwait?
Probably the biggest drawback to life in Kuwait (and most agree on this) is the driving. The roads are full of high performance cars driven at amazing speed and the result is a high level of road fatalities. The local taxis drive with little regard for others, rarely indicating or checking before pulling out. There is a strange mixture of fast cars and old bangers driven by poorly paid workers – neither indicates if it is going to pull over or out or just stop on the hard shoulder. Cars over- and undertake and cut in and out at high speed on our three or four lane highways which intersect the city. The heat in the summer months can be draining even though people do acclimatise. The other difficulty is honouring contracts, and many find their pay is late, or parts of their contracts are not honoured – we have seen quite a few friends leave for this reason. There is a feeling that if you are not happy, go, and a replacement for you can be found easily – this happens even in senior posts and occasionally happens to Kuwaitis themselves. Kuwait does have labour laws and these should protect you, but things can take a great deal of time to resolve, and relations between employee and employer are then so soured that returning to your job is not an option.

However, for most, Kuwait is an enjoyable posting. It is child friendly, has good schools, little crime, beaches, nowhere takes more than twenty minutes by car, and the Kuwaitis are friendly. Unlike other parts of the Gulf, expats have the opportunity to meet and make strong friendships with Kuwaitis – spending time in their homes, beach chalets, etc. Their hospitality is warm and generous. They have a reputation for not working very hard (in many cases only turning up for a couple of hours work a day) since their oil wealth arrived – and this fact is regularly highlighted in the press by Kuwaiti commentators – but old fashioned traditions of hospitality have not been lost. Residents enjoy a good standard of living with well stocked American-style supermarkets offering greater choice than supermarkets in the UK, and generally better quality. Kuwaitis demand the best of everything and a wide choice. In the six years we have been here we have never been able to get British beef (only Irish and American) because even pre-BSE, Kuwaitis found standards were not high enough when they visited farms and slaughterhouses in the UK (so one supermarket manager told me but this could just be local gossip). Most of the British shops – Debenhams, Mothercare, Laura Ashley, BHS, etc. and the US shops and fast-food restaurants are represented – so there is little you can't buy here.

Advice to those moving to Kuwait.
All belongings in your shipment will be searched, and often boxes and packing are cut open with knives with little concern for your property – so if something is particularly fragile or special – do not put it in your freight consignment. Naturally, alcohol is forbidden, and all videos are subject to censure (even children's videos will be taken to be checked) – so bring them in your hand luggage. Do as many of the vaccinations for children before you arrive, as your children cannot get residency unless they have all of them (otherwise they will need to have this done in a government clinic here). This includes BCG (anti-tuberculosis vaccine) which is given shortly after birth here. Spouses wishing to work will often need original copies of their degree certificates. Spouses can work if they agree to go under the sponsorship of their employer, and have to briefly leave the country (usually to Bahrain) and return on the new visa. When you arrive here it is worth taking the time to look for property because it is a renter's market with falling numbers of western expatriates. There are many landlords with empty properties, and some are more amenable to negotiation on price than others. There are many American and British schools which provide excellent education and achieve high results. There is one American School which has most of the children of American expats, and one British school, which only takes children up to age 13 and caters mainly for children of western expatriates – it is the only British school which takes the SATS tests at Key Stage 1 and Key Stage 4. The rest of the English and American schools have fewer western children, but offer the same or higher standards, and equivalent or superior facilities.

Ted & Mary Granger

Ted and Mary left America, wanting to raise their two small children in a country where life is lead at a slower pace and where they could gain an appreciation of another culture. They are both educators and attended an international recruitment fair, where they were offered teaching jobs in Kuwait.

What were your first impressions on arrival in Kuwait?
We arrived in August and found Kuwait to be very hot and dry. The desertscape seemed very brown. Luckily, the school employing us helped with all of the visa requirements. However, it was still a shock to go to the public medical facilities for the routine measures (i.e. complete health check including X-rays and HIV tests). Kuwait has impressive modern architecture, but the medical facilities and practices reminded us that we were 'not in Kansas' anymore!

How would you describe the standard of living?
The standard of living is good. Most western products can be purchased in Kuwait with the exception of pork, alcohol, and any books/videos/magazines that are not 'pure'. These products are available in abundance and can be found in many Kuwaiti homes, but they are not sold in stores. Prices are average for some local items and bargain for services. Imported items can be pricey.

What do you find are the major differences between Kuwaitis and Westerners?
There is a definite sense of a caste system in Kuwait. One can read about a Kuwaiti beating a Filipino maid to death and receiving a week in jail. However, if an unmarried Filipino maid is caught in an adulterous situation (with another unmarried non-Kuwaiti), she can receive up to ten years in jail. Kuwaitis are never at fault when in traffic accidents with non-Kuwaitis, etc.

Two major differences between Kuwaitis and westerners are the style of communication and family honour. Kuwaitis tend to be agreeable in business transactions, whether they intend to honour the agreement made or not. Westerners tend to be more direct and state when they won't be able to agree. In terms of family honour, it is important to maintain the name of the family sometimes at the cost of personal integrity. Lying is justified if it keeps the family from being dishonoured. Rarely does one read of a Kuwaiti dying of suicide, drug overdose, etc. These stories are changed before going to print, to preserve family honour.

Advice to those moving to Kuwait.
For families moving to Kuwait: we found it easier and more economical to purchase the children's clothes, Christmas presents, etc. and bring them with us. Holiday decorations (aside from Christmas) can be difficult to find. Also, it helps to remember that Kuwait went 'from an 1800s to 2000 mentality with the discovery of oil.' While the country appears very western, there is still in evidence much of the traditional Bedouin value system and thinking. Like any warm climate, it's important to avoid being out in the heat mid-day from May-September and to drink plenty of water.

It might be difficult for single people to live in Kuwait, if they look forward to an active nightlife as there isn't much of one! However, be sure to try the great Arabic and Indian food. Look for the restaurant named 'Canary' for economical and bountiful Arabic basics!

OMAN

Anne and Michael Collins

Anne and Michael Collins are in their sixties and intend retiring at the end of the present academic year after working abroad as teachers for almost forty years. Michael teaches English as a Foreign Language and Anne teaches Mathematics. They have worked in Turkey (where they first met), Tanzania, Saudi Arabia, Malawi and currently Oman. This is their seventh year in Oman. Their three children, now adult, were born abroad and educated in Tanzania, Saudi Arabia and Britain.

Why did you choose to work in Oman?
We were recruited to come to Oman by a British agency CfBT to work in a new, all age range private school for Omani children. We saw the advertisement in the Times Educational Supplement. The school needed native speakers of English to teach Maths, Science and English. All other subjects are taught in Arabic. The boys department of the school had many problems and Mike resigned and returned to

Britain after one year but some months later returned to Oman to teach at Sultan Qaboos University. I remained at the school. We both have single status contracts. Both our contracts make provision for medical care at a specific hospital but Muscat has many good private doctors and dentists should we need them.

What impression do you have of the country?

Oman seems to us to be the most attractive of the Gulf countries with interesting mountain scenery and a wonderful long coastline. It has been brought carefully into the modern world by the present Sultan but is still developing. Our first and lasting impression of Muscat, the capital where we work, is of a very clean, tidy, attractively landscaped city with few high rise buildings, good roads and in a very interesting location between the sea and stark rocky mountains. There is an old souk and scenic waterfront.

What difficulties did you encounter, if any?

We did not encounter any major difficulties in coming here since visas and other red tape was sorted out for us by our employer and sponsor. It is not really possible to come here to work without first having a job. A non-working spouse will be given a non-working visa which will have to be changed if they subsequently find full-time work. It is not easy to change jobs as you need a letter of release from your sponsor to do so and these are not willingly given. Work available locally e.g. secretarial work is poorly paid. Good jobs are few and far between. We were pleased to come to Oman, having long wanted to see it. However, salaries in education are low here and it would be difficult to make ends meet if we had our children with us.

What is the accommodation like?

Accommodation is generally good, often in new apartment buildings. Mike has a two-bedroomed bachelor house on the university campus which is about 40km outside the city and I have a furnished two-bedroomed flat supplied by my school in the city. (We get together often). Both our employers do allow teachers to opt for a housing allowance and find their own accommodation. There are plenty of places to rent, the cheaper places being further out of town.

What does Oman have to offer its expatriate residents?

While Muscat is not a shoppers' paradise like Dubai, most things are available here. At this end of the Gulf prices are higher as imported goods have further to come. Cars are a bargain compared to Britain and many expatriates, including us, have large 4WD vehicles in order to explore the country off-road. BHS and Mothercare have branches in Muscat. Good tailors are available and it is easy to get clothes made.

Mike and I belong to a sports club at one of the large hotels in order to use the swimming pool. I go several times a week. We belong to the Oman Historical Association and have been to some interesting lectures and on some interesting trips with them. Most sporting interests are catered for and there are some other groups for those with an interest in drama, music, Scottish dancing, gardening, and probably other topics. Muscat has less night life than Dubai or Abu Dhabi but the bigger hotels do have bars with live music groups. There are two or three public cinemas. There are many restaurants of all kinds including well known fast-food chains.

Although we teach Omanis, very few of our colleagues are from this country and we do not have much opportunity to get to know the local people socially.

Living in Oman is very easy, we really enjoy it. Any stress is usually work-related and never to do with the place. We particularly like the opportunity the country gives for exploring some beautiful natural features – the mountains, the desert and the coastline. It is easy to camp out in the wild. The winter climate is ideal. May to November is not so good and the mid-summer months can be very hot indeed but that is when we take our leave.

What is the situation like for women living in Oman?
Oman is one of the easier Islamic countries for western women to live in. Women can drive, should dress conservatively but do not have to completely cover up, can eat alone in restaurants and are generally not hassled. Many single women do work here and enjoy it.

Advice to others considering moving to Oman.
My advice to anyone offered a good job in Oman is to take it. Almost everyone likes the country. If you are coming here to teach in a school check your contract carefully. Ask what the teaching hours will be and what extra time you may be required to put in. Arabs do not plan far in advance and you can find a last minute weekend or evening duty assigned to you. Insist that you are sent an air ticket for first arrival. Don't agree to buying your own ticket for reimbursement later. It is a very different education system. Keep in mind that you are in another culture and it is 'their game, their rules' and you are not going to be able to change much.

QATAR

Louise & Angus Gray

Louise (51) is a housewife and her husband, Angus (54) is a Divisional Manager for an international company in Qatar. They have been in the country for over three years, having spent a five year period working and living in Bahrain. Prior to the contract in Bahrain, Louise and Angus had spent time in Nigeria together with a young family. After Nigeria, Angus had taken on a bachelor status contract in Saudi Arabia. Louise visited Saudi Arabia during the children's school holidays and whilst finding it a little restrictive enjoyed the brief visit.

Why did you decide to return to the Middle East after an interval of ten years?
The main reasons for returning to work in the Middle East in 1991 were because of the nature of Angus's work and the challenges possible in the Middle East, which were lacking in the UK. Since the family were now grown up and not dependent, it seemed an ideal opportunity to enjoy a challenging position within another culture.

What were your first impressions of Qatar?
Our first impression on arrival in Qatar was how much countries can vary in the Middle East. The airport is old and tired but with a friendly immigration staff. The shopping areas and souks are widely spaced and finding one's way around can be quite difficult. The driving is probably the worst in the Middle East. All new arrivals require a blood test, full medical and then a visit to the CID to register finger prints. All this in the first week! A temporary driving licence can be issued for the length of time the initial temporary visa is valid.

On arrival the world was a whirl whilst a very efficient Sudanese whisked us both through the red tape.

What were your thoughts after the first month?
Qatar is larger than Bahrain but much smaller than Saudi Arabia with most of the population living and working within Doha. However the Ras Laffan and other gas

fields are creating small townships in the north of the country. Qatar is fast catching up with the other more developed areas of the Middle East. With shopping malls and multi chain hotel complexes now under construction. There is not much work available for European wives. Secretaries can often find work, all be it poorly paid and often on split days, 8am to 12.30pm and 4pm until 7pm or often later.

A knowledge of the local custom and respect for the local culture can avoid embarrassment in such simple things as a visit to the souk or local supermarket. The local ladies are scornful of scantily dressed females, and on rare occasions can spit and hiss at a female considered to be improperly dressed. Remember that to a Muslim even showing more than the eyes can be seen as provocative. Covered arms and legs are best observed on visits to the souk or on any shopping trip, although abayas are not a necessity in Qatar.

However, this said, in the main the Qatari is a polite and courteous person with manners that would do many Europeans proud.

There is no restriction on women driving in Qatar, as in Saudi Arabia where ladies are not permitted to drive. But be warned, driving in Qatar is not for the faint-hearted. Qatar is a country of fast and furious 4WD vehicles and all driven by racing drivers. If driving worries one then taxis are available for anything from supermarket visits to a night out for very little money. Taxis take two forms: one being the hail and ride 'orange peril', all on fixed meters and so cheap it is unbelievable, the other being the limousine service complete with uniformed driver and available from a simple phone call. Even the limousine service is low cost being around 50 per cent of that charged in a UK city.

What is accommodation like?
Many local agents are available for the location of rental properties. Everything is bargainable and the term 'last price' is soon learnt. We opted for a large three bedroom, three bathroom independent house with membership of a local club for swimming and gym. The agreed property rental reduced by over 25 per cent at the end of the bargaining. Once inside them, many of the compounds are open plan living. Individual houses are usually surrounded by a two metre wall, great for privacy and the barbecue.

What about shopping in Qatar?
Shopping can be expensive if one wants to shop like a European, Sunblest Bread is available but at three or four times the cost of local breads, cereals come and go and panic buying when a particularly favoured item is available is often wise. Good quality clothes are available here and choice is improving.

What is the climate like in Qatar?
Great care needs to be taken in this climate due to the heat. Sun protection is needed all year round. Blue skies are the norm but fog does come in the winter, December to February, humidity can be a problem during June to September with temperatures in the 50 degrees centigrade region and humidity as high as 90 per cent. March to June and October to December are the activity months with a climate like a very good British summertime.

What activities are on offer in Qatar?
The opportunity for outdoor hobbies and especially water sports is terrific in Qatar. There are five marinas for mooring boats and one fair standard sailing club as well as a scuba diving club. Registration and insurance of boats is reasonable although mooring is not cheap. There are no hard standing moorings available in Qatar.

What are the options like for eating out?
Qatar is opening restaurants almost on a weekly basis with Italian, Indian, and Chinese, Thai, Japanese and several good fish restaurants now trading. There are also many fast-food chains such as McDonalds, Pizza Hut, Hardees and many more. The four main five star hotels also boast bars and licensed restaurants within their complexes.

Advice to those moving out to Qatar?
Qatar is a friendly and safe Country to work and live in as a family. However, when you step off the plane be ready for a culture shock. Think Qatar as you pass through immigration and the hustle of exiting the cool air-conditioned arrivals hall. Ignore the stares from hundreds of eyes and prepare yourself for the feeling of 'what have I done?' Think positive, think Qatar, and after three or four months you will be wondering 'why didn't we do this sooner?'

Qatar is a fairly strict Muslim community although accommodating to us Christians. Alcohol and pork meat is banned. The import of any form of alcohol is strictly prohibited. Alcohol can be bought from certain licensed outlets on a monthly basis, after obtaining a liquor licence. The liquor licence is only available after the issue of a work permit and allows you to buy a limited amount of alcohol per month. Drinking and driving is a definite 'no no', drunken driving will result in time in jail, a fine and possible deportation.

SAUDI ARABIA

Maren Hanson

Maren Hanson is 57 years old and has lived and worked in Saudi Arabia for the past ten years as an attorney. She currently works for a law firm in Riyadh. Her background is BA and MA in Economics from the University of Oklahoma, and a Justice Diploma from the University of San Diego School of Law. She obtained a Diplôme d'Etudes Approfondies in Public Law from the University of Tours, France, and a diploma from the University of San Diego School of Law, Institute on International and Comparative Law in Islamic and Middle Eastern Law.

What were your first impressions of Saudi Arabia?
The first impression I had of the Kingdom when arriving at Riyadh airport was the intense heat (and humidity if in Jeddah or the Eastern Province) present from April until November. The next thing I noticed was the long white dresses called 'thobes' of the Saudi men and the total black coverings of the women. I was surprised at the modern cities with architecturally beautiful buildings expecting something more exotic and disappointed not to see camels roaming loose. It was also quite strange to have all the shops close during the prayer times.

What are some of the differences in business practices between the Gulf and the West?
The first thing that comes to mind is that appointments frequently begin late. Time does not have the same importance in Saudi Arabian culture as it does in the West. During a meeting, your Saudi host may take numerous telephone calls and discuss certain matters or sign papers brought to him by the constant stream of people wandering through. This does not mean that he is not listening. Although everyone seems to be on the telephone all the time, to accomplish anything usually takes a personal visit. When we need information from a Ministry, someone from the office makes a visit to the Ministry. It is rare that we are able to get said information by a simple telephone call.

How much time is needed to acclimatise to living in Saudi Arabia?

I think it takes a while. The pace of living is very different in Saudi Arabia than in the West. It is slower, people are less active as they do not have to be 'doing' every minute (perhaps because of the heat). In fact, even now, it takes me several weeks to readjust whenever I return to Riyadh from the United States, I find everyone busy taking no time to relax and enjoy. You have to be doing something every moment of every day.

The initial cultural adjustment is also easier now than before because of instant communication through the internet, with e-mail, etc. so one does not have to feel so isolated at first until everything becomes familiar. Also, supermarkets carry American brands, French brands, English brands, etc. In fact, it is much easier to find familiar American products in Riyadh than in Paris where I previously lived. Major bookstores throughout the Kingdom have large selections of books in English, there is a local English TV station along with satellite TV. Current movies in English (and other languages to some extent) can be rented and it is rare that I am in a store where the sales person does not speak some English.

What about the social life in Saudi Arabia? What activities are available? How easy is it to meet others?

Generally speaking, there is not a lot of social interaction between Western and Saudi families, so the social life is an expat social life. Because most Westerners live in compounds, friends are made among the families living there and through the various international schools of the children. The newer compounds are no longer one company compounds, and are therefore like small communities. One also socialises with the expats met through work. Over the years, I have been active at American Community Services which offers all sorts of activities and classes, and includes a lending library. Organisations such as Toastmasters can also be found. Other major embassies have similar social organisations.

There is not a lot to do in the Kingdom, but I am always busy. There are no cinemas for example. I watch satellite TV and rent recent films on video for home viewing. Our social life is people orientated, having parties or get-togethers, going out to dinner, etc. When in Jeddah, we always go snorkelling in the Red Sea. The Red Sea has some of the best deep sea diving in the world. The Eastern Province has the Arabian Gulf for swimming and boating. Other popular pastimes are camping and hunting for desert diamonds.

What do you like least and most about living in Saudi Arabia?

I think that the answer most women would give for liking least is not being able to drive. For me, this is not a problem as I live in a villa and not a compound and have a driver so I do not feel the isolation some women talk about. I find the black abaya hot, especially in summer. Until recently, the lack of maintenance was probably my biggest complaint. You have something fixed and it breaks again within a month or so. My major complaint now though is the slow access and downloading on the internet. Internet providers are expensive so I cannot stay connected all the time. The time to download a file takes easily five to ten minutes so I can spend an hour and only visit three or four sites.

On the plus side, I love the hot, dry weather. We have a swimming pool which is in constant use most of the year. We have wonderful Saudi friends. Saudi Arabia is a great place to raise children (mine are now grown). The schools are good and there is less trouble for them to get into. Another plus is travel. While living in Saudi Arabia, I have been to India and Nepal, Japan and the Far East, Ethiopia, and all over Europe. I love being a lawyer in Saudi Arabia. Law firms in the Kingdom are not specialised so my work consists of a variety of assignments from drafting contracts to intellectual property work to licensing. I have a much wider range of assignments here than I would have working in the US.

What advice would you give to those considering moving to Saudi Arabia?
Moving to another country and culture is a great adventure and opportunity, so look at it as such. This is basic but very important.

Read books on cultural adjustment before you depart. Be aware that you will feel excited, everything in the new country will be 'exotic', you will become depressed since nothing works the way you are used to and you feel displayed, everything will then be bad in the new country, and adjustment – some things are better and some are worse. Knowing this before you leave will make each stage of adjustment easier to pass through.

Read books on Saudi Arabia so as to familiarise yourself with the background and customs of the country. There are many simple introductory books available once you are in the Kingdom.

Do not compare Saudi Arabia with your home country. Each country is different.

Do not assume motives and reasons for the way things are done in the new country. To give one example, it is easy to assume that women are second class citizens because they cover their faces and become 'invisible' in public. This is not true. They gain their identity through family and do not express their individuality through dress like Westerners whose image depends to a certain extent on their dress – sophisticated, working woman, hippie, punk, etc.

Get e-mail addresses for everyone back home. E-mail makes it easy to stay in touch with relatives and friends.

Saudi Arabia is conservative. Women should be covered at all times (if no abaya – long sleeves and long skirt or loose trousers). Carry a head scarf so that if one of the religious police tell you to cover your hair, you can. Say thank you and walk away.

The adjustment is hardest for women because of not being able to drive. My advice is to call your embassy to find out about groups and activities and to partake in an activity as soon as possible to meet other people so that you do not feel isolated.

Working women is another problem as women cannot work with men. That is why you see no female sales personnel or very few female secretaries. But there are jobs available. In Riyadh, there is always a list with American Community Services. Volunteer work is also possible.

Enjoy the experience! Not everyone has the opportunity to travel and to live in another culture.

John & Jenny Collier

John and Jenny have now been living in Jeddah, Saudi Arabia, for the past six years. Their children had completed their university education and so they felt that it was a good time for them to try something new.

What were your first impressions of Saudi Arabia?
When we first arrived in Jeddah, I was very surprised at how large and modern the city is. It also had lots of green areas where there are plenty of trees and grass. There are numerous palms and flowering bushes everywhere. Being a desert climate, you can imagine how much care goes into keeping it green.

Have you experienced any major problems living in Saudi Arabia?
Living in Jeddah has presented few problems for us regarding travel since we both

have multiple 'exit and re-entry' visas. Most people have to apply for a visa before they leave the country and therefore have a visa before they re-enter. One also needs a 'travel letter' in order to be able to move around the Kingdom freely. If one uses a company car, you have to have a letter stating that you are allowed to drive the vehicle. In most cases when a person arrives in the Kingdom, the employer takes the passport and keeps it until it is needed for travel. Also, when leaving the country you surrender your *iquama* in place of your passport.

Travel within the city can be quite a nuisance as it is against the law for women to drive. Some females are very fortunate in that the company sponsoring them supplies a driver. Most compounds have a limousine service available to residents as well as having a bus that takes them to the main shopping areas twice a day. There are also numerous taxis but we are advised not to use them. However, I have always used a taxi and never had a problem. The major concern is the fact that the drivers' English is very limited and so is their knowledge of the city. As long as you know where you are going and can direct them with hand signals everything is fine.

What is accommodation like?
Accommodation here is varied. Most westerners live in compounds catering to all their needs. Most of them have a supermarket on the premises as well as dry cleaning, video rental, library, nursery school, and in some cases playgrounds for the children and often a restaurant. There are pools, tennis courts, squash courts, and gymnasiums. I feel when one first arrives in Jeddah it is imperative to go to a large compound initially to get your bearings. Many of the compounds have activities where one can join in and meet people. They have various tennis tournaments, bowling leagues and many things for children. You can get involved as much or as little as you want. Having said that, we live in a private villa. We moved in May last year and I am loving it. I did live on a compound for six years though and made many friends and also know what there is available to do. One of the problems regarding living on your own is the fact that you have to do all of your own maintenance. On the compounds there is 24 hour maintenance, be it for your air conditioning, plumbing, etc. Tradesman are hard to find. Many do not speak English and when they come they do minimal work so that they can return often.

Is the cost of living in Jeddah very high?
The cost of living here is pretty much standard. You can go to a French restaurant and pay SR 150 per person or you can go to a Pakistani restaurant and pay SR 20 or even less per head. For any imported food such as cereals from the USA or imported vegetables you pay a very high price. Anything grown locally is very inexpensive. Believe it or not, there are quite a few items that are locally grown. Cabbage, beans, tomatoes and watermelon, just to name a few. Beans for instance are a very good buy. A good deal of the meat is imported from the USA as well as Ireland and of course there is lots of local lamb.

What's it like living in a Muslim country?
Living in a Muslim country is very interesting to say the least. Women wear an *abaya*, a sort of black housecoat. These can be very elaborate and are now being sold in colours other than black. I sometimes go out without one on but you have to make sure that your arms and legs are covered and not wear skin-tight trousers or revealing skirts. I therefore find it much easier to just cover up with the abaya. There are *matawa* in the kingdom – morals police that patrol the city making sure all is well and that people are paying heed to the religious rules and regulations. I have been told to 'cover your head' twice – I just nod and move on. I have never worn a scarf.

Ramadan is a strange time of year. During the month of Ramadan one is not allowed to eat, drink or smoke during daylight hours. This is strictly enforced and should you forget, you will be arrested and taken to jail. All restaurants and fast-food places are closed during the day. Supermarkets are open so that one can buy groceries. During the day, some businesses are also open. Some shops are open from about 2pm until 4.30pm and from 10pm to 2am. At midnight you can get your car repaired, get your hair cut, or even go to a dentist! This still seems weird to me. After the month of Ramadan is the 'Eid el Fitr' which is a celebration lasting for three days. During Eid there is almost nothing open with the exception of supermarkets.

One month after Ramadan is the month of 'Hajj' when Muslims from all over the world come to perform Hajj. During this time there are about 2.5 million people coming to Makkah and Madinah to carry out religious duties. All of these people fly into Jeddah so the airport is a zoo. Most people try to time their vacation breaks to avoid this. The airport has long queues and getting through immigration and passport control can be sheer torture. I have heard from some friends how they had to stand in line for eight hours. The longest time I've personally had to wait is one and a half hours. There is nothing to be done but to learn some patience. Losing your cool does nothing to alleviate the situation.

Five times a day prayers are said and everything shuts down during these periods. You can go to certain of the larger supermarkets that let you in so that you can shop throughout prayer times. However, you cannot get any assistance as there are no clerks on hand to help you to get produce weighed or get your groceries checked out. You are literally locked in and the doors will not open until after prayer.

What else do you think that those moving to Saudi should bear in mind?

When one comes to Jeddah there is usually a thorough search at customs and they do make sure that you are not carrying pork, alcohol or anything containing these items such as liqueur filled chocolates. Strictly prohibited in the Kingdom are alcohol, drugs, pornography and pork or any by-products. Believe it or not you are not even allowed poppyseeds or nutmeg because they are considered to be hallucinogens. Sleeping pills and any drug containing codeine are also not allowed.

Customs go through magazines to make sure that there is no pornographic material and will confiscate videos to be viewed and returned at a later date. Anything regarding Christmas is also a no-no. We did try to bring in a tree one year and it got taken away from us. One of my friends brought in a tree and some decorations. The tree was passed but they took her decorations. Another one did the same thing and they did the reverse – took her tree and left her decorations. Another friend of mine whose son got married had the wedding video taped. They took her tape away at customs and returned it a week later having edited the whole ceremony. As much as they say you are free to practise your religion, you can be arrested or deported for doing so. A couple of Filipinos were caught watching 'Christmas' videos and were arrested. You never know but some things aren't worth the risk.

It is illegal for more than eight women to be at a gathering. The way women's groups get around this is by arranging a local major hotel to sponsor their meetings. The hotel has to go to the emir of Makkah and get a special dispensation in order for the societies to go ahead with their gatherings. When the Canadian Ambassador was here recently there was a reception at one of the large hotels which had to get permission from the authorities because of the fact that there was going to be a mixed group of people – men and women in the same room!

The restaurants have dining areas for families and if there is a man or men on their own they are seated in special 'Men Only' areas. There are some stores such as music or video stores that do not allow women to enter. By the same token, there are many shops that do not allow men at all. Public beaches do not allow women to come in their bathing suits. There are numerous private beaches where women can go for a swim. In most cases when a boy turns 11 he is no longer considered a child and cannot be included with the women.

UNITED ARAB EMIRATES

Xavier Groult

Xavier (43), his wife, Christiane (46), and his two children, Emmanuel (19) and Elodie (15), all French nationals, first moved to Abu Dhabi city in 1993 for a period of two years. At the time of this book going to press, they are in the process of relocating there. Xavier worked as an electronic field engineer in one of the top French companies that sell advanced military systems to both domestic and international markets and is to work for the UAE Armed Forces. Christiane is a nurse. Prior to this first period spent in Abu Dhabi the whole family spent five years overseas, mostly in Jordan, Qatar and Egypt. Elodie was born in Qatar.

What were your first impressions of Abu Dhabi?
Our first impressions were that it appeared to be a city under permanent construction as far as the buildings and roads were concerned. However, we were surprised by the number of green areas despite the dry and hot weather conditions, and by the contrast of the growing urban modernity with the poor remote villages located in the middle of the desert. There were a high number of foreign nationals from the Far East (mostly male).

What were the major difficulties you encountered with the move?
The major difficulties encountered occurred during the first three months upon arrival in Abu Dhabi. We faced lengthy administrative regulations and procedures in order to set ourselves up, like obtaining the resident permit, the driving licence, accommodation, and so on. But it has to be said that all those things are for Europeans, much less difficult in comparison to the installation problems frequently faced by Pakistanis, Indian nationals, or Filipinos.

What are the main differences in business practices between the Gulf and the West?
The main differences are that in the Gulf: time is not important – one must always be patient, the Arabs are renowned (or perhaps more aptly 'infamous') for their adherence to the saying: *Inch Allah, Boukra, Malesh (IBM)*, 'If God wants what you ask me to do, it will be done tomorrow, and if not done tomorrow, it is not important, not a big deal, no harm'; everything can be bargained for; spoken words are as important as those written; never try to speed up things and never enter directly into the subject you wish to discuss; once an Emirati trusts you, this will be long-standing; local businessmen compensate their lack of technical knowledge by making an intensive use of personal understanding of the contractual/legal terms of every type of contract so that they can argue on any contractual point to always get the most out of a deal.

What is the social life like?
Since the end of the working day is around 2pm, the rest of the day can be used for socialising, hobbies, sport, cultural activities, etc. Hotels, clubs, and schools, are the

easiest places to meet people and make new friends.

How difficult was it to find work in the Gulf?
Only very few French people want to live in the Gulf so it is not difficult to find work there. For Christiane it was relatively easy to get a job as a nurse since the numerous Lebanese doctors working there prefer to work with French national nurses. Another opportunity for Christiane was to help in the French school as an assistant to the teachers of classes for young children.

What is the standard and cost of living like?
The standard of living for Europeans is of a medium to high level, mostly dependent on how much money you want to save out of the expatriation. It is so easy to spend all your earnings in Abu Dhabi as there is so much to do and so many things to buy (e.g. boats, 4WDs, eating in restaurants, enrolling in clubs, etc.). Local produce is cheap (fruit, vegetables, fish, meat) while imported food is expensive, sometimes twice the cost for the equivalent item found in France.

What did you like least about living in Abu Dhabi?
We found it most difficult accepting in-country customs such as the public slaughtering of animals (sheep and camels) to celebrate the end of Ramadan. Noisy neighbours in the middle of the night (locals do not distinguish between night and day) can also cause problems when it becomes a frequent occurrence.

What did you like most?
The fine weather, the absence of stress, more money to spend in restaurants, on entertainment and sports.

What is life like for women living in the UAE?
For women, the freedom in the UAE is almost identical to that experienced in Europe. There are neither restrictions nor constraints placed on clothing, driving cars (as found in Saudi Arabia), and working. There is no public sexual discrimination.

What advice would you give to others considering relocating to the UAE?
People whose extended family play a large role in their lives will most likely face the greatest difficulties living abroad. They may not succeed in the expatriation. Everyone must accept the in-country constraints (religion, customs) even if they are not as stringent as the other Gulf States. Before taking the decision to live abroad, ask for advice from people who have already spent some years overseas. Families with children of school age should always be aware of what schooling is available (or not).

David Wilkins

David is a British engineer and has been living in the United Arab Emirates on and off since 1996.

What were your first impressions of the United Arab Emirates?
Each Emirate has its own character. Since I arrived I have lived in the Emirate of Abu Dhabi, the largest of the seven Emirates. The Emirate has only two major urban centres, Abu Dhabi city and Al Ain. Abu Dhabi is a comparatively new city and like, say, Milton Keynes, the town planners have had an opportunity to give some thought to its layout. That thought has been influenced by US cities and so Abu

Dhabi is comprised of six-lane highways set out in a grid system, overhead traffic lights, central reservations, sidewalks, parks and fountains. It has both shiney new twenty storey tower blocks and crumbling old five storey blocks. There is nothing in between. Dubai, down the coast is a much older place and has therefore developed in a haphazard fashion, more along the lines of a British town.

The first impression of Abu Dhabi is that it is populated entirely by men from the Indian subcontinent. On further inspection you notice other nationalities: Arabs from around the Middle East – Egypt, Lebanon, Jordan, Syria, Arabs from Africa – Sudan, Somalia, then Filipinos, Europeans and finally UAE nationals, dressed in the national dress of white neck to ankle *dish dasha* with head dress of *agal* and *gutra*. UAE nationals are a minority – current estimates are around 10 per cent of the total population. Last of all you notice some women. Due to the huge numbers of male expatriates, the UAE has one of the lowest women to men ratios in the world.

What are the main differences in bureaucracy?
The civil service, slow in any country, in Abu Dhabi is so inefficient that you would have to laugh – if only your urgent papers weren't stuck somewhere in the system. By contrast, the government departments of Dubai are relatively business-minded and professional and at least give the impression of actually wanting to help. Things move quicker in Dubai.

Much of the bureaucracy encountered in the UAE relates to the fact that there are a huge number of expatriate workers. Other than the obvious visa and labour card issues, many other aspects of life will reflect the fact that, at any moment, you may depart the country, never to return. Some employers therefore have a practice of holding their employees' passports. There is nothing in the law permitting or obliging them to do this but it is for many employers a prerequisite to offering employment.

What is the accommodation situation like?
Much will depend upon whether your employment comes with or without an expatriate package. If you are a local hire, you may have to share accommodation. Fortunately, there is a surplus of new, vacant apartments. Rents average around £6,000 to £8,000 per annum for a two bedroom apartment (present rates). If you have an expatriate package you are unlikely to be obliged to share and the highly paid executives will get to live in villas. All in all, the accommodation is likely to be better than could be afforded at home.

Why choose to live and work in the Arabian Peninsula?
Tax-free pay, endless sunshine and the opportunity to live in a different culture. Apart from the UAE itself, the neighbouring countries include Oman which is truly beautiful. Iran is just across the Gulf and India, Jordan, Egypt, Syria and the Lebanon are all very close.

What is the social life like in the UAE?
The chief social activities are eating, drinking, sport and sunbathing and the UAE provides ample opportunity for the pursuit of them all. There are plenty of decent restaurants and bars concentrated mainly in the large hotels which also house most of the sports facilities. Water sports are rightly popular given that the main urban centres of Abu Dhabi, Dubai and Sharjah are all on the coast. The sun shines virtually every day of the year.

What do you like most about living in the UAE?
Abu Dhabi city is sufficiently compact so that work, restaurants, bars, supermarkets,

cinemas and sports facilities are all no more than a ten minute drive away.

The pace of life is gentler than back in the UK. Many shops and businesses close for lunch; employees pop home to have a meal with their family and a snooze; everything goes on hold when it's time to pray; there is the general attitude that if it happens it happens, if it doesn't it doesn't, or more to the point *insh'allah* – if God wills it. This can be frustrating on those occasions when you need something urgently but overall it means that expectations are more reasonable and life is that little bit less stressful.

The vast majority of the population are from cultures where civility and cordiality are still practised and so everyday dealings can be very pleasant.

I do not know what the statistics are, but the UAE feels like a very safe place. Certainly, in terms of street crime, Abu Dhabi must rank as one of the world's safest capital cities. The majority of residents are expats earning more than they could at home and to whom deportation would be a severe punishment indeed. Accordingly there is no motivation for crime. Leave your wallet in a taxi and you are almost certain to get it back. This may not be the case in Dubai which has more transients and casual visitors.

What do you like least?

The safety of the Emirates stops at the kerb. The driving is simply atrocious – the result of a combination of incompetence, carelessness and arrogance. If you enjoy driving at high speed through rush hour traffic, practising your slaloming skills, all the while chatting to your friends on a mobile phone and balancing a small child on your lap then you will feel perfectly at home in the UAE. Ditto if you enjoy dodgems.

The justice system is pretty medieval and, rather than being based on equitableness, seems to be based on nationality, name, influence, etc. Most expats try not to think what would happen if they were caught in a tangle with the authorities. There is nothing approaching the equivalent of the European Convention for the Protection of Human Rights and arrests are the usual first step in any police inquiry.

Expatriate menial workers from the sub-continent and the Philippines seem to get a particularly raw deal. Although there are employment laws offering a degree of protection from abusive employers, the prospect of visa termination and deportation is usually enough to make the employee suffer in silence. I personally have known of a case where the worker has been working twelve hours straight, seven days a week with no leave entitlement – all contrary to the law – and has not been paid for several months. It is extremely distressing to witness.

Advice to those considering the move.

Give it a go – the country is fascinating and the quality of life is superior to that in the UK. Do be prepared for the hottest summer you have ever known. Do be patient, polite and courteous – it will be greatly appreciated and any other approach will only result in frustration. Most problems encountered by expats in the UAE come from driving, drinking or offending UAE nationals. Don't behave exactly as you would in the UK.

APPENDIX II
Reading List

General Information on the Gulf

Arab Gulf States, Gordon Robinson, Lonely Planet.
Arabia Through the Looking Glass, Jonathan Raban.
Arabian Sands, Wilfred Thesiger, Penguin.
Courtesies in the Gulf, Donald Hawley, Stacey International.
Don't They Know It's Friday?, Jeremy Williams, Gulf Business Books.
Looking for Dilmun, Geoffrey Bibby.
The Arabs, The New Arabians(1981), Peter Mansfield.
Area Handbook for the Persian Gulf States, Richard Nyrop.
Bedouin, Nomads of the Desert, Alain Keohane, Stacey International.
The Closed Circle – An Interpretation of the Arabs, David Pryce-Jones.
Courtesies in the Gulf Area, Sir Donald Hawley, Stacey International.
Desert Driver's Manual, Jim Stabler, Stacey International.
Expats, Christopher Dickey.
The Failure of Political Islam, Oliver Roy.
A History of the Arab Peoples, Albert Hourani.
Inside the Middle East, Dilip Hiro.
Islam and the West, Bernard Lewis.
MEED Practical Guides, various authors, Middle East Economic Digest.
The Merchants, Michael Field.
Origins of Arabia, Andrew Thompson, Stacey International, 1999.
Sandstorms – Days and Nights in Arabia, Peter Theroux.
TIMES Guide to the Middle East, ed. Peter Sluglett and Marion Farouk-Sluglett, 1996.
Very Simple Arabic Incorporating Simple Etiquette in Arabia, James Peters, Stacey International.

Women in the Islamic World

Behind the Veil in Arabia – Women in Oman, Unni Wikan.
Beyond the Veil – Male/Female Dynamics in Modern Muslim Society, Fatima Mernissi.
The Hidden Face of Eve, She Has No Place in Paradise, Nawal El-Saadawi.
Images of Women – The Portrayal of Women in Photograhy in the Middle East 1860-1950, Sarah Graham-Brown.
A Mother Without a Mask, Patricia Holton.
Nine Parts of Desire – the Hidden World of Islamic Women, Geraldine Brooks.

Islam

Concise Encyclopaedia of Islam, Cyril Glasse, intro. Professor Huston Smith, Stacey International, 1999.
Islam in the World, Malise Ruthven.
The Koran Interpreted, AJ Arberry.
Mohammedanism – An Historical Survey, HAR Gibb.

Personal Narrative of a Pilgrimage to Al-Madinah and Meccah, Richard Burton, 1855.
The Venture of Islam, Marshall GS Hodgson.

Bahrain

Bahrain: A Heritage Explored, The Islands of Bahrain, Angela Clark.
Bahrain Through the Ages – The Archaeology, Shaikha Haya Ali Al-Khalifa & Michael Rice.

Kuwait

Kuwait: Vanguard of the Gulf, Peter Mansfield, 1990.
The Modern History of Kuwait 1750-1965, Ahmad Mustafa Abu-Hakima.
The Mother of Crimes Against Kuwait in Pictures, Ministry of Information.
Tides of War – Eco-Disaster in the Gulf, Michael McKinnon and Peter Vine.
Wildflowers of Kuwait, Linda Shuaib, Stacey International.

Oman

Birds of the Batinah of Oman, RA and GE Honeywell.
Field Guide to the Geology of Oman, Samir S Hanna.
Musandem – Architecture and Material Culture of a Little Known Region of Oman, Paolo M Costa.
Off-road in Oman, Heiner Klein and Rebecca Brickson.
Oman, Sir Donald Hawley, Stacey International.
Sea-shells of the Sultan Qaboos Nature Reserve at Qurm, Kathleen Smythe.
Snorkelling and Diving in Oman, Rod Salm and Robert Baldwin.
Sultan in Oman, James Morris.
The Sultanate of Oman, Raghid El-Solh, Ithaca Press.
Travels in Oman – On the Track of the Early Explorers, Philip Ward.
Whales & Dolphins Along the Coast of Oman, Robert Baldwin and Rod Salm.

Qatar

Arabian Time Machine, Helga Graham.
Bedouins of Qatar, Klaus Ferdinand, 1993.
Economic and Social Development in Qatar, Zuhair Ahmed Nafi, 1984.
Qatar, Martin Caiger Smith, Stacey International.
Qatar (Enchantment of the World), Byron Augustin and Rebecca A. Augustin, 1997.

Saudi Arabia

At the Drop of a Veil, Marianne Alireza, a Californian woman who wedded a man from a Jeddah-based merchant family in the 1940s.
Desert Treks from Riyadh, Ionis Thompson.
Fool's Paradise, Dale Walker.
The House of Saud, David Holden and Richard Johns.
The Kingdom, Robert Lacey.
The Kingdom of Saudi Arabia, Sir Norman Anderson et al., Stacey International.
Saudis inside the Desert Kingdom, Sandra Mackay.